"I have used my first edition copy of *A Hero's Welcome* in sermon preparation, class research, and personal study. I'm humbled to be able to endorse this exceptional work twenty years later to a new generation of believers." DR. KEITH R. KRELL, Senior Pastor, Fourth Memorial Church, Spokane, WA; Professor of Biblical Exposition, Moody Bible Institute-Spokane

"My first introduction to the subject of eternal rewards came from Dr. Ron Barnes, both in his classroom teaching and in this wonderful book, *A Hero's Welcome*. Dr. Barnes explains the subject with passion and lucidity. The format of the book is well suited for almost any reader. Advanced theological concepts are presented in the form of fun storytelling. The result is a book that will make the reader smile and laugh, while leaving a deep imprint on his or her spiritual life." PETE VIK, Professor of Biblical Studies and New Testament Greek at San Diego Christian College, Co-Pastor of Highpoint Church, San Diego, California, and author of the book, *Hope*

"A *Hero's Welcome* had a huge impact on my spiritual growth in college, encouraging me to serve God out of love for what He has accomplished on the cross, instead of fear. Reading it again last year, I was encouraged to keep an eternal perspective in the midst of suffering. This book has depths to be mined with multiple reads." ANDREA VIK, Highpoint Church, San Diego, California

"This book establishes that there is nothing this world can give that compares to the rewards possible at the Bema Seat of Christ! The book contains great examples of genuine love for God and our neighbor, showing us how to grow as Christians for the glory of God." REV. CLARK BURDETTE, Southern California Seminary student, Music Pastor at Beulah Land Cowboy Church, Martin, TN

"I thoroughly enjoyed this book and have recommended it to my wife. Dr. Barnes has an incredible ability to balance expository writing with deep, rich, exegetical study. My theology on eternal rewards has been greatly improved through reading this book." CARL CULVER, Southern California Seminary student

A Hero's Welcome

A HERO'S WELCOME

THE DOCTRINE OF FUTURE REWARDS AND THE BEMA SEAT OF CHRIST

RONALD BARNES

Southern California Seminary Press
El Cajon, California

A Hero's Welcome: The Doctrine of Future Rewards and the Bema Seat of Christ
2nd edition

Published by Southern California Seminary Press
El Cajon, CA

ISBN-10:0-9864442-2-7
ISBN-13:978-0-9864442-2-7

Previously published: *A Hero's Welcome: A Dissertation On the Doctrine of Future Rewards with Special Emphasis On the Bema Seat of Christ* by Graphic Business Solutions, El Cajon, CA, 1997.

Dedication

This book is dedicated to the Christ-exalting legacy of my dear mother, Florence Elaine Barnes, one of God's heroes of the faith.

Table of Contents

A Hero's Welcome

Acknowledgements

I thank Jesus, our Everlasting Rock, for Andrea Vik. In spite of formidable, physical health challenges, Andrea offered the precious gift of time to read the manuscript and her editorial wisdom to provide enhanced clarity of ideas as well as grammatical and punctuation correctness. Her work engendered considerable improvement to the final copy. As Jesus said, "whoever gives only a cup of cold water to one of these little ones in the name of a disciple, I tell you the truth, he will never lose his reward" (Matt. 10:42, NET Bible). Jesus has taken note of your help, Andrea, and will make your eternity all the richer for it!

I also commend Sean Rust, a gifted writer and brother in Christ, for his valuable editorial contributions. Thanks, Sean, for the quenching cup of cold water!

Dr. Joe Miller is a true scholar for The Teacher, The Lord Jesus Christ. Joe is also an excellent, published author; church planter; brilliant Information Technology Supervisor, and a diligent Director of Southern California Seminary Press. Check out Joe's engaging website at www.morethancake.org. I value your friendship, Joe, our endless brotherhood in Christ, your encouragement to publish this book and your valued editorial input. It is a joy to work with you as co-laborers in His Vineyard!

Finally, I want to honor Jennifer Ewing, the best Librarian and Researcher God ever made. Jesus did "all things well" (Mark 7:37). As does Jennifer–especially when it comes to written composition! Only our all-knowing God could know how many hours Jennifer invested in this book. Words are insufficient to properly thank you, Jennifer. Not only did you read the manuscript more than ten times, but your knowledge of proper grammar, punctuation, spelling, format, bibliographic citations, literary structure, literary integrity—where do I stop—inspires us all to pursue excellence in writing, to do "all things well." Your tireless efforts, creative input, reader-friendly heart and wise suggestions transformed this twenty-year-old, self-published book, into a book of professional quality! Name your favorite place to eat, and the dinner will be on my wife and me! We look forward to a time to celebrate all your hard work. And when you stand before Jesus at the Bema Seat, all saints of all ages will celebrate the eternal reward The Lord Jesus will give you for all He has done though you. As He promises, "Whatever you are doing, work at it with enthusiasm, as to the Lord and not for people, because you know that you will receive your inheritance from the Lord as the reward. Serve the Lord Christ" (Col. 3:23-24).

Foreword

Life is a series of evaluations. The moment you enter the world, you are evaluated. What is your length and weight? When will you take your first steps? As you mature, you are evaluated by your family, friends, teachers, employers, neighbors, and fellow Christians. Questions are posed such as: What do you want to be when you grow up? What is your GPA and SAT/ACT score? What do you do for a living? How much money do you make? Where do you live? What do you drive? How do you serve at your church?

All of these questions and the people who ask them share something in common—they are all flawed. People don't have all the facts, nor do they know the right questions to ask. Human thoughts, judgments, motives, and attitudes are sinful. Fortunately, there is one who is perfect in every conceivable way—the Lord Jesus Christ, who will one day evaluate our lives—our time, talents, treasure, truth, and relationships. The apostle Paul informs us that "we must all appear before the judgment seat of Christ, so that each one may be recompensed for his deeds in the body, according to what he has done, whether good or bad" (2 Cor. 5:10). These words are sobering and cut to the core. They remind us that this life is not all there is. Rather, once this life is over, we will give an account to the glorified and exalted Christ.

Martin Luther stated, "There are two days on my calendar: 'Today' and 'That Day.'" Luther sought to live each and every day in light of Christ's evaluation of his life. Living five centuries later, Dr. Ron Barnes, has devoted his life and ministry to living today in light of "That Day." Ron's overall aim in writing A Hero's Welcome is to motivate believers like you and me to pursue Christ's approval so that we can hear Him say, "Well done, good and faithful slave" (Matt 25:21, 23).

This book thoroughly challenges and motivates the believer to daily live in light of judgment day. I have used my first edition copy of A Hero's Welcome in sermon prep, class research, and personal study. I'm humbled to be able to endorse this exceptional work twenty years later to a new generation of believers.

Thank you, Ron, for writing this book. I am confident that you will have A Hero's Welcome. May your entry into the eternal kingdom of our Lord and Savior Jesus Christ be richly supplied to you (2 Pet 1:11).

Keith R. Krell, PhD
Senior Pastor, Fourth Memorial Church, Spokane, WA
Professor of Biblical Exposition, Moody Bible Institute-Spokane

1

Welcome to the Gallery of Virtue

Explion! ~
~ I'm hit . . . eject ~
Falling . . .

"Oh no! I've been spotted!"
On the ground...
...in enemy territory!

As precious life-blood was spilling on Eastern European soil, U.S. Air Force Captain Scott O'Grady found himself entangled in the brutal war in the Balkans. On this day his was just another routine sortie dispatched by NATO reconnaissance operations. But it would turn out to be anything but routine.[1]

As his F-14 bolted its way through Bosnian skies, suddenly "an SA-6 surface-to-air missile fired from a Bosnian-Serb stronghold" and struck his aircraft.[2] O'Grady hit the ejector button and quickly found himself plunging through cloud cover...and into the unknown. As he fell through the clouds, he saw below a small village in Bosnia Serb territory. He opened his parachute and landed several hundred yards inside a wooded area. Nervous that he had been seen, he flattened his body on the ground and covered his exposed skin with gloves.

For the next six days, time seemed suspended as armed men hunted him down like a fugitive. O'Grady later said, "For the most part, my face was in the dirt, and I was just praying they wouldn't see me or hear me."[3]

On the fifth night he prayed, "Lord, let me at least have someone know I'm alive and maybe come rescue me."[4] That night another pilot heard his radio call for help. The next morning a helicopter full of daring Marines marked his yellow flare, executed a flawless seven minute rescue maneuver and snatched him from the enemies' grasp.

O'Grady's gutsy evasion from the enemy gained him a hero's welcome as he touched down at Aviano Air Base in Italy. Loud cheers from the pleased crowd descended upon him as he deplaned. Along with his family, a distinguished military entourage greeted him with huge smiles of congratulations. A podium was placed in front of him—the people wanted to hear from their hero. In his remarks, O'Grady was careful to give due praise to his rescuers. But this would be his moment in the sun, his day to be honored for enduring such hardship and courageously discharging his mission in the battle.

I can still remember carrying that heavy brown pole with the Christian flag fastened to it.... And I can still hear them ringing in my ears..., the enthusiastic voices of 75 boys and girls at summer Vacation

Bible School: "Onward Christian soldiers...marching as to war...with the cross of Jesus...going on before." As a young boy growing up in the sleepy little logging town of Prospect, Oregon, I was schooled in the reality that Christians are in a war. Not a physical war against flesh and blood, but a spiritual war against Satan's evil forces (Eph. 6:1-13).

Since those early days, I've learned that as a good soldier of Jesus Christ, I must "endure hardship" (2 Tim. 2:3), and that one day the war will be over—I'll get to go home.[5]

But there's something else I've uncovered, and that only recently, one of the most profound truths I've come to know since enlisting in God's army. Here it is: I can have a hero's welcome when I touch down in heaven. Every true believer will arrive in heaven, but not every believer will have a hero's welcome. Some will. Some will not.

My name is Ron. Come with me on a journey through the pages of Scripture and discover how to have a hero's welcome as a soldier of Jesus Christ. Our journey begins in Petrine territory.

Words From The Foyer

I arrived late. Not that I intended to, but oh those red lights, one after another after another. Huffing and puffing from my sprint through the parking lot, I bolted through the door to the gallery just in time to hear the tour guide say...

"The mere mention of the name 'Simon Peter' conjures up numerous images, all at once. We envision Peter, the timid rabbit, as he denies his beloved Jesus three times. But when the God-appointed rooster crows to rebuke his disloyalty, a broken Peter quickly exits and weeps bitterly (cf. Matt. 26:69-75). Then, there's the eye-popping picture of this socially, unpolished fisherman from Galilee actually reproving Jesus when the Master foretells His destiny of death in Jerusalem—Jesus swiftly scolds Peter's Satan-like effort to divert Him from God's redemption agenda" (cf. Matt. 16:21-23).

"But for a final sketch, we see Peter on the Day of Pentecost, no longer the timid rabbit of days gone by, but the bold, lion-like man of the Spirit, unflinchingly heralding the gospel to the same religious leaders whose command drove the large spikes through Jesus' hands and feet.[6] All said, Peter, over time, allowed the Master Painter to paint a portrait of Himself onto the empty canvas of his heart, discarding the old flesh-colored painting filled with impetuous, chaotic lines and the immature brushstrokes of clashing colors. So now it's time to urge his fellow soldiers to do the same as he leads them into God's Gallery of Virtue."

I knew fear all too well and could surely relate to the Wizard of Oz' Cowardly Lion-Syndrome displayed by Peter. But I'd never pondered the 'second Peter' recreated by the Divine Artist. "Maybe there is hope for my own spiritual formation," I thought. Bursting with hope, I moved around the side of the small tour group to get a closer view of the guide whose name badge read Didaskolos. From a crash course in Greek the year prior, I recalled the meaning of that word: Teacher.

"In the second of two letters which bear his name," Didaskolos continued, "Simon Peter,[7] who describes himself as 'a servant and an apostle of Jesus Christ,'[8] pens a personal letter to 'those who have received a faith of the same kind as ours, by the righteousness of our God and

Savior, Jesus Christ.'[9] Here Peter assures his readers that as saints they receive equal honor with all God's family due to the impartial nature of Christ's work to save sinners.

"Then, on the heels of this warm and instructive affirmation, the apostle bears still more of his shepherd's heart in a prayer of intercession: 'Grace and peace be multiplied to you in the knowledge of God and of Jesus our Lord.'[10] The first seven words are parallel to 1 Peter 1:2b, but here, in keeping with part of the occasion for his writing, namely the false teachers of the day, Peter adds 'through the knowledge[11] of God and of Jesus our Lord.'[12] Such intimate knowledge of Christ will enable his fellow Christian soldiers to experience an outpouring of God's grace to help and God's peace to comfort when loyalty to Christ and sound teaching is contested (cf. 2 Pet. 2:1-3; 3:17). A steadfast faith will be the result."

"Just who were these false teachers?" asked a tall, darkly-tanned man named Allen.

"Thank you for asking," replied Didaskolos. "In brief, these pseudo teachers claimed to possess a superior knowledge of spiritual matters, available to a privileged few, which freed them from the demands of morality. However, they denied the deity of Jesus Christ (2 Pet. 2:1), practiced immorality (2 Pet. 2:10), secretly spread destructive heresies (2 Pet. 2:1), engaged in religious work with the same covetous spirit as Balaam (2 Pet. 2:15), despised angelic authority (2 Pet. 2:10), turned the grace of God into a license to sin (2 Pet. 2:18-19), twisted the meaning of Scripture for their own depraved intentions (2 Pet. 3:16), and, among other vices, scoffed at the future coming of Jesus Christ to earth (2 Pet. 3:1-7). This dangerous company preyed upon the saints of the first century like a hungry wolf stalks a flock of sheep in the open meadow."

"No wonder," said Allen, "that Peter warned his brothers and sisters in Christ about such dispensers of false doctrine."

"That's right, brother," said Didaskolos, shaking his head in agreement. "In fact, much of the New Testament contains a polemical tone. And our day is no different. We must learn to 'handle accurately the word of truth,' as Paul exhorts young Timothy (2 Tim. 2:15), and, in keeping with Paul's charge to Titus, detect and refute those who contradict what is sound doctrine" (Titus 1:9).

"Now then," said Didaskolos, "back to Peter's introduction to his readers. Having completed his gracious salutation and prayer of intercession in verses one and two, Peter shifts to a compelling exhortation in verses 3-11. To break this section down, verses three and four reveal the resources God has granted believers to insure their becoming portraits of His Son and verses 5-7 unveil the responsibility each believer has in the process. When such resources are appropriated and such responsibilities activated, a hero's welcome is in order.

"So then, just before he leads his partners in faith through the entry door to God's Gallery of Virtue, Peter, the transformed fisherman, feels he must remind them of the resources God has provided to exhibit these virtues. He declares in verse 3,

> Seeing that His divine power has granted to us everything pertaining to life and godliness, through the true knowledge of Him who called us by His own glory and virtue.[13]

"In these words, Peter explains the glorious outcome of our personal knowledge of Jesus, referred to in verse two. In essence, we have His very own power at our disposal, making a lifestyle of godliness possible. And it was the beauty of 'His own glorious person and moral excellence' [paraphrase mine] displayed before us in His incarnation–shining most brightly in His saving death–that moved us to accept His call into His kingdom."

Upon hearing these words, I couldn't help but think back on my own fear of death and hell as a non-Christian, only to hear from my blessed mother that Jesus had stretched out His arms and died for me. What grace. What mercy. What kindness. What an exhibition of love in that while I was yet a sinner, Christ died for me (Rom. 5:8) to rescue me from hell. The riches of His kindness led me to repentance (Rom. 2:4). Yes, I could see what Peter meant here: Christ's glory and moral excellence moved me to embrace His call of salvation. He was too marvelous to resist. Now, it was time to tune back in to our tour guide.

"But not only do we have His perfect power," declared Didaskolos, "but His precious promises as well. In verse 4 Peter adds,

> For by these He has granted to us His precious and magnificent promises, in order that by them you might become partakers of the divine nature, having escaped the corruption that is in the world by lust.[14]

"No doubt you are all asking the obvious question, 'To what does Peter refer when he says, "For by these?"' He looks back to God's 'glory and virtue' mentioned at the end of verse 3.[15] Not only did the disclosure of Christ's splendid nature through both His life and death make us run to Him for salvation, but as well it grants us precious promises. But how so? What's the connection here? Simply put, the fulfillment of God's promises to us are made possible by Christ. Speaking of Jesus, Paul writes in 2 Corinthians 1:20, '...as many as may be the promises of God, in Him they are yes...by Him is our Amen to the glory of God....'

"For instance, in his first epistle, Peter tells all Christians that they have been 'born again to a living hope through the resurrection of Jesus Christ from the dead, to obtain an inheritance which is imperishable and undefiled and will not fade away, reserved in heaven for you...' (1 Pet. 1:3-

4). But not only are we promised eternal security through the glorious resurrected Christ, but the following verses speak of His sure return and our being honored in His presence (1 Pet. 1:5-7). And this prospect of being honored in His presence is precisely what this tour is all about, helping each of you to see how that can be your experience when you stand before Him."

"I know we're all eager to move into the gallery of virtue, Didaskolos," said Janet, a blonde-haired woman who served God as a Sunday School superintendent, "but quickly can you tell us what Peter intends when he says that by these promises we 'might become partakers of the divine nature?'"

"By all means, my dear sister," answered Didaskolos. "You must know the meaning of this if you are to receive a hero's welcome from Jesus. In short, God's promise of the new birth in his first epistle (1 Pet. 1:3, 23) means that each believer shares in God's very nature, that is to say, the eternal life that causes God to exist, a life perfect in quality and endless in quantity, is imparted to each one who believes that Jesus alone can forgive him of sin and save him from hell. And consequently, possessing the nature of God enables the Christian to take flight[16] from the corruption that is in the world caused by the evil desires of sinful men.

"To perceive what this means in concrete terms you must wait to see the portraits in the Gallery of Virtue, just ahead. Each one is a display of God's own nature through the Christian. As such, each virtue presents the opposite of the corrupting influence of sin. Remember what Jesus said of Himself in John 8:36, 'If therefore the Son of Man shall make you free, you shall be free indeed.'

"So then, is it possible to reflect Jesus on the empty canvas of your life? Absolutely. You have all the heavenly resources you need: His divine power and His precious promises. But He has so arranged the process of spiritual growth that you must participate by accepting your human responsibilities."

Let The Tour Begin!

As we made our quiet exit from the foyer into the gallery, our gaze could not escape the wonderfully decorated plaque above the entrance:

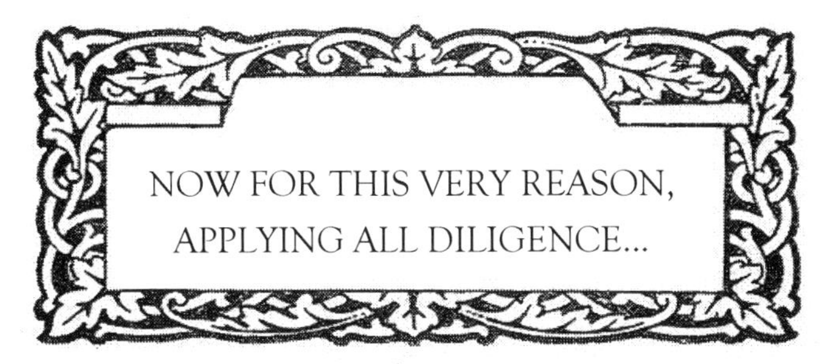

I scratched my head, puzzled. "What is the meaning of this?" I asked Didaskolos. In keeping with his helpful words in the foyer, his reply once again had us hanging on every word:

> Grace demands virtue. The sinner who receives (1) acceptance into God's family (2 Pet. 1:1c, d), (2) showers of heavenly help and inner peace (2 Pet. 1:2), and (3) all the power and promises needed to reflect God's image (2 Pet. 1:3-4), only then to spend most of his life snoozing in his carnal hammock, grieves his beloved Savior (2 Pet. 1:1e).

Then Didaskolos offered an analogy: "If a man saves his enemy from drowning, will not his enemy be moved to show appreciation for the rest of his days and avoid that which would offend the one who saved him? This only makes sense. So, you must see that grace demands virtue. Therefore, when Peter says, 'Now for this very reason,'[17] he links the Christian's rich position in Christ in verse 1, and his resources from

Christ in verses 2-4, to the Christian's logical responsibility before Christ in verses 5-7, namely, to portray the new nature he has received. And such responsibility on our part must be embraced with supreme diligence.[18]

"All said, it's a cause-effect relationship Peter speaks of: To experience God's grace in salvation is to desire to emulate God's person in sanctification. Let's view the first painting and begin learning how this all works out."

Above the portrait, engraved on a walnut brown-plaque were the words:

What could this mean? And how did it fit with the man in the portrait, someone we all recognized at once?

Seeing the puzzled lines on our faces, Didaskolos immediately launched his explanation:

"Your faith is the foundation[19] upon which you build the virtues displayed here in the gallery. Faith is the solemn confidence in God that what He has said is absolutely true.[20] As we gleaned from verse one, you obtained this faith from God to rely upon Jesus as your Savior, and now you enjoy equal standing with all believers as members of God's forever family. But now you must grow. You must exert your muscles of faith and climb the ladder of Christian maturity.[21] You must advance from spiritual infancy to adulthood.

"Have you all ever noticed that in many churches the largest department is the nursery—and I don't mean the place where they keep the babies during the service. I'm talking about physical adults who, spiritually, are still sucking on a milk bottle, eating smashed carrots and peas and drooling down their chin. In the words of Hebrews 5:12, by now they 'ought to be teachers' but 'have need again for someone to teach' them 'the elementary principles of the oracles of God' and 'have come to need milk and not solid food.' They are behind schedule."

At that statement, the faces around me turned solemn. I thought of several men in my own Sunday School class whose spastic attendance and grumpy spirits showed they are not as far along as they should be in spiritual character. Rather, they were spiritually underdeveloped, aged soldiers yet to graduate from boot camp. "Dear Lord," I whispered, "enlarge my heart to run the way of Your commandments (Ps. 119:32). Help me to grow according to Your schedule."

I couldn't get my mind off a certain word on the plaque. "I was wondering, Didaskolos, about that word 'supply.' What does it mean, 'in your faith[22] supply moral excellence?'"

"Great question, Ron. A most fascinating word indeed, this term 'supply.' It comes from the Greek word pronounced *epichoregein*. One author I read says it is a

> metaphor drawn from the Athenian drama festivals, in which a rich individual, called the *choregos*, since he paid the expenses of the chorus, joined with the poet and the state in putting on the plays. This could be an expensive business, and yet *choregi* vied with one another in the generosity of their equipment and training of the choruses. Thus the word came to mean generous and costly co-operation. The Christian must engage in this sort of co-operation with God in the production of a Christian life which is credit to Him.[23]

And straightaway, what God commands[24] His child to do is cooperate with Him in the production of moral excellence. This is the first rung on the ladder of spiritual maturity."

Moral excellence. When I heard that phrase it carried me back to a sermon I had preached in my first church. I even recalled the Greek term *arete*—all those flash card exercises were paying off. The word denoted whatever captures the unrivaled worth of a person or thing. In the Greek world it meant, in one word, excellence: land that was excellent in its ability to produce crops, or even the competency of the "gods" to achieve mighty works, or the quality that makes a man a good citizen, or friend, as one who has mastered the art of living.[25]

I, too, recalled that in Peter's first letter he had used the term to exhort all believers to "proclaim the excellencies" of God who has brought us out of the darkness of sin and into His marvelous light (1 Pet. 2:9). And from Didaskolos' message in the foyer, I remembered that Peter employed the term here in the first chapter of his second letter, verse 3: "seeing that His divine power has granted to us everything pertaining to life and godliness, through the true knowledge of Him who called us by His own glory and excellence." By His own excellent virtue of impartial mercy toward sinners, He made salvation possible. And now, saved sinners are to become portraits, by means of His power, of such moral excellence.

My private musing was interrupted when I heard Didaskolos offer a brief anecdote about moral excellence in action.

"I read once about a man called Eleazar who elected to die rather than deny the laws of his God and fathers. In fact, the story ends by saying that his death was a legacy of noble courage and moral excellence, an illustration of *arete*[26]—his Christian life was truly effective for God. So you see, a true believer resists temptations to become a hermit about his faith. On the contrary his pursuit of moral excellence is for public consumption as he is unwincingly bold, though not obnoxious, about his new life in

God."

With the detailed explanation of the text and the example of Eleazar, the phrase on the walnut-brown plaque, "in your faith supply moral excellence," now made sense as did its relationship to the man in the stunning painting below it.

There was no mistake who he was. As admiration filled our hearts, we each one looked up at the wavy haired evangelist: the dark suit, the fire and compassion in his eyes, an open Bible in one hand—the clear symbol of his faith—while the other hand gestured in earnest, obviously pleading with the crowd. Here was a man who stood for moral excellence.

Once a harlot covertly stationed herself in his hotel room awaiting in sniper-like fashion his return from an evangelistic crusade—a plot brewed in hell to destroy the unsoiled reputation of this man of God. But not ignorant of the devil's dark schemes, this choice servant of God always chose a fellow-soldier of the light to escort him to his room for these very occasions. Once discovered, the seductress was removed from the room and world-evangelist, Billy Graham, remained a portrait of moral excellence.

Stirred by these dramas in real life, I prayed, "Oh Lord, let me stand like steel for You. Let me unashamedly reflect the beauty of your moral excellence on the empty canvas of my heart so that all who see it may proclaim Your excellencies. Let them see my good works and glorify You, my dear heavenly Father. In Jesus' dear name. Amen."

Didaskolos, hands joined behind his back, now slowly made his way to the next portrait in the Gallery of Virtue. Eagerly, we followed.

In the painting was a middle-aged, black woman seated at a large desk, pouring over a tattered looking Bible. Her face combined exhaustion and fascination, and the plethora of books around her, both those strewn across her desk and on the shelves behind her, exhibited a soul thirsty for

God's truth. A plaque on the wall to her left bore the name of a conservative, evangelical Seminary and the degree, Th.M., Master of Theology.

But other photographs hanging from the same wall proved that all this acquisition of biblical knowledge had not lodged somewhere in her head, but had trickled down to her heart. In one picture you could see her standing smilingly in the middle of a group of raggedly-clad children in some indigent village. Several young girls smothered her in affection. One sat upon her shoulders, laughing, and two others extended their arms around her, their heads hugging her sides–she looked to be their hero.

"How many here have heard of the Greek term *gnosis*?" Didaskolos asked.

A few of us raised our hands. "Doesn't it mean knowledge?'" asked Janet.

You could tell that Didaskolos was pleased with her obvious study of God's word when he answered, "Yes, you're right. In surveying the use of this term, sometimes it refers subjectively to the knowledge that God himself possesses, the depths of which no man can chart (Rom. 11:33); in contrast, man's knowledge may be in view (1 Cor. 8:1, 7, 11). But as well, the knowledge of false teachers is indicted in 1 Timothy 6:20 since they championed a pseudo knowledge that stood opposed to the very pillars of truth seen in Christianity such as the deity and humanity of Christ. To these false teachers we have already been introduced."

"So how does Peter use the term here in 2 Peter 1:5?" Janet interjected.

"Actually, in neither of the above categories. The employment of *gnosis*[27] here is what we might call Christian knowledge, that is, the spiritual truths that form the content of true Christian living. This includes the believer's personal knowledge of (1) what God is like as gained through Scripture (e.g., God's glory, 2 Cor. 4:6), (2) God's plan of salvation (Luke 1:77) and (3) the 'grace and knowledge of Christ Jesus,' something Peter commands his readers to grow strong in (2 Pet. 3:18). But far more than the mere acquisition of biblical knowledge, *gnosis* includes the application of that knowledge. In his first epistle, the apostle John says, 'We know that we have come to *know* [emphasis mine] him if we obey His commands' (1 John 2:3, NIV). Paul declares in 2 Corinthians 8:1, and I'm paraphrasing, that '...knowledge all by itself only tends to give you a big head–you know, increase your hat size–but being lovingly sensitive to your brother, and not causing him to stumble, encourages him.'"

Having said this, Didaskolos turned slowly toward us all, and with somber countenance said quietly, but most intently, "Watch out for the Christian who commands a great deal of Bible knowledge, but isn't known for his love for others. There's no doubt about it: his heart is oozing with pride."

A hush fell over the crowd. I overheard Jim, a well-known writer of Christian books and Bible commentaries, whisper, "Yes, Lord, I needed that reminder."

After a few moments of soul searching, Janet broke the silence. "What connection, if any, are we to see then, Didaskolos, between the first portrait, Moral Excellence, and this second one, Knowledge?"

Didaskolos smiled and said, "A superb question, sister, the kind of question we who study Scriptures seriously must learn to ask. First, you may recall Peter's previous use of the same Greek term. In verse 2, first-hand experience of God's peace on the inside and God's grace to help us is dependent upon a personal 'knowledge of God, and of Jesus.' To know the Prince of peace is to know peace–it does not come to any man apart from the Source.

"Secondly, this personal knowledge of Christ is the seed that yields a harvest of holiness in our daily life, producing such virtues as moral excellence. You see, once we catch even a glimpse of what Jesus is like, we are moved to mirror His own moral excellence which, in the first place, drew us to drink of the living water.

"Conversely, it is precisely these acts of moral excellence which validate our true knowledge of Jesus in contrast to the false teachers of Peter's day and our day who, though they claim to know Christ, betray their own confession by immoral living. In fact, this explains Peter's four-fold use of the word in his second epistle,[28] a polemic against the pseudo *didaskoloi*, that is 'false teachers,' rebuffed in the rest of the letter.

"So then," Didaskolos continued with earnest, "grow in your knowledge of Jesus. Saturate your mind with Scripture like a heavy rain saturates the ground with water: Memorize it, read it, exert yourself to study it,[29] and feast on the messages of gifted Bible teachers. In short, know what you believe and why you believe it. To your faith add moral excellence and the knowledge of Christ to the portrait of your Christianity–such will aid you in securing a hero's welcome when you stand before the King."

Silence once again descended upon us as the morning dew. And as we slowly ambled to the next portrait, Nina, a housewife from nearby Mexico, quietly told me she had just begun an intense study program that would take her through every book of the Bible over the next seven years. I made a mental note to inquire later about her plan.

"The third painting is all about self-control," Didaskolos said. Then pointing up at the portrait, with quiet intensity, he said, "Now, if you look closely you can see the small black Bible in the young Asian sailor's left hand as he walks by the Adult Movie Theater. As a swarm of his sea mates gawk lustfully at the X-rated ads on the billboards and prepare to enter the slaughter house of immorality, this saint has tapped into God's power and said 'No!' to the wishes of his flesh. From Scripture he understands that his God-given sexual passions must be fulfilled only within the bonds of marriage (Heb. 13:4). He also comprehends Peter's declaration in 2 Peter 1:4 that having a share in the very life of God enables one to escape 'the corruption that is in the world through lust.' No doubt, too, he is familiar with Proverbs 7.

"To my knowledge of Christian truth I am to add self-control. While the false teachers to whom Peter wrote claimed that knowledge released one from the need for self-mastery, the apostle again yanks the pedestal from beneath their feet by affirming that authentic knowledge makes one morally ethical in all his ways."

"What is the term Peter uses here?" Janet asked.

"A rare word in the New Testament," replied Didaskolos. "It stems from a term that means 'strength' and implies dominion over oneself.[30] Alongside the word 'righteousness' it sparkles in Acts 24:25 as one of two jewels on a necklace of virtue. Righteousness denotes God's claims on our lifestyle, and by means of self-control these claims can be realized. The athlete, in view of 1 Corinthians 9:25, must possess such self-control if he is to win his competition—winners are not born, they're made.

"In Galatians 5:23, we see the term once more as part of the colorful cluster of Christian character produced by the Holy Spirit in the believer. Of course, the opposite of 'self-control' is being 'in want of strength,'[31] like the one who is as vulnerable as chickens cornered by a raccoon to sexual temptation perpetrated by Satan" (1 Cor. 7:5).

Alfred, a forty-something history professor at a nearby university asked, "Exactly what were the thoughts of Greek philosophers on this matter of self-control?"

"Great question, young man," responded Didaskolos, with obvious lines of pleasure on his face.

"Aristotle had no answer for how to rule one's immoral passions, though the Greeks esteemed such self-governing highly. The famous Greek philosopher said that 'divine virtue was beyond man.'[32] More specifically, 'in regard to a man and his passions' he distinguished four states in life:

> There is *sophrosune*, in which passion has been entirely subjugated to reason; we might call it *perfect temperance*. There is *akolasia*, which is the precise opposite...in which reason is entirely subjugated to passion; we might call it *unbridled lust*. In between these two states there is *akrasia*, in which reason fights but passion prevails; we might call it *incontinence*. There is *egkrateia*, in which reason fights against passion and prevails; we call it *self-control*, or *self-mastery*.[33]

"But Peter's rebuttal is that divine virtue is not beyond man, including the virtue of self-control which the Greeks acknowledged but did not know how to obtain. We have already heard Peter, the transformed fisherman, proclaim that via the impartation of God's nature at salvation, the believer has all the power he needs to master his lusts before they master him, and not just in matters such as food and drink, but on all battle-fronts, for 'everything pertaining to life and godliness...' (2 Pet. 1:3). God does not strip one's passions from him when He saves him since this would remove part of His image from within–the bank of emotions. No, He simply gives him the ability to make these passions 'his servants instead of his tyrants.'"[34]

Didaskolos paused briefly and then said, "But no doubt you're all wondering why Peter hangs this portrait of self-control where he does in the Gallery of Virtue."

I was about to inquire on that very note.

"You notice that self-control follows on the heels of knowledge

Very true!

suggesting as one man said, 'what is learned requires to be put into practice.'[35] What good is it to command vast knowledge of the things of God only to have them sit stagnant in the cerebral cavity? Such fills one to the brim with spiritual hubris, the worst brand of pride there is. As we've already learned from Paul, 'Knowledge makes arrogant, but love edifies' (1 Cor. 8:1b). And elsewhere the apostle echoes, 'And if I have the gift of prophecy and know all mysteries and all knowledge (*gnosis*),...but do not have love, I am nothing' (1 Cor. 13:2). And one thing love doesn't do is seek its own (1 Cor. 13:5). It allows those who embrace it to have dominion over selfish desires of any sort."

Just then, Clifford, an elderly man with snow-white hair, asked if he could share a personal illustration of how this virtue had been realized in his own life. Didaskolos gladly consented.

"I can relate to the young sailor in the painting," Clifford began, "for I, too, had to take a stand for holy living as a military man. The barracks were full of pornographic material and most of the guys bragged about their latest conquests. At times, I felt myself being sucked in like loose dirt into a vacuum by the strong urges to peek at those magazines and furtively check out one of those strip shows. Everyone else did it and more than one laughed at me for traveling on the straight and narrow. One night my will caved in to the peer pressure and I sneaked into an Adult Theater. I cried a river of tears that night, on my face before my dear Savior—my sin that night had sent Him to a cruel Roman cross.

"Broken and spilled out in the spirit of Psalm 51, I sought His forgiveness, and He washed clean the windows of my dirty soul. That night I made a choice to always think of two verses when sexual lust came knocking on the door of my heart: Matthew 5:6 and Romans 12:1. Matthew 5:6 speaks the happy news, 'Blessed are those who hunger and thirst for righteousness, for they shall be satisfied.' I realized that every time I chose the path of unrighteousness, I was conceding that my Shepherd's paths of righteousness really didn't satisfy. I needed a little sin to fill my cup. Seeing the absurdity of this warped conclusion, a conclusion that made the devil dance and sing, drove me to my knees in repentance.

"Romans 12:1 is one of those verses we all memorize, but I had failed to see that 'the mercies of God' Paul describes in living color in the first eleven chapters of Romans are designed, by their very nature, to motivate me toward personal maturity and productive ministry. They remind me of the righteousness God provided through Jesus' death and resurrection for me, a depraved man. Thinking on this, I realized, 'I need to preach the gospel to myself daily.'"

And then at once, with eyes closed and face directed heavenward—the sunbeams gleaming through the skylight of the gallery on his careworn face—Clifford, with a deep baritone voice, began softly singing the chorus of that sage, old hymn, "Lest I forget Gethsemane, lest I forget Thine agony, lest I forget Thy blood for me, lead me to Calvary."

"Could we all sing it together?" I asked.

"Most certainly," answered Didaskolos, already on his knees in a posture of worship.

As our voices rose like sweet-smelling incense to God, the Lord inhabited our praise and visited us with a strong sense of His pleasure. It was a moment not to be forgotten by anyone.

After a long pause, Clifford, whom we now cherished more than ever, asked if he could share one more thing. Of course, Didaskolos agreed.

"I once heard a story about Lewis Sperry Chafer, founder of that wonderful school, Dallas Theological Seminary, who stood on a street corner with a young student. As I understand it, a scantily dressed woman came into view across the street. The young man said to Dr. Chafer, 'Boy, it sure will be nice when I get old enough where I won't be tempted to look more than once at a woman like that.' Dr. Chafer, already in his eighties, replied, 'Yes, and so will I,' to the shock of the student."

"I wish to make it clear," Clifford continued, "that to this day, the two verses I mentioned have served me well, along with others, in curbing my appetite for sin, especially sexual sins. And though I turned eighty-six last weekend, the battle with this kind of lust still rages on occasion. But the spiritual satisfaction God provides through faith-driven obedience and the motivation that the mercy of the cross generates to offer my body, from head to toe, as a living sacrifice to Him, has made the strong and colorful brushstrokes of self-control more visible on the empty canvas of my life."

With his arm around Clifford, Didaskolos said affirmingly, "Your personal experience, my dear brother, provides a clear window through which this virtue of self-control can be seen—thank you very much. And no doubt each of you can think of other examples from Scripture where the portrait of self-control is missing. For instance, both Samson and David let their God-given sexual passions get out of control like a runaway train, and the results were destructive, not only in terms of their own lives and ministry, but to the nation of Israel as well (cf. Judg. 13-16 and 2 Sam. 11-20, respectively). And Demas allowed his affections, once captured by God, to prostitute themselves to the world (2 Tim. 4:10), his usefulness to God's kingdom washed out to sea. But (lines of hope were written all over Didaskolos' face), admire Joseph as he resists the daily seductions of Potiphar's wife (Gen. 39), and there you have a beautiful portrait of what Peter calls self-control.

"Well, that's enough to ponder for now. A lunch break is in order. We will resume at 1 p.m.—make sure you exercise the necessary self-control to be prompt," Didaskolos said half-smiling, though we knew he meant it.

Moved so deeply in my spirit by the truth of the last portrait, I elected to fast through lunch and assess my self-control, or lack thereof, in areas such as eating habits, sleep, TV viewing, exercise, the use of my tongue...and spiritual disciplines such as solitude. I spotted a densely wooded area about seventy-five yards beyond the parking lot and sat under a sweet-smelling pine tree. The solitude refreshed my soul like a tired deer drinking in new strength from the stream after narrowly escaping the hunter.

With insatiable appetites for more truth, most everyone returned early, and no one was late—except Didaskolos.

"I can't believe he's not here yet," blurted Janet with the same befuddled look as the rest of us. "He was so intent about our timeliness, and he's the one who is tardy...."

She had hardly finished the word "tardy" when through the large picture window in the foyer we watched a forest-green Ford Aerostar swerve somewhat hastily into the parking lot, as a cloud of dust kicked up behind it. Didaskolos bounded from the van and jogged to the building. Out of breath, and embarrassed, he said, "I sincerely apologize for my lateness, but I assure you it's not due to a lack of self-control. On my way here from the local taco shop, I saw an elderly woman on the roadside staring helplessly at the wounded tire on her car. I nudged my way through the crowded traffic and pulled up behind her. I asked if I could help and you should have seen her face light up with hope. Anyway, that's why I'm late...boy, I'd forgotten how much work it is to change a flat tire!"

"Sounds to me like you're on God's time, Didaskolos," Cliff quickly replied. You could tell that to a person, Cliff had spoken for us.

As we followed Didaskolos back into the gallery, Jack, a middle-aged

Caucasian, admitted to me that he, too, had seen the distressed woman on the boulevard, but chose to quench the Spirit's prompting to stop and help. "A lack of self-control on my part...too lazy and apathetic," he confessed.

En route to the next portrait, we each gazed once more upon the paintings already seen. Like any good teacher, Didaskolos briefly revisited each one with us.

"Adding to your child-like trust in the crucified, but risen Savior, Jesus Christ, as the sole source of your salvation from hell, allow the Master Painter to apply the beautiful brushstrokes of moral excellence onto the canvas of your heart. Do not be cloistered in your Christianity, but courageously proclaim Jesus to a world putrefied by sin. And keep your lives above reproach—no glaring inconsistencies.

"But in your pursuit of moral excellence, keep on adding knowledge from Scripture with which you can pilot your way through life's choppy seas with spiritual skill. After all, the Scriptures are not given for mere information, but for transformation. But don't forget that spiritual change occurs when you let the Painter take from His palate and brush on the virtue of self-control, granting the discipline you need to apply what you know. But this leads to yet another virtue that, if portrayed in your life, assures you a hero's welcome when you see your Master face to face."

The portrait now in front of us featured a man breaking through a yellow ribbon, the winner of a marathon race. The supreme exhaustion on his face was outshined by an unmistakable glow of satisfaction for having finished what he started, but more for his victory. But everyone's attention was stolen by the term on the ticker tape, *HYPOMONE.*

This time I beat everyone to the punch: "What's that word on the ticker tape, Didaskolos?"

"Very observant Ron. It's Greek for 'endurance.' Without it, you will not finish the Christian race in full stride. Far too many believers start well but finish poorly, slumped over somewhere short of the ribbon. Peter says we are to add to our self-control the virtue of endurance. And why? Because self-control empowers you to wait on God's promises and endure whatever difficulties the race may require of you. Let me explain.

"You should know that *hypomone* basically denotes resolve under pressure. It is 'distinct from patience' in the Greek world, being more active than passive in resisting adversity; for instance, heroic responses 'in the face of bodily chastisement, or the firm refusal of bribes' exemplify *hypomone*.[36] In the Old Testament the term pictures saints waiting on God with a sense of confident expectation, waiting for deliverance of some kind (e.g., Ps. 39:7; Mic. 7:7), but not in vain, because God is just and omnipotent (e.g., Isa. 51:5; Zeph. 3:8). Such firm hope, grounded in the person of God, creates courage in their hearts and outfits them to soar as eagles above the valley of despair (e.g., Ps. 27:13-14; Isa. 40:31).

"Such courage even quips one to stand like steel against the opposition and seductions of this evil world, even to the point of martyrdom, should this be required in one's loyalty to the God of all hope.

"Finally, the New Testament literature drops the Old Testament emphasis of waiting on God, at least in those words,[37] probably due to the focus on the Christian's genuine hope in God which implies a waiting for God to come through for him. He who remains faithful in spite of the howling winds of adversity understands that he is called to suffer for Christ (Acts 14:22) and progress in his spiritual maturity through it all (Rom. 5:3-5). And for his refusal to succumb to trials, he will be rewarded in the millennial kingdom with the fortune of helping Jesus execute His righteous rule on the earth (2 Tim. 2:11).

"Of course, the ability to endure such affliction is a fixed gaze upon

Jesus who grants all the power we need for 'life and godliness' (2 Pet. 1:3). After all, for the joy set before Him, Jesus endured the cross, despising the shame, and sat down at the right hand of the throne of God (Heb. 12:2). He finished the Father's work in full stride, and with His help so can we.

"In summary, one fellow-soldier describes the term Peter employs here in this way: 'The mature Christian does not give up. His Christianity is like the steady shining of a star rather than the ephemeral brilliance (and speedy eclipse) of a meteor.'"[38]

When I heard those words, "The mature Christian does not give up," a true story came to mind. Didaskolos warmly granted my request to share it:

"I had the unspeakable privilege of being one of the four children of a lady named 'Florence Elaine Barnes.' My brother and two sisters nicknamed her 'little, but mighty'—she was small in stature, but mighty in spirit, a woman of God if you ever saw one!

"Life was pretty much blue skies and sunshine for Mom until one day the black thunderclouds rolled in unawares, the lightning cracked and the rain began to pour.

"'...You have breast cancer,' the doctor said with a sigh. Gladly, but not before a mastectomy, the cancer disappeared. Sunny skies returned. She had praised God for the hard times, now once again she extolled Him for the good.

"But a few years later, the cancer awakened in her bones. Once more the fight was on. One fair afternoon I went for a drive with her and couldn't resist the question, 'Mom, do you ever get angry with God for allowing this cancer? I mean, you have served Him steadily for so many years, and then you get this. Others who don't even care about God are healthy and you're suffering.'

"'God can do as He pleases,' she replied. 'If He wants to heal me, that's fine. And if He wants to take me home, that's fine, too.'

"As I drove quietly along, my mother's words took root in my heart. I thought to myself, 'This resembles Job's response to his wife after she advised, "curse God and die" when God so bruised her husband with sorrow and pain. To this Job answered, "Shall we indeed accept good from God and not accept adversity?"' (Job 2:10).

"Two and a half years had expired since that unforgettable conversation when Mom's battle took her through the valley of the shadow of death to death itself, and not once did she lose faith, not once did she curse God. Confused perhaps by God's mysterious doings, but she endured to the end. She finished her race in full stride. In fact, as her pastor and close friends stood by, some of her last words were, 'Let's pray.' Not only had she shown her children and all who knew her how to live, but as well, how to die. For Florence Elaine Barnes, one of God's shining stars, a hero's welcome is in store."

When I finished this remarkable story, we all observed a few moments of contemplation. Everyone could think of saints who had let bitterness take root in their soul when God rained on them. Instead of enduring and maturing, they gave up and drowned in their disappointment with God.

So we just stood there, pondering the legacy of Florence Barnes, staring at the portrait of the marathon runner busting through the yellow ribbon, and praying silently, "Lord, I believe in You, help my unbelief. Help me endure faithfully for You, until my dying breath. May the word *hypomone* be the epitaph over my earthly life."

As our minds mused, our feet carried us around a corner to the final three portraits in the Gallery of Virtue. The first painting had inscribed over it the word *eusebeia*. A middle-aged gentleman stood enraptured gazing heavenward with a copy of the Scriptures lying open, yet balanced upon his upraised palm. His other hand reached out to touch the head of a frail female child in rags, the outline of her ribs in view. I stepped closer and spotted a small brown bowl of rice from which she ate with a worn silver spoon. On the man's shirt pocket was a black name badge which read, "George Muller, Director." Behind the man, just down a small dirt road, you could barely make out the sign in front of a red-brick building, ORPHANAGE. Below the painting a wooden plaque with the letters carefully routed read, "Pure and undefiled religion in the sight of our God and Father is to visit orphans and widows in their distress, and to keep oneself unspotted by the world." - James 1:27

"Anyone here ever heard of the man in the painting, George Mueller?" Janet nodded 'yes' and said, "He was a German-born Pastor who launched and steered a massive outreach to orphans in Bristol, depending solely on contributions for his support, and by 1875, he gave oversight to 2,000 needy children?"[39]

"You've done your homework, Janet," Didaskolos said affirmingly. "And our brother, George Muller who, at this very moment, enjoys the sweet presence of his Savior, is a picture of *eusebeia*—though dead, he still speaks. Peter says we are to add to our endurance, *eusebeia*, which some translators of our modern biblical text render, 'godliness'. A difficult term to interpret, the cardinal idea is that of 'heart to God, hand to man,'[40] as aptly depicted in the painting. He who possesses *eusebeia* has a clear conscience before God and man...and fulfills his biblical duties to both. The great commandments are his portion: 'You shall love the Lord your God with all your heart, and with all your soul, and with all your strength, and with all your mind; and your neighbor as yourself'" (Luke 10:27).

"Is it not true," Jim interjected, "that the Latin equivalent is *pietas*?"

"I believe you're right, my dear brother," answered Didaskolos. "Can you elaborate?"

"I'd be happy to," said Jim with obvious delight. "Warde Fowler describes the Roman idea of the man who possesses that quality," Jim began. "He is superior to the enticements of individual passion and of selfish ease. *Pietas* is a sense of duty which never left a man, of duty first to the gods, then to father and to family, to son and to daughter, to his people and to his nation.'"[41]

"Thank you for that backdrop, Jim," Didaskolos said warmly. "This concurs with the Greek world where the main sense of the term is reverential worship of the gods, and the resulting respect for others such as relatives, spouses, or emperors. In Judaism, we find the word in the Greek translation of the Old Testament, the Septuagint (LXX), in such places as Proverbs 1:7 where we read, 'The *fear* [emphasis mine] of the Lord is the beginning of knowledge; Fools despise wisdom.' As this verse and others in the LXX reveal, *eusebeia* entails deep respect for who the Lord is and my accountability before Him, bears the fruit of true spiritual knowledge in my life and takes me down a path opposite 'Fool's Way.' In the view of Philo, *eusebeia* 'embraces a true view of God and a turning from the sensory world to the spiritual world of true being.'"[42]

"In the New Testament, *eusebeia* denotes a lifestyle that exhibits the personal impact of being rescued from hell through the saving work of Jesus. Such a gracious gift instructs those who receive it to 'deny ungodliness and worldly desires and to live sensibly, righteously and *godly* [emphasis mine] in the present age, looking for the blessed hope and the appearing of the glory of our great God and Savior, Christ Jesus; who gave Himself for us, that He might redeem us from every lawless deed and purify for Himself a people for His own possession, zealous for good deeds' (Titus 2:12-14).

"Such godliness, as Peter shows, stands in contrast to the 'sensual conduct of unprincipled men' in Sodom and Gomorrah (2 Pet. 2:7). Peter clearly employs this example from the past to expose the false teachers of his day who had a form of godliness, but not the real thing as their improper behavior proves. True godliness is always grounded in sound doctrine (1 Tim. 6:3), so Peter asserts that true knowledge of God manifests itself in reverential submission to God and serving the needs of those around you. Of course, the Christian has all the divine power required to exercise such godliness, and those who do will find profit both in this world and in the world to come (1 Tim. 4:8)–as we will soon see, a hero's welcome awaits them."

Once again, I remembered a vignette from the life of my dear mother and asked if I could share it.

"Please do," Didaskolos said with anticipation.

"During her last few months on earth, my mother's energy level dipped severely due to a poor appetite from chemotherapy. But for as long as she could stand before them, she prepared her Sunday School lesson and taught God's eternal truth to her elementary class. On one occasion, she even made and delivered chicken soup to a sickly neighbor. In all, she is a picture of *eusebeia*; for one hand she raised heavenward in worship of her God, whom she trusted without question, and with the other hand she reached out to touch those in need around her, even when she herself was in greater need than they. 'Heart to God, hand to man,' that was my mother, Florence Barnes."

"Thank you, Ron, for sharing this story. The memory of your mother inspires each of us toward godliness." Then with a deliberate hand gesture to assert himself, Didaskolos said, "Now, we are ready to view the final two portraits. And as you would expect, they are not unrelated to what our spiritual eyes have seen to this point. For while the first five portraits: moral excellence, knowledge, self-control, perseverance and godliness, relate chiefly to the Christian's inner life and how he relates to

God, the last two concern how he relates to others. Please, walk with me down this brightly lit hallway to the first of these portraits."

The first portrait we saw featured two ladies, one in her late teens and an older lady in her fifties. The younger woman was bent forward, her face encased in her hands as tears streamed down over the fingers. The elder gentlewoman, eyes tightly closed and forehead wrinkled with concern, had one arm placed around her distraught friend, and her slightly open mouth suggested a prayer of intercession being lifted to God. Reaching down from heaven was the common anthropomorphic hand of God, depicting the answer to the prayer rising like incense to His throne of grace. Etched in a white pine-colored plaque above the portrait was the word *Philadelphia*.

"Certainly you all know what *philadelphia* means," said Didaskolos, "being familiar with what usually follows the mention of the fair city that bears that name–known as the 'city of...

"'...brotherly love,'" we all said in unison.

"Correct!" Didaskolos answered enthusiastically. "The term stems from two Greek words, *philos*, which means 'friend,' and *adelphos*, meaning 'brother.' In a broad sense it denoted love for one's blood brothers or sisters,[43] but in figure it stands for Christian brothers and sisters in God's eternal family, in this way distinguishing Christians from other people. Paul tells believers to be 'devoted to one another in *brotherly love* [emphasis mine]' which among other qualities entails 'rejoicing with those who rejoice and weeping with those who weep'" (Rom. 12:10, 14).

Then Nina inserted, "I once surveyed this term in my Bible concordance. I found 130 uses in Pauline literature[44] and learned in a word study tool called *Theological Dictionary of the New Testament* that *philadelphia* has Old Testament and Jewish roots (e.g., Matt. 5:22-23; Acts 2:29; 3:17, 22). Jesus also employs the term in Matthew 23:8 when He says, 'But do not be called Rabbi; for One is your Teacher, and you are all *brothers* [emphasis mine].' And to my joyful surprise, of those who know Him personally, He calls them 'His brethren' in Romans 8:29."

"Thank you sister for your inspiring example of serious research from God's priceless treasures in Scripture. And speaking of a studious mind, did anyone ponder the relationship between *eusebeia* and *philadelphia*? Why does Peter place 'brotherly love' on the heels of 'godliness?'"

"Could it be," I remarked, "that private devotion to God, the essence of *eusebeia*, shows up in how we treat other believers, especially reaching out to touch them at their point of need–like the lady in the portrait comforting and imploring heaven for the younger woman?"

"You couldn't be more right, Ron," Didaskolos said. "If someone says, 'I love God,' and hates his brother, he is a liar" (1 John 4:20). Since all God's children have become partakers of His nature (2 Pet. 1:4), they must, as one Christian scholar put it, 'show their royal birth in royalty of behavior towards other children of the King, whatever differences in culture, class and churchmanship.'"[45]

At this juncture Janet offered to share a note she had just written to a Bible teacher she'd sat under in a recent semester of demanding study. "This man is full of the Holy Spirit," she began. "As we have been exhorted today, he is appropriating God's power for life and godliness; in fact, as you will detect in my note, he depicts this aspect of God's nature called brotherly kindness." Reaching into her brown leather purse, Janet pulled out the note and began to read.

"Thank the Lord for you. This is to say thank you for being there for me in all those times I thought I would lose it. Your wisdom and prayers have been so appreciated during my time at the college. You'll never know how comforting you were the day you took time to pray with me in the hallway. Thank you for who you are. I am blessed to have known you."

"We are indebted to you, sister," said Didaskolos, "for sharing the personal encouragement you have received by a brother in Christ who has evidently visited God's Gallery of Virtue and allowed the Master Painter to color his life with the gorgeous brushstrokes of brotherly kindness. This concrete example of *philadelphia* is how it is portrayed in the New Testament.

"All said, in the pages of the New Testament this Christian kindness must be displayed with sincerity (1 Pet. 1:22), practiced routinely (Heb. 13:1), is a virtue that can always use improvement (1 Thess. 4:9-10), and includes such things as bearing each other's burdens—something seen in your story, Janet. But it also entails refraining from gossip, refusing to slander and looking for ways to honor the honorable character we see in other believers" (Rom. 12:10).

As we strolled contemplatively down the hallway to the final portrait, everyone sort of bunched together as we once again listened to our beloved teacher prepare us for the final viewpoint.

"In your mind's eye envision a dazzling rainbow, standing out in its full prism of colors amid the rain and the rays of the sun breaking through the clouds. Its impeccable arc and perfect fusion of colors has the fingerprints of God all over it. And please note, it's 'colors,' plural—not just blue, or red, or green, or yellow—but blue, red, green, yellow and perhaps other hues blended in lovely harmony.

"Love—*agape* love—is a rainbow of divine virtue with all the colors of God's grace shining through it for a whole world to see. Brotherly kindness, the portrait just behind us, is really a love for the brethren, but the term Peter selects here to describe the final portrait in God's Gallery of Virtue encompasses a love that knows no limits. It reaches out to touch anyone with a need, even a stranger—even an enemy!"

With this appetizer, Didaskolos then directed our eyes to the painting behind him. The scene was a raging river, parts of a collapsed bridge sticking out of the rapids, and near the edge of the river a group of slightly soaked men on horseback. But what arrested our attention was the inquisitive look on their faces as they gazed into the face of another man standing beside them, apparently saying something to the group.

"What is this picture all about?" asked Allen, speaking for all of us.

A coy look upon his face, Didaskolos replied, "I think I'll delay the explanation of this portrait until the conclusion of our discussion. Please don't let me forget."

"No chance of that," answered Allen.

"Now then, let's zoom in on this word *agape*; what does it mean?" Didaskolos quizzed.

"Isn't it true," inquired Nina, "that there are three basic words for love in the Greek culture?"

"Yes," said Didaskolos, "you're right. *Eros* is essentially physical satisfaction in the realm of sexual love. *Phileo*, as already discussed with regard to brotherly kindness, or *philadelphia*, focuses on the mutual encouragement friends can provide. This term is even used to depict the love that God the Father and God the Son have for each other and for believers (cf. John 5:20 and 16:7, respectively).

"I like how brother Michael Green put it: 'In both cases [*eros* and *phileo*] these feelings are aroused because of what the loved one is. With agape it is the reverse. God's *agape* is not evoked by what we are, but by what He is. It has its origin in the agent, not in the object. It is not that we are lovable, but that He is love.'"[46]

Jim then interjected an important question, "Didaskolos, I once heard that *agape* is not always used in the New Testament in a positive sense. Is that true?"

"Yes, brother, it is true," answered Didaskolos. "Paul sadly writes in 2 Timothy 4:10 that 'Demas, having loved this present world, has deserted me.' The word translated 'loved' there is *agape*. But in spite of this negative illustration of the term—a case of misguided devotion on Demas' part—for all intentions, the word *agape* stands for the disposition God maintains toward mankind and in reciprocal fashion, the attitude we ought to have toward Him."

Nina, evidently the ardent Bible student she claimed to be, then divulged some fascinating observations she had once made regarding God's *agape* love in John 3:16.

"God's love is unconditional: after all, who is this 'world' that He loved and still loves? It is a world of sinners like you and me."

"That reminds me," said Allen, "of Romans 5:8, a verse I just memorized. It says, 'But God demonstrates His own love toward us, in that while we were yet sinners, Christ died for us.'"

"Great correlation, Allen," Didaskolos inserted. "Nina, can you tell us more?"

"Well, God's love is also sacrificial. The verse says that '...God so loved the world that He gave His only Son....' But there's more...God's love is also very personal. We learn here that Jesus was given so that 'whoever believes in Him should not perish, but have eternal life.'"

Didaskolos then told us a true story about an elderly man who walked the beach at dusk one day. "Up ahead something caught his attention. A young man was tossing things into the foamy waves. Overcome with curiosity, he picked up his pace and when close enough inquired, 'What are you doing, young man, if I may ask?'

"'I'm throwing these star fish into the ocean before the morning sun bakes them to death.'

"'But there are millions of star fish along this beach,' the old man replied, still confused. 'What does all your effort matter?'

"The young man grabbed a starfish from the wet sand and said quietly, but soberly, 'It matters to this one!'[47]

"Each of us matter to God," Didaskolos continued. "Someone has said that the love of God is like the entire Amazon River flowing down to water just one daisy, and each one of us represent that one daisy. Please teach us more, Nina," said Didaskolos.

"God's love, according to John 3:16, is beneficial as well, extremely beneficial," she said with a big smile and eyes wide open. "Because God loves us the way He does, He has provided, through the gift of His Son, our blessed Savior, the promise of eternal life."

"It doesn't get any better than that!" exclaimed Clifford in a booming deep voice.

"These are profound insights, Nina," said Didaskolos. "Thank you once again. And from this we can grasp the depth of love God desires and requires to see in us for Him. Can we all say the Great Commandment from Luke 10:27 in unison?"

Most could recite from memory: "You shall love the Lord your God with all your heart, and with all your soul, and with all your strength, and with all your mind...."

"This intense and comprehensive love for God shows up, of course, in our adherence to His word. As John wrote, 'For this is the love of God, that we keep His commandments; and His commandments are not burdensome' (1 John 5:3). It is then obvious, is it not, what the opposite of loving God is—placing our own selfish wishes before God's wishes for our lives. This means that no person, place, possession, pursuit or position, can be more important to us than God. As God told Israel, in Exodus 20:3, 'You shall have no other gods before Me.' I would urge each of you, in a spirit of brotherly love, to get alone with God and allow the searchlight of His written word to expose any 'god' in your life, if there should be any at this time. Discard it, like a dirty diaper, and love Him with *agape* love."

"How then, does this kind of love express itself to others?" I asked.

"Excellent question, Ron," Didaskolos responded. "We certainly cannot bypass the second greatest commandment which is to love our neighbor as our self. What comes to mind straightaway is that potent summons by the apostle John in his first epistle, chapter 3 and verses 16-18: 'We know love by this, that He laid down His life for us; and we ought to lay down our lives for the brethren. But whoever has the world's goods, and beholds his brother in need and closes his heart against him, how does the love of God abide in him? Little children, let us not love with word or with tongue, but in deed and truth.'

"What stirs my spirit is how this theme of loving God and others weaves its way through the fabric of John's writings. Clearly the man was serious about the great commandments to love God and our neighbor as ourself. But just listen to what a life of love for God and others leads to in chapter 4, verses 16-19:

> And we have come to know and have believed the love which God has for us. God is love, and the one who abides in love abides in God, and God abides in him. By this, love is perfected with us, that we may have confidence in the Day of Judgment; because as He is, so also are we in this world. There is no fear in love; but perfect love

casts out fear, because fear involves punishment, and the one who fears is not perfected in love. We love, because He first loved us.

"Now then, let me summarize a few principles here. First, the believer who orders his actions and words by the standard of *agape* love is the same person who orders his life by the standards of God. After all, God, by very nature, is the epitome of love. Second, such a believer will have no fear or shame when he stands before Jesus at the judgment seat of Christ because 'as He is—He is love—so also are we in this world.' Like Him, we are known for our love for others. This is what John means when he says, 'perfect love casts out fear.' Thirdly, the believer resolved to love others recognizes that the reason he does so is a response to God's love for him.

"But let's get practical now. What does *agape* love look like in life? Any examples you can think of?"

Allen, the first to speak up, said, "The other day I clipped an article from the *San Diego Tribune* about a couple of guys who make a living aiding the less fortunate. Just listen to this selfless act of love: 'For eight years, tenant advocates Larry Wood and Rafael Sencion shared an office. When the city cut their financing, Sencion, a bachelor, agreed to be laid off in place of his friend...Wood's wife, Lori, was seven months pregnant at the time. The couple also had a three-year old daughter. "Larry, you're about to have a baby," Wood recalled his friend telling him. "You can't lose your job right now."'"[48]

"Excellent example, Allen." said Didaskolos. "Anyone else?"

"That reminds me of 1 John 3:17-18," said Jim, "the passage you quoted a moment ago, Didaskolos. The story comes from a Dallas Theological Seminary publication called *The Dallas Insider*, an informative newsletter for alumni. Roger Raymer, in his article entitled 'A Fellowship of Encouragement,' writes the following:

> Last fall a member of the Houston (alumni) chapter called me to let me know that after years of faithful ministry, he was out of a job. The severance package was woefully inadequate. Though he was now substitute teaching, the summer months had caused them to fall three months behind on his mortgage payments. He asked for prayer.... I prayed and then called a number of pastors in the chapter. In less than an hour we rallied both prayer support and financial help. By the end of the week we were able to write a check to cover back mortgage payments, some other outstanding bills, as well as a week's groceries. It was a beautiful illustration of the extended body of Christ reaching out in ministry to one who had served faithfully for so many years.[49]

"And thank you, Jim, for that fine illustration of *agape* love. How motivating. It brings to mind Proverbs chapter 3, verses 27-28, 'Do not withhold good from whom it is due, when it is in your power to do it. Do not say to your neighbor, "Go, and come back, and tomorrow I will give it, when you have it with you."'

"Not long ago I stumbled across a stellar example of biblical forgiveness, forgiveness that issues from a believer controlled by the Holy Spirit, a believer controlled by *agape* love:

> "Jim is a business man in his mid-forties. His company sends him to Japan a few times a year. He's unfaithful to his wife. He wants to be free, so he divorces his Christian wife of twenty-five years. She cries a lot and prays. But he is gone from her. He loves Haruka, a young, pretty Japanese girl, he says. His company continues to send him to the Far East on business. He can pick up the affair with the woman in Japan each time he visits Tokyo.
>
> "Haruka sends word she is pregnant. Jim sends them a small allowance.

"Suddenly one day back in Chicago Jim is taken violently ill. Doctors discover he has a rapidly spreading form of cancer. Surgery and chemotherapy don't help much and Jim grows weaker. He realizes he has no more than a few weeks.

"Mutual friends tell Helen, Jim's ex-wife. She went through the stages of anger and grief when Jim left. Still she can't forget she's a Christian.

"One day Helen appears at Jim's bedside in the hospital. She and Jim try to talk, but it is difficult. Finally, Jim breaks down and cries, asking for her forgiveness. Helen gropes for words. 'Is there anything I can do?' she finds herself asking.

"'It's Haruka and Jasmine,' Jim whispers. 'I've spent all my money on doctors and hospitals. I don't know what will happen to them. All my insurance is still being left to you.'

"Helen can't answer. She leaves Jim's hospital room and struggles in prayer for several days. A few days before Jim dies, she writes to Haruka inviting them to come to Chicago to live with her.

"A month after Jim's funeral, a moving scene takes place at O'Hare Airport. Helen takes into her arms a fragile Japanese girl and a frightened child. She welcomes them as family.

"Helen has made a home for them. Every day she thanks God for the way she has learned to appreciate His undeserved mercy, His constant love.[50]

"As Helen grasped hold of God's unconditional *agape* love for her, she mirrored that same kind of love toward her undeserving husband and his new family. Here's a woman who allowed Jesus, the Master Painter, to color her life with the resplendent brushstrokes of mercy, compassion, forgiveness and love. And here's the kind of woman to whom Christ will grant a hero's welcome when the day of reckoning arrives. He will reward her with the lavish commendation: 'Well done, you good and faithful servant' (Matt. 25:21).

"But it is not only such dramatic acts of love that warrant reward from the Lord. This *agape* love can have many expressions: watching a young mother's children, so she can have some time to herself for shopping, sleeping, or whatever; helping a friend move—perhaps this is the greatest exhibition of love known to man," said Didaskolos with a chuckle. "Maybe it's mowing a neighbor's yard while he's ill or gone on vacation, giving someone else the last piece of cherry pie, or warming up the car on a cold wintry morning so the family won't be so miserable as they drive off. As Jesus Himself said, even the gift of a 'cup of cold water to drink' to help any one of His servants is worthy of reward on Judgment Day" (Matt. 10:42).

"Let's not forget that amidst all the ministry of spiritual gifts being exercised by the saints in Corinth, *agape* love was strangely absent. So Paul sandwiches the famous chapter on *agape* love in I Corinthians, chapter 13. Verses 1-3 show the priority of love, verses 4-8a, the practical expressions of love, and verses 8b-13, the permanence of love. In fact, in the triad of faith, hope and love, 'the greatest of these is love.' Why? Because, by nature, love is eternal since it finds its source in the eternal God—God is love, as John says (1 John 4:8).

"Love, then, is the most important portrait in the gallery and is the summation of all of the portraits before it. Let me suggest some selected comparisons between the six preceding virtues and *agape* love as depicted in 1 Corinthians 13, verses 4-8."

Didaskolos presented the following chart:

2 Peter 1:5-7	1 Corinthians 13:4-8a

moral excellence	love does not rejoice in unrighteousness
knowledge	believes all things
self-control	does not brag
perseverance	bears and endures all things
godliness	does not seek its own
brotherly kindness	love is kind

"'A third-grade science teacher asked one of her students to describe salt. "Well, um, it's..." he started, then stopped. He tried again, "Salt is, you know, it's...." Finally, he said, "Salt is what makes French fries taste bad when you don't sprinkle it on." Can you imagine "pizza without cheese, strudel without apples, a banana split without bananas." The Christian life also has an essential element: love.'"[51]

Didaskolos paused for ten or fifteen seconds, then looked at us with all the sincerity he could muster and asked, "So what kind of entrance into heaven do you wish to have? Do you want to have a hero's welcome; the only kind of welcome our beloved Savior is worthy of? Or are you apathetic? Do you ever say to yourself, 'Well, I am eternally secure in Christ and don't need to climb the ladder of spiritual growth, I don't need to be serious about portraying the virtues I have seen in this gallery?'

"I don't want to shrink back in shame when I stand before Christ at His judgment seat.[52] I want to be able to look Him in the eye with a clear conscience, knowing I have cooperated with Him in painting onto the empty canvas of my life the beautiful virtues of His heart. I want to receive a hero's welcome.

"But you may be saying, 'Didaskolos, you have yet to show us where this idea of a "hero's welcome" comes from. Where in Scripture is this truth that some Christians will receive a hero's welcome and others will not?' I am so glad you asked," said Didaskolos with a grin that matched ours. "Let's finish Peter's paragraph here and the concept will unfold before your very eyes."

With the portrait of *agape* love forever impressed upon our minds, we eagerly trailed Didaskolos to the end of the hallway into a conference room where each took a seat to hear verses 8-11.

Endnotes for Chapter 1

[1] Adapted from: Kevin Fedarko and Mark Thompson, "All for One," *Time*, June 1995, 20.

[2] Ibid.

[3] Ibid.

[4] Ibid.

[5] The Christian will "go home" either at the time of his death or at the time of the Rapture, whichever comes first: cf. 2 Corinthians 5:1-9 and 1 Thessalonians 4:13-18, respectively.

[6] Such as Peter's sermon in Acts 2.

[7] Both nouns are nominative masculine singular, functioning as the subject of the sentence.

[8] Both nouns, "servant" and "apostle," are nominative masculine singular, serving in apposition to describe "Simon Peter." The conjunction "and" coordinates the two nouns. The phrase "of Jesus Christ" is a subjective genitive.

[9] Several observations should be made in verse 1 which are crucial to a correct understanding of Peter's emphasis in verses 10-11: (1) Peter identifies his readers as "those who have received a faith of the same kind of ours." The phrase "same kind of ours" is emphatic and translates *isotimos* which here means "equal in value," Brown, Driver, and Briggs, *Hebrew and English Lexicon of the Old Testament* (London: Oxford University Press, 1966), 382; or "equally privileged," Joseph B. Mayor, *The Epistle of St. Jude and the Second Epistle of Peter* (Grand Rapids: Baker, 1965), quoted in Cleon L. Rogers, Jr., and Cleon L. Rogers III, *The New Linguistic and Exegetical Key to the Greek New Testament* (Grand Rapids: Zondervan, 1998), 581. NIV renders it, "A faith as precious as ours" and Green points out the political background of the term: "All alike are sinners who owe their presence in the heavenly city...to the amnesty of the King." Michael Green, *The Second Epistle General of Peter and the General Epistle of Jude: An Introduction and Commentary*, Tyndale New Testament Commentary 18 (Grand

Rapids: Eerdmans, 1984), 60. *Isotimos* is a late compound adjective in the first attributive position and stems from two words, *isos* = equal, and time = honor or price, value; used only here in the NT; the best translation is "like precious" or "equal in honor" instead of "equal in value" which corresponds better to *polutimos*, the term seen in 1 Peter 1:7; 2:4, 6. Further support for "equal in honor" is found in the papyri, Josephus and Lucian. Archibald Thomas Robertson, *Word Pictures in the New Testament: The General Epistles and The Revelation of John* (Nashville: Broadman, 1933), 6:147. The plural pronoun "us" (*hemin*), is in the associative-instrumental case following *isotimon*. Referring to the original apostles of which Peter was one, the idea is "to those who have received a faith equal in honor with us." Thus, these second or third generation believers to whom Peter writes shared equal honors as recipients of the Christian faith with the original "eyewitnesses of His majesty" (cf. 1:16). The ground is level at the foot of the cross. (2) Peter says that this precious faith (*pistin* is accusative of direct object, and being *anarthrous* it carries the subjective sense here versus the objective idea of the body of doctrine Christians believe in, that is, in view is the believer's trust in Christ for the righteousness of God received in justificational salvation. The same sense is observed in the only other occurrence of the term in the epistle, 1:5, though there in connection with sanctificational salvation) shared by all believers has been "received," (second aorist dative articular participle, substantival use, from *lagchano*, "to obtain by lot, to obtain"). The aorist is most likely perfective in force denoting a past (unrepeatable) event with continuing results; and further, this faith is a gift from God (as per the reception of this faith just mentioned). (3) The grounds for this equal standing shared by all believers, Jew or Gentile, is the "righteousness of God" which here, in a subjective genitive form, emphasizes God's impartial justice, or fairness, as seen in Peter's use of *dikaiosyne* in the rest of the epistle, 2:5, 7, 8; 3:13 (versus the forensic nuance of the term observed in some of the Pauline corpus, e.g., Rom. 5:1). The noun "righteousness" is definite due to the preposition *en* before it and the genitive that follows. (4) The source and means of this salvific faith (the preposition *en* here could equal source or means) is "our God and Savior Jesus Christ." Since one article governs the two nouns (*ho theos kai soter* as in v. 3, *ho theos kai pater*), one Person is meant, namely Jesus. Elsewhere when Peter employs the term "Savior," an important name for God in the OT (Isa. 45:21), he clearly refers to Jesus (cf. 1:11; 2:20; 3:2, 18). In brief, we have here a classic declaration of the deity of Jesus Christ.

[10] "Grace" is *charin* and here does not stand for the undeserved favor of God that secures (past) justificational salvation for sinners, but the inward aid for (present) sanctificational salvation in His saints; cf. the same use of *charin* in Romans 12:3 and 1 Corinthians 15:10. Parallel to *charin* is *eirene* (peace); both are feminine singular nouns functioning as the joint subjects of the clause; *eirene* is the inward peace of

God (versus the peace with God seen in justification, see Rom. 5:1) available to the believers and especially significant in view of the potentially hostile environment of false teachers in the midst of Peter's audience. The following phrase "to you" signifies a dative of advantage. "Be multiplied" is a first passive optative of *plethuno*; in this form a wish or prayer is intended as in 1 Peter 1:2; Jude 2. And this grace and peace is multiplied in the believer's life by means of (the force of the preposition *en*) the full knowledge (*epignosin*) of God (objective genitive); *epignosin* is used again in 1:3, 8; 2:20.

[11] The term "knowledge" is *epiginosis*, literally, "full knowledge." With the attached preposition, *epi*, the idea becomes "thorough knowledge." This word and related words occurs eleven times in the epistle revealing the polemical nature of Peter's message: Though the false teachers of the day, namely the Gnostics, claimed knowledge of God, their actions betrayed such a reality (2:20-21). True knowledge finds its source in an understanding of and personal relationship with Jesus Christ.

[12] A large number of MSS read, "in the knowledge of our Lord," which is most likely the correct reading in light of three reasons cited by Green: (1) the shorter reading is generally preferable, (2) continuity with the singular "his" of verse 3, which follows, and (3) the fact that Jesus alone is the object of knowledge elsewhere in the epistle (cf. 3:18). Green, 62.

[13] The construction here is a genitive absolute with the subordinating conjunction, *hos*, functioning as a causal particle—the grace and peace just promised is available because of the reality now stated in verse 3. The participle *dedoremenes* is a perfect middle of an old verb, *doreo*, to bestow (*dorea* = gift), signifying that His gift of power, which follows, is the gift that keeps on giving. *Autou* (subjective genitive pronoun) is a reference to Christ who possesses *theias dunameos*, divine power. After all, He is *theos* (1:1). *Theias* found only here and in verse 4, which follows, and in Acts 17:29 where Paul uses *to theion* for deity. As Robertson observes quoting Bigg, "Peter is fond of *dunamis* in this Epistle, and the *dunamis* of Christ 'is the sword which St. Peter holds over the head of the False Teachers.'" Charles Bigg, *A Critical and Exegetical Commentary on the Epistles of St. Peter and St. Jude*, International Critical Commentary 42 (Edinburgh: T. & T. Clark, 1901), quoted in Robertson, 6:149. The phrase "all things that pertain to life and godliness" serves as the object of what Christ has given to us (dative of advantage). For a discussion of *eusebeia* go to page 26ff in this chapter. The participial phrase "of Him that called us" is an articular genitive aorist active form from *kaleo*. This is the divine call that summons sinners to salvation. Peter had experienced it and now informs his readers that they too are recipients of the true faith due to Christ's call. Some ancient texts read "through glory and virtue." According to Robertson, the texts B K L use *dia* while the texts Aleph A C P use *idiai* which can be translated as "by" or "to." The preferred reading is *idiai*,

"by His own glory and virtue"; *idios* (by own) is a favorite expression of Peter, employed 7 times in this epistle and also seen in his first epistle (cf. I Peter 3:1, 5). Robertson, 6:149.

[14] The term "these" translates the relative pronoun *hon* which could take "glory and virtue" as its antecedent or "all things pertaining to life and godliness," or also, as Robertson notes, the antecedent could be *hemin* meaning "through whom." Robertson, 6:149. Most commentators prefer the first idea. Alford renders it "through which (His attributes and energies)." Henry Alford, *The Greek Testament*, rev. by Everett F. Harrison (Chicago: Moody, 1968), 4:391. "He has granted" is the perfect indicative middle of *doreo*, same term as in verse 3, the perfect showing the on-going availability of what follows in the accusative construction, namely "His precious and magnificent promises." "Precious" is used in Peter's first epistle: in 1:7 to describe the Christian's faith, in 1:19 of Christ's blood, and here as an attribute of Christ's promises. In parallel to this term is the attributive adjective rendered "magnificent," an elative superlative. Robertson, 6:150. The subordinate purpose/result clause that follows is introduced by the *hina*. "By them" is the dative construction of the preposition *dia* and the demonstrative pronoun *touton* which takes us back to "His precious and magnificent promises." The phrase "might become" renders the term *ginesthe*, second aorist middle subjunctive of *ginomai*, showing the purpose for our divine calling, namely to be "partakers of the divine nature." "Partakers" is *koinonoi*, serving in the nominative case as the subject of the clause, "of the nature," which follows is a genitive of content or apposition. Elsewhere Peter says we are partakers of Christ's sufferings and will be partakers of His future glory (cf. 1 Pet. 4:13 and 5:1, respectively). Peter means here that we are in union with Christ. "Having escaped" is *apophugontes*, second aorist participle of *apopheugo*, only used here and in 2:18, 20. A perfective nuance may be the best choice here denoting the decisive transaction of "taking flight" (the essential idea behind the word) from the corruption that is in the world, and this condition continuing to the present. "Corruption" is *phthoras* from *phtheiro* and signifies "to destroy by means of corrupting and so bringing something into a worse state." W. E. Vine, *Vine's Complete Expository Dictionary of Old and New Testament Words*, ed. by Merrill Frederick Unger and William White (Nashville: Thomas Nelson, 1985), 130. Here it means "moral decay," the result of sinful lusts; this same nuance is seen in 2 Peter 2:12 regarding "the effect upon themselves of the work of false and immoral teachers." Vine, 131. In other uses it can equal physical decay such as the body in burial (1 Cor. 15:42), the current condition of the cursed creation (Rom. 8:22), or the destruction of animals (beasts) (2 Pet. 2:12). "Lust" is *epithumia* and denotes strong desire of any kind, not necessarily evil (e.g., Luke 22:15; Phil. 1:23), but in most every occurrence entails a bad desire, "a natural tendency towards things evil." Vine, 384. The term is associated

with "the pride of life" in 1 John 2:15, 17 and expressed as "lust of the eyes," and "lust of the flesh," respectively. Here, in the dative, Peter means that the corruption that is in the world is caused by lust. "Lust" stands in contrast with "divine nature" in verse 4 and with all the attendant graces of Christian character detailed in verses 5-7.

[15] "For by these" (literally, "through which things") renders the Greek *di hon* a genitive preposition of means followed by a neuter relative pronoun whose antecedent is the phrase "glory and virtue" just cited.

[16] "Take flight" is a rendering of *apopheugo* in verse 4; the term is also used in 2:18 of someone barely escaping from moral error and in 2:20 the word is in contrast with being entangled by the defilements of the world. In Hebrews 11:34 the root *pheugo* speaks of armies being put to flight as an effect of the power of the faith of God's people; the cognate *diapheugo* is found in Acts 27:42 of prisoners escaping.

[17] Literally, "'this very thing:' but just as *rí*, 'what,' has come to mean 'why?' 'for what reason?' so *auto*, or *touto*, or the strengthened demonstrative produced by the juxtaposition of both, has come to mean, 'wherefore,' 'for this reason.'" Alford, 4:391. Grammatically, *auto touto* is an adverbial accusative, "here, a classic idiom, with both *kai* and *de* (standing on either side of the accusative structure [parenthesis mine])." Robertson, 6:150. Theologically, the idea is this: because of our union with God in the impartation of the divine nature, and because of all the resources this brings—His perfect power and His precious promises—we have personal responsibility to work out the divine nature already worked in (cf. Phil. 2:12-13).

[18] Diligence renders the Greek term *spoude*, which denotes "earnestness, zeal, or sometimes the haste accompanying this" Vine, 169; used in Luke 19:5 as an imperatival participle where Jesus tells Zaccheus to "hurry and come down" in anticipation of His visit to the little man's house; with the attributive adjective "all" here the idea is similar to the exact construction in Jude 3: "make every effort." The Christian is to take serious measures to exercise his duty to cooperate with God in the production of godly character; note too, the imperatival use of the nominative participle *pareisenegkantes* here: "applying all diligence," the aorist signifying the urgency of the decision.

[19] Paul observes the same pattern in Romans 5, beginning with faith in verse1 and follows with the fruits of faith in verses 2-5. As Green comments, "The same holds good in the sub-apostolic literature as well. Barnabas puts faith first, with reverence and endurance, long-suffering and self-control as its allies; while Hermas not only puts faith first, but specifically says 'through her the chosen of God are saved.' Faith is here represented as a woman, who has several daughters (i.e. other virtues), and the culmination of them all, as here, is love." Green, 67.

[20] *Pistis* here equals confidence in God according to Walter Bauer, *A Greek-English Lexicon of the New Testament and Other Early Christian Literature*, trans. and adapt. by William F. Arndt and F. Wilbur Gingrich (Chicago: University of Chicago

Press, 1957), 668.

[21] Paul, too, employed lists to display various Christian virtues expected of the Christian (cf. Gal. 5:22-23, 1 Tim. 6:11, and Rom. 5:3f); such lists are to be found as well in the *Epistles of Barnabas*, 2.2, 3 and *The Shepherd of Hermas*, Vis. III, 8.1-7. Green, 66n2. As Green adds, "The practice of making lists of virtues was already well established among the Stoics, who called it a *prokope*, 'moral advance.'" Green, 66. Paul is not seeking to Hellenize the early church, but to find points of familiarity with his readers. Of course, the Christian has the divine nature within him to make these virtues a reality, whereas the religious efforts of the Stoics could never produce such spiritual fruit, being nothing but the anemic energy of the sinful flesh. Such legalism ever lurks in the shadows of the Christian who must be careful having begun with grace, in justificational salvation, not to abandon the same grace available for sanctificational salvation. This potential danger is precisely the occasion for Paul's polemical epistle to the Galatians.

[22] The prepositional phrase "in your faith" is probably best taken as a dative of association/accompaniment, that is, "in association with your faith, supply...." This nuance carries through all the parallel dative prepositional phrases in the ascending ladder of virtue: "in your moral excellence...in your knowledge...in your self-control...in your perseverance...in your godliness...in your brotherly kindness...in your love." The semantic value and corresponding concept in view, as per the term "supply," (see discussion in the text) seems to lend additional support to this exegetical choice regarding the dative.

[23] Green, 66-67.

[24] *Epichoregesate* is an aorist imperative, probably best taken as a constative nuance.

[25] Cf. William Barclay, *The Letters of James and Peter*, The Daily Study Bible Toronto: G. R. Welch, 1976), 301.

[26] 2 Maccabees 6:31, cited in Barclay, *James and Peter*, 302.

[27] Here the form is feminine, *gnosin*, an accusative of direct object following the implied repetition of the verb "supply"; "and [*de* functioning in a copulative role here in the continuation of the adding on of virtues] in your moral excellence, supply knowledge"; each of the accusative nouns in this section, *areten, gnosin, egkrateian, hupomonen, eusebeian, Philadelphian* and *agapen* function in like manner in Peter's parallel structure.

[28] See 1:3, 5, 8; 2:20. As Green comments, "Knowledge was, of course, one of the favorite words of the false teachers, but Peter was not, on that account, afraid to use it. He was confident that the God who had revealed Himself in Jesus was the God of truth. Knowledge, therefore, could never harm the Christian...The cure for false knowledge is not less knowledge, but more." Green, 68.

[29] Cf. 2 Timothy 2:15 and the imperative use of *spoudazo* there: "*Be diligent*

[emphasis mine] to present yourself approved to God as a workman who does not need to be ashamed, handling accurately the word of truth."

[30] The term used here, *enkrateia*, is part of a word group that takes its sense from the stem *krat*, signifying power or lordship. In brief, then, the word means "having power over all things and the self...." W. Grundmann, "enkrateia," in *Theological Dictionary of the New Testament*, ed. by Gerhard Kittel and Gerhard Friedrich, trans. and abr. by Geoffrey W. Bromiley (Grand Rapids: Eerdmans, 1985), 196. The same author goes on to say that the term plays "little role in the Bible." In the LXX, it is found in Sir. 18:30; Wis. 8:21; 4 Macc. 5:34, but does not occur in the Gospels. It is the word used in I Cor.7:9 where sexual self-control is in view, though, as Grundmann rightly concludes, "there is no extolling of asceticism as though marital sex were wrong. The sparse use of this ethical term is due to three things: (1) for Christians, life is directed by God's command so that there is no place for autonomous self-mastery; (2) belief in creation excludes dualism, for all things are good as they come from God; and (3) salvation in Christ leaves no place for meriting salvation by asceticism." Grundmann, 196.

[31] Cf. Vine, 215, in his discussion of *akrasia*.

[32] Green, 69, quoting Aristotle's *Nicomachean Ethics* (Nic. Eth.), vii. 3.

[33] Barclay, *James and Peter*, 302-303.

[34] Barclay, *James and Peter*, 303.

[35] Vine, 620.

[36] F. Hauck, "hypomeno, hypomone," in *Theological Dictionary of the New Testament*, ed. by Gerhard Kittel and Gerhard Friedrich, trans. and abr. by Geoffrey W. Bromiley (Grand Rapids: Eerdmans, 1985), 582.

[37] "The term *hypomonein* is mostly used in the absolute for "to endure," and only rarely" in the more concrete sense, "'to wait upon,' 'to expect,'" e.g., 2 Thess. 3:5; Rev. 1:9. Hauck, 583.

[38] Green, 69.

[39] William Barker, *Who's Who in Church History* (Old Tappan, NJ: F. H. Revell, 1969), 99.

[40] A phrase taken from Phil Keaggy, "Salvation Army Band," on True Believers, Sparrow Records, 1995, CD.

[41] Barclay, *James and Peter*, 304.

[42] W. Foerster, "sebomai," in *Theological Dictionary of the New Testament*, ed. by Gerhard Kittel and Gerhard Friedrich, trans. and abr. by Geoffrey W. Bromiley (Grand Rapids: Eerdmans, 1985), 1011.

[43] Bauer, Arndt and Gingrich, 866.

[44] H. von Soden, "adelphos," in *Theological Dictionary of the New Testament*, ed. by Gerhard Kittel and Gerhard Friedrich, trans. and abr. by Geoffrey W. Bromiley (Grand Rapids: Eerdmans, 1985), 22.

[45] Green, 70.

[46] Ibid.

[47] Loren Eiseley, "A Single Starfish," All-Creatures.org, accessed February 18, 2017, http://www.all-creatures.org/stories/starfish.html.

[48] This news story was from the Associated Press and printed in various versions on May 13, 2015 in newspapers across the United States.

[49] Roger Raymer, "A Fellowship of Encouragement," *The Dallas Insider*. Dr. Raymer was Alumni Director for DTS from 1988-1991.

[50] Ralph L. Lewis and Gregg Lewis, *Learning to Preach Like Jesus* (Westchester, IL: Crossway Books, 1989), 137-138.

[51] Dave Egner, "The Essential Ingredient," *Our Daily Bread*, March 4, 1995.

[52] Cf. 1 John 2:28. Several observations should be made here: (1) This passage is addressed to believers as John calls his readers *teknia* (little children), a favorite term of affection on his part for his brothers and sisters in the faith (in addition to this reference, cf. 2:1, 12; 3:7, 18; 4:4; 5:21; elsewhere only in John's gospel, 13:33, and once in Paul's epistle to the Galatians, 4:19). In fact, the term is used only figuratively in the NT (by contrast, *teknon*, of which *teknia* is a diminutive, can be used both in the natural and figurative sense). (2) John's present active command is 2:28 is to "continually abide [*mentee*] in Him [Christ]." (3) The purpose for a lifestyle of loyalty to Christ is signified by the *hina* clause, "so that when He appears, we may have confidence and not shrink away from Him in shame at His coming." This passage shows that for some believers–those who are not walking in consistent fellowship with Christ–the coming of Christ will mean a period of embarrassment. This will not be their eternal experience in heaven, but only as it regards their experience at the *bema* seat of Christ referred to later in 1 John 4:16-18. In that passage we are told that the believer who continually exercises *agape* love toward others will have no fear at the judgment of believers, because perfect (mature) love casts out fear. Obviously, this exercise of *agape* love is the essential proof of abiding in Christ, showing a clear link with 1 John 2:28.

2

Living This Day in Light of That Day

Each of us took a seat around the conference table and then Didaskolos dimmed the lights before he began to speak, "It is said that Martin Luther marked two critical days on his calendar–This Day and That Day, the day he would arrive in heaven, or, graduate to heaven.[1] But why should the believer have concerns about That Day? After all, everyone who believes that Jesus is God and trusts in Him alone as his Savior has the promise of eternal life. Luther understood, however, that not all graduations to heaven are created equal. Some will graduate Summa Cum Laude, others Magna Cum Laude, still others Cum Laude, but then...there will be those who graduate simply 'Laude.'

"God has left instructions in 2 Peter 1:5-11 to help us show up to our heavenly graduation in attire worthy of high honors. Why? Because this is what will bring the most honor to Him. Much honor from Jesus in the hereafter will mean that we honored Him much in the here and now. With verses 5 through 7 in clear view, we now discover in verses 8 through 11 how to live this day—indeed every day—in light of That Day. No one here wants to graduate simply 'Laude' does he?"

With a flip of a switch on the overhead projector, 2 Peter 1:8-10 appeared before us on the screen:

> For if these qualities are yours and increasing, they render you neither useless nor unfruitful in the true knowledge of our Lord Jesus Christ. For he who lacks these qualities is blind or shortsighted, having forgotten his purification from his former sins. Therefore, brethren, be all the more diligent to make certain about His calling and choosing you; for as long as you practice these things, you will never stumble.[2]

"Isn't verse 11 missing, Didaskolos?" Jane asked, confused.

"For now it is," answered Didaskolos with the kind of coy smile that let you know he was waiting for just the right moment to reveal that specific verse. "First, it is critical that we properly understand the flow of Peter's thoughts in verses 8-10.

"To start with, please don't miss the little term 'for' that begins verse eight. It's what we call a causal conjunction since it introduces why we must embrace God's call to holy living, in verse 5, with supreme diligence. Benefits abound. Again, look at what Peter declares in verse 8: 'if these qualities are yours and increasing, they render you neither useless nor unfruitful in the true knowledge of our Lord Jesus Christ.'

"You should know that classical Greek writers employed the term translated 'increased' to describe an excess of something, having more than is necessary, even to the point of exaggeration. But as one Bible student says, '...to fervent Christianity there can be no excess of good.'[3] In fact, there is no such thing as stagnant Christianity—each of us are either exhibiting the portraits in the Gallery of Virtue with increasing consistency or each portrait is slowly fading from the canvas of our lives. Don't forget, Peter has already told us in verse five to apply 'all diligence' as we embrace these virtues. For one quick example, due to such diligence on your part and the conjoining resource of God's power, you ought to possess more self-control now, in regards to your thought life, the way you use your tongue and your entertainment standards, than you did last year at this time."

This encouraged me because in recent months I had made a conscious effort with God's help to stop complaining so much about things in general, like the weather, traffic jams, and a meager balance in my checkbook. I had also quit watching two TV sitcoms and burned two old rock n' roll records, concerning which I no longer had a clear conscience before God.

"Now then," Didaskolos continued with fervency, "did you see the cause-effect relationship between possessing and increasing in these spiritual virtues and being delivered from being 'useless and unfruitful in the true knowledge of our Lord Jesus Christ?'"

"But what does Peter mean," asked Nina, "by the phrase, 'useless nor unfruitful in the knowledge of our Lord Jesus Christ'?"

"A very good question, Nina, and one I'm sure we all had," answered Didaskolos. "Peter uses the terms useless and unfruitful to assure his readers of what they won't miss out on if they allow the Master Painter to color His character onto the canvas of their lives, namely, the indescribable spiritual profit of knowing Christ as an intimate friend. It's true. If you wish to 'grow in the grace and knowledge of our Lord and

Savior Jesus Christ,' as Peter exhorts us to in chapter 3, verse 18, then you must imitate the qualities of His person. Otherwise, He will not reveal Himself to you. The unspeakable usefulness and fruit of such intimacy continually comes through obedience."

"That reminds me of a verse I memorized years ago," said Jim. "It's from John, chapter 14, verse 21, where Jesus declared to His disciples, 'He who has My commandments and keeps them, he it is who loves Me; and he who loves Me shall be loved by My Father, and I will love him and will *disclose* [emphasis mine] Myself to him.' From this I have learned that if I want my understanding of Jesus to grow deeper and deeper, I must resolve to do what He asks me to do. For He will not reveal the true knowledge of His person to those who resist His standards for their lifestyle."

"Thank you so much, brother, for that excellent correlation with John's words," said Didaskolos. "And if I could add one more thing to your thunder, I really like what a couple of fellow-citizens of the kingdom once wrote about the verse under discussion. Henry Alford said, '...the only way in any degree increasingly to see Him as He is, is to become increasingly like Him. He can only declare Christ, who reflects Christ.'[4] And then, from the pen of J. Moffatt, 'We learn of him *as* [emphasis mine] we live with him and for Him.'[5] So, do you really want to know Christ intimately? Then imitate Him ever-increasingly, and He will show Himself to you. Then you will have the true knowledge of our Lord Jesus Christ that the false teachers Peter rebuked claimed to have, but knew nothing of."

This concept would deserve more thought later, for I had never saw this cause-effect connection between being Christ-like and getting to know Christ better.

"Now then, a few thoughts on verses 9 and 10," said Didaskolos. "Notice in verse 9 that the Christian who fails to consistently portray Christ-like virtue, in contrast to the Christian who increases in the same, is, in Peter's words, 'blind or shortsighted....' The term 'blind' speaks of spiritual blindness, though it sometimes refers to physical blindness. The spiritual blindness Peter warns us of is precisely God's chastisement for failing to accept our responsibility and appropriate His resources for spiritual growth. Such blindness leaves us bereft of two things: the intimate knowledge of Christ, just promised to the obedient believer, and second, the aid of His guiding light that such knowledge brings. To be a carnal Christian is to be a spiritually dull Christian, one who lacks the insight necessary for escaping the corruption that fills this lustful world."

"But why does Peter add the term 'shortsighted' to the word 'blindness?'" asked Allen. "What's the difference, if any, between the two ideas? I mean, how can a man who is blind be said to be shortsighted?"

"I like your approach to the text, Allen," replied Didaskolos. "May your tribe increase. This second word 'shortsighted' is the Greek term from which we derive the English term, "myopia." It denotes, according to one author, 'the involuntary contraction of the half-closed eyes of a short-sighted man.'[6] Peter no doubt employs this image of a man who blinks and willfully closes his eyes to what's around him in order to portray any believers among his readers who, though they know Christ, as verse one reveals, are currently shutting their eyes to their duty to display the virtues of Christ. And, because they are taking a 'blinkered view' of the Christian life, they are therefore spiritually 'blind,' looking more like sinners than saints, and in danger of having less than a hero's welcome at their day of reckoning before Christ."

"But what causes such spiritual myopia?" I asked.

"Well, according to Peter's next line, such Christians had forgotten their purification from former sins. Most commentators believe Peter refers to the time of their water baptism, which in no way contributed to their salvation, nor does it ever, but gave public affirmation of their faith in Christ as personal Savior from sin and eternal judgment.[7] 'Former sins' would then mean pre-conversion sins, literally 'old sins,' from which they had been cleansed by the blood of Christ (cf. 1 Pet. 1:18). But this blessed forgiveness had been put out of their minds, created a severe lack of appreciation for their salvation, and left them looking for satisfaction in sin rather than in the Bread of Life of which they were partakers, according to verse 4.

"One of my favorite hymns as a young boy was 'Come Thou Fount of Every Blessing,' by Robert Robinson. The most stirring line in that song is: 'Prone to wander, Lord I feel it, prone to leave the God I love; here's my heart, Lord, take and seal it; seal it for Thy courts above.' Well, it so happens that Robinson himself 'lost the happy communion with the Savior he had once enjoyed, and in his declining years, he wandered into the byways of sin. As a result, he became deeply troubled in spirit. Hoping to relieve his mind, he decided to travel.' As H. G. Bosch relates:

> In the course of his journeys, he became acquainted with a young woman on spiritual matters, and [one day] she asked him what he thought of a hymn she had been reading. To his astonishment he found it to be none other than his own composition. He tried to evade her question, but she continued to press him for a response.
>
> "Suddenly he began to weep. With tears streaming down his cheeks, he said, 'I am the man who wrote that hymn many years ago. I'd give anything to experience again the joy I knew then.' Although greatly surprised, she assured him that 'the streams of mercy' mentioned in his song still flowed. Mr. Robinson was deeply touched. Turning his 'wandering heart' to the Lord, he was restored to full fellowship.[8]

"When we lose sight of how absolutely wonderful our salvation is, we are prone to wander from the path of heavenly virtue. This means, according to verse 8, that we will not enjoy a close friendship with Christ—if you don't grow in Him, you can't know Him well. It's a bad case of spiritual blindness and spiritual amnesia, as verse 9 reveals.

"In light of this dreadful, shameful possibility, Peter follows with a stern command in verse 10: 'Therefore, brethren, be even more diligent to make your calling and election sure, for if you do these things, you will never stumble.'

"In this context, the command, 'make your calling and election sure,' cannot be a calling into question the eternal security of Peter's readers who, according to verse 2, have 'received a faith of the same kind as ours, by the righteousness of our God and Savior, Jesus Christ.' As well, he calls them 'brethren,' here in verse 10. Rather, the word 'sure' refers to steadfast progress in holy living. Sanctification, not justification, is in view. Verse 10 does not pertain, then, to the assurance of one's salvation, but rather to diligently increasing in godly virtues in order to avoid stumbling into spiritual blindness and forgetfulness concerning justificational forgiveness (v. 9). It correlates perfectly with how Peter concludes his letter: 'You therefore, beloved, knowing this beforehand, be on your guard so that you are not carried away by the error of unprincipled men and *fall from your own steadfastness*, but *grow* [emphasis added] in the grace and knowledge of our Lord and Savior Jesus Christ. To Him be the glory, both now and to the day of eternity. Amen' (3:17-18).

"Keeping the immediate context in view is crucial to the correct interpretation of a given verse. And did you notice the element of consistency in the word 'practice,' in verse 10? If by God's power we zealously aspire to daily portray the virtues of Christ seen in this passage, they will be visible in us."

"But," declared Didaskolos, with his right arm in the air and with intensity in his voice, "there is one more thing that a steady display of Christian virtue affords us; not only an intimate friendship with Christ, and a sure escape from stumbling headlong into a life of sin, but also..."

—a deliberate dramatic pause

left us dangling in mid-air for a few seconds—

"...allowing the Master Painter to day by day color our lives with His character assures us a hero's welcome when we arrive in heaven. Verse 11 says it so clearly:

> for in this way the entrance into the eternal kingdom of our Lord and Savior Jesus Christ will be abundantly supplied to you.[9]

"To what does Peter refer when he says, 'for in this way'? asked Jim.

"Good question, Jim," said Didaskolos. "To track any author's flow of thought, it's imperative to understand such transitions. In short, this is a phrase that introduces the manner in which the ultimate result of doing what verse 10 declares, namely, practicing 'these things'—the virtues in verses 5-7—will come to me. And what is that marvelous result?"

"It is having my entrance into God's kingdom abundantly supplied to me," I blurted out.

"You're right on the money, Ron," answered Didaskolos.

And no sooner had he uttered these words that Nina shot out another question. "I see that verse 11 uses the term 'supplied' just as verse 5 does. Could it be that these are the same word in the original language?"

"Yes! Your guess is right," said a very pleased Didaskolos.

Grabbing another overhead transparency, Didaskolos displayed verse 5 and had us read it in unison:

> "Now for this very reason also, applying all diligence, in your faith supply moral excellence, and in your moral excellence, knowledge."

"You may recall that the term rendered 'supply' here in verse five is extracted from the world of music in the Greek culture. It denotes outfitting a chorus group with additional and complete supplies, even defraying their expenses far beyond what was expected. In verse 5 Peter exhorts us who have received the Christian faith to '*generously put ourselves out* [emphasis mine] in obedience to God,' [10] being beautiful portraits of Christ in a world uglified by sin. And now he proclaims that for those of us who so put ourselves out for God, God will put Himself out for us by giving us a hero's welcome when we enter His kingdom."

"But you may be wondering," continued Didaskolos, "where this concept of a 'hero's welcome' is found in the verse. In the Greek culture of Peter's day, a victorious athlete in the Olympic Games was paid high honors when he returned home. Caught up in the exhilaration of good ol' hometown pride for the success of one of their own, the citizens would welcome back their champion, not through the usual gate of entry, but through a section of the city wall broken down just for the occasion. Through this opening he would enter and be hailed as their hero."

Projecting once again the overhead transparency of verse 10, our most respected teacher said, "Note quickly that God's kingdom here is described as eternal, a future reality. With Abraham we are looking for a city whose builder and maker is God. In fact, God's country is our desire and our eventual destination (Heb. 11:10, 13-16), and, this kingdom belongs to Jesus Christ who is here called 'our Lord and Savior.' It is His kingdom and He is our[11] Lord and Savior. Though He is the Sovereign Master over all, we, nevertheless, enjoy this stupendous, personal relationship with Him via child-like faith in the impartial righteousness with which He offers to clothe us for eternity.

"But, though every believer is assured entrance into this fantastic kingdom, not every believer will be given a hero's welcome. One Christian author compares the carnal believer 'to a sailor who just manages to make shore after shipwreck, or to a man who barely escapes with his life from a burning house, while all his possessions are lost.'[12] By contrast, the obedient Christian, the one who allows the Master Painter to paint onto the empty canvas of his life the colorful brushstrokes of moral excellence, knowledge, self-control, perseverance, godliness, brotherly kindness and agape love, will have an abundant entrance into the kingdom. Like the triumphant athlete in the Olympic Games, God will go all out in welcoming him home."

That phrase, "God will go all out in welcoming him home." rang in our minds for several moments. What amazing grace that would save lost sinners, enable them to portray the beauty of Christ to this world so grotesquely deformed by sin, and then honor them for doing so.

No one said a thing. To a person, we knew that our salvation was purchased with the very life-blood of our glorious Savior, Jesus Christ, and nothing less than a diligent resolve to honor Him with an honorable life made any sense at all. He was worthy of a life that deserved a hero's welcome. And all the honor would ultimately be His, anyway.

After he could no longer stand the wait, Allen, like a young boy waiting to open his birthday presents, asked Didaskolos, "Now will you tell us what the portrait of the men on horseback is all about?"

"Yes, this is the appropriate time, Allen," answered Didaskolos. "Thank you for the faithful reminder."

We all followed Didaskolos back into the hallway and stood gazing at the last portrait in the Gallery of Virtue. The wooden plaque above it read:

Didaskolos began, "The painting in front of you is based upon a true event in our beloved country's history. As Chuck Swindoll tells it,

> During his days as president, Thomas Jefferson and a group of companions were traveling across the country on horseback. They came to a river which had left its banks because of a recent downpour. The swollen river had washed the bridge away. Each rider was forced to ford the river on horseback, fighting for his life against the rapid currents. The very real possibility of death threatened each rider, which caused a traveler who was not part of the group to step aside and watch.
>
> "After several had plunged in and made it to the other side, the stranger asked President Jefferson if he would ferry him across the river. The president agreed without hesitation. The man climbed on, and shortly thereafter the two of them made it safely to the other

side.

> "As the stranger slid off the back of the saddle onto dry ground, one in the group asked him, 'Tell me, why did you select the president to ask a favor of?' The man was shocked, admitting he had no idea it was the president who had helped him. 'All I know,' he said, 'is that on some of your faces was written the answer "No," and on some of them was the answer "Yes." His was a "Yes" face.'"[13]

After allowing a few moments for the impact of the story to sink in, Didaskolos asked a most penetrating question, "What does your face say, most often, 'Yes,' or 'No?' The world is full of people in need. They wonder, 'Will anyone help me? Will anyone take time to answer the burning questions that endlessly gnaw at my soul?' What response to their need do they read on your face? In John 13:34-35, Jesus said, 'By this all men will know that you are My disciples, if you have love for one another.' But beyond our love for His family, Jesus also told us to love our neighbor as ourselves, and that may include our enemies. It's anyone with a need: a need to be forgiven, to receive necessary food, drink and shelter, to have one's car fixed, to enjoy a break from the sometimes noisy, rowdy children, to receive a letter of encouragement or sympathy, and a thousand other needs.

"Whatever your vocation in life: a teacher, a business person, a construction worker, a writer, an astronaut, a plumber, a homemaker...it doesn't matter. Jesus is calling you to be a Good Samaritan, to serve the pressing needs of people in your web of life: the motorist with the flat tire, the abused child down the street, that unloved teenager from the broken home, the elderly shut-in next door, the bratty kid at the playground. Mauled by this cold-hearted world, they need the sunshine of His love; and He has chosen to radiate this love through you, His people.

"The portrait of Jesus reveals a 'Yes' face. Does your face reflect the same to the people you meet? Not all Christians will receive a hero's welcome, only those who consistently allow the Master Painter to paint His character onto the empty canvas of their lives. And what stands out the most in this portrait is our face: the eyes of compassion and forgiveness, the smile of hope, and in some cases even the wrinkles that mark the wisdom of a long following of the Savior; in all, a 'Yes' face. I ask you, is such a face your face? If so, yours will be a hero's welcome!"

Deep contemplation shaped the countenances of each person in the room. No one said a word. This tour had delivered more than we had expected; spiritually we would never be the same.

As for me, I heard the voice of solitude calling; a time for inventory, quiet moments with open Bible and heart bared before the Lord. The Spirit of God had brought to surface a few matters that must be dealt with. For one, there was that lonely widower across the street who had just lost his wife—he needed a "Yes" face.

My musing was interrupted when Didaskolos quietly said, "I sense from your spirits and reverent response that a hero's welcome is something you all desire, but there is more to receiving such a welcome from our precious Savior than just progressing in spiritual maturity. Certainly that is the essential requirement for such a heavenly reception, but the Scripture discloses other aspects of this truth which flow from it in a cause-effect relationship. So here's what I have in mind..."

Everyone waited intently.

"If you would like, we could continue our investigation of this matter at my home, say in a couple of months after I complete my summer tours here at the Gallery. Would that be something you would be interested in?"

We all nodded "Yes" in unison. "That would be marvelous," said Janet, expressing everyone's sentiment.

"Good enough," replied Didaskolos. "I will use the phone number on the card that each of you filled out to register for the tour to let you know when we will begin. I cannot wait to show you what else God has to say about this life-changing doctrine of future rewards for the believer. In fact, I will mail each of you some material entitled *The Bema Seat of Christ* which will answer four basic questions about that future event. Until then, be assured of my prayers for each one. It's been a long day, but one I shall never forget. By God's design and power, you have all contributed to the developing portrait of Christ-likeness in my own life, and for this I thank you."

Didaskolos stalled briefly and then said, "Clifford, would you be so kind to end our tour of the Gallery of Virtue with prayer?"

"I would be most honored to do so," answered Clifford.

"Our most blessed heavenly Father," he began, "we have known Your intimate presence today and are grateful for Your gracious dwelling among us. Thank you, Lord, for Didaskolos, for his gift to teach Your truths, but even more for his example of godliness before us. Never will we forget the 'Yes' face he displayed for the lady with the flat tire over our lunch break. May each of us allow you to work the same work you have worked in him. We love you, Father, and long to see Your face; and when we do, we pray that we will each have the privilege of honoring you by having lived an honorable life, one worthy of a hero's welcome. In the name of our coming Savior and King, Jesus Christ, Amen."

We gave one another friendly good-byes before parting. It seemed as if the summer would take forever before that study at Didaskolos house would begin, and the material on the *bema* seat couldn't come soon enough. But then again, learning to show the world around me the face of Jesus, namely, a "Yes" face, would occupy me every minute until then.

Endnotes for Chapter 2

[1] This quotation is unverified as to attribution.

[2] *For*–The *gar* here introduces the reason why the Christian should heed the imperatival idea in v. 5, "applying all diligence."

if these qualities are yours and increasing–The phrase *if these qualities are yours and increasing* contains two conditional circumstantial present active participles (*huparcho* and *pleonazo*) showing the habitual lifestyle expected in the display of holy character. *Pleonazo*, in classical Greek, is "a term of disparagement, implying excess, to be or to have more than enough, to exaggerate. But to fervent Christianity there can be no excess of good." Joseph B. Mayor, *The Epistle of St. Jude and the Second Epistle of Peter* (Grand Rapids: Baker, 1965), quoted in Fritz Rienecker, *A Linguistic Key to the Greek New Testament*, ed. by Cleon L. Rogers, Jr. (Grand Rapids: Zondervan, 1980), 769-70. The dative *humin* is locative of sphere, the idea being these qualities existing in you; these qualities are a contextual rendering of *tauta*, comprehensively summing up the seven virtues added to *pistin*, from verse 5. The conditional element also implies that it is possible that a believer will not have these spiritual qualities increasing in his life, and verse 9 reveals both the reality and the reason for such a carnal disposition.

they render you–The words *they render you* translate the present active indicative form of *kathistemi* (a combination of the intensive preposition, *kata* = down, and the verb, *histemi* = to set, place). The same word is found in James 3:6 where "the tongue is set among our members as that which defiles the entire body." It also used in Matthew 24:45, 47 of the servant who is put in charge of his master's possessions (cf. also in this vein, Acts 6:3). It is used intransitively here; the idea is having a spiritual disposition that is neither inactive or unfruitful.

neither useless nor unfruitful–From *argous*, here along with *akarpous*, functioning as an accusative predicative plural with *humas* being understood. Robertson, 6:152. *Argous* is from the alpha privative, *a* and *ergon*, meaning "not at work, idle, inactive, useless, barren." *Akarpous* stands in parallel with *argous* to declare the opposite of what is true about believers progressing in spiritual maturity. They are not (*ouk*) inactive, nor (*oude* per the indicative mood in the verb, functioning adverbially) unfruitful; cf. Matthew 13:22 where the same term describes those who hear God's Word but allow the worries of the world and the deceitfulness of riches to choke the divinely intended fruitful impact of Scripture.

in the true knowledge–*Epignosin*, that is, "full knowledge," the content of which is the Lord Jesus Christ—as we increasingly imitate Him, He discloses Himself to us, the result being a deeper personal knowledge of Him (cf. John 14:21-23 where Jesus reveals this very principle to the disciples during the Upper Room Discourse, no doubt on Peter's mind as he writes these words). Peter, too, undercuts the dangerous doctrine of the pre-gnostic wolves in sheep's clothing that lurked in the shadows of the believers to whom he writes by stating where complete and true knowledge lies, in the Lord Jesus Christ, whose deity these false teachers denied. Finally, it is noteworthy to trace Peter's use of *epignosin* to this point: 1:3 shows that the Christian experience commences with personal knowledge of Christ; 1:2 reveals how those who have such knowledge can possess and enjoy His grace and peace in abundance; and 1:8 tells of the ever-increasing personal acquaintance with who Christ is as the effect of imitating Christ in the routine of daily life (per the ladder of virtue in vv. 5-7). Paul, also, saw personal knowledge of Christ as the goal of the Christian walk (cf. Phil. 3:7-10). This is indeed the essence of eternal life (John 17:3).

of our Lord Jesus Christ. For—Again, Peter employs the coordinating conjunction *gar*, but in this case to explain (an explanatory *gar* may fit best here), why the realities of verse 8 are true, using the structure of contrast to do so: Grow in Christ and you will know Christ (v. 8), but not growing in Christ means you are spiritually blind and really don't appreciate His forgiving your sins; the result, by implication is that you will not get to know Christ better. It's grow to know (v. 8) versus don't grow, you won't know (v. 9).

he who lacks these qualities—Literally, "To whom [dative of possession] these things [*tauta*, which links itself contextually to the virtues detailed in vv. 5-7 and in that connection to the more recently referenced *tauta* in v. 8] are not" (*me* due to the indefinite relative clause).

is blind—Translates *tuphlos*, "blind," which can refer to literal blindness (Lev. 21:8 [LXX]; Mark 10:46 and in every occurrence of the term in his gospel) or figuratively to spiritual blindness; sometimes the latter is a visitation of God's judgment (John 12:40). Essentially, it entails being willfully blind to God's will (Matt. 15:14); even Satan has the ability to blind unbelievers from seeing the light of the gospel (2 Cor. 4:4); the Christians at Laodicea think they see well spiritually, but in reality are blind (Rev. 3:17). "Only Christ can cure this blindness of self-deception and complacency." W. Schrage, "typhlos, typhloo," in *Theological Dictionary of the New Testament*, ed. by Gerhard Kittel and Gerhard Friedrich, trans. and abr. by Geoffrey W. Bromiley (Grand Rapids: Eerdmans, 1985), 1199-1200. Here, in 2 Peter 1:9, *tuphlos* displays a contrast with *epignosin* in verse 8 in that true knowledge of Christ yields the light necessary for the Christian's trek through the maze of this spiritually dark world. Without this knowledge, one is left to stumble (see comments on *ptaisete* in v. 10), signifying that part of not experiencing the fruit (unfruitful, v. 8) of getting to know Christ better is a state of spiritual blindness for the believer who does not heed the call to diligence in verse 5.

or shortsighted–This term renders the present active participle *muopazon* which here modifies *tuphlos* by limiting it to a spiritual state of short-sightedness, a spiritual myopia, if you will. Aristotle used the word to describe a near-sighted man, able to see what is near, but not what is far off. This would fit well with the immoral lifestyle and lack of heavenly perspective of the false teachers, but as Green states, "probably Peter was thinking of the other meaning of *muopazein*, namely 'to blink,' 'to shut the eyes.'" Green, 72. Barclay concurs and says that the idea here is that of blinking and shutting one's spiritual eyes to the truth, to walk with a "blinkered view of life." Barclay, *James and Peter*, 306. Rienecker states that the word refers to "the involuntary contraction of the half-closed eyes of a short-sighted man and the word may be a correction or limitation of the idea of being blind (Mayor). On the other hand, the meaning may be 'shutting the eyes to the truth,' the intention being to emphasize the responsibility of the believer (Kelly)." Joseph B. Mayor, *The Epistle of St. Jude and the Second Epistle of Peter* (Grand Rapids: Baker, 1965), and J. N. D. Kelly, *A Commentary on the Epistles of Peter and Jude*, Black's New Testament Commentaries (London: Adam and Charles Black, 1969), quoted in Fritz Rienecker, *A Linguistic Key to the Greek New Testament*, ed. by Cleon L. Rogers, Jr. (Grand Rapids: Zondervan, 1980), 770. Peter warns, then, against looking away from God's call to maturity, depicting the dangerous state of a carnal believer. In this view the participial form here is causal, showing why the carnal believer is *tuphlos*.

having forgotten–The phrase having forgotten is from *lethen labon*, literally, "having received forgetfulness." *Labon*, second aorist active participle from *lambano*, has a causal force showing further reason (in concert with the causal *muopazon*) why the Christian portrayed here is *tuphlos*. Equally important is the decisive nature of the aorist tense here, signifying a calculated move to put out of one's mind the fact of his forgiveness at salvation. In that connection, *lethen* is from *lethomai*, "to forget," a *hapax legomena* and functioning as an accusative of direct object, telling us what has been actively received. A similar idea is found in 2 Timothy 1:5, "having received remembrance."

his purification from his former sins–Purification is articular pointing out a particular cleansing (*katharismou*), namely the forgiveness received at salvation via the sacrifice of Christ; the term is found in Hebrews 1:3. Peter spoke of this sacrifice in his first epistle as well (cf. 1:18; 2:24; 3:18). Some feel this is a reference to the believer's water baptism when he would make public confession of his following Christ. Even if it is, Peter is not making a case for water baptism as a condition for salvation. In this vein, cf. Acts 2:38 and 22:16; in both of these passages, the grammar does not allow for the so-called "baptismal regeneration" doctrine. Acts 2:38 could be rendered, "Repent and be baptized because [*dia* conveys a causal nuance] of the forgiveness of your sins." Acts 22:16, literally says, "Having arisen, be baptized; and wash away your sins, having called on the name of the Lord." In no instance do NT writers make baptism a requirement for justificational salvation, and even Paul said in 1 Corinthians 1:17, "For Christ did not send me to baptize, but to preach the gospel...." Here a clear distinction is made between the contents of the true gospel and water baptism. Concerning the phrase, *from his former sins*, the genitive is best taken in an ablatival sense. The Christian has been separated from his former (*palai*) sins, which refer to sins committed prior to conversion. As Green cogently states, "The man who makes no effort (v. 5) to grow in grace is going back on his baptismal contract. This could be the start of apostasy." Green, 73.

Therefore–Dio here is a subordinate conjunction inferring what follows from what precedes. Since within every Christian there is the inherent danger of not applying diligence to the call to virtue–and developing spiritual cataracts–be all the more on your guard. Of course, *dio* may reach back all the way to verse 3, inferring that God's gracious gifts of His power, His promises, and the personal knowledge of Christ, yield a sense of "oughtness" to our climbing the ladder of virtue. A sluggish response is nonsensical, morally reprehensible and, as verse 11 will imply, a response that will bring about the forfeiture of a hero's welcome.

Brethren–It is vital to note that Peter is addressing believers throughout this passage, indicated by the use of *adelphoi*, as the previous verse may tempt us to think otherwise.

be all the more–Translates *mallon*, an adverbial comparative adjective which modifies *spoudasate*: "Become diligent the more" (not less).

diligent–Renders the aorist active imperative (probably ingressive here) *spoudasate*, to be diligent (the same term found in v. 5, forming an inclusio in Peter's literary structure). The term stresses "the urgency of his plea that they should determine to live for God." Green, 73. Again, the decisive element in the aorist points up the kind of determined response for which the apostle calls. As noted in verse 5, *spoudazo*, the derivative here, means "to be in a hurry,...to exert effort." Rienecker, 770. The same attitude is mandated by Paul to young Timothy in the latter's study of the Word (cf. 2 Tim. 2:15).

to make–Present middle infinitive of *poieo*, "to make for yourselves."

certain–The term certain is *bebaios*; from *baino* it means "to go" denoting something that is fixed, certain, sure; figuratively, that upon which one may rely or trust; in the NT not used of persons, but of objects; Spiros Zodhiates, *The Hebrew-Greek Study Bible: King James Version* (Chattanooga: AMG Publishers, 1992), 1698; e.g., Hebrews 6:19, that which is immoveable and does not fail or waver, and therefore trustworthy (cf. Rom. 4:16 and Gal. 3:15 regarding the water-tight terms of the Abrahamic Covenant; Heb. 2:2 regarding the unalterable nature of the Mosaic Law mediated by angels; 2 Cor. 1:7 regarding Paul's sure hope that the Corinthian saints were sharers in both the apostle's sufferings and God's comfort). The papyri show this word to be a technical term for a "legal guarantee." Rienecker, 770. Here with the middle infinitive, the idea is "to make sure for yourself" your calling and election. In terms of NT usage, as Bob Deffinbaugh observes,

> One of the most critical texts is Romans 4:16: "For this reason [it is] by faith, that [it might be] in accordance with grace, in order that the promise may be *certain* [emphasis mine] to all the descendants, not only to those who are of the Law, but also to those who are of the faith of Abraham, who is the father of us all (Romans 4:16).
>
> In this text, Paul not only employs the term "certain," he also uses it in such a way that we can tell what Peter cannot mean where he employs the same term. Paul writes that God has designed "it" (justification) to occur "by faith," so that "the promise" (of justification or salvation) might be certain. In the context, Paul instructs us that if salvation were by our works, it would not be certain because it would depend on us. Justification by faith makes the promise of salvation—of the forgiveness of sins (see verses 7-8)—certain. We can therefore hardly suppose that Peter is now saying the opposite, namely, that we make our election and calling certain by our works, by working hard at the pursuit of holiness. ...
>
> Peter is not urging us to "make certain about" our election and calling. Our election and calling are from God, and they are not reversible (see Romans 8:29-30; 11:29). ...
>
> On the other hand, we are not to be passive in our salvation and sanctification. We must believe in the Lord Jesus Christ and receive the salvation God has provided through Him (see John 6:28-29; Acts 2:38; 16:31; Romans 10:8-15). Likewise, while faith is a gift from God (2 Peter 1:1), we must add to our faith through the provisions God has given to us (2 Peter 1:3-7).
>
> I believe the exhortation in verse 10 is but an intensified repetition of that given in verses 5-7. ...
>
> We are to continually strive to grow in our faith and in the godly qualities Peter spells out in verses 5-7. As we do so, we confirm, or establish, that which God began and which He is committed to establish in and through us. To make our calling and election sure is to make it stable. It is to set our lives on a course that cannot, and will not, be changed or moved away from the faith. It is to become so solid and stable that we will not be moved, especially by those who come to us with another gospel....
>
> It is certainly possible for a Christian to live in such a way that God removes him from this life (1 Corinthians 5:5; 11:28-30). I do not think one would expect a "Well done, good and faithful servant!" upon his arrival in the

> presence of God. He will be saved, yet as by fire (1 Corinthians 3:15). For the Christian who pursues holiness, there is a far better entrance into the kingdom of God. It is an entrance we eagerly anticipate (see Philippians 1:19-23; 3:14; 2 Corinthians 5:6-10). It is an entrance abundantly supplied to us. This is the reward of diligently seeking to confirm our calling and election.
>
> Robert L. Deffinbaugh, "Standing On The Promises–A Study in 2 Peter: 4. A Secured Faith That Keeps The Saints from Stumbling," Bible.org, July 3, 2004, accessed May 23, 2016, https://bible.org/seriespage/secured-faith-keeps-saints-stumbling-2-peter-18-11.

about His calling and choosing you–Calling and choosing you signifies the sovereignty of God in the salvation scheme. Calling (*klesin*) is the divine invitation to salvation (cf. also Rom. 11:29; 1 Cor. 1:26; Eph. 4:1, all which relate to this spiritual call, but note how 1 Cor. 7:20 employs the term to denote one's vocational call, that is, condition of employment, something which the Corinthians were told not to forsake unless it be immoral in disposition, as v. 24 implies). But, God's divine call comes chronologically (per Rom. 8:30) subsequent to and as a direct result of election (*eklogen*) which regards the actual acceptance of the sinner by God (Rom. 9:11; Eph. 1:4; 1 Thess. 1:4) as one selected from a number. The word is akin to *eklegomai*, to choose for oneself, not necessarily the rejection of what is not chosen, but giving favor to the chosen subject, with a view to a relationship with that subject. Zodhiates, 1712. Election must always be seen in view of its ultimate design, that of bringing glory to God who elects the spiritually dead sinner to salvation, and as the purposed effect, to bring the elected sinner into a holy life (cf. Eph. 1:4-6; 2:1-10).

For–The (always postpositive) *gar* here again has a syntactical force of yielding the reason for the aforementioned call to diligence.

as long as you practice–The phrase *as long as you do* translates the present active circumstantial participle, *poiountes* (doing), from *poieo*, functioning in a conditional manner, forming an hypothesis. See Alford, 4:394.

these things–Renders *tauta*, the third use of this pronominal demonstrative adjective in verses 8-10, in fact, this *tauta* answers to the former two, in like fashion referring once again in Peter's argument to the Christian virtues in verses 5-7. Here it functions in the accusative as a direct object of *poiountes*.

you will never stumble–The double negative here, *ou me*, rules out any possibility whatsoever of stumbling: "in no wise shall you ever stumble," completing the conditional participial clause, "if you do these things." The adverbial indefinite adjective *pote*, in concert with this absolute statement, means "never ever." Stumble is aorist active subjunctive second person plural (Peter still addressing the entire group of believers to whom he writes) from *ptaio*, "to stumble." "Of uncertain etymology, [this term] has such senses as 'to stumble against,' 'to collide with,' or in the more usual intransitive, 'to stumble,' 'to fall,' 'to suffer a reverse,' figuratively, 'to err,' 'to sin.' In the LXX, [the word] has the figurative sense 'to slip' in Sir. 37:12. Elsewhere it is used for the defeat of an army, e.g., 1 Sam. 4:2, 10. In Philo it means either 'to suffer misfortune' or 'to sin.' [The NT employs the word 5 times], the main meaning is the figurative one 'to slip'... [morally] (Jms. 2:10; 3:2 and [here, though Schmidt says Peter could mean to] 'suffer a reverse' [unfortunately Schmidt offers no explanation of the implications of that particular semantic value]." K. L. Schmidt, "ptaio," in *Theological Dictionary of the New Testament*, ed. by Gerhard Kittel and Gerhard Friedrich, trans. and abr. by Geoffrey W. Bromiley (Grand Rapids: Eerdmans, 1985), 968. In Romans 11:11 the sense is also figurative regarding unbelieving Jews who did not stumble so as to fall meaning that they may regain their balance and not fall into eternal ruin, a point the rest of the passage reveals (Israel's casting off is temporary in nature, they will be redeemed, regathered and restored to their land in the millennial kingdom). In the apostolic fathers, 1 Clement 51:1 gives one example of the term, "forgiveness is sought for what is done amiss through the snares of the adversary." Schmidt, 969. To this survey, Green adds that what Peter means here is that "the Christian will be spared a disastrous coming to grief. The metaphor is drawn from the surefootedness of a horse. A life of steady progress should characterize the Christian...." Green, 74. Continuation in the virtues of verses 5-7 insulates the believer from falling headlong into sin, though he will not attain sinless perfection, diligent as he may be to embrace this call to holiness. It should be noted that some interpret stumble here to mean "loss of salvation." Bauer, Arndt and Gingrich, 734. But, not only does this contradict NT teaching on the subject of the security of the believer but misses the intention of Peter to warn those who suffer the spiritual misfortune and profound moral reverse of not having these virtues "yours and increasing" (v. 8) that their entrance into the kingdom shall not be richly supplied to them (v. 11). And certainly, this is not the only place in the NT where such warnings are given (e.g., 1 Cor. 3:10-15; 2 Tim. 2:12-13).

[3] Mayor, quoted in Rienecker, 770.

[4] Alford, 4:393.

[5] J. Moffat, *The General Epistles: James, Peter and Jude*, Moffatt New Testament Commentary, quoted in Barclay, *James and Peter*, 304.

[6] Mayor, quoted in Rienecker, 770.

[7] See Green; Donald Burdick, "James," in *The Expositor's Bible Commentary*, ed. by Frank E. Gaebelein, vol. 12 (Grand Rapids: Zondervan Publishing House, 1984); Alford; and Barclay, *James and Peter*.

[8] H. G. Bosch, "377 Hymn Writer Lose [sic] Joy of Salvation," in *Encyclopedia of 7700 Illustrations: Signs of the Times*, [ed.] by Paul Lee Tan (Rockville, MD: Assurance Publishers, 1979), 183.

[9] *for*–Again the *gar* gives a reason for adhering to the previous imperative,

spoudasate (v. 10).

in this way–The phrase translates *houtos*, an adverbial adjective of manner introducing the kind of entrance into heaven that awaits those who progress in the spiritual maturity Peter calls for. NASB's rendering is preferable for its greater clarity to the KJV.

the entrance–The word is *he eisodos*, the same term seen in 1 Thessalonians 1:9, "For they themselves report about us what kind of reception we had with you...." The basic meaning is, "the way in, entrance." Rienecker, 770. *Eisodos* occurs approximately "50 times in the LXX for [words such as] 'entrance,' 'gate,' 'door,' 'entry,'" often linked with *exodos*, (exit). "'Going out and coming in' is a common phrase to denote fellowship (1 Sam. 29:6) or total activity (2 Sam. 3:25)." W. Michaelis, "hodos," in *Theological Dictionary of the New Testament*, ed. by Gerhard Kittel and Gerhard Friedrich, trans. and abr. by Geoffrey W. Bromiley (Grand Rapids: Eerdmans, 1985), 672. "The terms are rare in the NT, never occur together...*eisodos* in Heb. 10:19" speaks of the reality of the believer's confidence to "enter the holy place by the blood of Jesus..." Michaelis, 672. This is not a spatial use, but the idea of "access" to fellowship with the holy God via Christ. Acts 13:24 employs the term to describe the beginning of Jesus' earthly ministry: "After John had proclaimed before His coming a baptism of repentance to all the people of Israel." According to Michaelis, Peter's use here in 1:11 is not spatial either, but a figurative reference to the believer's access to the eternal kingdom. Michaelis, 672. It seems too difficult to separate the two elements, however, as the believer arrives in heaven after death. Used here with *eis* (governing the accusative of direct object construction, into the eternal kingdom), a preposition of location or sphere in this case (like the use in Matt. 9:7), a spatial idea may indeed be present with regard to *eisodos*. The cultural background to Peter's text may also lend to this more spatial interpretation; see comments under the word "abundantly." Finally, the particular time of entrance, whatever that may be (conceptual or literal, or both), is debated by commentators, but seems to be best taken as the believer's going to be with the Lord at death or at the Rapture whichever comes first. In support of this idea is Paul's reference in 2 Timothy 4:18 where he writes confidently at the eleventh hour of his life, "The Lord will deliver me from every evil deed, and will bring me safely to His heavenly kingdom...." Peter follows his exhortation to practice Christian virtue with a revelation of his own imminent departure from earth ("the laying aside of my earthly dwelling"), but this by itself, even though in close proximity, does not demand the idea of entering the kingdom at death in the sense of "absent from the body, present with the Lord" (2 Cor. 5:8). Elsewhere in the NT, the concept of being rewarded for godly character and faithful ministry is in the context of that future event called the *bema* seat of Christ (1 Cor. 3:10-15; 2 Cor. 5:10). It is the author's current position, though held somewhat tentatively, that Peter refers here to entrance into the kingdom at the time of physical death, though admittedly this would seem to make the passage irrelevant to those who never die but are translated at the Rapture. But even allowing this, God would certainly "make it up" to such deserving saints at the *bema* seat of Christ. Gangel says the time of this "abundant entrance" is when the believer "enters the Lord's presence in heaven." Kenneth O. Gangel, "2 Peter," in *Bible Knowledge Commentary: New Testament*, ed. by John F. Walvoord and Roy B. Zuck, 859-879 (Wheaton: Victor Books, 1985), 867; as does Neiboer, who calls this a "more glorious entrance than those who were content to be merely saved." Those whose life has been one of "devotion to Christ" will not only have a "victorious deathbed" experience, but "an entrance 'richly supplied.'" Joe Nieboer, *Practical Exposition of II Peter: Verse by Verse* (Erie, PA: Our Daily Walk Publishers, 1952), 72. DeHaan takes no clear position, seemingly blending both the believer's entrance into heaven after death with the rewards given at the *bema* seat of Christ. Richard W. DeHaan, *Studies in Second Peter* (Wheaten, IL: Victor Books, 1977), 37. Thiessen cites this verse under his brief discussion on the bema seat with no distinction between that future event and the believer's entrance into glory at death. Henry C. Thiessen, *Introductory Lectures in Systematic Theology* (Grand Rapids: Eerdmans, 1949), 456. Blum states that "Peter looks to future aspects of the kingdom of Jesus Christ that the believer enters at death or at the imposition of the kingdom." Edwin A. Blum, "2 Peter," in *The Expositor's Bible Commentary*, ed. by Frank E. Gaebelein, 257-289 (Grand Rapids: Zondervan Publishing House, 1984), 12:271. In either case, the believer is commended with a lavish "welcome home" for portraying Jesus in his earthly life. Trying to ascertain when this occurs is worth pursuing, though too much attention on the timing is to miss the point of Peter's message.

into the eternal–This is *ainion*, a first attributive adjective modifying *basileian*; it implies unlimited duration of time here (the opposite of that which is transitory). The term can denote specifically something which has neither beginning nor end (Rom. 16:26; Heb. 9:14) or something without end (Matt. 25:41, 46). Regarding the latter, Philemon 15 speaks of converted slave Onesimus now being Philemon's companion forever, a reference to the "endless ages of eternal life and blessedness." Zodhiates, 1685. Peter's use here is no doubt in this same vein, emphasizing the endless character of Christ's kingdom and rule. It should be noted that the descriptive phrase eternal kingdom is only here in the NT.

kingdom–*Basileian*, articular here to denote the specific kingdom of our Lord and Savior Jesus Christ, also functions as direct object of *eisodos*. The term is used often in the Gospels to refer to the kingdom of God, or the kingdom of heaven (unique to Matthew). The phrases are interchangeable essentially; spiritually the kingdom has a present form (Matt. 13:41, 47; 20:1), but has a future spiritual and literal aspect to it (Dan. 2:44; 7:13f) as Peter has in view here (cf. 1 Cor. 6:9-10; 15:50; Gal. 5:21). In Jewish thinking, what the apostle speaks of here is "the age to come," an age which would invade this present "age" where God would vindicate "Himself and His people." Green, 75. The last things have been inaugurated, and all that awaits is the consummation of the eternal kingdom. Blum adds, "In one sense, Christians are already in the kingdom (Col. 1:13). Yet, as Paul and Barnabas said, 'We must go through many hardships to enter the kingdom of God' (Acts 14:22). The kingdom is temporally limited in 1 Corinthians 15:24 and Revelation 20:1-6. But in this verse, Peter speaks of it as 'the eternal kingdom.'... Jesus is now the Lord (Acts 2:36), and as such He rules. In His coming to earth, His rule or kingdom will be visibly manifested and imposed (Matt 13:40-43). This will mark the end of this age and inaugurate the earthly messianic phase of the kingdom (Rev 20:1-6), which will last for a thousand years. Yet the kingdom does not end, for God's reign is eternal (Rev 11:15); and the mediatorial kingdom becomes the eternal kingdom of the triune God. Here, then, Peter looks to the future aspects of the kingdom of Jesus Christ that the believer enters at death or at the imposition of the kingdom." Blum, 12:271.

of our Lord and Savior Jesus Christ–The genitive phrase here identifies the kingdom of which Peter speaks as belonging to Jesus whose titles here are Lord, Savior and Christ. Jesus, the name given Him at birth in obedience to the angelic command and in connection with His role to "save His people from their sins" (Matt. 1:21), points up His humanity. It is joined here with His divinity signified first by the noun Lord; the term is *kuriou*, from *kuros* (might, power). It has the idea of supreme ownership, lordship; its widespread use includes a master of property (Matt. 20:8), head of a house (Matt. 15:27), a husband in a family (1 Pet. 3:6) and the Lord Himself who has authority over the harvest fields of the world, i.e., the peoples of mankind (Matt. 9:38), over the Sabbath (Matt. 12:8) and over all men as the King of Kings and Lord of Lords (Rev. 19:16). Peter's use here shows His Lordship over the eternal kingdom yet to come. The term Christ is from *chrio* which means "anoint." In the OT the term applied to everyone anointed with the holy oil, primarily to the priesthood (Lev. 4:3, 5, 16; 6:22); also applied to others acting as redeemers; the appellative occurs mainly in the Gospels, for example "Jesus who is called the Christ" (Matt. 1:16); used often in the Pauline corpus and in 1 Peter as a proper noun: "Christ" (e.g., Rom. 5:8; 1 Peter 1:11). Significant in Peter's use in 2 Peter 1:11 is the Messiah role Jesus will have in this future eternal kingdom, something predicted long ages ago (e.g., Isa. 11). Again, Peter's employment here is polemical in nature, refuting the false views of the pre-gnostics teachers of his day who denied the deity of Jesus (cf. 2 Pet. 2:1).

will be abundantly–The term is *plousios* and means "richly" functioning here as an adverbial adjective modifying the verb that follows, abundantly. The cultural backdrop here is intriguing. As Green states, "the metaphor of entry into the kingdom may well go back to one of the honours paid to a victor in the Olympic Games. His home city, in her joy and pride in his success, would welcome him back not through the usual gate, but through a part of the wall specially broken down to afford him entrance." Green, 75.

Supplied–This fascinating term was seen in verse 5 in the imperative referencing the believer's duty to supply in his faith the seven virtues which follow through verse 7. Now the term, in future passive form, is related to the divine side of the matter, and could in fact be deemed a divine passive since God is the one supplying in this case for the believer who has supplied virtue in addition to his foundational faith in Christ (v. 1).

to you–A dative of advantage in connection with the ones to whom this entrance into heaven will be so abundantly supplied.

[10] Green, 75.

[11] A genitive of relationship.

[12] J. A. Bengel, *Gnomon Novi Testamenti* (1773), quoted in Green, 76-7.

[13] Chuck Swindoll, *The Grace Awakening* (Waco: Word, 1982), 5-6.

3

So, What is This Thing Called "The *Bema* Seat?"

Nearly three weeks had passed since the tour at the Gallery of Virtue. Home for lunch, I was crunching on some cucumbers I had gathered the evening before from my first-ever-garden when I heard the familiar noontime sound of my mailbox lid opening and closing. I always enjoyed it when the mailman came; you never knew what surprises he might bring, especially news from friends or family. Of course, ever since the tour, I had been waiting for the handout on *The Bema Seat of Christ*. Could it have arrived today?

Still chomping on a lightly salted cucumber, I arose from the kitchen table to check the mailbox. Opening the front door, I saw a large manila envelope with Didaskolos' name on the return address bulging from the mailbox. Lifting up the brad, I was thrilled to find the handout inside.

I was also delighted that on this particular day, my boss had given me extra time for lunch due to some recent overtime. Perfect. I brewed some of my favorite peppermint tea, grabbed some fresh molasses-raisin cookies from the cookie jar, propped up my feet and began to read.

THE BEMA SEAT OF CHRIST

1. What does "Bema Seat" mean?
2. When does the Bema Seat of Christ occur?
3. Who are the subjects at the Bema Seat of Christ?
4. What are the issues at the Bema Seat of Christ?

WHAT DOES "BEMA SEAT" MEAN?

In the fifth chapter of Paul's second epistle to the saints in Corinth, he says, "For we must all appear before the judgment seat of Christ, so that each one of us may be recompensed for his deeds in the body, according to what he has done, whether good or bad."[1] The words "judgment seat" translate one Greek term, *bematos*, which is a possessive form—this is Christ's judgment seat—of the root, *bema.* Primarily, *bema* means "a step, or pace,"[2] that is, the single stride of one's foot. In Acts 7:5 we are told that when Abraham left his homeland in Ur of the Chaldeans, God gave him "no inheritance in it, not even a foot of ground," or more literally, "nor a space of a foot."[3] Israel would not possess Canaan just yet, in God's timetable, not even "a footstep[4] worth."

After this the term came to denote a raised platform, reached by steps like the well-known platform in Athens on the Pnyx Hill. From such platforms orators would speak. But the word was also used in the Greek culture of a tribunal, one for the accuser and one for the defendant.[5] As well, it was applied to the judicial bench of a Roman magistrate or ruler.

During the trials of Jesus, prior to His crucifixion, Matthew 27:19 tells us that while Pilate was sitting on "his judgment seat, his wife sent him a message, saying, 'Have nothing to do with that Righteous Man; for last night I suffered greatly in a dream because of Him.'" Pilate listened to the violent mob instead and sentenced Jesus to death.[6]

In addition to the political arena, "In Grecian games in Athens, the old arena contained a raised platform on which the president or umpire of the arena sat. From here he rewarded all the contestants; and here he rewarded all winners. It was called the '*bema*' or 'reward seat.' It was never used of a judicial bench."[7]

And it is precisely this latter sense of "reward seat" that becomes the sole focus of the event the New Testament calls "the *bema* seat of Christ"—but more about the nature of this crucial event later.

For now, with this backdrop, we can ask a second question,

WHEN DOES THE BEMA SEAT OF CHRIST OCCUR?

Several reasons exist for believing that the *bema* seat of Christ occurs on the heels of the Rapture of the church.[8] First, the two events are often juxtaposed in the New Testament. For instance, in 1 Corinthians 3, the *bema* seat of Christ is the subject of Paul's discussion. And as verse 13 tells us, "each man's work will become evident; for *the day* [emphasis mine] will show it...." The article "the" attached to the noun "day" indicates that this is not just any day on God's prophetical calendar; this is a day of particular identity.[9] As Paul continues his teaching on the *bema* seat, he reveals what this day is. According to 1 Corinthians 4:5 it is the day when "the Lord comes."

In 1 John 2 and 4 the Rapture and the *bema* seat of

Christ are again seen in conjunction. In 2:28 we read, "Now, little children, abide in Him, so that when He appears, we may have confidence and not shrink away from Him in shame at His coming." Then, 4:16-18 states, "We have come to know and have believed the love which God has for us. God is love, and the one who abides in love abides in God, and God abides in him. By this love is perfected with us, so that we may have confidence in *the day of judgment* [emphasis mine]; because as He is, so also are we in this world. There is no fear in love; but perfect love casts out fear, because fear involves punishment, and the one who fears is not perfected in love."

Essentially this passage shows us that the believer who consistently loves others is acting like God—"as He is, so also are we in this world"—and such conduct will allow him to be confident[10] rather than embarrassed and fearful when he sees Christ at His appearing.

There is, however, another reason to believe that the *bema* seat of Christ directly follows the Rapture. Not only are the two events often seen in close conjunction, but the mention of rewards is often connected with the Rapture. In many places in the New Testament, rewards are received from Christ at the time of the Rapture. And since according to other references it is at the *bema* seat of Christ that rewards are dispensed, it would be safely assumed that the *bema* seat is in view in those passages and, therefore, joined in a close time approximation to the Rapture. A few examples of these passages are as follows: 1 Thessalonians 2:19-20; 2 Timothy 4:8; 1 Peter 5:4.

A third reason why these two events should be seen in close relationship is because, according to Luke 14:14, rewards are linked to the resurrection. And since, according to 1 Thessalonians 4:13-17, the resurrection is a vital part of the Rapture event, rewards must be part of the scenario. In this same vein, when Christ returns to earth for his Second Advent, His bride is already rewarded. As Revelation 19:7-8 declares, "Let us rejoice and be glad and give the glory to Him, for the marriage of the Lamb has come and His bride has made herself ready. It was given to her to clothe herself in fine linen, bright and clean; for the fine linen is the righteous acts of the saints."[11] A few verses later reveal Jesus coming on a white horse with His saints, unleashing the wrath of God upon rebellious nations and setting up His one-thousand year rule on earth.[12]

To be sure, then, sometime between the Rapture and the return of Christ to earth, the *bema* seat of Christ will take place.[13]

But someone may well ask, "Why be so concerned about the timing of this event?" In short, the Rapture could happen at any moment; and since the *bema* seat follows, **TODAY** could be the day you stand at the tribunal of Christ. For example, the imminent nature of this appearing makes it imperative that the believer, with the alertness of a watchdog, guard his heart against selfishness and be on constant lookout for ways to treat others lovingly. If Jesus came today—right now—today would be my appointment at the bema seat of Christ.

But is the *bema* seat of Christ only for believers? That leads us to our third question,

WHO ARE THE SUBJECTS AT THE BEMA SEAT OF CHRIST?

Yes, everyone present at the *bema* seat of Christ is a believer from the church age only. Why is this so? First, since the *bema* seat occurs in conjunction with the Rapture, it would follow that those present at this judgment are only those raptured. And since those raptured are only believers from the time the church began in Acts 2 to the time of the Rapture itself, we would deduce that the *bema* seat is only for church-age believers. Some might argue that Old Testament saints could be present, and they may, but nowhere in Scripture do we have any evidence that this is the case. Apparently, they have their own time of reward.

In Romans 14, Paul refers to himself and the believers at Rome when he says, "For we will all stand before the judgment seat of God. For it is written, 'As I live, says the Lord, every knee shall bow to Me, and every tongue shall give praise to God.' So then, each one of us shall give an account of himself to God."[14]

Speaking to Christians in Corinth, the same apostle writes, "And I, brethren, could not speak to you as to spiritual men, but as to men of flesh, as to infants in Christ." Paul goes on to say that the *bema* seat of Christ will be required for those who have made Jesus Christ the foundation of their life, that is, they have trusted in Him as the exclusive source of their salvation. As verse 11 says, "For no one can lay any foundation other than the one already laid, which is Jesus Christ."

In Paul's second epistle to the Corinthians, he writes, in chapter 5, verse 10, "For we must all appear before the judgment seat of Christ...." No less than sixteen first person plural pronouns (we, us, or our) are found in verses 1-9. Contextually, then, the "we" that begins verse 10, above, is clearly referring to believers, who, unlike unbelievers, have (1) a heavenly house (i.e., a future resurrection body promised from God, vv. 1-4); (2) the presence of the Holy Spirit (v. 5); (3) the ability to walk by faith, not by sight (v. 7); (4) desires to be home in heaven with the Lord (v. 8) and (5) an all-consuming ambition to please God (v. 10). Beyond this, unbelievers have their own tribunal, at the Great White Throne judgment of

Revelation 20:11-15. In every New Testament reference to the *bema* seat of Christ, only believers are in view, never non-believers.

But what is the purpose of each believer appearing before the bema seat of Christ?

WHAT ARE THE ISSUES AT THE BEMA SEAT OF CHRIST?

The answer is actually two-fold. To start with, negatively speaking, the issue at the *bema* seat of Christ is not the reality of our salvation. 1 Corinthians 3:15 affirms that something other than salvation from hell is the issue at this event. The subjects, already believers, as 3:1 declares, are assured of being eternally saved regardless of how they fare at Christ's judgment: "If any man's work is burned up, he will suffer loss; but he himself will be saved, yet so as through fire." The NIV translators render this last phrase, "but only as one escaping through the flames."[15]

What's more, the very nature of our salvation proves that it is not the concern at the *bema* seat. For it is an issue already settled at the moment we trusted in Jesus as our Savior from hell. This decision, brought to pass in time, is the outworking of God's decision to save us in eternity past.[16] As such, we are presently sealed for God's future day of redemption (cf. Eph. 1:13-14; 4:30). As John writes, "We shall not come into condemnation *having already* [emphasis mine] passed from death to life" (John 5:24, NIV). But if the issue at the *bema* seat is not the reality of our salvation, what is it?

Positively speaking, the focus of the *bema* seat is rewards for saints. Muse on what God says in 1 Corinthians 3:6-8, 13-14: "I planted the seed, Apollos watered it, but God made it grow. So neither he who plants nor he who waters is anything, but only God, who makes things grow....his work is

> shown for what it is, because the Day will bring it to light. It will be revealed with fire, and the fire will test the quality of each man's work. If what he has built survives, he will receive his reward." Salvation is not the issue here, being a gift apart from human works, whereas the rewards at the *bema* seat are earned by good works.[17]
>
> So then, the question we are now compelled to ask is, What in our Christian lives is worthy of reward? In other words, what are the criteria for honor from our Savior on that Day? For what will we hear Him say, "Well done, good and faithful servant?" (Matt. 25:21). According to 1 Corinthians 3:12, He wants to see gold, silver and stone service, not wood, hay and stubble service. But what exactly does that mean? What do these look like? How do we embrace the one and avoid the other? These questions must be answered if we aim to do well on our final report card, the one issued by the Master Teacher at the bema seat of Christ.

Waiting for the Bible study to begin with Didaskolos would now be even more difficult. I wanted to do well on my final report card--certainly Jesus is worthy of nothing less! But I determined to start reading the New Testament on my own to see if I could discover the kinds of things for which Jesus would reward me at the *bema* seat. I would begin panning for these golden nuggets tonight after supper.

Endnotes for Chapter 3

[1] *For*–The *gar* explains the reason for Paul's ambition in verse 9 "to be pleasing to Him."

we must–This third person plural present active indicative impersonal verb denotes "compulsion of any kind," according to Bauer, Arndt and Gingrich who classify this particular use under "divine destiny or unavoidable fate" (cf. similar use in Rev. 1:1, "*the things which must* [emphasis mine] take place"). Bauer, Arndt and

Gingrich, 171. Each believer (indicated by the use of *pantas humas* in context) must appear before Christ's judgment seat—this appointment, by nature, is not optional.

all appear—The Greek is *phanerothenai*, aorist passive infinitive functioning here in the accusative case in a substantive role. The passive element is "we must all be made manifest," that is, as far as all Christians go, "They not only have to appear, but have to have their whole character made manifest." Alfred Plummer, *A Critical and Exegetical Commentary on the Second Epistle to the Corinthians* (Edinburgh: T&T Clark, 1956), quoted in Fritz Rienecker, *A Linguistic Key to the Greek New Testament*, ed. by Cleon L. Rogers, Jr. (Grand Rapids: Zondervan, 1980), 467. It is not just an appearance in the sense of appearing before a magistrate, but appearing "in our true light as we have never done before." Alford, 2:661. The term is used of Christ's appearing at the Rapture in Colossians 3:4; 1 Peter 5:4; 1 John 2:28.

before—The word is *emprosthen*, an adverb that can also function as a preposition, as here; it can mean: "in front of" (Luke 19:4; Phil. 3:14); "before, in the presence of, in the face" (Matt. 5:24; 23:14); "before, previous to," in a temporal sense (John 1:15, 27, 30); and from the Hebrew sense, "in the sight or estimation of" (Matt. 11:26; 18:14, and here, in concert with the meaning of *phanerothenai*; with the genitive it is translated "before"; perhaps a genitive of place is the best nuance, though it is more than just a location; it is an examination).

the judgment seat of Christ—Subjective genitive phrase.

so that—Coordinating conjunction, *hina*, introducing a purpose clause.

each one—The individual nature of this examination is denoted with the singular pronominal adjective, each one. Someone has said in effect, "It is possible to hide in the choir of life, but one day each of us will sing a solo before God."

of us may be recompensed—The term is *komiseta*, aorist middle subjunctive from *komizo*, "to bear, carry" (Luke 7:37); but in the middle voice, "to carry something off, to get something for oneself," here, to receive a recompense, "to receive back what is one's own." Philip E. Hughes, *Commentary on the Second Epistle to the Corinthians* (Grand Rapids: Eerdmans, 1977), quoted in Fritz Rienecker, *A Linguistic Key to the Greek New Testament*, ed. by Cleon L. Rogers, Jr. (Grand Rapids: Zondervan, 1980), 468. Colossians 3:25 employs the term when it says, "For he who does wrong will receive the consequences of the wrong which he has done, and that without partiality." In contrast to this negative judgment on unfaithful slaves or masters, Ephesians 6:8 declares, "knowing that whatever good thing each one does, this he will receive back from the Lord, whether slave or free." Here, the term shows the judicial nature of the *bema* seat corresponding well with what we read in Hebrews 6:10, "For God is not unjust [*adikos*] so as to forget your work and the love which you have shown toward His Name, in having ministered and in still ministering to the saints." Again, God does not owe His saints a reward, but has chosen out of His grace to do so, and His standard for doing so is *komizo* (in this connection, see the use of *misthos*, "wage, payment" in the NT, another word often found in the so-called "reward passages").

[2] Vine, 337.

[3] Bauer, Arndt and Gingrich, 139.

[4] Cf. Deuteronomy 2:5 where the term is so translated.

[5] Vine, 337.

[6] Cf. similar use of *bema* in John 19:13; Acts 18:12, 16, 17; 25:6, 10, 17. As Ryrie states, "Earthly *bemas* were raised, throne-like platforms on which rulers or judges sat when making speeches (Acts 12:21), or hearing and deciding cases (Acts 18:12-17)." Charles C. Ryrie, *Basic Theology* (Wheaton: Victor Books, 1986), 512.

[7] L. Sale-Harrison, *Judgment Seat of Christ* (New York: Sale-Harrison, 1938), 8, quoted in J. Dwight Pentecost, *Things to Come: A Study in Biblical Eschatology* (Grand Rapids: Zondervan, 1978), 220. Plummer states, "The...[*bema*] is the tribunal, whether in a basilica for the praetor in a court of justice, or in a camp for the commander to administer discipline and address the troops. In either case the tribunal was a platform on which the seat (*sella*) of the presiding officer was placed. In LXX...[*bema*] commonly means a platform or scaffold rather than a seat (Neh. viii. 4...). In N.T. it seems generally to mean the seat....But in some of the passages it may mean the platform on which the seat was placed. On the Areopagus the...[*bema*] was a stone platform...Fond as St. Paul is of military metaphors, and of comparing the Christian life to warfare, he is not likely to be thinking of a military tribunal here." Alfred Plummer, *A Critical and Exegetical Commentary on the Second Epistle to the Corinthians* (Edinburgh: T&T Clark, 1975), 156. Lehman Strauss concurs when he writes, "The word *bema* was a familiar term to the people in Paul's day, for in the large olympic arenas, there was an elevated seat on which the judge of the contest sat. After the contests were over, the successful competitors would assemble before the *bema* to receive their rewards or crowns. The *bema* was not a judicial bench where someone was condemned; it was a reward seat." Lehman Strauss, *God's Plan for the Future* (Grand Rapids, MI: Zondervan, 1965), 111.

[8] It is this writer's view that the Rapture of the church, referenced in 1 Thessalonians 4:16-18, occurs prior to the 7-year Tribulation era described in Revelation 6-19.

[9] This is the definitive use of the Greek article; cf. H. E. Dana and Julius R. Mantey, *A Manual Grammar of the Greek New Testament* (New York: Macmillan, 1955), 137-141.

[10] The term translated "confidence" in both 1 John 2:28 and 4:17 is *parresian*. It signifies boldness, assurance, freedom in speaking (cf. Acts 4:13, 29, 31; Eph. 3:12; Heb. 3:6).

[11] As Ryrie comments, "The good works of believers will constitute the wedding garment when the congregation of the faithful are joined to Christ in

marriage (2 Cor. 11:2; Eph. 5:26-27)." Charles C. Ryrie, *Ryrie Study Bible: New American Standard*, exp. ed. (Chicago: Moody Press, 1995), 2040.

[12] Cf. Rev. 19:11-20:6; it would seem that those who do not hold to a literal thousand year reign of Christ must also, to be consistent in their hermeneutic, take the rest of the personages, places and events in the passage symbolically, such as the angel, heaven, the Abyss, Satan, the nations, thrones, martyrs, Jesus, Word of God, first resurrection, second death, etc. In particular, why would the numerical values of this blessed resurrection and the contrasting death which has no power over those resurrected be literal if the thousand year era, mentioned here six times, is non-literal?

[13] Many commentators agree that the *bema* judgment takes place sometime in close connection with the Rapture (e.g., Pentecost, Ryrie, Baker, Chafer, and Thiessen).

[14] *For*–The *gar* introduces the reason for the exhortation (in the beginning of v. 10) to loving attitudes and actions toward Christians who hold different convictions than us regarding non-moral issues.

we–Translates *pantes*, which, in the wider context of this letter written from Paul to the believers in Rome (1:7), and in view of the immediate context where instruction is given regarding how Christians should treat one another, is restricted to Christians only.

will all stand–The tense of this verb, *parastenseometha*, shows the event named here, the *bema* seat, to be future.

before–The dative phrase is introduced with the *to*, a dative of location.

the judgment seat of God–At the end of the verse, some early manuscripts have *Christou* instead of *Theou*, probably to conform this text to the wording in 2 Corinthians 5:10, another central passage on the *bema* seat. The strong support for *Theou* leaves no reason to question the original nature of it and theologically points up the inseparable workings of Jesus, called Lord in the previous verse, and God, the Father. As Witmer rightly observes, "Because God judges through His Son (John 5:22, 27), this judgment seat can be said to belong to both the Father and the Son." John A. Witmer, "Romans," in *The Bible Knowledge Commentary: An Exposition of the Scriptures: New Testament*, ed. by John F. Walvoord and Roy B. Zuck, 435-503 (Wheaton: Victor Books, 1983), 493. *Theou* is a subjective genitive.

For it is written–An intensive perfect, *gegraptai* shows the certain and existing results of God's Word quoted here from Isaiah.

As I live, says the Lord, every knee shall bow to Me, and every tongue shall give praise to God–Paul draws from both Isaiah 49:18 and 45:23 to show that everyone will stand before God and give due homage, though in context he employs the quote for his own purpose to remind believers that each one of them will appear at God's tribunal for Christians. It's interesting to observe Paul's replacement of *kat' emautou omnuo* (the beginning words of Isa. 45:23 in the LXX) with *zo ego, legei kurios*; most likely, quoting from memory, "he inadvertently replaced one OT divine asseverative formula by another perhaps slightly more familiar." Matthew Black, "The Christological Use of the Old Testament in the New Testament," *New Testament Studies* 18, no. 1 (October 1971): 8, quoted in C. E. B. Cranfield, A *Critical and Exegetical Commentary on The Epistle to the Romans*, The International Critical Commentary (Edinburgh: T & T. Clark, 1979), 2:710. This quote by the apostle supports the statement of verse 10c.

So then–The *ara oun* forms an inferential element as Paul now draws his conclusion from verse 10 regarding the certainty of future judgment.

each one–The emphatic pronominal adjective here in the singular shows the individual nature of the judgment seat of God.

of us shall give–The tense of *didomi* signifies the future nature of this event called the *bema* seat.

an account–The term account translates *logon* (from *logos*). Used some 330 times in the NT, here the nuance is that of the "account which one gives by word of mouth." Vine, 10. The same sense is noted in Matthew 12:36.

of himself–In context, this is significant, for each believer will not give an account for the actions and convictions of others, but of himself. For this reason, judging another Christian for his personal standards on amoral issues is not acceptable; whether weak in faith (Rom. 14:1) or strong (the one looking down on his brother in v. 10), each saint will give an account of his personal convictions before Christ, the final judge on such matters. Treating those different from us in the body of Christ is a test of our love (v. 15). Elsewhere, a lifestyle of love toward others is a reason for confidence in the Day of Judgment (cf. 1 John 4:16-19).

to God–As Cranfield notes, *to theo* is most likely the correct reading (some omit it altogether) for its intrinsic probability; without it the necessary conclusion to the paragraph is deleted, though admittedly still implied without it. Cranfield, 2:710.

[15] The future tense of the verb "will be saved" signifies the glorification aspect of the salvation process, in contrast with past justificational and present sanctificational salvation.

[16] Cf. Ephesians 1:4, 13 respectively which reveal both God's sovereign election of who would be saved and the decision of the elect to choose salvation.

[17] Not that God owes them to us, in light of Luke 17:10, but that out of His grace He has decided to recompense our works. Of course, as will be seen, even these works we do are generated by the Holy Spirit, so that the reward for our works reminds us of the ultimate glory that is God's alone.

4

Do My Motives *Really* Matter?

It was my favorite kind of evening—the air was balmy and the moon played peek-a-boo behind white, puffy clouds. Of course, the most special thing about this evening was the launching of the new Bible study with Didaskolos. Before the tour at the Gallery of Virtue, I knew very little about being rewarded with a hero's welcome at the judgment seat of Christ. In fact, my knowledge of that future event and the doctrine of rewards wouldn't have filled a thimble. I now knew that to receive a hero's welcome I must progress in spiritual maturity. But according to Didaskolos, there were other criteria for future rewards, though each one is like a stream flowing from the headwaters of spiritual maturity. I was ready to discover those new streams.

What a reunion it was. Clifford, Allen, Jim, Janet, and Alfred were all there, and even Nina drove up from nearby Mexico. It had been two months since the tour, and we greeted one another with smiles, laughter and hugs as we walked up the red-brick sidewalk to the front door of our beloved teacher's house.

It was the kind of place you would expect Didaskolos to have. Neatly trimmed hedges bordered the sidewalk, the lush green lawn was carefully manicured, and window boxes decorated with a variety of colorful flowers stood out against the backdrop of a white house with yellow trim. The large porch with wooden railings displayed the congenial character of post-World War Two vintage.

I rang the doorbell. Everyone stood waiting for Didaskolos.

He had barely cracked open the door when a collective "Hello" rang out. Then one by one we filed in and embraced this wonderful saint of God. I immediately thought of Paul's advice in 1 Thessalonians 5:26 to "greet one another with a holy kiss," a visible display of the filial affection God's people should have for each other.

The inside of Didaskolos' home was as warm and personable as the outside, again a reflection of his own heart as one who, over the years, had allowed the Master Painter to color his life with the virtues of 2 Peter 1:5-7.

The dazzling glow and sound of the sparkling fire invited us into the living room where we all selected the chair of our liking. And no one could escape the mouth-watering aroma floating through the air from the kitchen. As we chatted, more than one tried to guess what Didaskolos had cooked up.

"So good to see each of you," he said. "I have been waiting for this moment like a young boy waits for Christmas morning. But before we begin our study, there are some goodies I've baked in the kitchen, so please help yourself and grab some coffee, herbal tea, juice, or whatever else you can find in the refrigerator."

Janet returned with a slice of homemade bread. Jim and I couldn't resist the big brown molasses cookies with raisins. Clifford fancied a dish of apple cobbler topped with a dab of vanilla ice cream, and the rest went for the homespun cherry pie. Some chose the freshly brewed coffee and others the various assortments of herbal teas. Taking our place in the cozy living room around the fireplace, we all realized the kind of time and love that had gone into these preparations. Each one's heart was stirred by the Christ-like portrait of *agape* love seen in Didaskolos.

"Would you please lead us in prayer, Clifford?" asked Didaskolos.

"Lord, you have said in your Word," Clifford began, "'Behold, how good and how pleasant it is for brothers to dwell in unity' (Ps. 133:1). We are grateful for this reunion, for these delicious treats that our beloved brother has prepared. We are thankful for the fragrance of You that exudes from him, and we ask You to visit with us tonight that, as the psalmist prayed, we may 'behold wonderful things from your law' (Ps. 119:18). For each one of us desires to be worthy of a hero's welcome when we stand before You. In the name of Jesus, our precious Savior and coming King, we pray. Amen."

Didaskolos took his seat in the middle of the circle, took a sip of his peppermint tea and then drew once again from his seemingly endless reservoir of illustrations:

"In one of Charles Schultz's *Peanuts* comic strips, Schroeder is playing the piano and announces to Lucy that he is learning all of Beethoven's sonatas. Lucy, leaning on the piano, says, 'If you learn to play them all, what will you win?' Schroeder is upset and says, 'I won't win anything.' Lucy walks away and says, 'What's the use of learning the sonatas if you don't win a prize?'[1]

"I know that each you wish to have a hero's welcome when you stand before Jesus on your day of reckoning. To make this wish come true, not only is it imperative that you progress in spiritual maturity, as we learned in the Gallery of Virtue, but as well you must practice your Christian Life with Spirit-led motives, motives that surpass the mercenary spirit of Lucy. And I am the first to confess, it is so easy to do the right thing for the wrong reason. Several Scriptures address this issue of the Christian's motivations for serving God. To start with, please open your copy of our Father's word to 1 Corinthians 4."

The rustling of the sacred pages was a pleasant sound to all; these people were truly in love with Jesus.

"To gain a proper backdrop for Paul's words here," Didaskolos began, "you should know that the carnal corral at Corinth had created their own Christian celebrity hall which in turn gave birth to chaos in the church. Look at chapter 1, verse 12 and you will see that some were saying, 'I am of Paul,' others, 'I am of Apollos,' another faction, 'I am of Cephas,' and still others, 'I am of Christ!' Cliques sprang up all through the Corinthian camp because they boasted in men instead of God, passing judgment on each leader among them. Such foolishness was conceived in pride, but in ignorance as well, as chapter 4, verses 1-5 reveal. Janet, would you mind reading those for us?"

"I would be delighted to," she replied.

"'Let a man regard us in this manner, as servants of Christ and stewards of the mysteries of God. In this case, moreover, it is required of stewards that one be found trustworthy. But to me it is a very small thing that I may be examined by you, or by any human court; in fact, I do not even examine myself. For I am conscious of nothing against myself, yet I am not by this acquitted; but the one who examines me is the Lord. Therefore, do not go on passing judgment[2] before the time, but wait until the Lord comes, who will both bring to light the things hidden in darkness and disclose the *motives*[3] [emphasis mine] of men's heart; and then each man's praise will come to him from God.'"

"A few observations are needful here," said Didaskolos. "First, the Master Teacher's examination of my ministry to others is continual–class is always in session. This is clear by the present tense in the word 'examines'[4] in verse 4. Second, note that verse 5 begins with the term 'therefore' which infers something from the preceding verses.[5] When you see a 'therefore' always go back and see what it's there for."

A few chuckled at the pun.

"Regardless of what others may say about us," declared Didaskolos, "God will make out our final report card. Others see what we do, God sees why we did it. As Proverbs 16:2 echoes, 'All a man's ways seem innocent to him, but motives are weighed by the Lord.' Therefore, don't render a final verdict on anyone's ministry; such action is outside your jurisdiction.[6]

"Thirdly, observe that the time of this 'final exam' will be 'when the Lord comes.'[7] Many New Testament passages link the dispensing of rewards to Jesus' sudden return at the Rapture (e.g., 1 Thess. 2:19-20; 2 Tim. 4:6-8). Even after a believer dies, his example may continue to inspire others in the Way. Like the smell of sweet perfume lingers long after the one wearing it has left the room, so the godly believer leaves behind the fragrance of his Savior. In brief, his influence may endure right up to the moment Jesus returns. Through something he has said, done, sung, prayed or written, etc., the final accounting of his Christian Life will be delayed until then. For then, and only then, will all the evidence be in."[8]

"Finally, did you notice, in verse 5, that the Lord will praise[9] His children when He comes again, but apparently not all of them. For in verse two, Paul states that God's servants must be found 'trustworthy.'[10] We will probe the depths of this passage some other evening, but for now, please understand that just as in the parables Jesus gave regarding faithful and unfaithful servants (Matt. 25:14-22; Luke 19:12-19), only the former will receive God's 'Well done!' Only those who serve Christ with Spirit-led motives deserve a hero's welcome."

"So what exact motives is God looking for in my life?" I asked.

"That's a crucial question, Ron," Didaskolos answered. "In Matthew 22:37-38, Jesus tells us that the first and foremost demand of the Law is to 'Love the Lord your God with all your heart and with all your soul and with all your mind'; and Doctor Luke adds, 'with all your strength...' (Luke 10:27).[11] James echoes this theme when he writes, 'Blessed is the man who perseveres under trial, because when he has stood the test, he will receive the crown of life that God has promised to *those who love Him* [emphasis mine]' (James 1:12). It's clear that to receive a hero's welcome I must serve God because I love God.

"We've all watched the newlywed couple gaze into each other's eyes, walking hand-in-hand everywhere they go. If separated for more than an hour, they run back to one another's arms and don't care who looks on. Oh, how the love flows between two people when the marriage has just begun."

Then Didaskolos asked the question, "Do you recall those early days in your relationship with Jesus when you were lost in the wonder of His love that forgave your sins and gifted you with His eternal life? No other person, place, pursuit or possession was as important to you as He. He was preeminent in your affection."

Then quietly and soberly he asked us, "How is it between you and your Savior tonight? Is your affection for Him still strong? Or, like chewing gum you have chomped on for some time, have you lost your original flavor of worship? Bible reading is as dry as crackers; church attendance a hollow obligation; prayer has become a chore seldom attended to; and carving out time in your busy schedule to befriend sinners to the Friend of sinners is as likely as a mid-summer snowstorm. Like the Ephesian believers, is it possible that some of us need to rekindle our first love for Jesus?" (Rev. 2:4).

After these soul-searching questions, Didaskolos allowed quietness to prevail. All of us appreciated the chance to let God's Spirit gently nudge our consciences with conviction, or, encourage us with affirmation: "You're doing well, I know you love above Me all else." As we sat there, the only sound was the occasional spark from the fire which now preached its own silent sermon, drawing from the exhortation Didaskolos had given to keep our love for God aflame.

Several soul-searching moments passed before Didaskolos asked, "Can anyone think of things that may become subtle substitutes for our love for God?"

"I confess," answered Jim, "that in my pursuit of biblical knowledge, sound doctrine and preaching skills, at times I have loved the study of Jesus and standing before others sharing what I knew more than I loved Jesus Himself. Perhaps it's because my intellect is satisfied and my self-esteem bolstered by such experiences. And while I'm confessing my shortfalls, I have certainly been guilty of being in love with teaching but not in love with the people I'm teaching; Paul says that such a disposition profits me nothing" (1 Cor. 13:1-3).

"What I think your saying, Jim," said Janet, "is that it's necessary to zealously defend the foundational truths of our faith; and it's good to love biblical research and teaching because that's the spiritual gift God gave you. But, one must be sure he falls in love with the Author of the text and faithfully shepherds the people he teaches. In brief, we must beware of right words without real worship."

"I like the way you expressed it, Janet," replied Jim.

Then Clifford chimed in, "That reminds me of something Francis Schaeffer once said:

> We must ask, 'Do I fight merely for doctrinal faithfulness?' This is like the wife who never sleeps with anybody else, but never shows love to her own husband. Is that a sufficient relationship in marriage? No, 10,000 times no. Yet if I am a Christian who speaks and acts for doctrinal faithfulness but do not show love to the divine Bridegroom, I am in the same place as such a wife. What God wants from us is not only doctrinal faithfulness, but our love day and night. Not in theory, mind you, but in practice."[12]

"But I've also found," said Nina, "that it's possible to have right works without real worship. I sometimes call it the Martha Syndrome. From Luke 10:38-42, we all remember how Martha fussed about having to do all the work when Jesus came to dinner while Mary feasted on Jesus' words. But Jesus corrected her saying, '...only one thing is necessary, for Mary has chosen the good part, which shall not be taken away from her.' Mary exhibits the highest priority in God's kingdom just expressed by Jesus, namely, loving God, which shows up in a 'Good Samaritan' lifestyle of loving one's neighbor (Luke 10:25-37). Martha's error was not in her work of hospitality, but in her lack of worship. Mary's choice of the latter would not be taken from her."[13]

"Excellent teaching, Nina," said Didaskolos with enthusiasm. "I'm sure we can all relate to the Martha Syndrome: right works without real worship. But there's even a third subtle substitute for really loving God—requesting things from God without real worship of God."

"What do you mean, Didaskolos?" Janet asked.

"Perhaps a story I once read in *Our Daily Bread* will illustrate. Paul Van Gorder writes,

> As a Christian, I find it so easy to become spiritually nearsighted, focusing on God's wonderful gifts while failing to center my love on God Himself. Sometimes my prayers sound like a 'wish list' just before Christmas. God tells us to present our needs to Him, and He delights in receiving our gratitude for what He bestows. But He longs that we love Him for who He is—not just for what He gives.
>
> "Bible teacher Leon Tucker told about taking a trip to Europe and promising his little daughter that he would bring her a doll from each country he visited. He purchased them in Ireland, Scotland, Belgium, France, and several countries. But on the way back to the States, the luggage containing these gifts was delayed and didn't arrive with him.
>
> "When Tucker got home, his little daughter greeted him with love and expectation. The look on her face said, 'Did you bring the dolls, Daddy?' Gently he told her about the mix-up. Momentarily her lip quivered and her eyes filled with tears, but then she threw her arms around his neck and said, 'I'd rather have you, Daddy, than all the dolls in the world!'[14]

"Then Van Gorder asks, "Is God more precious to us than all of His gifts? Our love and devotion should be centered on the Giver, not His gifts."[15] Finally, he cites a poem that drives home the point:

> Once it was the blessing, now it is the Lord;
> Once it was the feeling, now it is His Word;
> Once His gifts I wanted, now the Giver own;
> Once I sought for healing, now Himself alone.[16]

"This reminds me of a similar story from the life of Hudson Taylor when he tested missionary candidates' love for God:

> When Hudson Taylor directed the China Inland Mission, he often interviewed candidates for the mission field. On one occasion, he met with a group of applicants to determine their motives for service. 'And why do you wish to go as a foreign missionary?' he asked one. 'I want to go because Christ commanded us to...preach the gospel to every creature,' the candidate replied. Another said, 'I want to go because millions are perishing without Christ.' Others gave different answers. Then Hudson Taylor said, 'All of these motives, however good, will fail you in times of testings, trials, tribulations, and possible death. There is but one motive that will sustain you in trial and testing: namely, the love of Christ.'[17]

"Richard DeHaan tells of 'a missionary in Africa, [who,] when asked if he really liked what he was doing, responded, "Do I like this work? No. My wife and I do not like dirt. We have reasonably refined sensibilities. We do not like crawling into vile huts through goat refuse.... But is a man to do nothing for Christ he does not like? God pity him, if not. Liking or disliking has nothing to do with it. We have orders to 'Go' and we go. Love constrains us."'[18]

"DeHaan then concludes, 'We may not be serving the Lord under dangerous or unpleasant conditions, but the work He has called us to do has its own unique difficulties. In times of trials...only the love of Christ can strengthen us to go on.'[19]

"One of my favorite sketches shows the contagious nature of a person's love for God:

> There's a true story about 'an aged countryman [who] visited London for the first time. In a great art gallery, he [was overwhelmingly caught up] with a painting of Christ dying on the cross. As he gazed fixedly upon it, a deeper love for the Savior flooded his heart. With great feeling, he exclaimed, 'Bless Him! I love Him! I love Him!'

"Those standing nearby heard him. They saw tears glistening on his careworn face as he stood completely oblivious of the presence of others. Four of them came close to him and said, 'We, too, love Him, brother.' Though strangers to each other, they were drawn together in love and adoration for the Savior.[20]

"As a final illustration, listen to what Ben Patterson writes:

"I have a theory about old age....I believe that when life has whittled us down, when joints have failed and skin has wrinkled and capillaries have clogged and hardened, what is left of us will be what we were all along, in our essence.

"Exhibit A is a distant uncle....All his life he did nothing but find new ways to get rich....He spent his senescence very comfortably, drooling and babbling constantly about the money he had made....When life whittled him down to his essence, all there was left was raw greed. This is what he had cultivated in a thousand little ways over a lifetime.

"Exhibit B is my wife's grandmother....When she died in her mid-eighties, she had been senile for several years. What did this lady talk about? The best example I can think of was when we asked her to pray before dinner. She would reach out and hold the hands of those sitting beside her, a broad, beatific smile would spread across their face, her dim eyes would fill with tears as she looked up to heaven, and her chin would quaver as she poured out her love to Jesus. That was Edna in a nutshell. She loved Jesus and she loved people. She couldn't remember our names, but she couldn't keep her hands from patting us lovingly whenever we got near her.

"When life whittled her down to her essence, all there was left was love: love for God and love for people.[21]

"So then, why do I preach sermons, lead Bible studies, visit the sick and the bereaved, give money to missions, organize ministry programs, help a friend move, share the gospel, or offer someone a ride home? Because I love Jesus and am passionate about pleasing Him? Or out of mere duty, a hollow legalism fueled by the flesh? Do I serve God because I love God? What motivates me? What motivates you?"[22]

"To receive a hero's welcome I must have Spirit-led motives~serving God because I love God, but also, serving God for the glory of God.

As Dave Branon, in *Our Daily Bread*, tells it:

> A Grand Rapids woman was excited to have a visit from an old college roommate who lived in another part of the country. As she listened to her friend's story, though, she was touched by the problems her guest faced as a single mom struggling to keep things together.
>
> "The hostess decided to do something to help. She got on the phone to her friend's home church and told them of her concern. The people in that town 2,000 miles away immediately went to work. They cleaned the woman's house inside and out. They stocked the shelves and filled the refrigerator with prepared meals.
>
> "When the woman got home, she was stunned by what had happened. And not knowing who had taken care of her and why, all she could do was give the glory to God.[23]

"Branon then extracts the principal lesson when he writes, 'That's the great model of how our work for the Lord should be done—not for us to receive honor and praise but to let God receive the glory.... It's not easy to turn away from the applause after doing something for others. Yet if we want to do God's work His way, we will. Then we'll be sure who gets the credit.'"[24]

"No doubt each of you," Didaskolos continued, "are familiar with 1 Corinthians 10:31. Can someone quote it for us?"

"I will," said Clifford. "So whether you eat or drink or whatever you do, do it all for the glory of God."[25]

"Thank you, dear brother," said Didaskolos. "Many of us know this verse well, but do we understand the context in which it occurs?"

Jim spoke up, saying, "Isn't Paul imploring his spiritual family at Corinth not to misuse their Christian liberty and thereby cause a less mature believer to stumble?"

"Yes," said Didaskolos, "that is the general context. In matters of food, drink or any non-moral issue about which Christians may have different convictions, each believer is to do what will clearly bring honor to God, edification to God's people and a good testimony to the unsaved around him. Beginning with verse 23, Paul says,

> Everything is permissible—but not everything is beneficial. Everything is permissible—but not everything is constructive. Nobody should seek his own good, but the good of others. Eat anything sold in the meat market without raising questions of conscience, for, 'The earth is the Lord's and everything in it.' If some unbeliever invites you to a meal and you want to go, eat whatever is put before you without raising questions of conscience. But if anyone says to you, 'This has been offered in sacrifice, then do not eat it, both for the sake of the man who told you and for conscience sake—the other man's conscience, I mean, not yours. For why should my freedom be judged by another man's conscience? If I take part in the meal with thankfulness, why am I denounced because of something I thank God for? So whether you eat or drink or whatever you do, do it all for the glory of God. Do not cause anyone to stumble, whether Jews, Greeks or the church of God—even as I try to please everybody

in every way. For I am not seeking my own good but the good of the many, so that they may be saved' (1 Cor. 10:23-33, NIV).

"Here Paul reflects the Jewish philosophy of the day, and that of the Old Testament Scripture," continued Didaskolos, "that real meaning in life is achieved by investing only in that which holds eternal value.[26] Even in routine matters such as dining with others, the Corinthian saints are exhorted to be sensitive to the personal convictions of others who may not feel at ease eating meat sacrificed to idols. Such consideration would show brotherly love and in turn give glory to God who is Himself love and commands His children to love others. As one Christian writer comments, 'This [the glory of God] is the ruling motive in the Christian's life, not just having his own way about whims and preferences.'"[27]

Then Nina asked, "Didaskolos, I think I understand what doing something to God's glory means, but in case I'm in a fog and don't know it, could you clarify?"

"I would be glad to," replied Didaskolos. "The term 'glory' is the Greek term *doxa*. In a nutshell, it refers to the honorable recognition that a person deserves. As such it is the opposite of shame or dishonor. Applied to God, as it is here in 1 Corinthians 10:31, and in many other texts, it entails seeing who God is in all His perfect attributes and ascribing to Him the unspeakable place of importance His reputation demands. It is recognizing the immeasurable renown, honor and fame God so deserves.[28] And once again, it is the attribute of God's kind and considerate love that stands out, like a gorgeous full moon on a cloudless night, when one Christian denies his own freedom to eat, drink, or do anything for that matter, in order to avoid the risk of offending another believer who does not have freedom in that area."

"What are some quick examples of such denial in our day?" asked

Allen.

"Good question, my brother," responded Didaskolos. "To start with, I know a devout Christian man in his fifties who, not for a lack of trying, still cannot swallow the idea that today's Christian contemporary music scene is from God. For him, the driving beat, wailing electric guitar rifts, and occasional wild vocal lines, sound too much like worldly music. Perhaps we might call such thinking 'old fashioned,' but in spite of the biblically-based lyrics, he cannot get past a sound that reminds him of music that clearly offends God.

"So, when his Christian friends, who happen to feel comfortable listening to upbeat Christian tunes, invite him over, they are obligated to respect his convictions, and not become a stumbling block to him. This means they must refrain from using their favorite CD for background music. Instead, in a spirit of brotherly love that glorifies the God of love, they would be prudent to select the kind of music he would prefer. Once he leaves, they are free to crank up their own style of music.

"But beyond the arena of musical taste, there are plenty of other fronts where Christians differ in their convictions, Swindoll provides this list:

- Going to movies or live theater,
- Wearing cosmetics,
- Playing cards or billiards,
- Watching television,
- Going to the beach,
- Not having personal devotions in the morning,
- Going to a restaurant that serves alcohol,
- Dancing—even square-dancing,
- Getting a face lift,
- Working out in leotards,

- Mixed bathing, or
- Eating pork.[29]

"Once a youth worker, in an ethnic community, attended a church that had Scandinavian roots. Being a rather forward-looking and creative young man, he decided he would show the youth group a missionary film—we're talking simple, safe, black-and-white religious-oriented movie. That film projector hadn't been off an hour before a group of the leaders in the church called him in and asked him about what he had done. They asked, 'Did you show the young people a film?' In all honesty he responded, 'Well, yeah, I did.' 'We don't like that,' they replied. Without trying to be argumentative, the youth worker reasoned, 'Well, I remember that at the last missionary conference, our church showed slides—' One of the church officers put his hand up signaling him to cease talking. Then, in these words, he emphatically explained the conflict: 'If it's still, fine. If it moves, sin! You can show slides, but when they start movin', you're getting' into sin.' In spite of this rigid approach to visual education, the youth worker did not look down his nose at these leaders for their different convictions, an attitude that brought glory to a God of love and understanding.[30]

"As Paul told the believers at Rome,

> Don't undo the work of God for a chunk of meat. Remember, there is nothing wrong with meat, but it is wrong to eat it if it makes another stumble. The right thing to do is quit eating meat or drinking wine or doing anything else that offends your brother or makes him sin. You may know that there is nothing wrong with what you do, even from God's point of view, but keep it to yourself; don't flaunt your faith in front of others who might be hurt by it. In this situation, happy is the man who does not sin by doing what he knows is right." (Rom. 14:20-22, Living Bible)

"Bringing glory to God, does this mean that instead of 'showing off' myself, I am to show off God to the world?" asked Janet.

"That's a contemporary way of putting it, Janet," answered Didaskolos, "and I think it communicates the concept well. There are plenty of occasions where we are tempted to be religious showboats. We must instead be consumed with the desire to point others to how absolutely glorious God is. One of my favorite passages of Scripture is Psalm 29:9 where we are told that in His temple everything says, 'Glory!' Overwhelmed by the magnificence of who God is, the residents of heaven, angels and saints alike, cannot stop saying 'Glory!' as they think of God.

"But we don't have to wait until heaven to catch this spirit of ceaseless praise. We can now join David's chorus when he invited God's people to 'magnify the Lord with me, and let us exalt His name together' (Ps. 34:3). Elsewhere he exhorts, 'Let those who love Your salvation say continually, "The Lord be magnified"' (Ps. 70:4). And, my life-verse is 1 Chronicles 16:24: 'Tell of His glory among the nations, His wonderful deeds among all the peoples.' When we finally realize that our chief role as humans is to take every opportunity we have to tell others how marvelous God is–who He is and what He's done for us–then, and only then, have we begun to live, and I mean really live. Of course, showing God off to the world is not limited to words from our lips. Our actions and attitudes can manifest the 'sweet aroma of the knowledge of Him in every place' (2 Cor. 2:14).

"Contrary to what society teaches us, this is our reason for existence, to bring renown, fame and glory to God, not to ourselves. As one man said, 'Few people need voice lessons to sing their own praise,'[31] and someone else, 'The man who sings his own praises always gets the wrong pitch.'[32] Again, 'job one' for each of us is to sing His praises instead of our own."

"This sounds a lot like Jesus' warning to His disciples in Matthew 6:1-17," said Nina.

"You are so right, sister," replied Didaskolos with great delight. "You certainly exhibit before us the portrait of Knowledge we observed in the Gallery of Virtue. Your diligent research in our Father's Word stimulates us to do the same. Let's take a brief survey of that passage; but be prepared: Your true motives for serving Jesus will be exposed," said Didaskolos with a wry smile.

"Now then, just before we pan for the gold nuggets of spiritual truth in Matthew 6, may I remind you all that only a few moments prior Jesus had exhorted the Twelve, 'Let your light shine before men in such a way that they may see your good works, and glorify your Father who is in heaven' (Matt. 5:16).

"Jesus is saying that our good works, concrete examples of which are detailed in the Sermon, should be done in such a way that the world looking on will get a good opinion of Him.[33] In Jesus' day, the tiny wicker oil lamps gave little light in the average home, which had few windows. Thus, they would be most efficient when set on a lampstand. It follows that placing something large over them would likely extinguish the light altogether.[34]

"So, to let our light shine, we who believe must, for example, resolve to be peacemakers in a tense world; view persecution as a joyful privilege; pray for our persecutors; let the enemies of God who sue us have more than they ask for; go two miles when they ask us to go one; and graciously lend to those in need (Matt. 5:9-12, 40-42, 44). Such good works will point them to our gracious and forgiving Father who 'causes His sun to rise on the evil and the good, and sends rain on the righteous and the unrighteous' (Matt. 5:45). And as they see Him in His true light, they will glorify Him. But, as we discharge these good works, we must take regular inventory of our motives, for it's possible to do them out of pride, as religious showboats, and not with the intent of showing God off to those looking on. Thus, Jesus says what He says in what follows: Matthew 6:1-17. Let's take a quick break, then pan for more gold."

From the fireside to the kitchen, a light buzz of conversation filled the house. Holding a cup of Apple Orchard tea and peering out the large picture window in the living room, I overheard Alfred's baritone voice telling Janet that though he knew drinking wine was okay as long as it did not lead to intoxication, he had recently been insensitive by drinking in front of a new convert, named John, who had struggled for years with alcoholism.

"John seemed uneasy when I offered him a wine cooler at my apartment yesterday," said Alfred. "He told me later that he had burned every bridge to his old lifestyle, including any ingestion of alcohol, lest he once again fall headlong into addiction. I realize now that when John's around I must give up my personal freedom before Christ to drink—for sure I would be a stumbling block to him. But beyond that, I am wondering if I ought to give up drinking wine altogether since it may appear inconsistent with Christianity to my unbelieving family. What do you think, Janet?"

"Before my husband died," replied Janet, "we would often have a glass of wine for special occasions like anniversaries, but would never drink when others were around for the very reasons you just gave. But also, just as Didaskolos' pointed out tonight, such consideration for others 'shows off' the sensitivity of our most kind God and by this glorifies His character before others. Certainly God would honor your motive for denying personal freedom in that area. Whether you ought to abstain entirely is between you and Him; you ought to begin praying about it."

With refills of tea, coffee, juice and some with second helpings of homemade molasses cookies and blueberry muffins (including me on the cookies), we all resumed our places around the fireplace which had a fresh supply of chunks of ponderosa pine. As the fire popped in the background, Didaskolos once again served us in breaking open the Bread of Life.

"Please turn in your Bibles, if you have not already done so, to Matthew, chapter 6. And by way of reminder, Jesus is now going to tell us how to execute our good works in such a way that will bring glory to God, and not ourselves. Would someone please read verses 1-4?"

"I'll read," said Jim: "Beware of practicing your righteousness before men to be noticed by them; otherwise you have no reward with your Father who is in heaven. So when you give to the poor, do not sound a trumpet before you, as the hypocrites do in the synagogues and in the streets, so that they may be honored by men.[35] Truly I say to you, they have their reward in full. But when you give to the poor, do not let your left hand know what your right hand is doing, so that your giving will be in secret; and your Father who sees what is done in secret will reward you."

"Now, a few observations here," said Didaskolos. "First, you should know that in verses 1-18, Jesus discusses three practices of the Pharisees central to their religious lifestyle: Giving, praying and fasting.[36] Second, the general warning, found in verse one, applies to all three of these duties. We might paraphrase it like this, 'Stop being a religious showoff.' Such motivation signifies the kind of intent behind religious duties that will result in no reward from the Father in heaven.

"Third, it is imperative to understand this term translated 'reward.' It is the Greek word, *misthos* and basically means, 'payment, or wages.' When used as an adjective it means hired servant. In Romans 6:23, God tells us that 'the *wages* [emphasis mine] of sin is death, but the free gift of God is eternal life through Jesus Christ our Lord.'

"Judas, we're told, purchased a field with the reward he received for his wicked betrayal of Jesus—a *misthos* of thirty pieces of silver. And there he committed suicide out of regret for his dastardly deed. Here in Matthew 6, and in many other places in the New Testament, *misthos* speaks of the reward God graciously elects to give His children who practice righteousness for His honor, not their own. Not that God owes them this honor (cf. Luke 17:10), but out of His grace He chooses to justly reward them.[37]

"Following His general exhortation in verse one to avoid religious showboating, in verse 2, the Master Teacher gives specific illustrations of what He means."

"Isn't this an example of deductive teaching style?" asked Jim.

"Yes, it is," affirmed Didaskolos. "More often than not, Jesus gives the illustration first, and then extracts a general principle; this is what we call inductive teaching style.[38] But in this case we find the general principle followed by specific examples."

"Now then, did you see how verse 2 begins, with the comparative conjunction, 'so'? This shows us that Jesus is drawing an application from the imperative in verse 1:

> *So* [emphasis mine] when you give to the poor, do not sound a trumpet before you, as the hypocrites do in the synagogues and in the streets, so that they may be honored by men. Truly I say to you, they have their reward in full.

"Here Jesus explains how not to give, that is, don't advertise your generosity to needy others for the purpose of enhancing your own reputation. The motive for giving, in the minds of these hypocrites, was 'that they may be honored by men.'"[39]

"I have three questions," said Allen. "First, did these people really blow a trumpet when they made their donation? Second, what does Jesus mean when he says, 'They have their reward in full?' Third, what does the command, 'Do not let your left hand know what your right hand is doing' mean?"

"Excellent questions," replied Didaskolos. "Since blasting a trumpet was not part of giving alms, perhaps a play on words is in view since charity boxes were sometimes shaped like trumpets.[40] Similar to Jesus' pedagogy elsewhere, this is most likely symbolic language, here of the hyper-arrogance of these folk who, in pretending to give to the poor, really intended to receive honor for themselves. Their giving was simply an occasion to advertise their piety, a motive which Jesus soundly condemns.

"As for the meaning of 'they have their reward in full,' this is the language of complete repayment in ancient business receipts.[41] Jesus is saying that one cannot seek both the honor of men and God at the same time. Giving to impress others totally exhausts one's opportunity for future reward from the Father; in terms of remuneration for 'work done,' he is paid in full.

"Conversely, he who embraced the Jewish tradition of entering the secret chambers in the temple to deposit his gifts so the poor could receive them in secret would be rewarded by the omniscient Father who always sees[42] what we do 'in secret.'[43] Such non-showy giving, done behind the public scene, is what Jesus means by not letting your 'left hand know what your right hand is doing.' That is, since one hand always knows what the other hand does and the two act in unison in work and play, Jesus' curious statement symbolizes a state of ignorance between the left hand and the right hand. So what does this mean practically?

"Essentially, the giver not only keeps his voluntary contribution a secret to others, but to himself as well in the sense that he readily forgets what he gave, refusing to dwell on his act of charity, refraining from patting himself on the back. Both others and himself are 'ignorant' of the whole matter. Doing his good works in this way displays his true righteousness before God and gains a reward from God. After all, the motive behind such giving is to bring glory to God, not the giver. This manner of giving is then, an application of what Jesus said in Matthew 5:16:

> Let your light shine before men *in such a way* [emphasis mine] that they may see your good works, and glorify your Father who is in heaven.

"Too often," continued Didaskolos, "those who contribute to various Christian endeavors yield to the offer that their names be placed on a plaque or in published literature of some kind to commemorate their act of charity. Or what about hoping people around us will notice when we place our gift into the offering plate as it floats down the row? If any act of charity seeks the applause of men on earth, we forfeit any eternal reward for our deed. Of course, this does not mean that giving in public is categorically wrong—the issue is our motivation.[44] But not only must we monitor our motives when we give, but when we pray as well."

"In Matthew 6:2-4," Didaskolos continued, "Jesus reveals the don'ts and do's of giving, and now in verses 5-15, the don'ts and do's of prayer. Looking at verses 5 and 6, can you see structural similarities with verses 2-4?"

After a minute or so, Nina spoke up. "In both cases Jesus begins with a prohibition not to imitate the religious hypocrites who give and pray to gain notoriety with men. This is followed by Jesus' emphatic and authoritative phrase, 'Truly I say to you,' which introduces the negation of any future reward for such ostentatious behavior."

"Good observations, Nina," affirmed Didaskolos. "Any other parallels here?"

"Yes, there's the positive instruction," said Janet, "on how to pray in such a way that gains reward from our heavenly Father, and once again His omniscience, grace and justice are cited as the basis for reward: 'your Father who sees in secret will reward you.'"[45]

"Thank you, Janet, for those excellent insights," said Didaskolos. "Please do not misunderstand Jesus here, He is not condemning public prayer but rather motives that wish to impress those who hear us pray. In His day, pious Jews had set times for private devotions; according to Josephus, the famous Jewish historian, prayers were offered in the temple 'twice a day, in the early morning and at the ninth hour.'[46] There was also a sunset service. If one could not, however, make it to the temple, then the synagogue or standing on the street corner would have to do. By the way, standing was a common posture for prayer.

"Now then, what is Jesus point in all this? He is simply issuing a sentence upon those who went out of their way to have their private devotions within view of others who could admire their piety. In fact, this is exactly the point of Jesus' parable in Luke 18:9-14 where the proud Pharisee, instead of securing some out of the way street corner, stands in full view of the crowd, hoping to be honored by men for his spiritual disposition. The publican, by contrast, 'standing some distance away,' pleaded with God to be merciful to him as a sinner. And it's the publican who is commended by Jesus in verse 14:

> I tell you, this man went to his house justified rather than the other; for everyone who exalts himself will be humbled, but[47] he who humbles himself will be exalted.

"Back to Matthew 6, notice what verses 7 and 8 add to this matter of prayer:

> And when you pray, do not use meaningless repetition as the Gentiles do, for they suppose that they will be heard for their many words. So do not be like them; for your Father knows what you need before you ask Him.[48]

"You should know that, in Jesus' day, Jewish scholars debated the use of fixed prayers, and these were okay, as long as one's motive was sincere. By contrast, Greek prayers were not so rigid, piling up 'as many titles of the deity addressed as possible, hoping to secure his or her attention.'[49] The priests of Baal called on their god from morning till noon (1 Kings 18:25-29) and the pagans in Ephesus thought they could win their idol's favor by lengthy petition. For two hours they shouted, 'Great is Artemis (Diana) of the Ephesians!' (Acts 19:21ff).

"For some, prayer is often viewed as a magic formula; and the more words, the better the chance of getting an answer. Jesus condemned those who 'for appearance's sake offer long prayers' (Mark 12:40)—not that He was against long prayers since Scripture records extended prayers from godly people (e.g., 2 Chron. 6:14-42; Neh. 9; Ps. 18; 89; 119). But who among us has not been fooled on occasion into thinking that Jesus is more pleased by an hour-long petition than a five-minute petition?"

That question provoked me to reassess my current resolve to spend at least 30 minutes a day in prayer—at least I needed to take stock of my motives. The subtle undercurrent of legalism has a way of pushing you unawares into dangerous waters.

"Some of the most profound prayers in Scripture," Didaskolos continued, "are brief and pithy. The prayers of Moses (Ex. 32:31), Solomon (1 Kings 3:6-9), Elijah (1 Kings 18:36-37), Hezekiah (1 Kings 19:14-19), Jabez (1 Chron. 4:10), Agur (Prov. 30:7-9), the publican (Luke 18:13), the dying thief (Luke 23:42), Stephen (Acts 7:60), and even the so-called 'Lord's Prayer' in Matthew 6:9-13 serve as examples. But even some have turned the Lord's Prayer into a rote formula of meaningless repetition absent the spirit of sincere worship.

"The bottom line of all this is captured well by our brother in the faith, Haddon Robinson, who writes,

> Jesus wasn't opposed to public prayer. He was against the motive that turned it into a performance.[50] That's why He admonished His followers to go to a room and close the door. In the Jewish homes of the first century the only private place where the door could be locked was the storeroom, and that's the word Jesus used (in verse 6). In a private place no one can see us, showmanship disappears, and we are more likely to talk with God.[51]

"As Jesus concludes in verse 8, we are not to mimic the hollow prayers of a religious showoff, nor the petitions of those who think that God must be informed of their need and cannot be sufficiently placated without going on and on about their situation. He tells us, 'So do not be like them; for your Father knows what you need before you ask Him.'"

"Does this mean," Allen asked, leaning forward on the light blue sofa, "that I must accept the reality that God knows everything there is to know, including all my personal needs and wants, before I can pray correctly?"

"That's a profound question, brother," replied Didaskolos, "and you couldn't have said it better, except to add that He longs for you to think of Him as your heavenly Father, not just your all-knowing Maker. And once you comprehend His omniscience and His personal care as your heavenly Father, then your petitions will be sincere, not showy; meaningful, not meaningless; reverent, not flippant; and full of trust, instead of strained cries fraught with fear, distrust and a vacillating hoping against hope that for your long-winded pleading you will be heard."

Then Nina asked, "Is the 'Lord's Prayer,' which follows in verses 9-13 meant to be corrective, then, in light of the misguided motives for prayer in verses 1-8?"

"Yes, that's a helpful way of expressing the force of the inferential term, 'then,' in verse 9: 'Pray, *then*, [emphasis mine] in this way,' says Jesus—not that we are required to use the exact words of His prayer, but the manner of our praying should entail certain elements. In essence, our prayers should display, above all else, a motivation to adore God. The words, 'Hallowed be thy Name,' in verse 9, reflect the very reason for our existence, namely, to bring glory to God's Person which is what 'His Name' stands for. In concert with this, we ask that His promised earthly kingdom 'may come' so that His will may be done on earth as it is now in heaven. Of course, presently, God's children can 'hallow,' that is, 'show to be holy,' their heavenly Father's name by living out His will in their lives. The opposite is true when they exercise their own selfish will—they profane His Name among unbelievers, bringing it into disrepute (cf. Jer. 34:15-16; Rom. 2:17-24).

"But in addition to adoration for God's Person and petition for

God's covenantal Program, our omniscient Lord knows we have daily, personal needs for food, forgiveness, and, for protection from the Evil one, Satan himself. So, in verses 11-13, He invites us to petition Him in a spirit of child-like dependency.

"And did you notice that the only part of this model prayer that's stressed is our need to forgive others who offend us? As verses 14-15 state: 'For if[52] you forgive others for their transgressions, your heavenly Father will also forgive you. But[53] if you do not forgive others, then your Father will not forgive your transgressions.'"

"This seems to imply that a Christian can lose his salvation by not forgiving the one who wrongs him, or that forgiveness from God is earned by forgiveness of others," said Janet with a puzzled look.

"It does seem that way," answered Didaskolos, "but Jesus is not talking about the forgiveness that leads to salvation, but the kind that maintains fellowship in God's family, both with God Himself by obeying His command to forgive and with those who require your forgiveness. In other words, an unforgiving spirit blocks your intimacy with God and the Christian brother or sister in the situation. In reality, these verses further explain what Jesus said in verse 12,

> And forgive us our debts, as we also have forgiven our debtors.

"Notice that the request for forgiveness is grounded in[54] our previous forgiveness[55] of others as the comparative adverb 'as' indicates. Since salvation is clearly depicted as an unearned gift elsewhere in Scripture (e.g., Rom. 6:23; Eph. 2:8-9), this verse has to do with forgiveness for one already in God's family even as the words 'Our Father' reveal. A non-Christian cannot call God his Father.

"To sum up verses 5-15, Jesus is telling us that prayer which aims to show God off—all the wonders of His Person and kingdom program—and express faith-driven dependency on the heavenly Father to meet personal needs, is the kind of prayer that merits reward. Such prayer is void of the spiritual pride of the hypocrites and the meaningless repetition of the pagans."

This fresh look at prayer and the motives behind it prodded me to evaluate both my own private prayers and my prayers offered in public. Too often, God the Holy Spirit has convicted me of praying to impress others, especially new believers—putting on display how well I have learned to pray. On occasion a few have even said, "Wow, I wish I could pray like that!" Anyone watching could have noticed my head enlarge, my hat size increase. And when around "giants of the faith" I sometimes yield to the proud ambition of offering something eloquent, usually inserting lots of Scripture, to persuade them of how spiritual I am. How nauseating that must be to the nostrils of God, anything but a sweet-smelling sacrifice rising to His throne.

What's more, I could sure celebrate God more than I do; most of my prayers are requests for personal needs. I decided to make it a point to spend at least 15 minutes a day just praising Him for who He is, perhaps taking some praise Psalms, such as Psalm 100, and making them my own prayer to God.

"Please, Lord, show me Your glory, then make my passion in life to declare Your glory to the nations."

"In Matthew 6:16-18, the same basic literary format continues," said Didaskolos. "Jesus says,

> Whenever you fast, do not put on a gloomy face[56] as the hypocrites do, for they neglect their appearance so that they will be noticed by

> men[57] when they are fasting. Truly I say to you, they have their reward in full. But you, when you fast, anoint your head and wash your face so that your fasting will not be noticed by men, but by your Father who is in secret; and your Father who sees what is done in secret will reward you.

"Again, some brief observations are in order: First, the word 'whenever' indicates Jesus' assumption that His followers will engage in the spiritual discipline of fasting, just as He assumed that they would give and pray. Second, Jesus begins with what not to do when you fast, pulling back the curtain on those who fast to impress others with their piety. Such hypocrites would 'neglect their appearance' to be noticed by men.[58] In fact, the phrase 'neglect their appearance' literally means 'they disfigure their faces.' But what is the cultural background here? As one writer states, 'Jewish fasting required abstinence not only from food but also from other pleasures, which would include the usual practice of anointing one's head with oil to prevent dry skin; avoiding all these practices made fasting obvious.'[59]

"As another author says, 'Pharisees wanted everyone to know they were fasting, so they did not wash or trim their hair and sometimes put ashes on their heads.'[60] These hypocrites will gain the reward of applause from men: perhaps a compliment here or there, a chief seat in the synagogue, or a building named after them, but no lasting reward from the omniscient God who not only sees what we do but why we do it.

"After exposing such evil motives, Jesus tells us how to fast without anyone knowing you are fasting: 'But you, when you fast, anoint your head and wash your face,'[61] He says. Such humble motives will be honored by our Father who 'sees what is done in secret.'[62] He is far more interested in what we are on the inside than what we do on the outside. As Isaiah 58:3-12 shows, God never settled for outward fasting only."

I would make it a point to read that passage in Isaiah when I got home.

"So then," continued Didaskolos, "you can see from these few passages that doing what we do in God's service must be done with a desire to show Him off instead of making a name for ourselves. Otherwise, we have no future reward.

"In his book, *Comeback*, former Major League pitcher, Dave Dravecky, rehearses his varied motivation as an athlete. He states,

> Growing up, I had always been at the center of attention. That was exactly how I had wanted it. My performance had been for me, and no one else. I had to be the star. That kind of motivation can keep you going strong, as long as you succeed. But it's not so good for dealing with failure or with forces beyond your control. Seeing Jesus Christ as your audience shifted the pressure off yourself. You did your best to bring glory to God, not yourself. If you lost, the loss would hurt, but it wouldn't change anything fundamental. God would still be there."[63]

Stirred by Dravecky's testimony, Jim then said, "I confess, there have been too many times when I wanted to be the star of the show in the morning service, hoping people would say, 'Wow, what a sermon!' If I understand Scripture correctly, those particular acts of preaching will get incinerated at the judgment seat of Christ, rewards forfeited."

"Thank you so much for your transparency, Jim," said Didaskolos. "We can all relate to clamoring for the spotlight. And when others praise us for something, it is a major test of character to see how we handle the praise. As Proverbs 27:21 reveals,

> The crucible is for silver, and the furnace for gold, and a man is tested by the praise accorded him.[64]

"When someone commends your sermon, some kind act, your fine leadership, or something else you've done or said, I advise you to return a courteous 'Thank you for your encouragement,' then quickly and privately pass the compliment heavenward to Him who ultimately deserves the credit."

"Do you enjoy sports?" Didaskolos continued. "Then determine to play in a way that honors God—be wholehearted, unselfish, and honest. Do you play a musical instrument? In addition to your own enjoyment, play for the enjoyment and spiritual edification of others; and play skillfully as Psalm 47:7 exhorts; this will show the excellence with which God does things. When He finished creating the world in six, literal, twenty-four hour days, He saw everything He had made and it was 'very good' (Gen. 1:31).

"And here's some other food for thought," said Didaskolos. "When you pray, do you ever hope others will be impressed by how well you've learned to pray? Monitor your motives before you pray in public. And, have you ever felt hurt when, after doing something wonderful for your church, no one recognized you for it? Maybe you wanted to be the star, you know, get your name 'in the lights.' Even as you do your job, do you seek to impress your colleagues or boss, or do you do your work heartily 'as for the Lord,' as Colossians 3:23 instructs?[65] After all, locking your sights on the Lord as your Employer will purge your motives from self-glorification."

At this point, Didaskolos read a prayer by Ruth Harms Calkin, called *I Wonder*:

> You know, Lord, how I serve You with great emotional fervor in the limelight. You know how eagerly I speak for You at a women's club. You know how I effervesce when I promote a fellowship group. You know my genuine enthusiasm at a Bible Study. But how would I react, I wonder, if you pointed me to a basin of water and asked me

> to wash the calloused feet of a bent and wrinkled old woman day after day, month after month, in a room where nobody saw and nobody knew.[66]

"As someone has put it, 'To reflect God's light, don't seek the limelight.'[67] When all is said in this matter of showing God off instead of ourselves, perhaps the prayer of the psalmist sums up what should be the continual prayer of our hearts, "Not to us, O Lord not to us, but to Your name be the glory, because of your love and faithfulness" (Ps. 115:1).

Didaskolos concluded this life-changing evening with the following recap:

"When you stand before Jesus, He will be happy to reward you for serving Him with the right motives, motives produced by the Spirit of God as you yield to Him. First, there is the motivation that says, 'I serve God because I am in love with God, I feel deeply affectionate toward Him and my highest ambition is to bring a smile upon His dear face.' Second, there's the motivation that says, 'May others glorify God as they see His character in me; may others see my good works and extol my Father in heaven; my mission in life is to declare His glorious Person to the nations.'

"Is this your true confession? If so, you can anticipate His praise; you can look forward to a hero's welcome."

As we sat there staring into the fire, now reduced to a few gentle flames rising from a bed of hot, orange coals, more than one of us, including myself, felt sorely convicted about our concern that others be impressed with our spirituality. This evening would be used of God as a turning point in my motivation for Christian living.

"Nina," said Didaskolos, "would you mind closing our time in a word of prayer?"

"I'd be honored to," she replied. "Our most gracious heavenly Father, we are unspeakably grateful for meeting with us tonight and for showing us how important our motives are in Your eyes. Help each of us to do what we do because we love You and want nothing more than to bring a smile upon Your dear face. Help us, too, dear Father, to become passionate about showing You off to others around us. I, for one, yield too often to the temptation to show off my own piety. Deliver me. Deliver my brothers and sisters, here. With the psalmist we pray, 'Not to us, O Lord, not to us, but to Your name be the glory, because of Your lovingkindness and Your truth.' I pray in the name of our precious Savior, Jesus Christ, Amen."

As we returned our dishes to the kitchen, Alfred and Janet volunteered to stay and help Didaskolos clean up. He gladly welcomed their servant spirit, the same portrait of *agape* love he had taught us in The Gallery of Virtue and had modeled by his own hospitality.

The rest of us stepped out into the gentle breeze of the night, exchanged friendly good-byes and drove home thinking about that day when we would each stand before Jesus. What could be better than having a hero's welcome on that fine day? And next week it would be even more clear how this could be possible.

I slept well that night.

Endnotes for Chapter 4

[1] Haddon Robinson, *The Christian Salt and Light Company* (Grand Rapids, MI:

Discovery House Publishers, 1988), 93.

[2] The Greek construction of the negative particle *me* present imperative *krinete* indicates that such inappropriate judgment was going on and needed to stop.

[3] The Greek term is *boulas*, used twelve times in the NT, often referring to God's purposes and intentions (Acts 2:23), but here of man's intentions. The locus of these intentions is said to be in the heart (*kardia*), emphasis mine.

[4] The phrase is *ho anakrinon; anakrino* means "to question, to examine, to interrogate, used of a judicial examination before the final verdict is given." Johannes Weiss, *Der erste Krinther Brief* (Gottingen: Vandenhoeck & Ruprecht, 1910), quoted in Fritz Rienecker, *A Linguistic Key to the Greek New Testament*, ed. by Cleon L. Rogers, Jr. (Grand Rapids: Zondervan, 1980), 396. The tense of the articular substantival participle is present, and in conjunction with the present tense verb, *estin*; the idea is the continual examination of each of the Master-Teacher's pupils. Each day is under the watchful eye of His omniscient scrutiny, His grade book always in hand.

[5] The term is *hoste*, a common inferential conjunction which here introduces an independent clause.

[6] The construction here is a present imperative preceded by the negative *me*, which signifies action going on that needed to cease. The final verdict on someone else's ministry is not for us to make; only the all-knowing God has that right.

[7] The word "comes" translates *elthe*, most likely a dramatic aorist.

[8] First, the adverbial adjective of time, "then" is *tote*. Second, one reason for the reality that judgment must await Jesus' return is what we find, in principle, in Hebrews 11:4 in reference to Enoch, that "though he is dead, he still speaks." Of course, in His omniscience, Jesus would not only know the on-going impact of a believer up to the time of the *bema* seat but their future impact as well throughout the Tribulation period and the millennial age. For instance, the influence of a Christian book written by a believer prior to the Rapture that continues to be read through these time periods would be included in Jesus' final evaluation at the *bema* seat.

[9] Translates *ho epainos*, functioning here in the nominative case as the subject of the independent clause. *Epainos*, which means "praise, approval, recognition" can be used of praise coming to God (Eph. 1:6), of men praising men for good character (Rom. 13:3; 2 Cor. 8:18; 1 Pet. 2:14), of praiseworthy thoughts (Phil. 4:8) or, as here, of praise coming from God to men (cf. also Rom. 2:29; 1 Peter 1:7). Bauer, Arndt and Gingrich, 281. The word "from" renders the preposition of source, *apo*, in this verse: "...each man's praise shall come to him from God."

[10] The term is *pistos* and means "faithful, dependable." Rienecker, 396. "Because stewards [see *oikonomois* in same verse] were trusted to handle their masters' finances, purchase slaves and goods, and make wise investments, it was most important that they be 'trustworthy' or 'faithful.'" Craig S. Keener, *The IVP Bible Background Commentary: New Testament* (Downers Grove: IVP, 1983), 459.

---

[11] Judaism repeatedly emphasized love for God and others; in fact, this "great commandment" (cf. Matt. 22:36) was so paramount in Jewish society that it was regularly recited. "In the Greek language, adjectives like 'great' had come to be used sometimes for superlatives like 'greatest.'" Keener, 107. It should be noted as well that "heart, soul, mind and strength" compose the various aspects of one's entire self–everything about me should be consumed with a passionate love for God. The concept of "mind" was implicit in the Hebrew understanding of the term "heart." Keener, 107.

[12] Francis A. Schaeffer, *A Christian View of the Church*, vol. 4, The *Complete Works of Francis A. Schaeffer: A Christian Worldview*, 2nd ed. (Wheaton, IL: Crossway Books, 1994), 41-42.

[13] Verses 41-42 present a textual problem; of the choices, according to Liefeld, the most plausible are: "(1) 'few things are needed,' (2) 'one thing is needed,' (3) 'few things are needed–or only one;'" TR concurs with (2) as does NIV for its text: RV, RSV, NASB and NEB follow suit; UBS gives the same reading a "C" rating. Walter L. Liefeld, "Luke," in *The Expositor's Bible Commentary*, ed. by Frank E. Gaebelein (Grand Rapids: Zondervan Publishing House, 1984), 8:945. Marshall supports (1) because "it is indirectly attested in the good MSS which have the conflate reading" (this is the chosen variant in the NIV footnote). Contextually, Marshall points out, as well, that if "few" equals "few dishes of food" then Jesus' switch from "few" to "one" is comprehensible. I. Howard Marshall, *The Gospel of Luke: A Commentary on the Greek Text*, The New International Greek Testament Commentary (Grand Rapids: Eerdmans, 1979), 453-54. Scribes were more apt to conclude that Jesus was not teaching Martha about hospitality but about spirituality, thus the contrast between "few dishes of food" and "one" necessary spiritual goal of listening to Him. Such was the goal Mary had chosen which would not be taken from her. It should be noted, too, that Jesus' words to Martha, though a rebuke in nature, were given in sympathy, per the use of the double vocative, "Martha, Martha." As Walter Liefeld remarks concerning the difficulty of the textual problem here, "In any case the basic meaning is clear–Martha's and Mary's priorities are contrasted." Liefeld, 945.

[14] Paul Van Gorder, "The Gift or The Giver," *Our Daily Bread*, June 14, 1990.

[15] Ibid.

[16] Ibid.

[17] Richard DeHaan, "Week 50: Wednesday," *Our Daily Times with God: Favorite Selections from Our Daily Bread* (Grand Rapids, MI: Discovery House Publishers, 1988), 408.

[18] Ibid.

[19] Ibid.

[20] Walter B. Knight, "3222, We Too Love Him," in *Encyclopedia of 7700 Illustrations: Signs of the Times*, [ed.] by Paul Lee Tan (Rockville, MD: Assurance

Publishers, 1979), 763.

[21] Craig Brian Larson, ed., *Illustrations for Preaching and Teaching: From Leadership Journal* (Grand Rapids, MI: Baker Books, 1993), 187.

[22] Cf. the author's article: Ron Barnes, "Why Your Motives Count Forever," *Kindred Spirit* 19, no.4 (Winter 1995): 10-11. A quarterly publication by Dallas Theological Seminary.

[23] Dave Branon, *Our Daily Bread*, July 24, 1995.

[24] Ibid.

[25] "So" renders the inferential conjunction *oun*; the three-fold repetition of *eite*, a combination of the conditional particle *ei* and *te*. Bauer, Arndt and Gingrich suggests the translation "if–if, whether–or," reveals a parallel structure. Bauer, Arndt and Gingrich, 219. A wooden expression would be, "Whether, then, you eat (*esthiete*), whether you drink (*pinete*), whether whatever (*ti*, indefinite pronoun) you do (*poiete*), all things (*panta*), with a view to (*eis*, accusative, purpose nuance; cf. Dana and Mantey, 104, for this use of *eis* apart from the normal *eis* + *to* – + infinitive) the glory that belongs to God (*doxan theou*, subjective genitive), do as a way of life (*poiete*, pres. active imperative, suggesting habitual action in concert with the three present indicative verbs above)."

[26] Keener, 474.

[27] Archibald Thomas Robertson, *Word Pictures in the New Testament: The Epistles of Paul* (Nashville: Broadman, 1933), 4:158.

[28] Bauer, Arndt and Gingrich classify the use of *doxa* here in 1 Corinthians 10:31 under "fame, renown, honor." Bauer, Arndt and Gingrich, 203. In general *doxa* signifies the idea of "brightness, splendor, radiance." Bauer, Arndt and Gingrich, 202. It is used of the radiance of (1) literal light (Acts 22:11), (2) the heavenly bodies in the sky (1 Cor. 15:40f), the angels (Luke 2:9), especially of God Himself (Ex. 24:17; 40:34), and subsequently "of those who appear before [Him] Moses, 2 Cor. 3:7ff., and Christians in the next life...Col. 3:4." Bauer, Arndt and Gingrich, 202. Beyond this literal meaning, *doxa*, in figure, can include the might and "majesty...of God" (e.g., "Christ was raised fr. the dead" through the glory of the Father, Rom. 6:4). Bauer, Arndt and Gingrich, 202. There is also the moral nuance of *doxa* seen in Romans 3:23 where all men have missed the mark of attaining God's holy perfection: They "fall short of the glory of God." Also in the figurative vein, *doxa* can refer to the future blissful state of true believers in heaven, a reality that motivates them to endure, by contrast, any suffering for the gospel this side of heaven (Rom. 8:17-18). Further, man retains his own glory and dignity, in spite of the Fall, since he still possesses, in some measure, the image of God (1 Cor. 11:7). Finally, *doxa* can signify "anything that catches the eye;" such as "fine clothing (Sir 6:31...), of a king..." in his royal disposition (Matt. 6:29), or man in the various expressions of human splendor (1 Pet. 1:24). Bauer, Arndt and Gingrich, 203.

[29] Adapted from Charles R. Swindoll, *The Grace Awakening* (Waco: Word, 1982), 159.

[30] Ibid., 160-1.

[31] E. C. Mckenzie, "524 Epigram," in Tan, 211.

[32] "524 Epigram," in Tan, 211.

[33] In Vine's definition of *doxa*, he points out that the word comes from *dokeo*, "to seem" and therefore primarily signifies the idea of an opinion, an estimate. In this case, the believer's good works, if done absent an ostentatious spirit, leave people with a good opinion of who God is. Vine, 267.

[34] Keener, 57.

[35] *Beware*–Beware translates *prosechete*, which means "to give heed to, to watch out for," but according to Robertson, "The Greek idiom includes 'mind' (noun) which is often expressed in ancient Greek and once in the Septuagint (Job 7:17). In the NT the substantive nous is understood. It means to 'hold the mind on a matter,' take pains, take heed." Archibald Thomas Robertson, *Word Pictures in the New Testament: Gospel According to Matthew; The Gospel According to Mark* (Nashville: Broadman, 1933), 1:50. The present tense calls for a constant guard against showing off your spirituality.

of practicing your righteousness–Dikaiosunen is the correct reading here; *eleemosynen* (alms) is likely a gloss on this term, since in the LXX "righteousness," in Hebrew, was often translated "alms." As Carson concludes, "If 'alms' were in fact original, then v. 1 should be read with vv. 2-4, not as the introduction to vv. 2-18; and this would break the carefully wrought structure...Moreover the external evidence strongly supports *dikaiosynen*." D. A. Carson, "Matthew," in *The Expositor's Bible Commentary*, ed. by Frank E. Gaebelein (Grand Rapids: Zondervan Publishing House, 1984), 8:163. Regarding the meaning of *dikaiosynen*, used with *poiein* (present infinitive functioning as a complement to the imperative beware), it refers to the practice of piety which conforms to God's moral will.

before men to be noticed–The phrase to be noticed renders the Greek term *theaomai*, from which we derive the English word "theater." *Theaomai* is an aorist passive articular infinitive of purpose as the object of the preposition *pros*, revealing the improper motives for pious living; "by them" is dative of agency: the seeing is accomplished by those looking on, as the passive indicates.

by them; otherwise you have no reward with your Father–"Literally, 'beside your Father,' standing by His side, as He looks at it." Robertson, 1:50. The dative prepositional phrase begins with *para*, here a locative use; "your Father" is a subjective genitive showing the personal relationship the believer possesses with God.

who is in heaven. So when–So translates *oun*, an inferential conjunction introducing instruction based on the warning given in verse 1; "when" renders *hotan*, an adverb of time, introducing a temporal clause and showing that Jesus assumed (when not if) each (the number in *poies* is singular: "when each of you give to the needy") of His disciples would contribute alms to the poor.

you give–The term give translates *eleemosynen*, a "kind deed, alms, charitable giving (BAG). Nothing is more marked in rabbinic ethics than the stress laid upon charity in every sense of the word (Montefiore and Loewe, A *Rabbinic Anthology*, 412)." Bauer, Arndt and Gingrich, 249; and G. C. Montefiore and H. Loewe, A *Rabbinic Anthology* (New York: Schocken Books, 1974), 412, quoted in Rienecker, 17. Rienecker recommends G. C. Montefiore and H. Loewe, A *Rabbinic Anthology* (New York: Schocken Books, 1974), 412-39; and George Foot Moore, *Judaism in the First Centuries of the Christian Era: The Age of Tannaim* (Peabody, MA: Hendrickson, 1997), 2:162-179, for further details on "rabbinic views of charity." Rienecker, 17.

to the poor, do not sound a trumpet–The words do not sound a trumpet form a prohibitionary subjunctive with the presence of the negative *me*, or it could be an aorist imperative. If the latter, the *me* would indicate the prohibition of an action that had not yet begun.

before you, as the hypocrites–Hypokritai is "an old word for actor, interpreter, one who personates another...to wear a mask. This is the hardest word that Jesus has for any class of people and He employs it for these pious pretenders who pose as perfect." Robertson, 1:50.

do in the synagogues and in the streets, so that they may be honored–The purpose clause here is introduced by *hopos* + the subjunctive; how ironic that *doxa* (here translated "honored") is what these hypocrites are after, the very thing that they forfeit since God alone is ultimately worthy of it.

[36] Keener observes, "Judaism stressed that one should not perform deeds for the sake of reward but nonetheless promised reward, as Jesus does here...at the day of judgment...Prayer, fasting and gifts to the poor were basic components of Jewish piety (Tobit 12:8), and many rabbis listed qualities (e.g., virtues on which the world was founded) in sets of three." Keener, 61.

[37] For a detailed look at *misthos*, see Appendix A.

[38] As Ralph and Gregg Lewis assert, this is the most common method of Jesus' pedagogy. Ralph L. Lewis and Gregg Lewis, *Learning to Preach Like Jesus* (Westchester, IL: Crossway Books, 1989); see especially chapter 3.

[39] The words by men translate *hupo ton anthropon*, a prepositional phrase of agency: These hypocrites hope to receive glory via others who observe them. This is the most common use of *hupo* according to Dana and Mantey, 112.

[40] Keener, 61.

[41] Ibid.

[42] The word "sees" is *ho blepon*, an articular present participle functioning here as a substantive, modifying *ho pater sou*.

[43] The phrase is dative, locative of sphere; the TR added *en toi phaneroi* (openly), but this is a gloss intended to complete the antithetic parallel structure, but Jesus does not guarantee any public notoriety for piety. Carson, "Matthew," in *Expositor's*, 8:164, and Robertson, 1:51.

[44] A balanced perspective is offered by Wiersbe who asks, "Does this mean that it is wrong to give openly? Must all giving be anonymous? Not necessarily, for everyone in the early church knew that Barnabas had given the income from the sale of his land (Acts 4:34-37). When the church members laid their money at the apostle's feet, it was not done in secret. The difference, of course, was in the motive and manner in which it was done. A contrast is Ananias and Sapphira (Acts 5:1-11), who tried to use their gift to make people think they were more spiritual than they really were." Warren Wiersbe, *The Bible Exposition Commentary* (Wheaton: Victor Books, 1989), 1:25.

[45] The verb is future, *apodosei* (same form as v. 4) and though it probably refers to the *bema* seat of Christ (2 Cor. 5:10), it could include some moment in the future in the believer's earthly existence. Humility comes before honor whether here and now or in the hereafter.

[46] William Hendricksen, *Matthew*, New Testament Commentary (Grand Rapids: Baker, 1973), 322.

[47] A mild adversative denoted by *de* creating a structure of contrast and comparison in Jesus' pedagogy.

[48] *And when you pray*–The term pray is *proseuchomenoi* (circumstantial participle of time: contemporaneous), from *proseuchomai*, a combination of the preposition *pros* (to) and *euchomai* (to wish, pray, vow). The term denotes the act of praying and the preposition *pros* implies praying to God whether for the obtaining of good or the averting of evil (Matt. 6:9; 24:40; 26:36, 39, 44; Luke 1:10). The term comprehends both thanksgiving and request, though the Greek word for worship is *proskuneo*; as well, *proseuchomai* is in contrast with *deesis* which means "supplication" to anyone, not only God, for specific benefits. Zodhiates, 1753.

do not use meaningless repetition–The construction of the negative *me* + the aorist imperative *battalogesete* prohibits the beginning of this activity. The term *battalogesete* is used of "stammerers who repeat the words, then mere babbling or chattering, empty repetition. The etymology is uncertain, but it is probably onomatopoetic like 'babble.'" Robertson, 1:51.

as–The word as renders *hosper*, a comparative adverb to introduce the comparative clause, pointing up the contrast between how not to pray and how to pray.

the Gentiles do, for–Inferential use of *gar* to give a reason for the preceding imperative, *battalogesete*.

they suppose that they will be heard-for their many words. So–Inferential *oun*.

do not be like them–The imperatival construction here contains the negative *me* plus the aorist command *homoiothete*, signifying prohibition against beginning such inappropriate action.

for–Another inferential use of *gar* (introducing a reason for the previous imperative).

[49] Keener, 62.

[50] In the practice of the early church we find examples of public prayer (Matt. 18:19-20; Acts 1:24; 3:1; 4:24-30).

[51] Haddon W. Robinson, *The Solid Rock Construction Company: How to Build Your Life on the Right Foundation* (Grand Rapids, MI: Discovery House Publishers, 1989), 20.

[52] The if (*ean* + subjunctive *aphete*) introduces an anticipatory element, a third class conditional sentence, a probable situation in the future.

[53] A mild contrast introduced by coordinating conjunction *de*.

[54] *Hos* is here a conjunction/adverb of manner. Robertson states, "We ask forgiveness 'in proportion as' (*hos*) we also have forgiven those in debt to us, a most solemn reflection." Robertson, 54. A causal nuance is also possible: "Forgive us because we have forgiven...."

[55] In view of the past time of the indicative aorist, *aphekamen*, a perfective nuance may fit best here.

[56] The phrase gloomy face is *skuthropoi* (compound of *skuthros*, sullen, and *ops*, countenance) only here and Luke 24:17 in the NT.

[57] The dependent clause, "so that they may be noticed by men," repeats the same Greek construction seen in verse.5.

[58] *Aphanizo* is probably a clever play on words here with *phanosin*, "they neglect their appearance in order that they may appear." Rienecker 18.

[59] Keener, 62.

[60] Ryrie, *The Ryrie Study Bible*, 1522.

[61] *But*–Jesus employs the mild adversative conjunction *de* to depict the contrast between how not to fast and how to fast.

You–The singular nominative pronoun *su* is emphatic joining with the *de* to paint the contrast that should exist between the hypocrites and Jesus' disciples.

anoint your head and wash your face–"Anoint" and "wash" are both aorist imperatives in the middle voice giving a reflexive idea: "anoint your head yourself... wash your head yourself."

[62] The word secret is *kruphaio*, a *hapax legomena*; it does occur four times in the LXX.

[63] Dave Dravecky, and Tim Stafford, *Comeback* (Grand Rapids, MI: Zondervan Pub. House, 1990), 89.

[64] *The crucible*–The word crucible is the Hebrew term *masrep* (nominative masculine singular here to denote the subject), found only here and in Proverbs 17:3 in a similar statement. A container made of a substance that can resist great heat for melting or fusing metals; KJV renders it "refining pot."

is for silver–The term silver is *kesep* (predicate nominative position following the implied stative verb, equating crucible with silver); silver freshly mined and smelted as material for vessels, trumpets, idols and currency (shekels of silver); silver alloy purified by heat as impurities skimmed off (e.g., Prov. 25:4).

and–*Waw* conjunction introducing synonymous parallelism in next line.

the furnace–The word furnace translates *kur* (functioning as the second subject in this declarative compound sentence), used nine times in the OT; a smelter's furnace for the refining of metal (cf. example of this process in Ezek. 22:20).

for gold–King Solomon's ivory throne was overlaid with gold (*zahab*), 1 Kings 10:18. Here the term gold functions as a predicate nominative in parallel with silver.

and–*Waw* disjunctive with a circumstantial nuance introducing the spiritual analogy: "The crucible is for silver and the furnace for gold, while a man is tested by the praise accorded him." Most translations use "and" instead of "while" for a smoother rendering.

a man is tested–The word tested is *bochen* (from *bachan*), to examine, try, prove, often parallel to *nasah* (put to the test) and *sarap*, ("to refine" from which *masrep*, above, is a derivative). *Bachan* denotes examining something to determine essential qualities, especially integrity. The term usually has God as its subject, as here and in Proverbs 17:3 and almost always found as a spiritual metaphor. In fact, nineteen times it refers to God's scrutiny of His people (cf. Job 23:10; Zech. 13:9; see also 1 Pet. 1:7 in this same vein). In all this, the advantage of adversity for God's people stands out.

by the praise accorded him–Literally, "by the mouth of his praise"; perhaps an objective (adverbial) genitive best reflects the idea here.

[65] The force of the conjunction as (*hos*) here is well stated by O'Brien, "...the slaves are reminded of the ultimate reason for their conduct (*hos*, "as," often appears with a participle to indicate the reason or motivation for something happening; but the NT, like classical Greek, in abbreviated expressions will omit the participle when it is clear from the context as to what is meant: e.g. 2 Thess. 2:2, see Robertson, Grammar, 1140; BDF, para. 425[4])." Peter T. O'Brien, *Colossians, Philemon*, Word Biblical Commentary 44 (Waco, TX: Word Books, 1982), 228.

[66] "If Nobody Knew," *Our Daily Bread*, July 1, 1994.

[67] Ibid.

5

Adversity Has Its Advantages

Once again the air was electric as we arrived at the cozy home of our beloved teacher, Didaskolos. Every way you turned was met with the warm embrace of brotherly kindness, one of the seven portraits we had come to be so familiar with since that life-changing tour at the Gallery of Virtue.

On this night, this portrait of kindness was especially visible in Janet who brought both a peach pie—my favorite—and a cherry pie—a close second. Both were homemade, but that wasn't all that was homemade.... Alfred surprised us all with a huge batch of homemade ice cream. What a combination: Fruit pie, still warm from the oven, and homemade ice cream! As usual, in the manner of Jesus Himself, Didaskolos donned the 'servant's towel' and prepared a variety of beverages: coffee, assortments of herbal teas and two kinds of juice for those who preferred cooler drinks. His sensitivity to the interests of others, particularly his notable effort to learn the very things we each fancied, provoked us, in the spirit of Hebrews 10:24-25, to love and good works.

We each chose a refreshment and a seat around the crackling fire. Didaskolos, through all his preparations for the evening, had a way of making us feel so welcome. It reminded me of Peter's exhortation,

> Be hospitable to one another without complaint. (1 Pet. 4:9)

Waiting patiently for everyone to settle in, Didaskolos then asked Nina to open the study in prayer. "Our gracious Lord and Master," she began, "how grateful we are once again to meet together. As You have before, we ask you to visit us with Your blessing tonight. Open our spiritual eyes to behold wonderful things from Your word (cf. Ps. 119:18), but as well, empower us, Holy Spirit, not to be mere hearers of Your truth, but doers as well (cf. James 1:22-25). We praise you, our kind Father, for this wonderful food and drink and for the loving hearts that prepared it. Now, please give our teacher Your wisdom to instruct us accurately in the Scriptures. In the name of Jesus, our precious Savior, we pray. Amen."

"Prior to discovering a new truth tonight," said Didaskolos, "related to the future rewards of the believer, it would be good to review what we've learned so far. First, from the tour at the Gallery of Virtue and our exposition of 2 Peter 1:1-11, what does God require of us to insure a hero's welcome when we arrive in heaven?"

"Progressing in spiritual maturity," Jim piped up without hesitation.

"That's correct," replied an obviously pleased Didaskolos. "In proportion to the length of your Christian Life, God will reward you for allowing Him to consistently paint the image of His Dear Son, Jesus Christ, onto the empty canvas of your heart. For the saint who has known Christ for 20 years, this portrait should be quite developed, whereas someone saved only a few months to a few years may not reflect His image with the same clarity, but God will take into account the appropriate schedule for growth."

"Where does this idea of proportionate growth emerge in 2 Peter 1? I don't recall any discussion of that," asked Alfred.

"Well, you're right, brother," replied Didaskolos. "The thought is not explicitly revealed by Peter, but one example elsewhere would be Hebrews 5:11-14. Here, the writer of this epistle confronts Jewish brethren being tempted to renounce Christianity and fall back into Judaism. He says,

> Concerning him we have much to say, and it is hard to explain, since you have become dull of hearing. For though by this time you ought to be teachers, you have need again for someone to teach you the elementary principles of the oracles of God, and you have come to need milk and not solid food. For everyone who partakes only of milk is not accustomed to the word of righteousness, for he is an infant. But solid food is for the mature, who because of practice have their senses trained to discern good and evil.

"Without going into a detailed analysis of this text, suffice it to say for our purposes here, these believers were behind schedule in terms of progressing in spiritual maturity. Still on the bottle, they needed to go back to the basics, whereas they should have been on 'solids' and even teaching the word of righteousness to others. Coupled with this reality, there is the fact of varying quantities of life for each Christian. Each one's days are numbered differently (cf. Ps. 139:14-16; 2 Tim. 4:6; 2 Pet. 1:12-15). It would seem safe to say, then, that God puts together the quality of spiritual maturity He expects to see with the quantity of time each saint has lived. His granting of a hero's welcome is in response to the kind of 'character and time stewardship' each believer has kept in regards to portraying Jesus in his daily experience.

"But beyond our opportunity to receive a hero's welcome for progressing in spiritual maturity, what is another criteria for reward that emanates from such maturity?"

"Practicing our Christian life with the right motives," I answered.

"That's correct Ron," said Didaskolos. "When we stand before the *bema* seat to receive recompense for what we have done for the Lord, He will not only look at what we did, but why we did it. And since our motivation for Christian living is a barometer of our spiritual maturity, we discussed maturity and motives in that precise order.

"But now we come to another cause for reward, and like the motives the Holy Spirit produces as an offshoot of our pursuit of Christian maturity, this third criteria also blossoms from the same seed."

As Didaskolos paused, we all wondered what new truth from Scripture would flower before our eyes tonight.

"Our search begins in Matthew's Gospel, the fifth chapter. This is the famous Sermon on the Mount. Now you should know that a small camp in Christendom view this particular sermon as having no direct application for Christians today since it was given to Jews anticipating Messiah's earthly kingdom, a kingdom postponed until His second advent due to the nation's rejection of Jesus as Messiah. But James' many allusions to the Sermon shows that he thought it to be relevant and applicable in his day, and if in his day, ours too, since the rest of his epistle is for believers today. For instance, the exhortation to be 'patient until the coming of the Lord,' in 5:7, is obviously relevant since that event has yet to happen. In all, James refers to the Sermon no less than fifteen times.[1] I mean no sarcasm by this, but if the Sermon on the Mount was good enough for James' practical use, it should be good enough for ours. With this view, let's consider Matthew 5:10-12."

"Isn't this passage part of the well-known Beatitudes?" inquired Alfred.

"You're right," answered Didaskolos. "These words form the eighth proclamation of blessing in Jesus' Sermon on the Mount. He states, 'Blessed are those who are persecuted[2] because of righteousness, for theirs is the kingdom of heaven. Blessed are you when people insult you, persecute you and falsely say all kinds of evil against you because of Me.[3] Rejoice and be glad because great is your reward in heaven, for[4] in the same way they persecuted the prophets who were before you.'[5]

"The term 'blessed,' employed twice here, means 'to pronounce happy, to be fully satisfied';[6] it describes one who is fortunate and even envied by others because of his blessed state."

"Is this 'blessedness' something beyond what we commonly call 'happiness?'" Nina asked.

"Good question, sister," replied Didaskolos. "Indeed it is, 'happy'[7] portrays someone who has good luck come his way, favorable circumstances such as a paycheck, a new car, plenty of food, a clean bill of health from the doctor's office, etc. There's nothing wrong with being glad about such things, but what if the sky turns black and life rains on you, then what of your happiness? Usually it's washed away with the rain down the gutter. In brief, the 'blessedness' Jesus defines here is an inward contentment unaltered by earthly conditions. This is clear by the kind of person He describes here as 'blessed'–one persecuted for doing what is right in God's sight. Certainly, such treatment would not naturally produce happiness.

"Once again, listen to Jesus' words, 'Blessed are those who persecuted because of righteousness....' I emphasize the causal phrase to show the reason for the persecution.[8] Specific expressions of persecution are mentioned by Jesus, namely, insults and false accusations of an evil nature. Such is hurled our way, not for obnoxiousness, but for righteousness. A mighty big difference, wouldn't you say? But why is ill-treatment from unbelievers the cause for unconditional happiness?"

"For one," said Jim, "the kingdom of heaven is their possession."

"Exactly," said Didaskolos. "If you are willing to endure suffering for Jesus, you establish the irrefutable reality that you are His, and if His, a citizen of His heavenly kingdom. But why else this blessedness?"

"Because of the reward waiting in heaven," declared Janet.

"Right again," Didaskolos answered with intensity. "But not just a reward. Did you see the adjective before it? It will be a great reward.[9] And the sphere where rewards are received is heaven.[10] In conjunction with what we have already seen regarding the time of reward, Jesus no doubt has in mind the *bema* seat of Christ as the occasion for such a great reward for suffering in the cause of Christ.

"But there's yet another thing worthy of mention here. For believers who endure persecution for their willingness to please their King, they are in select company, and noble company at that. Jesus says, 'for so they persecuted the prophets who were before you.' As Hebrews 11:36-38 reports, some of the saints of old experienced 'mockings and scourgings, yes, also chains and imprisonment. They were stoned, they were sawn in two, they were tempted, they were put to death with the sword; they went about in sheepskins, in goatskins, being destitute, afflicted, ill-treated (men of whom the world was not worthy), wandering in deserts and mountains and caves and holes in the ground.'

"What a privilege should we be called to own the same reputation as the likes of Abel (God's first martyr), David, Jeremiah, Daniel, Meshach, Shadrach and Abednego and a host of other men and women who tasted agony, torture and in some cases, death itself, due to their unswerving devotion to the true God. And since we share this present bliss of being numbered with the likes of these and anticipate the future glory of great reward in heaven, Jesus imparts the two-fold logical imperative: 'Rejoice and be glad....' The term 'glad' means literally 'to skip and jump with happy excitement.'[11] The blessed, inner disposition of the believer is concretely illustrated, then, right here in this remarkable attitude toward suffering, an attitude far removed from circumstantial happiness.

"Such an attitude is splendidly displayed by John Chrysostom, a godly preacher in the fourth-century. Chrysostom preached so fervently against sin that he offended the unscrupulous Empress Eudoxia and numerous other church officials. According to one writer,

> When summoned before Emperor Arcadius, Chrysostom was threatened with banishment if he did not cease his uncompromising preaching. His response was, "Sire, you cannot banish me, for the world is my Father's house." "Then I will slay you," Arcadius said. "Nay, but you cannot, for my life is hid with Christ in God," came the answer. "Your treasures will be confiscated" was the next threat, to which John replied, "Sire, that cannot be, either. My treasures are in heaven, where none can break through and steal." "Then I will drive you from man, and you will have no friends left!" was the final, desperate warning. "That you cannot do, either," answered John, "for I have a Friend in heaven who has said, 'I will never leave you or forsake you.'" Chrysostom was indeed banished, first to Armenia and then farther away to Pityus on the Black Sea, to which he never arrived because he died on the way. But neither his banishment nor his death disproved or diminished his claims. The things that he valued most highly not even the emperor could take from him.[12]

"Chrysostom lost his material possessions and was banished, but he rejoiced because he knew he had treasure in heaven they could not touch. Beyond this Polycarp demonstrates his steadfast joy of knowing the true

God even under the threat of death:

> Polycarp, that aged bishop of Smyrna, dragged by the mob to the Roman tribunal was given the choice: sacrifice to the godhead of Caesar or die. 'Eighty and six years,' came the immortal reply, 'have I served Christ, and He has done me no wrong. How can I blaspheme my King who saved me?' So they brought him to the stake, and he prayed his last prayer: 'O Lord God Almighty, the Father of the well-beloved and ever-blessed Son, by whom we have received the knowledge of Thee...I thank Thee that Thou hast graciously thought me worthy of this day and of this hour.'[13]

"Certainly, this kind of Spirit-led response to persecution will bring great reward to John Chrysostom and Polycarp at the *bema* seat of Christ."

"And isn't this same kind of reward promised in Revelation 2:10?" Alfred asked.

"Yes," answered Didaskolos. "It would do us well to compare what's there with Matthew 5:10-12."

With eager anticipation, each one shuffled the pages of his Bible to Revelation 2:10.

"Revelation 2:8-11 is penned to the church at Smyrna," Didaskolos began, "one of seven Asian churches (see Rev. 1:4) addressed by the apostle John. The seaport city of Smyrna was about 35 miles north of Ephesus (present day Izmir), the center of the imperial cult of Rome. No doubt these believers would not acknowledge Caesar as Lord, and such a spiritual stand canceled their opportunity to work at the guilds as unemployment and poverty became their lot. As well, a significant Jewish community resided in Smyrna who did not have to patronize the Roman system, since their religion was tolerated by Rome. But Rome certainly would not cooperate with the Christian faith.[14]

"With this historical backdrop, it should not surprise us to read what Jesus says to His followers in Revelation 2:9: 'I know your afflictions and your poverty, yet you are rich! I know the slander of those who say they are Jews and are not, but a synagogue of Satan.'[15] Their maligned condition leads Jesus to then give the following exhortation in verse 10:

> Do not fear what you are about to suffer. Behold the devil is about to cast some of you into prison,[16] that you may be tested, and you will have tribulation ten days. Be faithful until[17] death and I will give you the crown of life.

"Staring persecution in the face, these saints were in need of supreme encouragement, therefore the imperative, 'Do not fear' or more literally, 'Stop being afraid!'[18] The grammar here implies that fear existed in these saints, not surprisingly so, and John urges them to put an end to their fears. But don't miss the point that this stern command is grounded in the promise of future reward for enduring such trials, a promise that enables them to face their opponents with courage."

"I was wondering," said Janet, "what is meant by the indicative statement, 'you will have tribulation for ten days.' Is that ten literal days, or some figure of speech for a period of time?"

"Excellent question, sister," answered Didaskolos. "And just before we answer it, let me briefly point out several things here: First, this suffering is about to[19] come upon them—it lurks just around the corner. Second, this suffering is from the devil himself.[20] Third, it is targeted toward some,[21] not all, in the church; fourth, it comes for the purpose of testing them;[22] and fifth, by nature, this suffering will entail imprisonment for ten days.

"Now then, in answer to Janet's question, is this ten literal days or should we assign a figurative meaning? Some suggest an allegorical interpretation—a reference to the so-called ten periods of church history, beginning with Nero and ending with Diocletian. It seems better, however, to take the phrase as an indefinite, though limited period of suffering just as the phrase 'ten days' can mean elsewhere in Scripture.[23]

"Now then, regarding the reward, notice the requirement for reward, that is, faithfulness. John says, 'Be faithful until death, and I will give you[24] the crown of life.' The words 'be faithful' literally mean 'prove yourself loyal and true.'[25] And here, loyalty to Christ may mean being willing to die for Him as a martyr. And what is the specific reward for such loyalty?"

"The Crown of Life," I replied.

"Yes, exactly, Ron," answered Didaskolos. "But what is this Crown of Life? To begin with, it's important to see what follows this promised reward in verse 11:

> He who has an ear, let him hear what the Spirit says to the churches. He who overcomes will not be hurt by the second death.

"So what is this 'second death?'"[26]

"It's the lake of fire, isn't it?" asked Jim.

"You're right, brother," said Didaskolos. "According to Revelation 20:11-15, those whose names are not written in the Lamb's Book of Life will be thrown into the lake of fire, which verse fourteen calls 'the second death.' Jesus warned of this eternal judgment of literal fire on those who reject His gift of salvation (cf. Matt. 26:41; Mark 9:42-50). In brief, the 'Crown of Life' contrasts, in the most profound sense, the 'second death' since it is literally, 'the crown that consists of eternal life.' Though eternal life is not earned, since Jesus grants it as a gift to those who trust Him alone as their Savior, in some sense this crown is the future reward of those who remain true to Him amid the fierceness of the battle.[27] What great encouragement and comfort the promises of verses 10 and 11 would be to such believers, not only to avoid the lake of fire, hell itself, but to be honored at Christ's tribunal with a hero's welcome."

"Is that what the crown symbolizes? Honor from Christ?" asked Nina.

"The term is *stephanos*,"[28] replied Didaskolos, "which, in part, symbolizes honor bestowed on military victors. For example,

> When Romania became a kingdom in 1881, King Charles realized that there was no crown for him to wear. He instructed his soldiers to go to the arsenal and secure some iron from a canon which had been captured from the enemy. They melted it and fashioned it into an iron crown. His intent was that this crown would be a token of that which was won on the field of battle. It had been bought and paid for with many Romanian lives.[29]

"The crown John speaks of here is borrowed from the Greek culture of his day where crowns, woven of such things as oak, ivy, parsley, spruce, myrtle, or olive, were given to honorable servants of the state, those who conquered in war and to victorious athletes in the games. As well, they became symbols of festive gladness at wedding feasts, etc. This is not the royal crown given to kings,[30] but in this passage and others in the New Testament where future rewards are in view, it is a crown earned through conquering. In this case, it is conquering the desire of the flesh to recoil from suffering and instead endure it by God's power.

"Examples of suffering abound in the pages of church history: James was beheaded in Jerusalem in AD 44. Philip was cruelly scourged and then crucified. Matthew died by the sword. Enemies of the cross dragged Mark by his feet through the streets of Alexandria, then burned him to death the following day. Luke lost his life at the end of a rope in Greece. In India, a spear pierced through Thomas and claimed his life, and on and on it goes.[31]

"Here is a modern example:

> Zufan lives in Ethiopia. Growing up, she embraced Islam, but then a Christian told her about Jesus, and she trusted in Him as God and as her Savior. Then, her family disowned her and her friends shunned her. Zufan became the target of vicious insults and slurs from the community. How is Zufan responding? She says, "I preach the gospel courageously everywhere, whatever dangers and risks come to me."[32]

"Jesus says to the persecuted believers at Smyrna, 'Be faithful until death, and I will give you the crown of life.' Those who honor Jesus on earth in their hour of affliction will be honored in heaven with the Crown of Life.

"Now then, before we close, what kind of persecution might we face in our American culture? Certainly, none of us have been flogged or scalded in hot oil for our Christianity, but are there subtle forms of opposition? Did not Paul say to Timothy, 'All who live godly in Christ Jesus will suffer persecution'" (2 Tim. 3:12).

Didaskolos paused for a moment, then said, "What sort of misery has God allowed to pay you a visit of late? But the more important questions are, 'What is your attitude toward this misery? Are you growing bitter, or are you getting better as a believer because of the trial? Has God permitted someone to treat you unfairly and apparently bring to an end the dream God gave you?' As a result, you may have no choice but to sit patiently in God's waiting room, for the moment, as He sovereignly orchestrates circumstances to insure your being in His place when He's through.

"Joseph can help us wait with courage instead of pacing the floor. 'Just rest quietly,' he would say were he here tonight, 'enjoy the piped-in-music: The promises of God. He will fulfill the dreams He's given you. In His own way. In His own time (cf. Gen. 37-50; especially 45:1-11; 50:15-21). Such patience will grant you the Crown of Life when you see Jesus.'

"Like Job, you may have lost your material possessions, your children, or your health—or like Job perhaps you've lost all of these. Will you abandon your moral integrity and curse God, as Job's foolish wife urged him to do? Or, like Job, will you view God-sent adversity with the eye of faith, from heaven's portico, and meekly accept God's dealings with you (Job 2:9-10)? Electing Job's response versus that of his wife's will assure you a hero's welcome when you see Jesus face to face.

"Or perhaps you are feeling the oppressive heat of immediate family members, in-laws, neighbors, or work associates due to your stand for Jesus, for doing right in a world of wrong. Be strong in the strength of His might (Eph. 6:10). You're in swell company: The prophets of old. They too endured suffering for going against the grain of sinful society, and with them you are promised 'great reward' (Matt. 5:10-12, previously discussed in detail) when you stand before Jesus at the *bema* seat. The proud smile on His face will be worth it all!

"Remember, not only will Jesus grant you a hero's welcome for progressing in spiritual maturity (see ch. 1, 2 Pet. 1:5-11), and for practicing your Christian life with Spirit-led motives, but as well for persevering in suffering. Keep that in mind when life deals you a lemon, and God will teach you how to make lemonade."

At that clever analogy, a few faint chuckles could be heard around the room, but not without the truth of God's word settling deep into our souls. This evening's message would change the way we viewed adversity. After all, who among us wanted to stand before the *bema* seat embarrassed at the way we had responded to the sour experiences with which our all-wise and sovereign God had afflicted us on earth for His own good purposes (cf. Ps. 119:71; Rom. 5:3-5; Heb. 12:5-11)? Whatever we would have had to endure for His name's sake would be well worth it to hear Him say, "Welcome home, and well done, My good and faithful servant. Enter into the joy of your Lord" (cf. Matt. 25:21).

Most everyone sat forward, head in their hands, staring at the soft flickering flames of the fire. As silence prevailed, the precious Person, the Holy Spirit of God, prevailed even more abundantly. He encouraged me to not grow weary in God's waiting room as I awaited a full-time job, and He convicted me about my attitude toward someone whom I felt (as did many others) had treated me dishonestly in causing me to lose the job I had. I had to resolve in my spirit that God causes all things, yes all things, to work together for good to those who love God (cf. Rom. 8:28). This divine viewpoint enabled me to bury my potentially bitter feelings and join the hands of faith with Joseph who asked rhetorically of his brothers, "Am I in the place of God?" (Gen. 50:19).

Sensitive to the Spirit's wishes to speak to our hearts about the word we'd just heard, Didaskolos allowed us to reflect for several moments and then said, "It's time we put a period on our session, but do take this truth with you and routinely assess your attitude toward the misery God allows in your life—not the miseries you bring on yourself through sin, of course—but those God allows for His own designs, designs which are sometimes past finding out. And to aid a godly response and thereby a hero's welcome for each of you, I have copied a study I did several years ago. It's called *An Exposition of James 1:12*; this is another passage that mentions the Crown of Life. It's a bit on the technical side, but I think you'll benefit from it.

"Now then, there are two more aspects of gaining a hero's welcome I'd like you to see in Scripture before our study ends. For the first of these, there just happens to be a guest speaker lined up to be at our church the next couple of Sunday nights who plans to address the very subject. If you're all agreed, we could attend together and see what he has to say."

Only Jim's church had a Sunday evening service (an event seemingly on the brink of extinction in modern-day American Christianity), and he would do his best to cover his duties there so he could join us. We would mark next Sunday night, 6:30 p.m. sharp, on our calendars.

As we carried our dishes and silverware back to the kitchen, the place buzzed with intrigue as to what these last two principles regarding a hero's welcome would be. As difficult to wait as a young girl waiting for her birthday, we would have no problem, however, consuming our thoughts with the message fresh on our minds: Persevering in suffering....or the way I now preferred thinking of it: How to make lemonade when life deals you a lemon.

Each one exchanged friendly good-byes and picked up the paper on James 1:12 on his way out the door. I admit I exceeded the speed limit on the way home, anxious to start reading my copy.

"Please, forgive me, dear Lord."

Endnotes for Chapter 5

[1] Compare the following: James 1:2 with Matthew 5:10-12; 1:4 with 5:48; 1:5 and 5:15 with 7:7-12; 1:9 with 5:3; 1:20 with 5:22; 2:13 with 5:7; 6:14-15; 2:14-16 with 7:21-23; 3:17-18 with 5:9; 4:4 with 6:24; 4:10 with 5:3-5; 4:11 with 7:1-2; 5:2 with 6:19; 5:10 with 5:12; 5:12 with 5:33-37. List from J. Ronald Blue, "James," in *The Bible Knowledge Commentary: An Exposition of the Scriptures: New Testament*, ed. by John F. Walvoord and Roy B. Zuck (Wheaton: Victor Books, 1985), 818. Beyond James' copious use of Jesus' teachings in Matthew 5-7 to his own readers, it is equally true that many of the teachings of Matthew 5-7 declare what God has always expected of His followers, such as "You cannot serve God and money" (6:24). As Barbieri states, "While the passage must be understood in the light of the offer of the messianic kingdom, the sermon applies to Jesus' followers today for it demonstrates the standard of righteousness God demands of His people." Louis A. Barbeiri,

"Matthew," in *The Bible Knowledge Commentary: An Exposition of the Scriptures: New Testament*, ed. by John F. Walvoord and Roy B. Zuck (Wheaton: Victor Books, 1985), 28.

[2] The passive participle here raises questions per the force of the perfect. Broadus maintains that it applies to the fact the "chief rewards of such sufferers do not so much attend on the persecution as follow it." John A. Broadus, *Commentary on the Gospel of Matthew*, An American Commentary on the New Testament 1 (Valley Forge, PA: Judson Press, 1886), 92, quoted in Carson, "Matthew," in *Expositor's*, 8:136. Other commentators treat it as a Hebraizing prophetic perfect, though of course it must be kept in mind that persecution had already broken out on the early church at the time of Matthew's writing. As Carson points out, we must ask why the same tense is not used in Matthew 5:4, "Blessed are those who mourn...." Perhaps the perfect here is more aoristic and the participial use here merely adjectival in function (cf. C F. D. Moule, *An Idiom Book of New Testament Greek* (Cambridge: University Press, 1959), 14). Carson, "Matthew," in *Expositor's*, 8:136.

[3] Note how Matthew moves from the general to the particular with verse 10 showing the general reality of persecution and verse 11 the specific forms it may take.

[4] The *gar* points up the reason for the imperatives "rejoice" and "be glad." We are in great company when afflicted for our faith, sharing the same reputation of faithfulness held by the prophets of old.

[5] Opposition from the world is normal fare for the true disciple; cf. John 15:18-25; 2 Timothy 3:12; 1 Peter 4:13-14.

[6] Zodhiates, 1735. As John MacArthur notes, "Homer used the word to describe a wealthy man, and [in the same vein] Plato used it of one who is successful in business. Both Homer and Heisod spoke of the Greek gods as being happy (*makarios*) within themselves... [being] unaffected by the world of men—who were subject to poverty, disease, weakness, misfortune, and death." The word connotes then, an inward state of contentedness unqualified by circumstances, the very disposition God desires for His children. John MacArthur, *Matthew 1-7*, The MacArthur New Testament Commentary (Chicago: Moody Press, 1985), 141-142. Further, this term is used to introduce all nine beatitudes here and the four in Luke 6:20-22. As Marshall states, "In the LXX it usually translates '*asere*', the construct plural of '*eser*', 'luck, happiness', and is found in the form 'O the happiness of....' It is thus accompanied by a statement which gives the reason why the person named is to be praised as being happy. The happiness, however, is the result of a state of divinely given salvation, so that a statement of blessing is in effect...a statement predicating salvation." Marshall goes on to compare the difference between *makarios* and *eulogetos* (used to render the Hebrew *barak*). In brief, the latter is employed more frequently and expresses "God's act of favour to men, shown in material or spiritual gifts to them, but it can also be used of men blessing God in the sense of praising him....In

the NT the corresponding words are used much more of praise being offered to God, but while *makarios* is rarely used of God, *eulogetos* is always used. As applied to men, however, in the OT *baruk* and *asere* are synonyms, the latter tending to replace the former in course of time....; the former is more a prayer for blessing, the latter a statement that someone is blessed." I. Howard Marshall, *The Gospel of Luke: A Commentary on the Greek Text.* The New International Greek Testament Commentary (Grand Rapids: Eerdmans, 1979), 248.

[7] From the English root *hap*, favorable circumstances. Zodhiates, 1735.

[8] The phrase is in the genitive, an adverbial of reference, introduced with the causal *hoti*.

[9] The term great is *polus*, a second predicate adjective here, following the articular noun *misthos* (see Appendix A for the word study).

[10] The last phrase of the causal clause reads *en tois houranois*, a dative of sphere construction.

[11] Zodhiates, 1680. The term is a compound of *agan*, very much, and *allomai*, to leap; cf. the same word in John 5:35 and Acts 16:34; often the word is placed after *chairo*, a term of less intense delight (in this regard, cf. 1 Pet. 4:13 and Rev. 19:7).

[12] MacArthur, *Matthew 1-7*, 232-233.

[13] William Barclay, *The Gospel of Matthew*, The Daily Study Bible (Toronto: G. R. Welch, 1975), 115.

[14] Wiersbe, *Bible Exposition Commentary*, 2:573.

[15] True Jews are so inwardly, not merely outwardly, having been circumcised in the heart, not just the flesh (cf. Rom. 2:27-29).

[16] It should be noted that the prisons of the ancient world were a place where the accused awaited sentencing which resulted either in execution or banishment. No wonder Jesus seeks to calm their fears.

[17] The idea is "even to the point of death." Alan Johnson, "Revelation," in *The Expositor's Bible Commentary*, ed. by Frank E. Gaebelein, 399-603 (Grand Rapids: Zondervan Publishing House, 1984), 12:438.

[18] The present imperative preceded by the negative pronominal cardinal adjective, *meden*, implies that fear existed in these people and John meant that it should cease.

[19] A rendering of *melleis*, present active indicative verb, "to be about to."

[20] *Ho diablos*; and see endnote 22.

[21] Translates *ex humon*.

[22] The word is *peirasmos*, and can be used negatively regarding solicitation to evil, as in James 1:13 (something God is incapable of doing), or in a positive sense to bring about further change in spiritual character (something God does frequently in the lives of His children, Gen. 22:1; James 1:2). Here Satan seeks to show these believers as unapproved, as spiritual failures in spiritual warfare (cf. the same use of

the term in Satan's strategy in 1 Cor. 7:5 and compare the concept with the book of Job where Satan tries earnestly to entice Job to curse God by afflicting him with loss of possessions, progeny and physical health). The Greek here shows the coordinating conjunction *hina* plus the subjunctive mood indicating a purpose clause: "cast some of you into prison that you may be tested."

[23] See Genesis 24:55; Numbers 11:19; Nehemiah 5:18; Job 19:3; Jeremiah 42:7; Daniel 1:12; Acts 25:6. Alford, *The Greek Testament*, 4:567, concurs, as does Alan Johnson who writes, "it may be a Semitism for an indeterminate but comparatively short period of time." Alan Johnson, "Revelation," in *The Expositor's Bible Commentary*, 12:438. But it may refer to a rather long period of time as history shows that "many Christians were martyred in Smyrna over the next several centuries." Keener, 770.

[24] The form here of *doso* signifies the future (tense) certainty (indicative mood) of this personal bestowment by Christ (first person, singular) on His suffering servants.

[25] *Ginou pistis; ginou* is present middle imperative; *pistis* sometimes carries this meaning of "faithfulness," seen elsewhere in Matthew 25:21, 23; Luke 16:10; 1 Corinthians 1:9; 4:2; Ephesians 6:21; Revelation 1:5. The parallel words and ideas would be "true, just, trustworthy, and observant of and steadfast to one's trust, word, or promises"; the quality is applied to both God and His children (cf. Zodhiates, 1749).

[26] How significant that Jesus introduces Himself to this particular group of suffering saints as "the First and the Last, who died (literally, 'became a corpse') and came to life again" (v. 8b). These saints could find extreme consolation in the fact that the One who, as the First and Last—Creator and Lord of history, was also able to bring them to life again as they faced impending death. In fact, their persecutors could take their bodies, but they would never ever (the double negative in the Greek in v. 11 affirms the absolute certainty of this promise) have the ability to hurt them with "the second death," an obvious reference to the lake of fire (cf. Rev. 20:14; 21:8). Jesus is faithful to reveal Himself to us in accordance with our current needs and concerns.

[27] The second predicate genitive here, *tes zoes*, could be purely descriptive, "a living crown," in contrast to the perishable crowns of the day, or it could be appositional in force, "the crown is life." Most commentators prefer the latter, but in what sense could eternal life be earned via suffering? The NT teaches salvation by grace alone. Certainly the language of Revelation 2:8-10 addresses believers who are part of God's universal church, localized in Smyrna, "rich" spiritually, though poor materially (v. 9). Joseph Dillow admits that this crown is given subsequent to saving faith and therefore suggests a greater quality of life in the eternal state, but how would this be fair to those who never had the opportunity to suffer and die for Christ?

Dillow, *Reign of the Servant Kings*, 577. Still this view has merit since, according to the first class conditional sentence of 2 Timothy 2:12, "If we endure, we will also reign with Him." That is, believers who fail to endure the suffering God allows will lose privileges of position and authority in the eternal state. We could say that the future tense of "I will give you the crown of life" is not necessarily eschatological. Perhaps it refers to a greater quality of spiritual life on earth, here and now, due to obedience, the abundant life Jesus spoke of. But in this case, what good would it be, and what consolation would it bring to these soon-to-be suffering saints to have such a promise when they may soon be dead? So, the crown must be eschatological, given at the *bema* seat of Christ for those who endure persecution for righteousness (cf. Matt. 5:10-12 and James 1:12). Called "the crown of life," it is the specific way in which Jesus honors who honor Him in suffering.

[28] See the Appendix A for further details on *stephanos*; also cf. William Barclay's excellent discussion on the cultural implications for the meaning of the term. William Barclay, *The Revelation of John: Chapters 1-5*, The Daily Study Bible (Toronto: G. R. Welch, 1976), 1:82-83.

[29] Erich Sauer, *In the Arena of Faith* (Grand Rapids: Eerdmans, 1966), 66, quoted in Dillow, 574.

[30] There are instances in Scripture where *stephanos* refers to a kingly crown (e.g., 2 Sam. 12:30; Matt. 27:29; Rev. 14:14), but as Trench observes, *diadema* is the more common term in these contexts. Trench does, however, prefer to regard "the crown of life" as a royal crown, since we reign with him. Richard Chenevix Trench, *Synonyms of the New Testament* (Grand Rapids, MI: Eerdmans, 1953), 78. And it could be argued in view of passages such as 2 Timothy 2:12 where faithfulness to Christ gains one the privilege of co-rulership with Him in the future, that *stephanos* means priestly authority in Christ's kingdom. Yet as Mayor concludes, based on the strong emphasis in Greek culture on the *stephanos* received for victory in the games, public honor for distinguished service, or festal ornamentation, "the idea of a kingly crown seems less appropriate...than a crown of merit or victory." Joseph B. Mayor, *The Epistle of St. James* (Grand Rapids, MI: Zondervan, 1954), 49. Mitton concurs when he states, "In the Greek world its chief purpose was to reward prowess in athletic contests, and it was made out of leaves. In itself valueless, it denoted a high honour. The Jews cared little for athletic skill, and for them the crown was more often a symbol of joy on some festive occasion (Ezek. 16:12; Wisdom 2:8), or a sign of special dignity...(Prov. 16:31...Wisdom 5:16)." C. Leslie Mitton, *The Epistle of James* (Grand Rapids: Eerdmans, 1966), 44-45.

[31] Cf. John Foxe, *Foxe's Christian Martyrs of the World* (Chicago: Moody Press, 1960), 24-35.

[32] Adapted from: Wycliffe Associates, "I Preach The Gospel Courageously," *Involved* (May 2016): 3.

6

The Crown of Life: Who Qualifies?

An Exposition of James 1:12

As James pens his epistle to certain persecuted Christians in the first century, he senses the need to instruct them about adversity. This instruction includes (1) the proper response to adversity: be joyful (vv. 2, 9-11); be pliable (vv. 3-4); and be prayerful (vv. 5-8); (2) the nature of adversity: multifaceted, that is, they come in all shapes and sizes (various trials); (3) the reality of trials: "Count it all joy, my brethren, when you encounter various trials..." (v. 2); and (4) the reward for a proper response to adversity (v. 12). The reward mentioned in verse 12 will be our focus in this paper.

In this verse, James begins by saying, "Blessed is the man who perseveres under trial...." The adjective translated blessed is the Greek term *makarios* and is placed at the beginning of the Greek sentence for emphasis. In spite of the trials his readers are facing for their Christianity, James wants their attention to be on the reward awaiting them in the future, so he places the word "blessed" first. This is the same term rendered "blessed" in the beatitudes Jesus gave in Matthew 5:3-12. It describes someone who is inwardly happy, though external circumstances are not an occasion for happiness. Such inward joy causes others to envy those who possess it. Placed in the predicate position, "blessed" makes an assertion about the noun it modifies, namely, "man": "Blessed is the man...."

The noun "man" is the Greek term *aner*, generally a strict reference to the male gender, but here employed in a generic sense.[1] The context demands this interpretation since those addressed are called "brethren," a word used elsewhere in the New Testament to refer to a whole group of believers (see for example, Rom. 12:1). As well, James uses *aner*, in a few verses prior, 1:7, when he says of the believer who prays without faith in God's ability to answer, "For let not that *man* [emphasis mine] suppose that he will receive anything from the Lord."[2] Obviously, the term man here is meant to include males and females in the congregation, not just males.[3] But who qualifies to be 'blessed?"

"Blessed is the man who perseveres under trial..." declares James. The word translated perseveres is *hupomonei* and carries the idea of bearing up under difficult circumstances with patient endurance and constancy.[4] You can find this particular term 17 times in the New Testament; in fact, James employs it three other times in his letter: In 1:4 ("Let endurance have its perfect result") and twice in 5:11, one of which speaks of the perseverance of Job. In short, the English word "perseverance" serves, then, as a good translation of this Greek term.

The next word "trial" comes from the term *peirasmon* which means "to put to the test." Here it is used in a positive sense in contrast to 1:13 where it refers to solicitation to do evil.[5] The trials spoken of in 1:12 are the "various trials" of verse 2 since there is a reward for a godly response to them. Chapter 5 then depicts the form these trials have taken with regard to these believers—persecution from wealthy unbelievers who are unfairly exploiting these materially poor saints (cf. 5:1-6). Of course, because he chooses Job as a model of enduring adversity, the variegated trials James speaks of could include the kinds of things Job faced: losing possessions, posterity and physical health.

The next word in verse 12 is the preposition "for"[6] which introduces the reason why the Christian in view is "blessed," namely because, as James affirms, "after being[7] approved, he shall receive the crown of life." The word "approved" is the Greek term *dokimos* which means "to be approved after [a time of] testing."[8] In the Greek version of the Old Testament, the Septuagint, the term is used of coins and metals which underwent the removal of impurities (alloys, etc.). For instance, in Zechariah 11:13 we read, "Cast them (30 pieces of silver) into a furnace and I will see if it is good (approved) metal." As such, the word "approved" is parallel to the previous word *peirasmon* (trial) as part of the contextual motif of God testing His people, via the furnace of adversity, to see if they possess true spiritual character. And those who pass the test are promised the Crown of Life in the future.

In *Our Daily Bread*, Joanie Yoder writes,

> Do you believe God is good, even when life isn't? Mary did, and I gasped with amazement the day I heard her pastor share her story at her funeral. She, being dead, yet speaks!
>
> Mary had been a widow, very poor, and totally

> housebound because of her ailments in old age. But...she had learned to praise God amid her hardships. Over the years she had come to savor with deep gratitude every good thing He sent her way.
>
> Her pastor said he occasionally would visit her at home. Because of her crippling pain, it took her a long time to inch her way to the door to let him in. So he would call on the telephone and tell her that he was on his way and the time he would get there. Mary would then begin the slow, arduous journey to the door, reaching it about the time he arrived. Without fail, he could count on her greeting him with these triumphant words: 'God is good!'
>
> I've observed that those who speak most often about God's goodness are usually those with the most trials. They choose to focus on the Lord's mercy...rather than on their troubles, and in so doing they taste His goodness.
>
> Mary not only challenges us to taste and see, but to taste and say that the Lord is good—even when life isn't.[9]

Yoder concludes her article with these insightful words, "those who bless God in their trial will be blessed by God through their trial."[10]

Our Christian sister, Mary, now in the presence of the Lord, learned how to make lemonade when life dealt her a lemon. In the fire of adversity, her character was proven to be of supreme spiritual quality, to the extent that the Master Goldsmith, Jesus, could see His own reflection in her. Passing such a test of character will gain Mary a Crown of Life at the bema seat.

Now then, back to the text. The words, "he shall receive the crown of life" contain the future tense and the absolute certainty of what is said.[11] By contrast, the double-minded, doubt-driven saint of 1:6 will receive "nothing from the Lord."

Their unbelief not only negates their getting the heavenly wisdom they need to handle their trial (cf. v. 5), but proves their lack of spiritual character and robs them of the Crown of Life on judgment day. This sobering reality is apparently implied in this context, a truth confirmed elsewhere in the New Testament several times (e.g., 1 Cor. 3:10-15; 2 John 8).

But what is this "Crown of Life?" Serving as the direct object of the sentence, it should be noted that this is a particular crown, not just a reference to crowns in general. This is clear by the definite article, "the," in front of the noun rendered "crown."[12] In brief, the word "crown," based upon its historical background and biblical usage, signifies a figurative expression of spiritual victory, honor and gladness. Here, the particular application is (1) a believer's personal triumph over the temptation to wilt under the blistering heat of life's adversities, (2) the resultant honor God grants for such perseverance and (3) the personal joy possessed by the believer for such a reward.

But what can be meant by the word "life" here? The Greek term is *zoe* and emphasizes the quality of life that comes from God alone. Is God giving the saint who, with God's help, makes lemonade out of life's lemons, a special quality of spiritual life in the eternal state? This would have to be the case since these readers had already received the gift of eternal life at conversion. He calls them "brethren" in verse 2, and fourteen more times in the rest of the letter. As already seen, this promise is future. And because such crowns, in the New Testament,[13] are associated with the bema seat of Christ following His coming, the future would not seem to be some time following the trial, but the future meeting with Christ at the *bema*.

So then, in what sense is the persevering believer given a greater quality of spiritual life in the eternal state following his examination at the bema seat? We are not precisely told, but just as there will be degrees of punishment in hell, as Matthew 11:20-24 reveals, so also there are degrees of bliss in heaven. The believer who perseveres in trial, showing his steadfast love for God, will be given a higher quality of eternal life, a greater capacity for joy throughout the long tomorrow. Donald Burdick rightly observes the following about the Crown of Life: "It is evident that this 'life' that God has promised is more than the eternal life given to every believer at the time of his salvation (John 5:24). Since it is a reward for an accomplishment subsequent to initial faith, it must refer to a still higher quality of life."[14]

In this sense, the phrase "Crown of Life" is appositional, in nature, that is, the crown itself is life.[15] This concept is consistent with God's gracious decision to justly compensate those who follow Him faithfully with greater reward and responsibility both here and in the hereafter. Many Old Testament and New Testament passages confirm this general idea.[16] Certainly, every believer will be morally like Jesus, according to 1 John 3:2, but there will be degrees of reward. As Jesus tells us in Luke 19:11-19, some believers will be honored as rulers over eleven cities, while others will rule only five cities. Heaven will be wonderful—without even a thimble full of sadness—for all believers (see Rev. 21:4), but in terms of the quality of each believer's eternity, differences will abound.

At best, we can be sure that those who respond to God-sent trials by being (1) joyful in light of the prospect of personal spiritual progress and their position in Christ (James 1:2, 9-11), (2) pliable in cooperating with God instead of contending with God (vv. 2-4) and (3) prayerful due to their need for wisdom (vv. 5-8), can be (4) hopeful in view of their future reward (v. 12, the Crown of Life) for such a Spirit-led, faith-generated response. What the detailed nature of this crown entails, beyond its obvious symbol of honor, spiritual triumph and gladness, may be too difficult to uncover this side of heaven, but both the requirement and reality of it are as clear as the crystal river in the New Jerusalem, that splendid place Jesus is now preparing for us (cf. Rev. 22:1ff.).

The final phrase of the verse unveils the motive God is looking for in His child's reaction to the misery He allows. Once more, James writes, "Blessed is the man who perseveres under trial, for once he has been approved, he shall receive the crown of life, *which the Lord has promised to those who love Him* [emphasis mine]."

The relative pronoun "which" refers back to the Crown of Life; and the phrase it introduces—"the Lord has promised"—is an indicative statement of absolute reality. The Lord has assured us that such a reward is in store for the saint who meets the criteria of perseverance in trials. But the ability to meet such a requirement would be impossible without the motivation of a fervent love for Jesus, in brief, a whole-hearted embracing of the Great Commandment: "Love the Lord your God with all your heart and with all your soul and with all your strength and with all your mind..." (Luke 10:27, NIV). And those who have a passion to live out this great commandment will be the recipients of the Great Commendation, which in reference to trials shall be the Crown of Life.

The phrase "those who love Him" suggests a lifestyle of loving God, an idea supported by the general context. And the litmus test of how genuine our love for God is occurs when God rains upon our parade. Are we mere fair-weather saints, as Job's wife seems to have been, at least in her initial response to Job's sickness (Job 2:9), or will we accept both good and adversity from God? If the latter, then God can still brag on us when Satan, the accuser of the brethren, discusses our situation with God.[17] Any believer can say, "I love God" when there is sunshine and blue skies, but when the clouds blacken, the thunder rumbles in the distance and the lightning strikes home, we discover how true we will remain to God.

> William Drummond told a story of a young woman he knew whose face always seemed to radiate Christian joy. Her actions too made it evident that she was a devout follower of Christ. But she also had one other identifying feature—she always wore a little gold locket around her neck. Such oval or heart-shaped cases usually contain the picture of a loved one, which the wearer gladly shows to anyone who inquires. This girl, however, never showed anyone what was inside hers.
>
> One day, during a time when she had become seriously ill, one of her closest friends was permitted to open the locket. Drummond said, "Instead of seeing the photograph of the girl's mother or of some male admirer, she found inscribed the words, 'whom having not seen, I love.' The secret of her consecrated life was revealed. She had given her full devotion to Jesus, the Lover of her soul, and all her actions had been beautified by His presence."[18]

Here then, is a gorgeous portrait of how one's love for Jesus enables him to endure adversity permitted by Jesus, a love that will be rewarded with the Crown of Life.

With haste I tossed the whole document on the walnut coffee table in front of me and ran to my computer desk in my bedroom–there it was, the journal I'd been keeping for the last few years, tracking my thoughts, prayers and God's intimate dealings with me. I knew just the entry I wanted to read after reading Didaskolos' paper. By far, the most difficult words I'd ever penned....

> It was a Sunday morning. I lay there on our dark blue couch, depressed, disillusioned with God, angry with God. Another long drawn out day as the prisoner of fatigue stood before me, fatigue brought on by an inability to get even one night of quality sleep. And this due to an irritation in my bladder called interstitial cystitis which woke me up several times a night. My body owed a sleep debt two years and running.
>
> I just lay there on that blue couch of ours. I didn't want to go to church. Not only was my energy tank on empty but I was mad at God. My prayer went something like this, 'Lord, I have served you loyally, though certainly not perfectly, for 20 years. And you allow this condition! I can barely do my job, and if this gets any worse I may lose my job; I can't function as father, or as a husband the way I should. This whole thing is a 500-pound weight on the back of my wife, Ginny. Lord, if it wasn't for a wife and three children, I might even end my life and be released from this prison and into the freedom of Your presence. I know that would grieve you, Lord, but I feel trapped. I don't agree with Your treatment of me.'

As these dark, disturbing thoughts once again haunted my soul, I recalled actually considering throwing down the baton and quitting the Christian race. It had now been a couple of years since that scary moment on the dark blue couch. And, though there had since been some brief times of depression and discouragement, four basic thoughts from Scripture had rescued me, not only from the slough of despondency on that couch, but from many occasions where the temptation to be embittered at God dangled before me like a deadly hook before a fish! These four thoughts were as follows: (1) Though I cannot fully understand God, He is worthy of my full trust. (2) When I seriously think about it, my personal love for Him will not let me do anything that would hurt Him. (3) One glorious day—and it could be today!—Jesus will come, snatch me away from this cursed world, give me a brand new body absent of any sickness or disease, and void of any capacity to sin; and when I see Him, perhaps a Crown of Life shall be mine for loving Him even when He allowed life to deal me a lemon. And (4) from my study of the book of Job, I couldn't stand the thought of anybody but God having bragging rights on me. That Satan could ever say, "I finally achieved control of Ron's decisions and he's bitterly cursing You, God, to Your face," sobered my spirit.

These thoughts had fed my faith and moved me off the couch, back into church and on with life under God's perfect, sovereign and all-wise plan. Yes, indeed, I could count on it: All things do work together for good to those who love God.[19]

As my tired body and mind fell off to sleep I whispered, "Thank You, my dear and precious Lord, for keeping me in love with You, for keeping me true to You, despite the tough times you've permitted me to know with my less than perfect health. If you should never choose to heal me from it, please help me to draw upon Your sufficient grace, so that the glory of Your strength can be seen through my weakness. I love you Lord."

My condition stole some of my sleep that night, but God answered my prayer and granted the necessary stamina for the next day. What a precious promise I cling to from Deuteronomy 33:25: "As your days, so shall your strength be."

Endnotes for Chapter 6

[1] Cf. Bauer, Arndt and Gingrich, 66.

[2] A literal translation.

[3] See this same use in Romans 4:8.

[4] Rienecker, 723; cf. also Zechariah 6:14 in the LXX: "*Ho de stephanos estai tois hupomenousin.*"

[5] As Ropes aptly observes, "Inner enticement to evil would have to be *resisted*, not *endured*." James H. Ropes, *A Critical and Exegetical Commentary on the Epistle of St. James*. The International Critical Commentary (Edinburg: T. T. & Clark, 1954), 150.

[6] Greek, *hoti*, here functioning in a causal sense.

[7] Translates *genomenos*, an aorist participle functioning temporally here, antecedent in time to the following verb, "he shall receive."

[8] Rienecker, 723.

[9] Joanie Yoder, "Taste and Say," *Our Daily Bread*, May 5, 1995. This article is based on Psalm 34:8.

[10] Ibid.

[11] The indicative mood of the future verb *lempsetai* affirms the absolute certainty of this promise.

[12] The term is *stephanos*; as Hailey writes, "A crown of flowers was worn by the pagan worshiper (Ramsay), a crown adorned the patron goddess, as indicated on the coins of the city, and the city had a crown of buildings on the crown-shaped acropolis of Mount Pagos. But all of this would fade away. In contrast, the faithful Christian would be given a crown of life." Homer Hailey, *Revelation, an Introduction and Commentary* (Grand Rapids: Baker Book House, 1979), 128.

[13] See 1 Corinthians 9:25; 1 Thessalonians 2:19-20; 2 Timothy 4:8; 1 Peter 5:4; Revelation 2:10.

[14] Donald Burdick, "James," in *The Expositor's Bible Commentary*, ed. by Frank E. Gaebelein (Grand Rapids, MI: Zondervan, 1981), 12:171.

[15] Representing the common position on the genitive construction here, Moo says, "Life should be taken as identifying the reward—'the reward that is life.' This life is, of course, not physical life, but eternal life, the enjoyment of God's presence on into eternity." Douglas J. Moo, *The Letter of James: An Introduction and Commentary*, Tyndale New Testament Commentaries (Grand Rapids, MI: Eerdmans, 1985), 70-71. Ropes adds, "Eternal life as the reward for the friends of God was a fundamental idea

of later Jewish and of Christian eschatology, cf. Ps. Sol.13:10; Enoch 58:3; 4 Ezra 8:52ff. Mk. 9:43; Jn. 3:15...." Ropes, 152. Jesus spoke of such special intimacy as a reward for obedient believers: "You are my friends, if you do whatever I command you" (John 15:14). The "Crown of Life" would certainly include such intimate friendship with Jesus.

[16] E.g., Daniel 12:3; Matthew 25:14-30 also teaches varying degrees of responsibility and privilege in serving Christ in the future kingdom based on faithfulness, or the lack thereof, here and now; see also 2 Timothy 2:12; and again, as 2 John 8 intimates, it is absolutely possible to lose out on one's "full reward."

[17] "Who has bragging rights on me?" seems to be a key issue in the book of Job. For instance, consider the real intent behind the conversation between God and Satan regarding Job in Job 1:6-11 and 2:1-5.

[18] Henry Bosch, "The Love Locket," *Our Daily Bread*, August 12, 1990.

[19] Adapted from Romans 8:28.

7

Are You One of God's "Impact Players?"

Portraying the self-control we had learned of in the Gallery of Virtue, everyone promptly arrived at East San Diego Bible Fellowship's Sunday evening service, where Didaskolos attended. As always, smiles and warm embraces were plentiful, and each one awaited what was to be learned from God's messenger on this night. It was now clear in our minds that receiving a hero's welcome would not be the privilege of every believer when he saw Jesus, only those who progressed in spiritual maturity. And the fruits of such maturity would be practicing our Christian walk with Spirit-led motives, and it would show up most profoundly in the way we persevered in suffering. But, according to Didaskolos, Scripture revealed other criteria as well for future rewards.

Friendly ushers greeted us as we meandered in. We filled an entire row together and prayerfully prepared ourselves for the instruction we were about to receive. After expressing our worship of God by both singing and contributing to the offering, the speaker was introduced and began his message. Curiously, the title printed in the bulletin was "C'MON, LET'S PLAY BALL!" With faces turned upward and notepads in hand, we were ready for the feast.

"A few years ago, the world of sports hatched a new phrase: 'impact player.' And just what is an impact player? An impact player is one who has made a marked contribution to a given sport, elevating the level of skill, the performance standard and the success of his team. In fact, when sports fans evaluate how a particular sport should be played, they point to these gifted and disciplined athletes as the yardstick.

"And who are they? For a sampling, Michael Jordan, Henry Aaron, Walter Payton, Jack Nicklaus, John McEnroe, Wayne Gretzky, Carl Lewis and Peggy Fleming come into view as we erect posters of impact players on the walls of our mind. Such are the caliber of competitors for which pro scouts are combing the college campuses, and in some cases, even the outback of foreign countries.

"And though the achievements of these athletes don't mean squat in terms of eternal values–unless, of course they are done for God's glory–this concept, 'impact player,' warrants our contemplation as Christians.

"God wants to see us suit up for the game, not sit in the grandstands. But not just suit up–He wants to see us down in the mud, butting heads with the 'enemy,' making a difference in the final score.

"God wants to see us make a mark on our family, our neighborhood, our nation. Yes, even our world.

"God wants to see us leave a lingering fragrance of Him for the generations that follow us down the corridor of history. Agents of spiritual change, that's what He wants us to be. In brief, impact players!

"And should we allow His Spirit to make us people of impact, He is eager to reward us for the same. He will honor us at the *bema* seat of Christ. In fact, one way He wants to reward us is by giving us what Paul, in 1 Thessalonians 2:19, called the 'crown of exultation.' But who, in particular, qualifies for the Crown of Exultation? What kind of impact qualifies me for the Crown of Exultation? The question before us is, 'Who qualifies for the Crown of Exultation?' But we cannot answer it so quickly.

"To start with, we need to discover the significance of the term 'crown' itself, in particular the one referred to here by Paul. In the Greek culture of New Testament days, a crown was a wreath woven of oak leaves, ivy, parsley, myrtle, olive, violets, or of roses. These crowns were given to the victor in the Greek athletic games. For instance, the runner who was the first to cross the finish line, the competitor who hurled the discus the farthest, or the wrestler who conquered his opponent by pinning him to the mat, received a literal crown to wear on his head.

"Beyond the sports arena, crowns were given to servants of the state whose work deserved public notoriety. And finally, a crown was something worn at occasions such as wedding feasts. To sum up, historically speaking, a crown in New Testament times portrayed at least three things: victory, honor and an adornment of festive gladness.

"Now, with this backdrop, I believe it is possible to see all three of these meanings attached to the rewards God will dispense at the *bema* seat of Christ. That is, every reward will signify spiritual victory in the life of the recipient—victory over Satan and sin. Every reward given will be God's way of honoring honorable service for Him. And lastly, every reward received will be attended with unspeakable gladness for the privilege to have served the blessed Savior. Indeed, both the Lord and His servants will share a time of celebration around this heavenly tribunal.

"So, again, we ask, 'Who qualifies for this Crown of Exultation?' But, en route to discovering the full answer we must find out what is meant by the term 'exultation?'

"Basically, the word means 'to boast, to glory in something.'[1] For example, in the New Testament God tells us to boast in Him (e.g., Rom. 5:11), that is, we should recognize that He alone is our source of ultimate joy. We are also told to rejoice in trials, because they are designed to make us more like Him (e.g., Rom. 5:3). Our spiritual blessings in Christ should cause great exultation (e.g., James 1:9). And, other Christians are to be an occasion for our joy (see Ps. 16; 133; Rom. 16; Col. 4:7-15; 3 John 1-8).

"Let's now read 1 Thessalonians 2:19-20 and see which of these occasions for exultation fits best. Paul writes, 'For who is our hope or joy or crown of exultation? Is it not even you....?'[2] Then skip down to verse 20: 'for you are our glory and joy."[3] So, what is the cause for exultation here? The Christians at Thessalonica, right?

"But, who qualifies for the Crown of Exultation? There is yet one more question which, I promise you, will lead us to our desired destination. We're getting hot!

"The question is, 'Why does Paul call the Thessalonian believers his, Silvanus' and Timothy's Crown of Exultation?' What is the connection between these believers, these three men, and this crown? The answer is two-fold.

"First, these three men had befriended these people of Thessalonica and won them to Jesus. In chapter 1, verse 5, Paul declares, 'For our gospel did not come to you in word only, but also in power and in the Holy Spirit and with full conviction....' Chapter 2 and verse 13, then reports the response of these people to the gospel–'And for this reason,' says Paul, 'we also constantly thank God that when you received from us the word of God's message, you accepted it not as the word of men, but for what it really is, the word of God, which performs its work in you who believe.'

"So why does Paul call these saints his Crown of Exultation? In part, because he was their spiritual father. They were his spiritual children. But that's not all. Not only had he befriended these people to Christ, the Friend of sinners, but he had also brought them up to be like Christ. And how did he do that?

"Briefly, he did it the same way the Master mentored others: (1) The personal example of godliness, and (2) the proclamation of God's word. This process entailed both the demonstration and impartation of truth. You cannot have one without the other to be an effective disciple-maker. Of course, it would be amiss not to mention the element of intercessory prayer in this process, something Paul routinely practiced on behalf of the saints in Thessalonica, as 1:2-3 reveals.[4]

"Chapter 2, verses 10-12, make the issue clear: 'You are witnesses, and so is God, how devoutly and uprightly and blamelessly we behaved toward you believers; just as you know how we were exhorting and encouraging and imploring each one of you as a father would his own children, so that you may walk in a manner worthy of the God who calls you into His own kingdom and glory.'

"The evidence of God's impact on these people, via the disciple-making efforts of Paul and his friends, is obvious in chapter 1 where the apostle commends these believers for several things: For imitating Christ Himself, for being spiritual examples to others, and, according to verse 3, for their 'work of faith and labor of love and steadfastness of hope....'

"Now, let's try to put all this together. If Paul calls these saints, whom he had befriended to Christ and then brought up to be Christ-like, his Crown of Exultation, what is the criteria for receiving such a crown on judgment day? Who qualifies for the Crown of Exultation? Those who are faithful stewards of the Great Commission, right?

"The Great Commission. Let's review it, quickly: 'Go, therefore, and make disciples of all the nations,' Jesus commands, 'Baptizing them in the name of the Father, and of the Son, and of the Holy Spirit, teaching them to obey whatever I have commanded you; and behold, I am with you always, even to the end of the age' (Matt. 28:19-20).

"Is it not true that, in terms of our ministry to others, the Master has left us but two basic assignments: (1) Befriend sinners to the Friend of sinners; this is implied in our duty to make disciples (you can't make one until he's converted), and (2) Bring up the saints to be like the Savior. That's Matthew 28:19-20 in a nutshell. And that's precisely what Paul did in Thessalonica.

"But this is of no surprise; that's what Paul did on his first missionary journey in Europe. Paul's first point of spiritual impact there was Philipi. Subsequent to his church planting ministry in this small Roman colony, the apostle penned a warm-hearted letter from his prison cell. He wrote, 'Therefore, my beloved brethren, whom I long to see, my joy and crown, so stand firm in the Lord.' He had befriended them to Christ and brought them up to be like Christ. Like the Thessalonians, he regarded them as his crown.

"Paul took Christ's commission to make disciples seriously. This was his lifestyle wherever he sojourned. And such a lifestyle assured him of a Crown of Exultation when Christ returns at the Rapture to reward His church. Again, verse 19 says, 'For who is our hope or joy or crown of exultation? Is it not even you, in the presence of our Lord Jesus at His coming?'[5] Both congregations are referred to as his crown.[6] Therefore, both represent (1) the spiritual victory that every believer possesses in

Christ, (2) an occasion for Christ to honor Paul at the judgment seat, and (3) an occasion for unspeakable gladness.

"Who qualifies for the Crown of Exultation? Those who are faithful stewards of the Great Commission. As a way of life, such people befriend sinners to the Friend of sinners and bring up the saints to be like the Savior.

"While pastoring in Calgary, Alberta, Canada, I started a co-ed softball team in our church. One lady in our church had an unsaved husband named Mike. Mike wasn't interested in church, but he did agree to play softball with us. Through this weekly contact with Mike, I was able to cultivate a friendship. This led to squaring off against one another on the racquetball court each Tuesday evening.

"Prayers continued to ascend for Mike's salvation. And as they did, God's power began to fall. Mike, impressed by the life of Christ he saw in the members of our church softball team, started showing up on Sunday mornings. About a year later, Mike was sitting in the service as the Spirit of God began His marvelous work of regeneration. During my closing invitation, Mike received Christ as his personal Savior. We joined the angels in 'party-time' for Mike. What a day of gladness it was. But I didn't leave the 'party' saying, 'Well, Mike, I hope you do well in your new Christian life. See you around, brother.' I did not leave this new spiritual baby on the proverbial doorstep.

"No.

"In addition to feeding this precious, new sheep, via Sunday morning sermons and small group Bible Study, I ran errands with Mike, spent time together playing racquetball, and discussed how to live out his new life as a Christian. I was God's chosen vessel for spiritual impact. Mike has been baptized and continues to grow in Christ today. And one of these days, I will stand around Christ's heavenly throne with Mike at my side. He is my Crown of Exultation. Of course, a sincere love for God and for others is the all-consuming motive as we strive for the Crown of Exultation. As Paul told the saints at Corinth, '...though I have all faith, so that I could remove mountains, but have not love, I am nothing' (1 Cor. 13:2).

"Bill Otto, Dave Heaney, Joe Palmer, Darwin Cloud, Joan Martin, Travis Buckeye, Kim Harms, and Mike and Jeanette Parker are strangers to you, but each one holds a special place in my heart. These are a few of the people God has graciously impacted for eternity, using me to lead them to Christ and/or help them to grow in Christ.

"Whatever your vocation: Engineer, housewife, schoolteacher, student, plumber, pastor...ask God to help you see the real business of your life to be the Great Commission. Take time to befriend sinners to the Friend of sinners. Whether through sports, a sewing class, aerobics at a local gym, computers, etc., make contact with lost people with the prayerful intent of leading them to our precious, Savior, The Lord Jesus Christ. Remember: No contact equals no impact.

"In addition, find someone to be your 'Timothy,' or 'Tiffany,' someone you can bring up to be like the Savior. Teach them how to study Scripture, how to lead someone to Jesus, how to use their spiritual gift, how to keep in step with the Holy Spirit, and how to be a Christ-honoring employee and family member. And once the Great Commission becomes the Grand Devotion of your life—instead of the Great Omission of your life—you will be forever honored by Jesus. And the fruit of your spiritual impact will compose a more beautiful festal garland than ever graced the brow of any Greek athlete.

"You may never be able to fly through the air and dunk a basketball like the impact player, Michael Jordan, but you can be an impact player for Jesus. You may never wow the crowd with a towering homerun in the vintage of Henry Aaron, but you can be an impact player for Jesus. You may never possess the power and grace to outrun a host of clawing defenders like Walter Payton, but you can be an impact player for Jesus. You may never, ever, sink a birdie on the golf course—a feat Jack Nicklaus has done many times, but you can be an impact player for Jesus.

"And how do you become an impact player for Jesus? It's simple. Like Paul, get serious about the Great Commission: Take time to befriend sinners to the Friend of sinners, and bring up the saints to be like the Savior. And the eternal impact God makes through you will yield an everlasting reward called The Crown of Exultation."

During the closing prayer I resolved before God to lovingly pursue the conversion of my friend, John, at work. I also resolved to love him as a person, even if he never embraced Jesus as Lord and Savior. I had prayed for his salvation and been kind to him when opportunities arose, but I had never presented the good news of salvation through Jesus Christ to him. And, I had not spent time with him outside the workplace. I would find out what his interests were and seek occasions to deepen our friendship. As well, I could accelerate my intercessory prayers for his salvation, and even fast on behalf of his need for Christ. I realized my level of seriousness in befriending sinners to the Friend of sinners was quite low, though I did spend a good deal of time bringing up the saints to be like the Savior through my small group Bible study and spending time mentoring the young, male believers.

As our group slowly made its way to the parking lot, I discovered that I wasn't the only one whose lifestyle was less than evangelistic. Nina confessed that, though a believer for several years, she was not helping any other believers grow in their faith—the Great Commission was not the real business of her life.

With a spirit of contemplation evident among us, Didaskolos suggested we all make a commitment to pray for one another in these regards, something everyone was eager to do. But that wasn't all he said.

"What do you say we pair off and keep one another accountable, in a spirit of loving encouragement?" he asked. "You know, call one another, and pray for those we are befriending to the Friend of sinners. But not only should we storm heaven together on behalf of lost souls, but gently ask each other, 'Have you spent any time lately with your unsaved friend, or family member?' In Hebrews 10:24-25 we are told to 'consider how to stimulate one another to love and good works,' and this would certainly be one application of that."

This degree of loyalty to the Lord in evangelism was something we all needed, and having someone to whom we were each accountable was wise advice in view of the Hebrews 10 passage.

"Jim, would you dismiss us with a word of prayer, please?" Didaskolos asked.

"Dearest Lord," he began, "how we have been moved tonight by your Word in 1 Thessalonians 2. Each of us senses the need to aspire for the Crown of Exultation. The Great Commission is the assignment You have left us to do. I confess my lethargy, even my apathy toward lost souls around me who need the life-giving Bread You alone offer. We simply ask You to remind us of the day when we shall stand before you at the bema seat so that we will not be embarrassed for our lack of devotion to the Great Commission. Use each one of us to win many to You and help many to grow into Your likeness. Help us to live each day the way we will wish we had lived each day when we stand before You on that day! To this end we pray, in the beautiful name of Jesus. Amen."

Several endorsed Jim's fervent, sincere prayer with their own quiet, "Amen."

"Well, now you can see," said Didaskolos, "that not only does the Lord wish to grant us a hero's welcome for progressing in spiritual maturity, for practicing our Christian lives with Spirit-led motives, for persevering in the suffering God sends us, but also for persevering in a Spirit-led ministry. And to be sure, if we're ordering our lives by the Holy Spirit, He will prompt us to be about the business of heaven: Befriending sinners to the Friend of sinners and bringing up the saints to be like the Savior."

"But there is one final criteria for reward I'd like you to know about. So, if you wish, let's meet again next Wednesday evening; same time, same place, and discover that for which our gracious God wishes to honor us."

We couldn't wait.

But, as we drove out of the parking lot, we wouldn't forget how profoundly the Spirit of God, through His Word, and His preacher-servant, had moved us on this night—toward Spirit-led ministry in the lives of both sinners and saints in our circle of influence.

Endnotes for Chapter 7

[1] The Greek noun here is *kauchesis*, "the act of boasting." Vine, 268. It sometimes signifies a sinful boasting (James 4:16), but can also signify a "glorying" in that which God is proud of—as in Paul's boasting here regarding the converted saints at Thessalonica whose presence with Paul at the *bema* seat will represent "success and triumph and stimulate true exultation in the heart of the missionaries. It denotes the inward feeling of joy as well as its outward expression." D. Edmond Heibert, *The*

Thessalonian Epistles: A Call to Readiness (Chicago: Moody Press, 1971), 129. In 2 Corinthians 8:24, the same apostle longs for the occasion to glory in the generous heart of the saints at Corinth for their financial contribution to God's work.

[2] *For*–Translates *gar*, a subordinating conjunction indicating the reason Paul so desired to see these believers, a desire revealed in verse 17.

who–The Greek is *tis*, a pronominal interrogative form in the nominative case (introducing the subject), neuter, singular. As Heibert observes, "...*tis* may be rendered 'what' or 'who.' Because the three nouns are non-personal it is generally rendered 'what,' but since persons constitute the hope, joy and crown it would be better to render 'who' (Moffatt, Phillips, Berkeley, NASB)." Heibert, *Thessalonian*, 128-129.

is our–"Our" is *hemon*, a subjective genitive pronoun, first person plural (referring to Paul, Timothy and Silvanus), emphatically placed here.

hope–Translates *elpis*, nominative feminine singular; the term means "expectation, prospect." Bauer, Arndt and Gingrich, 252; here the Thessalonians being Paul's "object of hope"; the same emphasis is seen in other places such as Christ as our hope (Col.1:27) Bauer, Arndt and Gingrich, 252. Zodhiates adds that hope is the "desire of something good with expectation of obtaining it" (e.g., Acts 16:19; Rom. 5:4; Titus 1:2). Zodhiates, 1713.

or joy–*Chara* following the noun *elpis* and the coordinating conjunction *e*. *Chara*, from *chairo* ("to rejoice") means "joy." (cf. Matt. 2:10; 25:21; 1 Pet. 1:8). Here the Thessalonians are the "cause or matter of joy or rejoicing." Zodhiates, 1768. Heibert says, "'Our joy' looks forward to the joy and gladness Paul anticipates in that future day. They will be true objects of the missionaries' joy when their hopes for them are realized and the beloved converts are glorified with them on that day." Heibert, *Thessalonian*, 129.

or crown of exultation? Is it not even–An ascensive use of the *kai*.

you–The interrogative sentence contains the negative *ouchi*, a strengthened form of *ou* and implies a strong affirmative answer to this rhetorical question.

[3] *for*–The *gar* gives reason for the assertion of verse 19.

you–The nominative plural pronoun, *humeis*, is emphatic: "indeed it is really you who are our glory and our joy." Heibert, *Thessalonian*, 131.

are–The present tense in *este* confirms that the Thessalonian saints were even now Paul and his associates' joy, while the mention of Christ's future *parousia* shows that this same intense glorying over these believers will be present then as well, especially in view of the crown of reward seen in verse 19.

our–As well as showing the personal nature of future rewards, the personal pronoun, "our," "intensifies the glory or esteem in which the Thessalonian believers are held, while *joy* [emphasis mine] points to the inner feeling of delight which the missionaries have in them." Heibert, *Thessalonian*, 131.

glory–Doxa, parallel conceptually here with the concepts of *elpis*, *chara* and *kauchesis*, refers to the esteem these believers have in Paul's eyes. Bruce concurs and states that *doxa* here implies "that in which one takes pride" and cites similar uses in 1 Corinthians 11:7 where "the woman is the glory of the man" (or perhaps "a man's wife is his glory"), and possibly 2 Corinthians 8:23, where two messengers sent to Corinth with Titus are described as *doxa Christou*, "a credit to Christ" (or "men in whom Christ can take pride"). F. F. Bruce, *1 & 2 Thessalonians*, Word Biblical Commentary 45 (Waco, TX: Word Books, 1982), 57.

[4] This was typical of Paul's ministry (cf. Eph. 1:15-19; Phil. 1:9-11 and Col. 1:9-12).

[5] *of*–The genitive prepositional phrase "in the presence of" translates *emprosthen* which conveys the idea of being "before, in front of," used of "place or position only." Vine, 56. Similar uses are found in Matthew 6:1; Luke 19:27 and John 12:37.

our Lord Jesus at–The preposition *en* functions as a dative of location.

His–The *autou* is in the first attributive position modifying the dative feminine noun *parousia*.

coming–The term *parousia*, literally "a presence," can refer to the physical presence of a human (Phil. 2:12), the first stage in someone's appearing (2 Macc 8:12; 2 Cor. 7:6f; Phil. 1:26) and as a technical term for the coming of Christ and antichrist (the former represented here and the latter in 2 Thess. 2:9. Bauer, Arndt and Gingrich, 635. The word is a combination of two Greek words, *para*, (with) and *ousia* (being, from *eimi*, "to be") and denotes "both an 'arrival' and a consequent 'presence with.' The presence of Christ at the Rapture continues to be with His saints on into eternity." Vine, 111. In extrabiblical Greek we find references to a ruler's visit to a certain place. It may refer to "the moment of arrival to initiate a visit or it may focus on the stay initiated by the arrival. In the NT the word applies to the return of Jesus Christ. The various facets of this future visit are defined by the contexts in which *parousia* appears. In this instance it is Jesus' examination of his servants subsequent to his coming for them (4:15-17) that is in view." Robert L. Thomas, "1 Thessalonians," in *The Expositor's Bible Commentary*, ed. by Frank E. Gaebelein (Grand Rapids: Zondervan Publishing House, 1984), 11:262.

[6] The same idea is seen in respect to Paul's ministry and relationship with the Corinthians and Philippians (cf. 2 Cor. 1:14 and Phil. 2:16).

8

You Mean God Is Grading *My* Sermons?

> Behold, how good and how pleasant it is for brothers to dwell together in unity! It is like precious oil upon the head, down upon the beard, even Aaron's beard, coming down upon the edge of his robes. It is like the dew of Hermon coming down upon the mountains of Zion; for there the Lord commanded the blessing–life forever.

These words from Psalm 133 ran through my head as we again gathered at the home of our teacher, Didaskolos. The precious and sanctifying nature of our bond as Christians, symbolized by the oil of priestly consecration mentioned in the psalm, and the spiritual refreshment signified by the mountain dew, were realities we embraced as we contemplated another evening of life-changing study together.

When everyone had arrived, Didaskolos began by saying, "You'll recall from the sermon we heard last week at my church that God will grant a hero's welcome for those who practice a Spirit-led ministry. And that entails, at least essentially, what two areas of focus?"

"Befriending sinners to the Friend of sinners and bringing up the saints to be like the Savior," said Nina without hesitation.

"That's right, sister," Didaskolos said affirmingly.

"And could I add," Nina continued, "that the accountability we agreed upon has been like a good old cattle prod in motivating me toward love and good works, namely, to practice a Great commission-lifestyle. This past week, after Janet called me and prayed with me concerning a couple of my co-workers, I had the opportunity the next day, over lunch, to share the sweet news of Jesus' offer of salvation with the very ones we prayed for. I'm following up now with fervent intercession, fasting once a week, and plan to invite them over for a barbecue next Friday for more conversation."

"But that's not all," said Nina. "I also signed up to teach the Jr. High Sunday School class at church to help disciple the young believers God has given us. I'm a little nervous about all this, but God is giving me incredible courage."

"Fantastic," said Jim.

"That's wonderful news," I chimed in.

"We all rejoice with you, sister," said Didaskolos, "and will uphold your on-going efforts with prayer, even as Moses prayed for Joshua and the Israelites as they battled the Amalekites (cf. Ex. 17). This is the kind of permanent spiritual change God makes in our lives as we obey His word by the power of the indwelling Holy Spirit, that marvelous person of the Godhead who energizes us for ministry.

"Now then, just before we leave this principle of rewards for Spirit-led ministry, let me say briefly that our speaker did not have time to address a particular crown revealed in 1 Peter 5:4, the Crown of Glory, though this crown is certainly related to our ministry for the Lord. But in the truest sense of the word, this crown is reserved for a special group we often call pastors, though the biblical term is a function, not an office (cf. Eph. 4:11-16). There's not time to examine this crown tonight, but I have copied a handout of a study I once made of 1 Peter 5:1-4 for your interest. Please pick one up in the foyer as you go home."[1]

I had spent some time in the pastorate myself and looked forward to seeing what this Crown of Glory was all about.

After a brief opening prayer, Didaskolos began our study, as he often would, with an anecdote he'd read somewhere:

> For 131 years one of the world's richest treasures—perhaps a billion dollars in fine gold—lay lost and out of reach in the frigid, lightless depths of the Atlantic, entombed in the wreck of a once elegant 19th century steamer, the S.S. Central America. As the side-wheeler sank in a monstrous hurricane off the Carolina coast in September 1857, hundreds of California gold miners slipped into the sea alongside their fortunes. Shortly after the news reached bankers in New York, who were anxiously awaiting a fresh shipment of gold, the recession of 1857 became the Panic of 1857, a financial crisis that helped set the stage for the Civil War. Until recently, the riches of the Central America lay far beyond the grasp of man or machine—8,000 feet below the surface. Then in 1985 an unlikely trio from Ohio—a research engineer, a geologist and a journalist—began a cautious but brilliant search for the ship, using cutting-edge technology and a revolutionary undersea robot. In October their research vessel docked in Jacksonville, Fla., having recovered enough gold to make

everyone involved fabulously rich.[2]

Then Didaskalos transitioned to true riches when he said, "While there's nothing inherently wrong with going for the gold of earthly riches, make sure you're going for the gold of heavenly riches—rewards at the bema seat of Christ. For as God tells us in 1 Corinthians 3:11-15, '...no man can lay a foundation other than the one which is laid, which is Jesus Christ. Now if any man builds on the foundation with gold, silver, precious stones, wood, hay, straw, each man's work will be evident; for the day will show it because it is to be revealed with fire, and the fire itself will test the quality of each man's work. If any man's work which he has built on it remains, he will receive a reward. If any man's work is burned up, he will suffer loss; but he himself will be saved, yet so as through fire.'"

"Go for the gold my brothers and sisters. Not for the gold this earth yields—at least that should not be your obsession—but for heaven's gold. Let that be your pursuit, not for the reward itself, but for the honor it will bring to Jesus to have lived an honorable life.

"Paul's instruction to the saints at Corinth, here in chapter 3 of his first letter, is, no doubt, the most familiar passage on the bema seat of Christ. But what exactly is the context of these words, and what is the criteria for reward here? That's the quest of this evening. And though I could try and lead you through the territory before us, I have decided instead to bring a guest speaker by way of cassette tape. This man's voice you will immediately recognize. It belongs to Dr. Chuck Emert, the dear brother we listened to at my church last week.[3] He has done a series of messages on the *bema* seat of Christ, and they are now in wide circulation. So, take some good notes, jot down any questions that come to mind along the way, and once the message ends, we'll have some discussion.

"Anyone wish to get a refill on tea or juice before we press 'Play?'"

I got up, walked briskly to the kitchen and placed my eager paws around some molasses-raisin cookies, fresh and still warm from the oven. Didaskolos remembered my fondness for this treat and never failed to make them for me. I was again reminded of the sensitive, loving man God had allowed us to learn from, by his exhortation to be sure, but much more by his example. Everyone was a bit amused to see me return with more of my favorite dessert.

With everyone completely content, Didaskolos started the tape.

"There was chaos in Corinth!

"Disunity had erupted in the church due to exalting the messenger instead of the Message; the servant instead of the Master. According to 1 Corinthians 1:12, some were saying, 'I am of Paul'; another, 'I am of Apollos'; another, 'I follow Cephas'; and still another, 'I follow Christ.' But what's more, these carnal Christians placed too much emphasis on human wisdom, as 1:18-2:5 reveals. Therefore, they needed a lesson on the primacy of God's wisdom disclosed through the agency of the Holy Spirit—a wisdom taught by the Spirit and received by those who are spiritual.[4] And here's precisely where the root of the Corinthians' problems lie.

"In one word, they were not spiritual, they were carnal!

"If one spent a week with these saints, he might leave with this question in mind, 'Are these folks really Christians?' Yet as the apostle Paul commences his first letter to these people, he says, 'to the church of God in Corinth, to those sanctified in Christ Jesus...' (cf. 1:2).

"Though positionally 'in Christ,' practically, they were worldly. In fact, as Paul starts chapter 3, he says, 'Brothers, I could not address you as spiritual[5] but as worldly—mere infants in Christ' (3:1, NIV).[6] Believers? Indeed. Mature believers? No way!

"That Paul calls them 'worldly'[7] means that their style of living was ruled by the promptings of indwelling sin,[8] an outlook on life dominated by selfishness and independence from God's Spirit. And of the many proofs of the carnal flavor of their Christianity were the divisions among them. This induces Paul to fire the stinging, rhetorical question, 'Are you not acting like mere men?' words which expose their worldly disposition. But he doesn't stop there. On the heels of his exhortations to spiritual maturity in 3:1-4, in 3:5-9, he explains who these leaders of the church truly are. It is a perspective the Corinthians desperately need!

"In verses 5-6, he quizzes, 'What, after all is Apollos? And what is Paul? Only servants,[9] through whom you came to believe—as the Lord has assigned to each his task.[10] I planted[11] the seed, Apollos watered it,[12] but God made it grow.'[13] Now then, let's pause for a moment and extract an important principle from these two verses, namely: Evangelism is a partnership between God and His people. And this partnership entails two perspectives.

"First, there is the God-ward side as God 'assigns each to his task,' and causes 'the work done to grow.' Then second, the man-ward side is to plant and water, figurative expressions for preaching the gospel, as 2:1-5 unveils. Thus, notice what Paul says of himself and Apollos: We are only 'servants through[14] whom you believed.'[15] Once again, evangelism is a partnership between God and His people.

"A second vital truth emerges from verse 7: The fruits of evangelism exalt God, not His servants. The inferential conjunction 'so,' which begins the verse shows that since God makes the work of His evangelists grow, 'neither he who plants nor he who waters is anything, but only God, who makes things grow.'[16] The carnal Christians at Corinth were exalting

God's servants, not God. Paul sought to correct their misguided viewpoint.

"A third reality surfaces in verse 8: God rewards His servants for their faithful labor. Paul continues, 'The man who plants and the man who waters have one purpose,[17] and each will be rewarded[18] according to his own labor.'

"God rewards faithful endeavors to win people to His Son; and these rewards are dispensed individually. The term 'each'[19] confirms this, a truth precisely illustrated by two individuals, Paul and Apollos, each of whom did their assigned task from God of planting and watering. Also noteworthy in this regard are the emphatic words 'his own reward.' The term 'own' translates *idion*[20] and highlights the personal nature of God's rewards.

"Verse 8 also discloses two other truths. First, note the future timing of God's disbursement of rewards: 'each one *will* [emphasis mine] be rewarded....' And what is this future time? Chapter 4, verse 5, says the time of reward is juxtaposed with the return of Christ at the Rapture. And, as a final observation, please observe that the basis for rewards is, in part, God's justice: 'each will be rewarded *according to his own labor* [emphasis mine].' Surely, these rewards issue from God's gracious heart. He does not have to reward anybody. But once He decided to honor honorable service, that is, service done by the power of the Spirit, as chapter 2 instructs, and service done for His glory, as 10:31 mandates, His standard is grounded in fairness. To say it another way, the Christian life is a stewardship of various responsibilities, as we'll see later in chapter 4, including the duty to evangelize unbelievers as Paul and Apollos did. And he who discharges his assignments faithfully will be justly recompensed, which is the precise meaning of the term rendered 'reward' here.

"Having established, then, the reality of rewards in verse 8, Paul explains the reason for rewards in verse 9: 'For[21] we are God's fellow workers; you are God's field,[22] God's building.' Since we work with God in this partnership and with His servants as fellow workers—'he who plants and he who waters are one'—God will not let our labor go unnoticed, much less unrewarded. As the writer to the Hebrews penned, 'God is not unjust; He will not forget your work and the love you have shown Him as you have helped His people and continue to help them' (see Heb. 6:10). The word 'unjust' means doing contrary to what is right,[23] and is used elsewhere of unjust judges of the pagan world (cf. 1 Cor. 6:1). God is certainly unlike such unfair, dishonest and untrustworthy judges, a fact explained by the phrase, 'He will not forget your work...and love.'[24]

"Now then, it is important to pay attention to the continued agricultural metaphor employed by Paul in verse 9: 'you are God's field,' an allusion to 'I planted...Apollos watered...God made it grow,' in verse 6. But the metaphor changes in the last part of verse 9: 'you are God's building.' Most likely this clever switch in figures is culturally linked to the many temples and buildings in Corinth. Furthermore, this alteration in metaphors is significant in that it serves to introduce Paul's point in verses 10-15 concerning the *bema* seat of Christ—an event all Christians should be serious about, but especially carnal Christians like those at Corinth! For at this event Jesus will pass out the rewards spoken of above. There will be rewards for those who are spiritual, but a forfeiting of rewards for those who are carnal. In particular, verses 10-15 discuss the divine resources for spiritual labor, the nature of spiritual labor and the rewards for spiritual labor. Let's view them in that order.

"In verse 10, the apostle manifests the divine resources for spiritual labor. He says, 'By the grace God has given me, I laid[25] a foundation as an expert builder, and someone else is building on it. But each one should be careful how he builds.' The building metaphor, introduced in verse 9c, is now extended. And Paul is keenly aware of the means by which he, as a wise master builder,[26] laid a foundation[27] in Corinth. It was by God's grace, here not a reference to the undeserved mercy God bestows upon the sinner (the kind of grace spoken of in Eph. 2:8-9), but to God's enabling power imparted to His servants to do their assigned tasks, per verse 5.[28] But what foundation did he lay?

"This figurative expression references his joint efforts with Apollos in winning the Corinthians to Christ, as verse 5 says. Of course, laying this foundation meant preaching Christ crucified as seen in 2:1-5; in fact, Paul says in verse 12, 'no one can lay any foundation other[29] than the one already laid, which is Jesus Christ.' In brief, Paul preached the glad news about Christ to the Corinthians, and they believed the message.[30] And this he did, not only by God's grace, but as well by God's wisdom (cf. 1:18-2:5).

"In this regard, he calls himself a 'wise master builder' in verse 10, an indirect rebuke, perhaps, to the carnal Corinthians' emphasis on embracing the human wisdom of their day and their subtle rejection of God's wisdom.

"But now someone else was building[31] upon the foundation Paul had laid, once and for all. And due to the sacred and true nature of this foundation laid—Jesus Christ Himself in the hearts of the Corinthians—and due to the coming judgment of rewards, referenced in verses 12-15..., 'each one' (who is building) must be careful how he builds,' as verse 10c says. The words 'each one'[32] remind the reader of the aforementioned reality that God's rewards are individually dispensed. Each believer is accountable to God for how he has labored. But what is the criteria for acceptable labor? What kind of labor is worthy of reward? And which kind is not? Such questions are answered in verses 12-15.

"First, the context around these verses shows that those Paul exhorts to 'be careful' here are actively building on the foundation of faith in Jesus Christ. What's more, the context also emphasizes teaching God's truth, as 4:1-2, 15-17 make evident. It seems safe to say, then, that Paul's definitive focus is on those teaching God's word to the saints in Corinth. Each teacher's message is being evaluated to see if it represents gold, silver and costly stones, metaphors for that which is valuable and enduring in God's eyes, namely sound doctrine about Jesus Christ..., or, wood, hay and straw, metaphors for that which is worthless and of no lasting value, namely, false doctrine.[33]

"Further comparison, in light of Paul's previous words in chapters 1 and 2, would lead us to conclude that 'gold, silver and precious stones service' most certainly entails the qualitative labor that only the Holy Spirit can produce through us. Again, 2:1-5 illustrates this kind of labor in Paul's ministry to the Corinthians. The apostle's discussion about receiving the Spirit at conversion, the subsequent understanding of what God has given us (2:12), and then teaching God's wisdom as you are 'taught by the Spirit' (v. 13), correlates perfectly with the labor of 'gold, silver and stone' quality."

"By stark contrast, wood, hay and straw would signify low quality labor, that which is done in the flesh—things such as false doctrine, ministering with impure motives[34] and in general any service to others not done in the power of the Spirit. Culturally, the Corinthians knew that costly stones, such as marble and granite, were used to erect strong, quality buildings such as palaces, and straw as building material for thatched roofs of low quality such as mud huts.

"Verse 13 then continues the thought of verse 12: 'his work will be shown for what it is,[35] because[36] the Day will bring to light.' These words teach us that this judgment will occur on a well-known day since the noun 'Day' has the definite article preceding it. But what day is in view? I

Corinthians 4:5 has the answer: 'Therefore, judge nothing before the appointed time; wait till the Lord comes. He will bring to light what is hidden in darkness and will expose the motives of men's hearts. At that time each will receive his praise from God.'

"It is obvious that both passages have the same event in mind. Given this fact, 'the Day' spoken of here in verse 13 is clarified in 4:5 as Christ's coming at the Rapture (see 1 Thess. 4:13-18). And on that day each man's work will be brought to light, that is, manifested[37] in its true character. Has it been done in the energy of the flesh, a hollow religiosity? Or, in the power of the Holy Spirit, the actual work of God in, through and for men? And according to the end of verse 13, the reason it will be so clearly manifest is that 'with fire[38] it will be revealed, and the fire will test the quality of each man's work.'[39]

"'Fire' symbolizes the thorough examination by the omniscient Christ, who, according to 1 Corinthians 4:5, will even take into account the very motives in the believer's heart—He will not only judge what we do, but also why we do it! Note too, the word 'quality' here which translates a term that was used of testing metal for genuine character.[40] Once put through the fire, the metal was found to be approved or disapproved.

"So also, Christ will examine the messages we preach, the Bible studies and counsel we give, and see if it rightly divides His truth, in the spirit of 2 Timothy 2:15. If it does, we will individually be approved for reward as verse 14 promises: 'If[41] any man's work which he has built upon it remains,[42] he shall receive a reward.'[43] Such sound teaching is done in the power of the Spirit (cf. 1 Cor. 2:1-5), honors the Lord who gave it by the same Spirit (cf. 1 Cor. 2:6-16), and is, therefore, of great worth and enduring quality—like gold, silver and costly stones!

"But not every believer will be found faithful to those things 'taught by the Spirit' (cf. 1 Cor. 2:13). They will see their messages and counsel go up in smoke, as verse 14 declares: 'If any man's work is burned up,[44] he shall suffer loss; but he himself shall be saved, yet so as through fire.'

"The verb 'burned up' has the idea of total consumption by fire. But note that the unrewarded work is not to be confused with the eternal security of the worker! True, the errant teacher of God's Word will suffer loss of potential reward,[45] but he himself[46] shall be saved.[47] True, his teaching will be non-durable like wood, hay and straw, but his salvation is as stable and secure as the Christ who gave it. This fact is further confirmed by the last phrase of verse 15: 'yet so as through fire.' The idea here is that of a man who 'dashes through the flames safe, but with the smell of fire still upon him.'[48] In the words of Thomas Schreiner and Ardel Caneday, "some will be saved that have done shoddy work."[49]

"As we arrive at verses 16-17, Paul continues his warning to those whose teaching is not reflective of the careful master builder of verse 10. First, he asks the rhetorical question, 'Do you not know that you (plural, referring to the church at Corinth) are a temple of God, and that the Spirit of God dwells in you?' The answer expected is 'Yes, this is a fact.'[50] The Corinthians had received the Spirit, according to 2:12, and needed to know that as part of God's people, they were the special dwelling place of the Spirit. This aspect of their position in Christ is a continuous reality as signified by the present tense in the verb 'you are' (*este*).

"The noun 'temple' sustains the building metaphor and denotes the idea of an inward shrine or sanctuary. Used forty-six times in the New Testament, it sometimes refers to the temple in Jerusalem and the holy of holies. God's people are now God's holy of holies. The Spirit's indwelling presence makes us sacred—we are the 'house of the Lord.' This reveals Paul's high view of the church and sets the stage for the polemical words of verse 17: 'If any man destroys the temple of God, God will destroy him, for[51] the temple of God is holy,[52] and that is what you are.'

"In context, this loud siren-like warning has to be addressed to those whose work as teachers was akin to wood, hay and straw. Observe the parallel phrase that begins verse 17 and verses 14-15: 'If any man....' The term 'destroys' (*phtheirei*) here in verse 17 is employed in 1 Corinthians 15:33 of bad company destroying, or corrupting, good morals. In his second letter to these same believers, the apostle asks them to make room for him in their hearts, for he had wronged no one, corrupted no one, nor taken advantage of anyone (see 2 Cor. 7:2). Elsewhere, the term speaks of the old self being corrupted with deceit (Eph. 4:22), the harlot of Revelation 18 corrupting the earth with her immorality, and in Jude 18 it speaks of the eternal destruction of the ungodly.

"So what is Paul's use of the term here? True to the context, the apostle is affirming that anyone who causes the collapse of a local church is subject to the severe discipline of God.[53] It's worth noting that the verb 'destroy,' found twice in this sentence–once of the effects of the errant teacher and once of God's chastisement toward such a teacher–is actually juxtaposed in the Greek sentence.

"But what is the exact content of this corrupt teaching that threatens to destroy God's church in Corinth? Most assuredly, it includes the divisive ideas of making celebrities of Christian leaders, noted in chapter 1. Beyond this, the letter on the whole addresses such issues as worldly wisdom so highly prized by the Corinthians (cf. 1:18-30), misunderstandings about the Spirit's ministry (cf. 2:1-16), and God's servants (cf. 3:1-4:21; ch. 9), immorality (ch. 5; 6:12-20), litigation in pagan courts (see 6:1-11), marriage and divorce issues (ch. 7), matters regarding the proper use of Christian liberty (chs. 8 and 10), the role of women in worship and abuses of the Lord's Supper (ch. 11), and the doctrine of the resurrection (ch. 15).

"To sum up, a myriad of incorrect beliefs and eye-popping practices were alive and well, spreading through the body like a malignant cancer. And errant teachers were the ones responsible for such false doctrine. Paul, therefore, informs the saints of the *bema* seat of Christ (1) to lend encouragement to those who, as careful master builders, were building up the church by speaking those things 'taught by the Spirit' and (2) to give firm admonition to those whose teaching was as worthless as wood, hay and straw, which cannot survive the test of fire, and was consequently destroying the stability of the church.

"In the final verses of the chapter, verses 18-23, these destructive teachers in Corinth are exhorted to embrace God's wisdom. This would make them wise master builders (compare vv. 18-20 with 2:6-3:10) and embrace the right perspective on God's servants, Paul, Apollos, and Cephas (see vv. 21-23). And it is this need for divine viewpoint that propels the apostle into his discussion in chapter 4 regarding the faithfulness required of those who proclaim the mysteries of God's truth; for the Master Teacher continually examines them[54] and will reward them fairly at the *bema* seat in accordance with His absolute knowledge of not only their message, and its content, but also their very motives.[55]

"Contemplate the sobering reality that God is listening to your sermons, your biblical advice on the telephone or in a letter, and your outline and interpretation of Scripture as you lead the home Bible study or Sunday School class. As James 3:1-12 affirms, those who teach will incur a stricter judgment due to the profound influence of the tongue. But don't let this intimidate you, rather let it inspire and invigorate you to heed the words of 2 Timothy 2:15, 'Do your best to present yourself to God as one approved, a workman who does not need to be ashamed and who correctly handles the word of truth.' Then when you stand before Jesus at the bema seat, you will receive a hero's welcome for teaching His word accurately–after all, such teaching is as good as gold!"

I had never heard this passage taught in such detail, and though some of it, due to its technical nature, left me a bit overwhelmed in trying to assimilate all the information, there was no missing the big idea: God was listening to my sermons and giving me a grade. I reflected on a recent message where I had taken a verse out of context and led some people to believe that if we would just lift Jesus up, that is, exalt Him before others, He would draw all men to Himself. The text was John 12:32. Someone showed me after the sermon that verse 33 defined this 'lifting up' as the means by which He would die, namely, the cross. I felt embarrassed for my lack of diligence and care in handling the Scriptures.

As we opened the discussion, I found I was not the only one who felt that more than a few of our Bible messages and counsel would be burned up in the fires of Christ's omniscient judgment.

Jim said, "Without knowing the law of context, I failed to see the authorial intention behind Matthew 18:20: 'For where two or three have gathered together in My Name, I am there in the midst of them.' Often, people quote this verse when only a few show up for prayer time. But, the context of Matthew 18 regards church discipline. Verse 20 simply promises Jesus' guiding, supportive presence when two, or three, members of His church prayerfully gather to confront and restore another saint who needs to repent of sin."

"I recall," said Alfred, "teaching that Jesus and His church were pictured in *The Song of Solomon*, you know, an allegorical interpretation of that book of the Bible. Someone then showed me Ephesians 3 which teaches that the church was a mystery in the Old Testament and that *The*

Song of Solomon is meant to be taken literally as a love story between Solomon and the Shulammite woman. It reveals God's wisdom for courtship, the sexual relationship between a married couple, and even how to work through marital conflict. I looked at the book differently once I understood this literal approach. I also formerly used Revelation 3:20 to urge non-Christians to invite Jesus into their hearts. Then, my pastor showed me that, in context, Jesus is inviting lukewarm Christians to restore their intimate friendship with Him. Even the idea of 'inviting Jesus into your heart' is not a biblical concept. He indwells us as a result of conversion, not as a condition for conversion (see Col. 1:27)."

Others confessed how they had once taught that a believer could lose his salvation through patterns of disobedience, when in reality, what is lost is close friendship with God and rewards at the *bema* seat.

"Salvation," said Nina, "is a gift and cannot be earned through our obedience. Jesus' work of redemption paid the price of our sins in full. We can add nothing to it. As Jesus cried out on the cross, 'It is finished!' Righteousness is God's gift to the one who doesn't work for his salvation (see Rom. 4:5), but simply believes that Jesus is God in human form and trusts Him alone to forgive his sin and grant eternal life (see Acts 10:43). And since it is the very eternal life of God granted to the believing sinner, it cannot be lost. My motivation for serving Christ changed once I realized that salvation, by nature, is totally by grace. I now serve Him out of gratitude, not out of fear I may lose my salvation via too much sin in my life. And this study on the *bema* seat provides even more motivation to serve Him well. For He is altogether worthy of my living a life worthy of reward."

Before we closed the meeting, Didaskolos gave an amusing illustration, but one that drove home the point of the evening even deeper:

> It was late at night but Leroy Shively couldn't sleep. He was in Chicago for a convention, and across the street from his hotel a new building was being constructed. At the moment, workers were laying the foundation in the half-block-sized hole. Gigantic forms had been laid. Cement truck after cement truck wheeled in, waited in line, dumped its load, and drove off for another load. Workers had begun at dawn and were still going strong.
>
> "As he was tossing and turning, Leroy wondered what was going to be built on that foundation. It surely had to be a skyscraper. Then he thought, 'Wouldn't it be funny to come back in a year and find a hot dog stand on all that concrete!'
>
> "Strong foundations aren't intended for small buildings. The same is true in the Christian life. Jesus Christ is the solid foundation on which we must build our lives, as we learned tonight. But what are we building on that foundation? Is it a palace worthy of Him, built of gold, silver and gemstones of Spirit-generated good works and the sound teachings of our faith? Or is it a shabby little structure of the sticks and straw of legalistic works? Careless, yes, even destructive interpretations of His Word? Activities and words generated by the flesh?
>
> "A solid foundation gives a building strength; the right materials give it lasting value. 'Lord, help me to build my life into something that is worthy of the foundation on which it stands.'[56]

In my heart, I echoed this same prayer to my precious Savior. I'm sure others did the same.

A Hero's Welcome

"So there you have it," said Didaskolos. "At the *bema* seat, the criteria for being rewarded with a hero's welcome will at least be our progression in spiritual maturity, practicing our Christian lives with Spirit-led motives, persevering in God-sent suffering, practicing a Spirit-led ministry and finally, proclaiming a sound message. Jesus will grant a hero's welcome for those of His followers, who by the power of the Holy Spirit, pursue these heavenly values. For those who do not, lazily going through life in the flesh, theirs will be an embarrassing experience when they stand before Him to receive their final report card—rewards forfeited. As John warned his Christian readers, 'And now, little children, abide in Him, that when He appears, we may have confidence and not be ashamed before Him at His coming' (see 1 John 2:28). And again, 'Look to yourselves, that we do not lose those things we worked for, but that we may receive a full reward' (see 2 John 8). Salvation is free, paid for by the crucified, risen Lord Jesus Christ. Rewards are earned by perseverance in sound living and sound teaching.

"The question that now begs answering is: What is the content of the rewards God grants us on that day and into eternity? We have been diligent to consider the criteria, but what will these rewards consist of? What will be the nature of a hero's welcome? In next week's lesson, we will begin our search."

Next week couldn't come soon enough. But in the interim I needed to carefully prepare my small group Bible study for the coming weekend—like a wise master builder, handling accurately the word of truth.

Endnotes for Chapter 8

[1] See Appendix B: 1 Peter 5:1-4.

[2] Tim Noonan, "The Greatest Treasure Ever Found: Gold," *Life*, March 1992,

32.

[3] Dr. Charles Emert serves as the Vice Chancellor for Southern California Seminary. He taught Bible at Christian Heritage College (El Cajon, CA, now called San Diego Christian College), Baptist Bible College (Clark's Summit, PA), and Southern California Seminary (El Cajon, CA) and with his wife, Loretta, was a missionary in Romania, Albania and Russia.

[4] See 1 Corinthians 2:6-16, especially verses 15-16.

[5] According to Mare, "The adjective *pneumatikos* applies to believers who are spiritually mature Christians–i.e., those led into maturity by the Spirit in contrast with the immature ones still controlled by the fleshly prejudices and viewpoints dominating the unsaved of the world." W. Harold Mare, "I Corinthians," *The Expositor's Bible Commentary* (Grand Rapids: Zondervan Publishing House, 1984), 10:205. This is what the Corinthians, though saved, were not.

[6] This version (NIV) is used throughout this passage in 1 Corinthians 3. To be a babe in Christ is not wrong, unless spiritual infancy is prolonged (cf. 1 Cor. 14:20; Heb. 5:11-14).

[7] The Greek term is *sarkinois*. "It is not wrong to be *sarkinos*, for we all live in the flesh (*en sarki*, Gal. 2:20), but we are not to live according to the flesh (*kata sarka*, Rom. 8:12)." Robertson, 4:92.

[8] See Romans 7:15-25, where the struggle between the new nature the Christian receives at conversion (implied) and indwelling sin is manifest.

[9] The term translates *diakonoi*, from *dia* and *konis*, "raising dust by hastening." John 2:5 employs the term to describe the waiter at the wedding at Cana. Spiritually, Paul refers to himself as a "servant" in Colossians 1:23, 25; and the technical sense of "deacon" comes later in Philippians 1:1; 1 Timothy 3:8, 12. Paul leaves out the verb here: "Servants ("only servants," NIV) through whom you believed," showing that that's all they were, nothing more, nothing less. No Christian should be idolized, but regarded for simply what he is, a servant of God. Yet, too often in today's Christian sub-culture, one feels uncomfortable calling some significant Bible teacher, or missionary statesman, by his first name. We feel obligated to address them according to title or degree: "Excuse me, Dr. ——, I was wondering if you could answer this question...." Have we forgotten we are brothers and sisters in the same forever family?

[10] No servant of God has any basis for pride or conceit, since God sovereignly and graciously extends occasions and assignments for ministry. Paul retained this humble and dependent perspective throughout his ministry even as Colossians 4:3 requests, "And pray for us, too, that God may open a door for our message, so that we may proclaim the mystery of Christ, for which I am in chains."

[11] *Pheuton* could be taken as a constative aorist, or perhaps a consummative sense fits even better.

[12] Apollos "irrigated" the church, as seen in Acts 18:24-19:1.

[13] The imperfect verb, *euxamen*, stresses the continuing blessings of God in the past upon the work of Paul and Apollos' in Corinth.

[14] *Dia*, a preposition of means, here in the genitive.

[15] The ingressive aorist here signifies the act of becoming a believer.

[16] Present participle with a causative active nuance, "The one causing things to grow." This understanding of the active voice separates Christianity from the errant doctrine of Mormonism which views God as ever increasing in His development as a being.

[17] Literally, "are one," the neuter indicating that their aim and result are identical; they work in harmony, not in competition. C. K. Barrett, *A Commentary on the First Epistle to the Corinthians* (London: Adam and Charles Black, 1968), quoted in Rienecker, 394. It is also striking to note Paul's use of the neuter here in connection with the neuter interrogative *ti* in verse 5: "what is Apollos or Paul...?" and the neuter indefinite *ti* in verse 7: "neither is anything the one who plants nor the one who waters...."

[18] This is *misthos*.

[19] *Ekastos*, singular pronominal adjective modifying the previous singular substantival participles, *phuteuon* and *potizon*.

[20] Attributive adjective, modifying *misthon*.

[21] The *gar* introduces the reason for the previous affirmations regarding rewards.

[22] The background here is the farming going on in the plain below the city of Corinth. "There the land was plowed, the crops reaped, the grapevines tended, and the grapes gathered–a crop 'for which Corinth has for centuries been famous (our word 'currant' is a medieval corruption for Corinth).' (Broneer, "Corinth," B A, Vol SIV 1951, p.96)." Mare, "1 Corinthians," *Expositor's*, 10:206.

[23] See Bauer, Arndt and Gingrich, 18; regarding *adikos*.

[24] The term forget is *epilathesthai*, an aorist infinitive functioning epexegetically here to explain the contents or nature of *adikos*.

[25] The *etheka* is the correct reading, not the perfect *tetheika*. Robertson, 4:95.

[26] *Architekton*, skilled craftsman. Robertson states, "This is the only New Testament example of the old and common word *architekton*, our architect. *Tekton* is from *tikto*, to beget, and means a begetter, then a worker in wood or stone, a carpenter or mason (Matt. 13:55; Mark 6:3).... *Architekton* occurs in the papyri and inscriptions in an even wider sense than our use of architect, sometimes of the chief engineers. But Paul means to claim primacy as pastor of the church in Corinth as is true of every pastor who is the architect of the whole church life and work. All the workmen...work under the direction of the architect (Plato, *Statesman*, 259)." Robertson, 4:95.

[27] Of course, much depends upon the wisdom and expertise of the architect in the laying of the crucial foundation of any structure. By sharp contrast, the foolish builder of Luke 6:49 is condemned for building his house on the ground without a foundation (*themeliou*, the same term Paul uses here).

[28] See also 1 Corinthians 15:10 for this same semantic value of *charis*.

[29] The adjective *allon* is masculine here because it refers to Christ. There is no room for anyone but Jesus on the platform of salvation–not Buddha, Mohammed, Krishna, New Age philosophy, Joseph Smith, nor anyone else, nor any other ideology. All believers, according to 1 Peter 2:5, are living stones in God's temple, but there is only one foundation: Jesus Christ.

[30] This is the message of the cross; cf. 1:18; 2:2.

[31] The present tense of *epiokodomei* denotes the continual activity of spiritual input into these saints at Corinth, in contrast to the aoristic action of *etheka* on Paul's part; regarding the latter, a culminative or perfective nuance is suggested.

[32] Again, *ekastos* is used.

[33] The building materials of the day were temples made from gold and other valuable metals, but in stark contrast there were frames of ordinary houses built of wood. In the latter, the walls were constructed with hay or dried-grass, mixed with mud, and the roofs created with straw or stalks. The imagery Paul selects would easily communicate the idea of pure doctrine versus the kind of insipid teaching symbolized by the lesser materials, material which would not endure the fire of God's judgment at the *bema* seat.

[34] Cf. 1 Corinthians 4:5 in this regard.

[35] The phrase what it is renders the adjective *phaneron*, "to make visible," modifying to *ergon*.

[36] The causal clause introduced by the *hoti*.

[37] *Phaneroo* is found in both 1 Corinthians 3:13 and 4:5, linking the two passages.

[38] The prepositional phrase with fire is *en pur*, a dative of instrumentality.

[39] Elsewhere, fire is a metaphor of testing (cf. Dan. 7:9f.; Mal. 4:1; Matt. 3:12; Luke 3:16f.).

[40] An adjective, *opoion*, "what sort of, what kind of." Rienecker, 394.

[41] First class conditional sentence, assuming the statement as fulfilled, true.

[42] *Menei*, future indicative from *meno*, "to abide, remain."

[43] Literally, "a reward he shall receive," as *misthon* is emphatically positioned.

[44] As Henry Alford states, "It is possible that this whole image, as addressed to the Corinthians, may have been suggested, or at least illustrated, by the conflagration of Corinth under Mumious: the stately temples (one of them remaining to this day) left standing amidst the universal crash and destruction of the meaner buildings." Alford, 2:494.

[45] The passive voice of the verb, "suffer loss," shows that Christ, the Judge, will exact His impeccable penalty.

[46] Emphatic.

[47] Again, the future passive shows God's work of preserving (*sothnsetai*, from *sozo*) even His most carnal child from the eternal loss of soul.

[48] Rienecker 394-395; also, the first class conditions in both declarative sentences in verses 14-15, introduced by *ei*, assume both cases to be true. "Those whose works are consumed by the fire will themselves escape the flames (as if they were to jump out of the burning wooden structure they had built) and will be saved alone, without any works of praise to present to Christ." Mare, "I Corinthians," *Expositor's*, 10:208.

[49] Thomas R. Schreiner and Ardel B. Caneday, *The Race Set Before Us: A Biblical Theology of Perseverance & Assurance* (Downers Grove, IL: InterVarsity Press, 2001), 51.

[50] The negative sentential particle, *ouk*, expects the affirmative.

[51] The *gar* introduces the reason for God's severity toward those who destroy His people through errant teaching.

[52] *Hagios*. "The Corinthians themselves in their angry disputes had forgotten their holy heritage and calling, though this failing was no excuse for the ringleaders who had led them on." Robertson, 4:99. The city of Corinth was, of course, filled with pagan temples, against which saints in Christ stand in great contrast.

[53] This cannot be spiritual death (as Alford asserts), since these were saints, and since they are promised salvation in verse 15, in spite of their potentially poor review on the Day of Judgment. It must then be temporal death (so Meyer; cf. also 1 Cor. 5:5 for an example of this form of God's punishment) or some other manifestation of chastisement short of death; both expressions of divine discipline are illustrated later in 1 Corinthians 11:27f. Temporal death was the punishment delivered for defiling the material temple of the OT (Ex. 28:43; Lev. 16:2).

[54] Cf. the present participle, *anakrinon*, in 1 Corinthians 4:4.

[55] See 1 Corinthians 4:5. The detailed treatment of this passage and the whole issues of motives is found in Chapter 3 of this work.

[56] This entire anecdote adapted from Dave Egner, "A Palace or a Shack?" *Our Daily Bread*, April 15, 1993.

9

God Wants To Give *Me* A Standing Ovation?!

Wednesday nights seemed to come slower than they used to before this study began. The expectations were again high as we thought about how our future rewards would present themselves. But, until then, there were rewards to be enjoyed here and now—like Nina's homemade egg rolls which scored a big hit. But not to be outdone was Jim with his peach cobbler, still toasty from the oven. Didaskolos provided the homemade ice cream to go with it. And I brought my rookie batch of molasses-raisin cookies, following the recipe Didaskolos had stuck in my pocket on the way out the door our last meeting. If they tasted half as good as his, I'd be happy this first try.

I grabbed some decaf coffee, and, of course, a couple of my cookies, then I took my usual place on the cozy burgundy loveseat near the fireplace.

"Tonight," Didaskolos began, "we will survey the content of our future rewards, that is, what they will consist of. But first, let's briefly recap the criteria for rewards observed in our previous meetings, starting with the tour at the Gallery of Virtue and up to last Wednesday's discussion."

The reminder of the tour brought a wave of nostalgia over all of us. That day had been the beginning of our collective, but highly personal, journey through the pages of Scripture in discovering this doctrine of eternal rewards. This journey had radically changed our perspective on Christian living. To a person, we desired to live a life worthy of a hero's welcome, the only kind of welcome suitable for such a worthy Savior. Nothing less made sense in view of His redeeming sacrifice and glorious resurrection for wrath-deserving sinners.

Our private musings were interrupted by a question from Didaskolos: "So, what are the five, general criteria for eternal rewards? Can anyone recall?"

No one was quicker than Janet: "Progressing in spiritual maturity, practicing our Christian lives with Spirit-led motives, persevering in suffering, practicing a Spirit-led ministry, and, proclaiming a Spirit-led message."

"You're memory is perfect, sister," said Didaskolos, with a smile of obvious pride for his student. "These are the essential criteria for reward revealed in Scripture, at least as I see it at this juncture in my study. Other specific matters could be discussed such as the use of our money, our time, our spiritual gifts; how we raise our families, our labor in the marketplace, and even something as seemingly insignificant as giving someone a drink of water. But, each could fit under one of these major categories. I would encourage each of you to read Scripture and begin making a list of passages where rewards are discussed and you will easily fill a notebook. If this study has whet your appetite for further research in this often overlooked point of doctrine, then I am well pleased.

"But for this evening, our goal is to introduce just how our rewards will be meted out. We have, of course, noted the nature of rewards along the way–it's been inevitable–but we need to be specific now and also ponder a few matters that we have yet to see at all. With that in mind, I invite you to find 1 Peter, chapter 1, in your copy of our Lord's Word.

"Like James, Peter pens his first epistle to a group of persecuted saints. So, it should not surprise us that the first matter of importance is the doctrine of salvation. What else brings more comfort in their afflicted state? The sovereign orchestration of the Godhead in making salvation possible is visible in verses 1-2: The selection of the Father, the sanctifying work of the Spirit and the sacrifice of the Son. Contemplation of God's amazing grace toward the sinner should evoke adoration from the sinner made a saint.

"'Blessed be the God and Father of our Lord Jesus Christ,' declares Peter, the transformed fisherman from Galilee, 'who according to His great mercy has caused us to be born again to a living hope through the resurrection of Jesus Christ from the dead, to obtain an inheritance which is imperishable, undefiled and will not fade away, reserved in heaven for you....'

"Then, after stating the believer's eternal security in verse 5, in verse 6 Peter begins with two words: 'In this.' To what does 'in this' refer? It refers to the stupendous realities of verses 3-5: the believer's living hope, secure inheritance and expectation of glorification.[1] 'In this you greatly rejoice, even though now for a little while, if necessary, you have been distressed by various trials.' Their bright future in Christ brings stability amid adversity, but so does another reality.

"In verse 7, Peter uncovers part of God's design for sending misery into our lives, namely, 'so that the proof of your faith, being more precious than gold, which is perishable, even though tested by fire, may be found to result in praise and glory and honor at the revelation of Jesus Christ.' Wow! Did you get that? 'Praise and glory and honor at the revelation of Jesus Christ.' We must ponder that statement, but first things first.

"You should know that the term rendered 'proof' is the word *dokimon*, the same one James employs in his discourse on rewards for trials. Perhaps you recall our study of James 1:12. In case you don't, the term means 'to approve after examination,' picturing the gold refiner's fire as he tests precious metals for their genuineness. Here, Peter applies the cultural backdrop of the goldsmith to the hot furnace of God-sent adversity. In this furnace, God provides Himself with a laboratory of sorts to display the genuine faith of His children. It's worth noting, at this juncture, that the original phrase, 'that the proof of your faith,' finds the noun 'faith' in a place of emphasis. The believer's faith far outweighs even gold in terms of what is truly valuable; it is most precious to God. And so, He tests it to purify it from the dross of unbelief and whatever other sins may challenge its continued operation. And the end result is that the believer who responds to being in God's furnace with joy and keeps loving Jesus—the focus of verse 8—will be venerated before God when Jesus comes. How interesting, is it not, that Peter, like James, points up the Christian's love for his Savior as the motive for his attitude of gratitude, even when the sky turns black. Of course, this is when our love for Jesus is best proven, while on God's anvil.

"As you ponder this precious passage," said Didaskolos, with a deep breath, "do you have any questions or comments?"

"What," asked Jim, "is the significance of the words 'may be found' in verse 7: 'that the proof of your faith may be found to result in praise and glory and honor at the revelation of Jesus Christ'?"

"These words," answered Didaskolos, "stem from the Greek term *heurisko*, 'to find something by searching for it and/or inquiring about it,'[2] even as the shepherds sought to find Mary and Joseph and Jesus (cf. Luke 2:16). Here, the verb appears in the passive voice, signifying that this discovery of the kind of faith that deserves to be rewarded because it passes God's severe test is, ultimately, His discovery. In His omniscience, He knows all about our sufferings for righteousness and, as well, He takes full note of our faith-driven reaction to suffering and promises to honor us for it. In fact, the small word 'to' in verse 7: 'may be found to result in praise and glory and honor...' denotes the goal God has in mind for those who exercise unflappable faith amid adversity. He is saying to us here, 'You honor Me on earth with a godly response to trials I send your way, and I'll honor you in heaven.'"

"But just how will he honor us?" asked Nina. "Are there any particular differences between the terms, 'praise and glory and honor'?"

"I'm so glad you asked that question, sister," said Didaskolos, "because that's our intention tonight. We want to see the content of our rewards from Christ. But it was necessary to expose you to the details of this passage which I believe provides a panoramic viewpoint for at least two major categories of future reward.

"The word 'praise' (*epainon*) tells of the recognition or approval that believers can receive from Jesus at His coming. Of course, if their works are burned up at His *bema* seat due to His work being carried out in the energy of the flesh, including harmful teaching and carnal motives—the possibility we observed in 1 Corinthians 3 and 4—they will forfeit any praise. What a terribly sad moment, though not a burden to be borne into eternity since in the New Jerusalem there will be no more crying or mourning (see Rev. 21:4). Their shame will be real (see 1 John 2:28), though temporary. No doubt, when you think of verbal praise from Jesus, you think of the parable in Matthew 25 when the master says to two of his three servants, 'Well done, you good and faithful servant…' (cf. vv. 21, 23). And of course, a review of 1 Corinthians 4:5 is in order here: 'Therefore, do not go on passing judgment before the time, but wait until the Lord comes, who will both bring to light the things hidden in the darkness and disclose the motives of men's hearts; and then each man's *praise* [emphasis mine] will come to him from God.'[3]

"The other content of reward found here is the idea of positions of honor in Messiah's future kingdom. As some have suggested, the terms 'glory and honor' in verse 7 are meant to focus on this part of our reward,[4] in addition to the verbal praise just noted. Certainly, both elements of verbal praise and positions of honorable rank are observed in the parable Jesus taught in Matthew 25. And both seem to exist here in Peter's words. Peter simply echoes what he heard Jesus teach about future rewards.

"Let's consider, then, a few closing thoughts on verbal praise. Then, next week we will contemplate the prospect of positions of honor and rank in the future kingdom.

> Rudolph was a young musician in Vienna with a burning desire to write a symphony. Finally the time came when he was able to do so. After writing and rewriting it many times, he showed the score to some friends and asked for their opinion. Without exception they agreed that it was an excellent work. But Rudolph continued to labor over it, polishing and perfecting what he hoped would be a masterpiece. At last, he was ready to present it to the public.
>
> "The orchestra performed his symphony beautifully. After the last movement ended, there was a brief pause. Then the audience broke out in thunderous applause. Rudolph, however, seemed unmoved until an old white-haired man approached him. Placing his hands on

> the young man's shoulders, he exclaimed, "Well done, Rudolph! Well done!" Only then did the young musician smile with satisfaction. He had received approval from the one he wanted to please the most—his respected mentor.
>
> "That's how we should view our work—as service for our Master. Recognition from people is encouraging. But we should long to hear above anything else our Lord's 'Well done, good and faithful servant.' It's the Master's approval that really counts![5]

"As we think on this whole matter of receiving verbal praise from Jesus, it is imperative to compare it with our study of Matthew 6 on the issue of Spirit-led motives. You remember that service done for Christ for the praise of men will not receive praise from God. We cannot serve two masters, God and money. And, in this vein, neither can we embrace two motivations at the same time, one to gain men's applause and the other, God's.

"When Teresa Edwards of the gold medal-winning US women's basketball team reflected on her great reward, she burst out saying, 'Oh, man, this is sweet. This is so sweet, you can't describe it.'

"To acquire this world's gold may be sweet, but it can never compare to going for and obtaining the 'gold' that comes to the Christian when he or she hears the Master say, 'I'm proud of you, child. You did well. You did right in My sight—your conduct was good and faithful; you stayed true to Me even when you felt like quitting. Well done, My dear child. I praise you.'"

"But though such verbal praise from Jesus Himself is a most exhilarating reality, this is not all our dear Master has in store for His faithful servants. There are, as well, positions of honorable service in His future kingdom. For how many of you is this a new concept?"

Several hands went up.

"Well then, next week will prove to be a most illuminating time together. Until then, imagine yourself standing before Jesus and Him saying to you, 'I praise you, My blood-bought child. For your God-exalting life on earth, I honor you. You responded in a manner worthy of My immeasurable grace that rescued your soul from eternal separation from Me. For honoring Me on earth, I now honor you in heaven. Your honor here will forever remind all angels and saints here that honoring Me is the purpose of time and eternity.'

"How does that make you want to live the rest of this night...and the rest of your lives?"

Slowly we gathered our things...

And departed.

Joyfully...

Thoughtfully....

Endnotes for Chapter 9

[1] The masculine or neuter relative pronoun, *ho*, found in the prepositional phrase *en ho agalliasthe* ("in which you currently greatly rejoice") that begins verse 6, cannot find its antecedent in the feminine noun *soterian* in verse 5; if it be masculine, perhaps its link is to the masculine phrase, God the Father, in verse 2—of course, the biblical precedent for rejoicing in God exists in many places (e.g., Rom. 5:11). But the distance between the two phrases makes this improbable. Some, like Bigg, see a temporal element here, connecting *en ho* with the prepositional phrase which ends verse 5: "in this last time." Bigg, *St. Peter and St. Jude*, 102-3. The close proximity of the words is noteworthy as is the concept of suffering believers finding cause for joy in spite of their adversity; but it proves too much since this last time may not come in these believers' lifetime (and didn't), making their anticipation one that Hiebert calls "mistaken." Hiebert, *First Peter*, 54. Further to this, the verb "rejoice" would have to

be future since the glorification of the believer, though imminent, is still to come and, again, may not come during his time on earth. As Heibert aptly concludes, "it seems best to regard the relative as neuter and to understand the expression *en ho*...as a summary of the picture drawn in vv. 3-5....That widely accepted view is consistent with the relative clause construction that closely connects those two sections." Heibert, *First Peter*, 54.

[2] Zodhiates, 1719.

[3] Emphasis added. A detailed look at this passage in its context is found in chapter 3 of this work.

[4] So says Heibert, *First Peter*, 58; also see Mason who writes, "Praise is the *language* that will be used about these men's faith; 'honour,' the *rank* in which they will be placed; 'glory' the fervent *admiration* accorded to them...." A. J. Mason, Alfred Plummer, and William M. Sinclair, *The Epistles of Peter, John, and Jude: With Commentaries*, Layman's Handy Commentary, ed. by C. J. Ellicott (Grand Rapids: Zondervan Pub. House, 1957), 13.

[5] Richard DeHaan, "The Master's Approval," *Our Daily Bread*, September 6, 1993.

10

Begin with the End in Mind

"Tonight," Didaskolos began, "it is once again my privilege to have you in my home. Practicing hospitality without complaint, as Peter exhorts (1 Pet. 4:9), has not always been my strong suit. But in times of solitude with Jesus, He has taught me that stimulating fellowship is part of the process that He, as the Head of the church, has ordained to cause His body to grow (cf. Eph. 4:11-16; Heb. 10:24-25). But hospitality is also good for other reasons. For instance, it requires a denial of self—a denial of what I might rather do with my time and my material provisions. Further, I learn, as Jesus said, that it is 'more blessed to give than to receive' (Acts 20:35). Of course, what we gain most through hospitality is how to love people on a personal basis, the same way the Lord loves us. And our brief look at 1 John 4:16-18 has shown us that to do well at the *bema* seat we must consistently treat others with love. If love for others does not characterize our reputation before God and others, we are, in reality, zero in terms of what really matters to God. For, God is the epitome of love (1 John 4:8). You may be the greatest Bible teacher, the most effective evangelist or organizer your church has, but if you do not have love, it profits you nothing on God's scale of true values (cf. 1 Cor. 13:1-3).

"Well, I assure you I did not plan to say all that. But perhaps, since I prayed much in preparation for this evening, the Holy Spirit wished to remind us all of the priority of having a reputation for loving others. Is that your reputation? Hospitality is, then, one way to express such love."

Didaskolos' testimony was in our hearts like a cowboy's gentle kick into the flanks of his horse. I needed this prodding and I sensed that others did too. It was far too easy to be zealous for preaching good sermons and leading others in a course of spiritual direction without really taking time to show personal care for those who listened and followed. This prelude to our study would not be forgotten—after all, what good would it do me to preach wonderful sermons but get a poor grade on my final report card in the 'course' entitled, "Love your neighbor as yourself"? That wouldn't honor my Savior who gave me the passion and ability to teach His Word, but never wanted me to just love teaching and not the people I teach.

"Please turn in your Bibles," said Didaskolos, "to the twenty-fifth chapter of Matthew's Gospel. Our focus will be on verses 14-30 where

Jesus continues His similes on the kingdom of heaven by telling a parable, the so-called 'Parable of the Talents.'

"You'll notice that verse 14 begins with the conjunction 'for' which connects this parable with Jesus' imperative in verse 13, 'Be on the alert, for you do not know the day or the hour.' So, The Parable of the Talents serves to generate spiritual readiness for Christ's Second Coming to earth, which is the subject of the previous parable, The Parable of the Ten Virgins, in verses 1-12.

"Now then, the parable tells us, in verse 14, that the kingdom of heaven is 'just like[1] a man about to go on a journey, who calls his own slaves, and entrusted his own possessions to them.' To one he gave[2] five talents, to another two, and to another, one, 'each according to his own ability.' No doubt you know that a talent was a measure of weight, the size varying anywhere from 58-80 pounds. Customarily it was used to weigh precious metals. And what's more, one talent was worth about 6,000 denarii, one denarius being one day's wage. This was indeed a bundle of money. And in this story, the possessions entrusted were silver, as the term for 'money' indicates. So what kind of stewards would these three men be? That's the issue here.

"The first man immediately traded[3] with his five talents and gained five more. Likewise, the one receiving two talents doubled his money, as verses 16-17 state. In stark contrast, however, verse 18 reads, 'But[4] he who received the one talent went away, and dug a hole in the ground and hid his master's money.'

"Bad decision!

"After a long while,[5] the master returned to settle accounts with his servants. The phrase translated 'settled accounts' renders *sunario logon* in the Greek language. Found only here and in Matthew 18:23-24, this was a commercial term of the day that meant 'to compare accounts, to make a reckoning.' Clearly it denotes the principle of accountability.

"The first man proved his faithful stewardship by revealing ten talents in contrast[6] to the five with which he started. And for this, he was honored with verbal praise from his master, 'Well done, good and faithful servant....' But that's not all; the master continues the content of his reward, 'you were faithful with a few things, I will put you in charge[7] of many things,[8] enter into the joy of your master.'

"The term 'servant' is in the vocative case here, drawing special attention to the man. Then, the two attributive adjectives, 'good' (*agathe*) and 'faithful' (*piste*), follow to depict the kind of servant he was. The reward, then, you see, is both verbal and practical in nature. Not only is he praised, but he is promised greater responsibility in the master's kingdom rule. Of course, the ultimate reward is coming into the full joy of his master's presence.

"The second man hears the same chorus of praise from his master as the first man—this is intriguing. For though the two men received different abilities and opportunities, they received the same reward. So what's the point? Faithfulness! That's the requirement for future rewards, rewards of verbal praise and practical opportunities for sharing in the future rule of the master. The master was simply looking for fidelity to the individual stewardships given.

"But the beautiful chords of fidelity played by the first two men are followed by the dissonant sounds of the third man's song. This man proves to be a poor steward of his master's gifts, evidenced in his fear-driven act of hiding his talent in the ground. His judgment of his master as 'hard' and 'unfair,' and the thought that his master may never return (he could then keep the talent for himself) prompted such foolish action and the result was severe.

"First, his master rebukes him, calling him a 'wicked, lazy slave' (*doule, ponere kai oknere*) in contrast to 'good and faithful servant' above, and advises him as to what he should have done: 'put my money in the bank,[9] and on my arrival I would have received my money back with interest.'[10] Next, he strips his lone talent from him and gives it to the first man, who now has eleven talents. Then comes the explanation for such swift and scalding retribution: 'For to everyone who has shall more be given, and he shall have an abundance; but from the one who does not have, even what he does have shall be taken away.'[11] But the axe cuts deeper still on this man's unfaithful stewardship.

"Verse 30 concludes with, 'And cast out the worthless slave into the outer darkness; in that place there shall be weeping and gnashing of teeth.[12] Most believe this is a reference to final and eternal doom in hell, in parallel with Matthew 13:47-50 and other places where Matthew describes the unbeliever's future judgment with these terms.[13] Others, emphasizing the fact that each of three servants belong to the master, as verse 14 indicates,[14] believe this third servant represents a carnal believer who forfeits governmental privileges in the future rule of the King.[15] Whatever the identity of the third servant, the point of the parable is that faithfulness here grants honorable duties in the hereafter. Further, since the era in view is the Tribulation (see Rev. 6-19), those depicted by the parable would be tribulation saints, not church saints who are already present with the Lord via the Rapture. Does this mean that church saints will not share in Messiah's future rule? I think not. Jim, would you please read 1 Corinthians 6:1-3?"

Jim's low, baritone voice was pleasant to hear.

"Does any one of you, when he has a case against his neighbor, dare to go to law before the unrighteous and not before the saints? Or do you not know[16] that the saints will judge the world?[17] If the world is judged by you, are you not competent to constitute the smallest law courts? Do you not know that we will judge angels? How much more matters of this life?"

"Thanks so much, brother," said Didaskolos. "As one author states, 'it is possible that the litigants of 6:1-8 are the father and mother of 5:1. If so, such litigation would clearly be displaying the church's dirty laundry before the world.'[18] Most commentators believe, too, that noncriminal property issues are in view here.[19] Whatever they were, they were not criminal matters since such were handled by the government, according to Romans 13.

"In brief, Christians were taking each other to court, courts run by the pagan standards of the Roman Empire. 'What about God's standards?' Paul seems to ask. They should have been settling certain disputes in their home Bible studies, not in court, though some cases may have needed to go to court.[20] The point Paul makes is that these saints were failing to use their prerogative to resolve such conflicts themselves. And the basis for his admonishment is the fact that in the future God's people will judge not only the world, but angels as well."

"Isn't it interesting," said Janet, "that the term 'saints,' in verse 2, stands in contrast with the term 'unrighteous' in verse 1? And the word 'unrighteous,' if I recall from a word study I once did, basically means 'injustice.'"[21]

"Yes," affirmed Didaskolos, "it does mean that. In exact opposite fashion of the unfair and undependable[22] rulings of the secular judges of this world, saints will rule with perfect equity and righteousness in the future reign of Messiah. The specifics of their co-rulership is not stated here, just the fact that they will execute authority over both the unrighteous world and angels."

"Which angels?" asked Nina.

"I knew someone would ask that intriguing question," replied Didaskolos with a smile. "By using the word 'angels' without the definite article, 'the,' before it, Paul probably has in mind a certain class of angels, most likely fallen angels. For why would we judge good angels?[23] Fallen angels, the devil included, will receive their judgment at the close of the millennial age when the devil is cast into the lake of fire to endure eternal torment. 2 Peter 2:4 and Jude 6 indicate that some angels are currently imprisoned awaiting their day of final judgment. Of course, numerous demons are now loose and serve as Satan's cohorts to oppose God and His people. Like their leader, they seek to deceive mankind, in general, until their predicted eternal doom becomes reality (Eph. 6:10-18).

"Will all saints share in this co-rulership with Christ?" Alfred asked.

"This question has been debated by more than a few," answered Didaskolos. "The interrogative sentences we just read in 1 Corinthians 6:2-3 expect an affirmative response: 'Yes, I know the saints will judge the world,' and, 'I know we will judge angels.' The articular phrase 'the saints' seems to point to every member of God's holy family—the term itself denotes those set apart and consecrated to God. It entails not only what a Christian is in His perfectly sanctified standing in Christ, but his practice of holiness in character and deed.[24] In this context, God's people are set apart unto the holy duty of co-ruling with Messiah in the future earthly kingdom as other Scriptures clarify. But before we assume that this means every saint, it is important to compare other passages on the subject.

"For example, Matthew 19:27-30 declares that the original apostles will have special ruling positions in millennial age as a reward for their earthly faithfulness to Christ. Their honor will be presiding over the twelve tribes of the nation, Israel. This duty is not for every believer, but relegated to the apostles. Matthew 20 goes on to state that to sit on Jesus' right and left is 'for those for whom it has been prepared' by the Father.[25] The Parable of the Minas, in Luke 19, shows that our future positions and privileges are in proportion to our present faithfulness to the opportunities and resources God gives us.

"In short, a nobleman imparts ten minas each, a measure of money worth about three months wages, to his servants; then, he leaves town. When he returns, the first servant had doubled his money and in turn is granted authority over ten cities.[26] The second servant is likewise good and faithful, but not to the degree of the first servant, earning only five minas. Accordingly, he was honored with less responsibility: five cities instead of ten. The third servant earns nothing and therefore receives no authority to rule in his master's kingdom. In fact, the minas originally given him were handed over to the first servant. Jesus summarizes the meaning of the parable in verse 26: '...I tell you that everyone who has, more will be given, but as for the one who has nothing, even what he has will be taken away.'"

"The difference between this parable and the one we studied in Matthew 25 is interesting," said Jim. "In the latter, each servant received a number of talents according to his ability whereas in Luke 19 each one received the same amount of minas. Is it safe to say, then, that the minas signify the equal opportunities our Master gives us as Christians during the course of life, and the talents represent the different gifts and talents He gives individuals?"

"Yes, I would concur with that," replied Didaskolos. "In both cases, faithful stewardship is required, and in both cases rewards are the result of such fidelity. But, Luke 19, in contrast to Matthew 25, shows that our future rank in the kingdom is dependent on our present service, an idea that may be new to some of you. There will be degrees of opportunity in heaven. God's partiality, if we may call it that, is, however, as one author put it, 'justly partial.'[27]

"I believe then," continued Didaskolos, "that not all believers will be given authority to rule in Jesus' future, earthly kingdom. The saints will judge the world and angels, but only the faithful saints. Remember, it's possible for a Christian to come up empty at the *bema* seat, according to 1 Corinthians 3:15, experience shame,[28] and forfeit rewards.[29] If this be possible, and if governmental positions, along with verbal praise, are part of the content of future rewards, then it follows that not all will rule, though they will be heirs of the kingdom."

"Is this what Paul meant," I asked, "in his second letter to Timothy when he says, in verses 11-12, 'It is a trustworthy statement: For if we died with Him, we will also live with Him; If we endure, we will also reign with Him; If we deny Him, He also will deny us; If we are faithless,[30] He remains faithful, for He cannot deny Himself'?"

"I couldn't agree more," said Didaskolos. "That line, 'If we endure, we also reign with Him'; leaves no room for doubting that only Christians who endure faithfully in their earthly pilgrimage for Jesus will have the privilege of reigning with Him in the future. And the context further defines the endurance required. There's the loyal soldier willing to undergo the hardships of military duty, the disciplined athlete and the hard-working farmer. Applying these word pictures to his own gospel ministry, Paul states, in 2:10, that he endures 'all things for the sake of those who are chosen, so that they also may obtain the salvation which is in Christ Jesus and with it eternal glory.' The soldier earns the approval of the one who enlisted him, the devoted athlete wins his competition, the diligent farmer reaps a bountiful harvest, and the believer who endures whatever suffering is required to remain true to his Lord, gets to reign in his glorified state."

"I was thinking," said Alfred, "that the faltering of Demas in 2 Timothy 4:10 depicts just the opposite of the enduring faithfulness Paul speaks of here."

"Yes! A superb observation," declared Didaskolos. "Demas, in light of Colossians 4:14, had been a companion of Paul's and obviously tracking for the Lord—though admittedly no commendation is given regarding him—but, the verse you mentioned says, 'Demas, having loved[31] this present world, has deserted me and gone to Thessalonica....' And again, what a difference between Demas and Paul. Paul, according to 2 Timothy 4:6-8, came to the end of his earthly life and looking back, said 'I have fought the good fight, I have finished the course, I have kept the faith; in the future there is laid up for me a crown of righteousness, which the Lord, the righteous Judge, will award to me on that day; and not only to me, but also to all who have loved his appearing.'

"Will the Demas's of God's fold, those who fall out of love with Jesus in exchange for a love affair with this present world, receive the Crown of Righteousness at the *bema* seat? No! This would contradict the just standards of the Righteous Judge, Jesus Christ. This particular crown is reserved for those who endure faithfully to the end of their Christian journey. And why do they endure? Because they love Christ, and His appearing. They consistently do what is right in His sight.[32] But, believers who have not endured hardship like a good soldier, a disciplined athlete and a hard-working farmer, will forfeit the rewards of such loyalty. And so, it follows that neither will they have opportunity to reign with Christ in His kingdom, according to 2 Timothy 2:11-13."

Then Janet spoke up. "I heard of a Christian lady," she said softly, "that became a prisoner of discouragement and extreme depression. Her mind began to flirt with thoughts of suicide. Then someone shared this truth that Christians who fail to endure will forfeit rewards and the right to rule in the age to come. Saved still? Absolutely, as 1 Corinthians 3:15 makes clear. But not rewarded, or, at least not receiving the full reward John speaks of.[33] Through this teaching, the benevolent Shepherd began wooing back His little stray lamb, and restored her soul to a spirit of enduring faithfulness. She realized that the sweet deliverance from her sin through Jesus' death and resurrection demanded one logical response: 'I will love Him because He first loved me. I will live a life now that is worthy to be honored later.'"

"What a moving illustration of the power of this truth that faithfulness here and now brings the reward of reigning in the hereafter. Thank you, sister, for that story." Didaskolos paused and then said, 'What do you say we take a break..., get a refill on coffee, or whatever you like?"

Most everyone took seconds on the homemade cinnamon buns Nina had brought—a perfect counterpart to the French Roast gourmet coffee Didaskolos had brewed.

After gently tossing a fresh log on the fire, Didaskolos said, "Now please turn in your Bibles to Revelation 2:26 as we continue this discussion about the faithful believer's governmental authority in the Millennial Age."

I'd always had questions about this particular passage ever since my pastor did a series on The Seven Churches of Revelation.

"Would someone please read that for us?" Didaskolos asked.

Jim took the initiative: "He who overcomes,[34] and he who keeps My deeds until the end, to Him I will give authority[35] over the nations."

Didaskolos continued. "As one commentator puts it, 'Christ promises believers who are faithful that they will join Him in His millennial rule.'[36] Then observe verse 27 where the nature of the believer's rule is described by Jesus: 'And he shall rule them with a rod of iron, as the vessels of the potter are broken to pieces, as I also have received authority from My Father.' The same author states that the word '"rule" (*poimanei*) means "to shepherd," indicating that they [believers] will not simply be administering justice but will...be dealing with His sheep and protecting them as well.'[37] Though Psalm 2:9, the verse John quotes here, refers to Christ's future rule over the nations, the apostle applies it to the believer's honored position in the kingdom—but only to those believers who characteristically keep[38] His words.[39]

"Revelation 3:21, in this same vein, promises the believers at Laodicea, 'He who overcomes, I will grant to him to sit down with Me on My throne, as I also overcame and sat down with My Father on His throne.' Observing the comparative clause here, one author puts it like this: 'As Christ overcame through his suffering and death (John 16:33) and entered into the highest honor God could bestow, that of being seated at this "right hand" of sovereignty (Mark 16:19; Acts 2:22ff; Rev. 22:1), so believers who suffer with Christ even to the point of death will share in the honor of Christ's exalted position.'[40] Of course, suffering is not mentioned in Jesus' description of the Laodicean church, but it is in 2 Timothy 2:11-13, as already noted. What is emphasized here is the intimate fellowship with Christ missing in the church at Laodicea. That's why Jesus says what He does in verse 20, 'Behold, I stand at the door and knock; if anyone hears My voice and opens the door, I will come in to him and will dine with him, and he with Me.' Many have used this verse to urge unbelievers to receive Christ for salvation from hell, but is that an accurate handling of the passage when saints are clearly addressed, the church at Laodicea? Surely, it is not! This verse contains an invitation to spiritually lukewarm saints[41] who need to dine with Christ, a figure for close communion with Christ. For those who say 'yes' to this invitation will overcome their carnal state and be rewarded with opportunities to co-rule with Christ in the future kingdom. The apostles have their promise of co-rulership with Christ (cf. Matt. 19:28), martyred saints of the Tribulation will reign with Christ in the Millennium,[42] and, as we've seen, loyal church saints will share in the same. Old Testament saints will have a portion in Christ's rule, as well, with David serving as a co-regent of Christ,[43] though it is does not seem to be stated as clearly as in the New Testament.[44]

"So you see, then, that the content of our future rewards is both verbal praise and governmental positions in Christ's kingdom. Further to this, though we have essentially discussed these matters, there are specific honors Christ chooses to graciously bestow upon His people. These are symbolized in crowns. There is the Crown of Righteousness in 2 Timothy 4:8 for those who do what's right in God's sight faithfully to the end of their lives. I Corinthians 9:25 reveals the imperishable crown for those who exercise spiritual discipline, the Spirit-produced virtue called self-control. One writer even calls it 'the crown of mastery.'[45] And you should know that the context of 1 Corinthians 9 applies such self-control to an evangelistic lifestyle. This should not surprise us since befriending sinners to the Friend of sinners requires a great deal of discipline. Discipline is required to make time for non-Christians, and be compassionate and loving instead of calloused and legalistic. After all, the holy huddle is so warm, cozy and comfortable. Being with Christ-insulting people takes a Christ-loving Christian out of his comfort zone.

"Then, Peter tells of another honor, the Crown of Glory. This crown is given to faithful shepherds of God's flock.[46] You recall, no doubt, our study of the Crown of Exultation in 1 Thessalonians 2:19-20 for those who faithfully embrace the Great Commission. And finally, James 1:12 and Revelation 2:10 speak of the Crown of Life for those saints who endure the various trials permitted by God in their earthly journey.

"Of course, as Revelation 3:11 and 1 Corinthians 9:27 warn us, these crowns can be lost due to severe moral, or doctrinal lapses, that forge a firm path into the way of carnality. And finally, these crowns are not for our glory ultimately, but we will cast them at the feet of our beloved Savior. He wore a crown of thorns so we could be with Him in perfect fellowship and co-reign with Him in His kingdom. As Revelation 4:10 prophesies, 'the twenty-four elders will fall down and worship before Him who sits on the throne, and will worship Him who lives forever, and will cast their crowns before the throne, saying, "Worthy are You, our Lord and our God, to receive glory and honor and power; for You created all things, and because Your will they existed and were created."'"[47]

"With all this in view, are we to believe there will be differences in eternity future, regarding the status of each believer?" Janet asked.

"I believe so," answered Didaskolos. "At first this disturbed me, then I realized that God, who, out of His grace chooses to reward us, does so in line with His perfect justice and omniscient awareness of our faithfulness, down to our very motives. Not that our sovereign, generous God has some contractual arrangement to which He is bound to grant specific rewards for specific services—The Parable of the Vineyard Owner in Matthew 20:1-16 throws out any such thinking. [48] But, in some sense, as Hebrews 6:10 puts it, 'God is not unjust so as to forget your work and the love which you have shown toward His name, in having ministered and in still ministering to the saints.'

"But beyond the doctrine of God which is where all theology must begin, the teaching of the New Testament is so clear that rewards are dispensed according to the quality of each man's work (cf. 1 Cor. 3:13-14), that each will receive his own reward according to his own labor.[49] And how this difference is expressed is seen, for example, in the amount of responsibility we will have in Jesus' future reign, per the Parable of the Minas in Luke 19. But perhaps the distinctions will be made manifest in others ways as well. As one author suggests, 'Inasmuch as reward is associated with brightness and shining in many passages of Scripture

(Dan. 12:3;[50] Matt. 13:43;[51] 1 Cor. 15:40-41, 49), it may be that the reward given to the believer is a capacity to manifest the glory of Christ throughout eternity. The greater the reward, the greater the bestowed capacity to bring glory to God.... Capacities to radiate the glory will differ, but there will no personal sense of lack in that each believer will be filled to the limit of his capacity to "show forth the praises of him who hath called you out of darkness into His marvelous light (1 Pet. 2:9)."'[52] Since the very purpose of our existence is to bring glory to our Maker and Savior,[53] this variance in 'shining' may very well be part of our individual status in heaven. What's more, internally, there will be differences as well—everyone's cup will be filled to the brim with spiritual joy and satisfaction, but everyone's cup will be a different size. This again reflects God's perfect justice and the varying degrees of rewards He dispenses. After all, why should the carnal believer have the same depth of spiritual joy as the spiritual believer?[54]

"The content of our reward is further described by the writer to the Hebrews by the term 'rest.' Of the redeemed, but disobedient children of Israel, God said, 'So I declared on oath in My anger, They shall never enter My rest' (Heb. 3:11). A careful study of this concept in Hebrews shows that entering God's rest is not a guarantee for every believer, otherwise why would 4:10-11 say, 'For anyone who enters God's rest also rests from his own work, just as God did from His. Let us, therefore, make every effort to enter that rest, so that no one will fall by following their example of disobedience.'"

"What is the comparison going on here?" I asked.

"It's basically this, Ron," replied Didaskolos. "The Exodus generation failed to enjoy their promised inheritance of the land of Canaan because they listened to the voice of fear. Remember the majority report of those who returned from spying out the land: 'And they spread among the Israelites a bad report about the land they had explored. They said, "The land we explored devours those living in it. All the people we saw there are of great size"' (Num. 13:32, NIV). By contrast, Caleb's faith in our great God sent his fears packing. In fact, he silenced the majority and said, 'We should go up and take possession of the land, for we can certainly do it' (Num. 13:30, NIV). Guess who, then, got to enter 'God's rest'?"

"Caleb," said Alfred.

"And Joshua," Didaskolos said with emphasis, "who also fixed his spiritual eyes on his powerful God rather than the powerful peoples of Canaan. But the rest of the nation, including Moses, who lost his temper too many times and dishonored the Lord in front of His people (cf. Num.20:9-12), failed to enter the rest of Canaan due to their unfinished business of conquering the peoples there. Unbelief gave birth to disobedience, and they forfeited the inheritance God had in store for them. But please note, entering God's rest did not just mean entering the land of Canaan, but as a matter of cause-effect it entailed the spiritual condition displayed by Joshua and Caleb required to enter that rest. Likewise, the apostle Paul's Spirit-controlled life enabled him to 'finish his course' and be eligible for the 'crown of righteousness' (cf. 2 Tim. 4:6-8).

"Israel's failure to receive her full inheritance-rest serves, then, as a warning to us. As Hebrews 10:35-37 states, 'Therefore, do not throw away your confidence, which has a great reward. For you have need of endurance,[55] so that when you have done the will of God, you may receive what was promised. For yet in a very little while, He who is coming will come, and will not delay. But my righteous one shall live by faith; and if he shrinks back, My soul has no pleasure in him.' It is indeed possible for God's 'righteous one' to stumble in his faith, a reality which gives occasion for the book of Hebrews. And such slippage will mean the forfeiting of rewards in the likes of the nation, Israel; our salvation is a gift, but our inheritance in God's rest is earned."

"But what specifically would that mean?" Janet wanted to know.

"I believe your question can be answered from Hebrews 2:5-8," declared Didaskolos. "Would you please read that for us, sister?"

Janet eagerly turned there and read, "For He did not subject to angels the world to come, concerning which we are speaking. But one has testified somewhere saying, 'What is man, that You remember him? Or the son of man, that You are concerned[56] about him? You have made him for a little while lower than the angels; You have crowned him with glory and honor, and have appointed him over the works of Your hands; You have put all things in subjection under his feet.'[57] For in subjecting all things to him, He left nothing that is not subject to him. But now we do not yet see all things subjected to him.'"

Didaskolos continued. "The pronoun 'him,' as one Bible scholar comments, '...refers to man...who was given dominion over the creation (Gen. 1:28), but who lost it when he sinned (Rom. 8:20), and will regain it in the future millennial kingdom because of Christ's death for sin.'[58] But it's only those who endure, who persevere in God's will, who will receive what is promised here. Those who shrink back from loyalty to Christ, as the Hebrew Christians were tempted to do by their unbelieving Jewish countrymen, will know God's displeasure and disinheritance from His rest. Again, 'let us be diligent to enter that rest.'

"In sum, all believers will inherit eternal life, according to Titus 3:7, but not all will be enjoy co-rulership with Christ in His kingdom, as we have already seen in 2 Timothy 2:11-13.[59]

> "In the eleventh century, King Henry III of Bavaria grew tired of court life and the pressures of being a monarch. He made application to Prior Richard at a local monastery, asking to be

accepted as a contemplative and spend the rest of his life in the monastery.

"'Your majesty,' said Prior Richard, 'do you understand that the pledge here is one of obedience? That will be hard because you have been a king.'

"'I understand,' said Henry. 'The rest of my life I will be obedient to you, as Christ leads you.'

"'Then I will tell you what to do,' said Prior Richard. 'Go back to your throne and serve faithfully in the place where God has put you.'

"When King Henry died, a statement was written: 'The king learned to rule by being obedient.'

"When we tire of our roles and responsibilities, it helps to remember God has planted us in a certain place and told us to be a good accountant or teacher or mother or father. Christ expects us to be faithful where He puts us, and when He returns, we'll rule together with Him.[60]

"But please permit me," said Didaskolos somewhat apologetically, "to add one last illustration before we move on; I want this concept of entering God's rest to be clear. As you know...

The last words of great men are often significant. Often when a man comes to the end of his life, wisdom is distilled and challenging comments are made. Perhaps one of the most moving illustrations of such a final exhortation came from the lips of General Douglas MacArthur before the corps of cadets at West Point in 1961. MacArthur was, perhaps, the greatest military genius in history. He was without doubt the greatest military strategist and fighting General the United States has ever produced. His brilliant "island-hopping" strategy enabled him to overcome superior Japanese forces in the Pacific war. With enlightened statesmanship and compassion he single-handedly created the new Japan. He is the author of the Japanese constitution. During his tour there he ruled for many years as an American Caesar. His final military contribution was in the Korean War where his military maneuvers are still studied as classical examples of battleground genius.

"MacArthur went to West Point and once served as commandant of the corps of cadets. His last and most memorable good-bye was given there. Addressing the corps of cadets, he took as his text the academy's motto: Duty, Honor, Country. Speaking without notes, striding back and forth, he closed his message with a passage that no one who was on that plain that noon will ever forget. There was not a dry eye in the corps as he said:

"'The shadows are lengthening for me. The twilight is here. My days of old have vanished, tone and tint; they have gone glimmering through the dreams of things that were. Their memory is one of wondrous beauty, watered by tears, and coaxed and caressed by the smiles of yesterday. I listen vainly, but with thirsty ear, for the witching melody of faint bugles blowing reveille, of far drums beating the long roll. In my dreams I hear again the crash of guns, the rattle of musketry, the strange mournful mutter of the battlefield. But in the evening of my memory, I always come back to West Point. Always there echoes and re-echoes in my ears—Duty, Honor, Country. Today marks my final roll call with you. But I want you to know that when I cross the river my last conscious thought will be of the Corps, and the Corps and the Corps. I bid you farewell.'

"MacArthur had completed his life work and could look back on a career spanning over fifty years and know that he had done his best. Likewise, the desire of God is that every Christian should similarly be able to say at the end of life, 'I have finished my work.' This accomplishment was termed 'entering into rest' by the writer of the Epistle to the Hebrews."[61]

"For the first time I think I understand this concept in Hebrews," said Nina, "but what about that passage in Matthew, where Jesus spoke of laying up treasure in heaven?"

"I'm so glad you reminded me of that, sister," said Didaskolos. "That is yet another descriptive phrase of the content of our reward. Jesus said in Matthew 6:19-21, 'Do not store up for yourselves treasures on earth, where moth and rust destroy, and where thieves break in and steal. But store up for yourselves treasures in heaven, where neither moth nor rust destroys, and where thieves do not break in or steal; for[62] where your treasure is, there your heart will be also.'"

"What is the cultural backdrop to these words?" Jim asked.

"Well," said Didaskolos, "since in Jesus' day, 'thieves could [easily] dig through walls and steal a [so-called] "strongbox"'—a safe of sorts—those who could afford it, protected their wealth in other ways: 'investing money with moneychangers, depositing it in a temple for safekeeping (even most robbers balked at "robbing gods") or burying it in the ground or in caves, where, however, moth (for expensive apparel) or rust (for coins) could destroy its value.'"[63]

"What, then, is meant by 'laying up treasures in heaven'?" Jim continued.

"Jewish writings," replied Didaskolos, "'spoke of "laying up treasure" with God (e.g., Tobit 4:7-10). Sometimes this meant that the generous person could trust that God would help him in time of need; sometimes it referred (as here) to treasure in the world to come.'[64] Certainly, in view of Jesus' focus on rewards for godly motives in verses 1-18, the concept of treasure in heaven furthers that motif. The Pharisees, of course, believed that a sign of godliness was material prosperity, the same gross error some preach today. So Jesus confronts their covetous eyes in verses 22-23 and then, in verse 24, concludes by saying, 'No one can serve two masters; for either he will hate the one and love the other, or he will be devoted to one and despise the other. You cannot serve God and wealth.' 'Greed or God, which will it be?' asks Jesus.

"In his book, *I Talk Back to the Devil*, A. W. Tozer writes, 'Money often comes between men and God. Someone has said that you can take two small ten-cent pieces, just two dimes, and shut out the view of a panoramic landscape. Go to the mountains and just hold two coins closely in front of your eyes—the mountains are still there, but you cannot see them at all because there is a dime shutting off the vision in each eye.'[65] As Craig Brian Larson adds, 'It doesn't take large quantities of money to come between us and God; just a little, placed in the wrong position, will effectively obscure our view.'[66]

"So you see—and this may surprise you—you can 'send it ahead' in a sense, that is, if your spiritual vision sees eternity in time and seizes the moments. True, there are no U-haul trailers at graveside services...but before they put you six feet under, you have the chance of a literal lifetime to lay up for yourselves treasures in heaven. For instance, 'during his exceptionally long ministry, which spanned most of the eighteenth century, John Wesley earned a considerable amount of money from his published sermons and other works. Yet he left only 28 pounds when he died, because he continually gave what he earned to the Lord's work.'[67] He sent it on ahead.

> "Charles Spurgeon and his wife, according to a story in *The Chaplain* magazine, would sell, but refused to give away, the eggs their chickens laid. Even close relatives were told, 'You may have them if you pay for them.' As a result, some people labeled the Spurgeons greedy and grasping. They accepted criticisms without defending themselves, and only after Mrs. Spurgeon died was the full story revealed: All the profits from the sale of eggs went to support two elderly widows. Because the Spurgeons were unwilling to let their left hand know what the right hand was doing (see Matt. 6:3), they

> endured the attacks in silence.[68]

"The Spurgeons were storing up treasure in heaven, and the location of their treasure proved where their heart was.

"And if you don't mind, I can't resist just one more story here."

"No complaints, here," said Alfred, who spoke for all of us.

Didaskolos continued:

> "Two elderly sisters in the faith, Elsie and Helen, had already retired from their vocational Christian jobs when the Lord led them to help plant a Hispanic church in a certain city. This would require, however, the selling of the home they had lived in for many years and move to this city. It was obviously a big undertaking to move at their age, but Elsie, quite matter-of-factly remarked that a house is a material thing that soon passes away, but ministry in the lives of people will last.[69]

Didaskolos asked the group, "Have you ever had someone point out a problem and your reaction was over-the-top? Perhaps you have ignored biblical teaching because it conflicts with what you want?

> "When you go to a doctor for your annual check-up, he or she will often begin to poke, prod, and press various places, all the while asking, 'Does this hurt? How about this?' If you cry out in pain, one of two things has happened. Either the doctor has pushed too hard, without the right sensitivity. Or, more likely, there's something wrong, and the doctor will say, 'We'd better do some more tests. It's not supposed to hurt there!' So it is when pastors preach on financial responsibility, and certain members cry out in discomfort, criticizing the message and the messenger. Either the pastor has pushed too hard, or perhaps there's something wrong. In that case, I say, 'My friend, we're in need of the Great Physician because it's not

supposed to hurt there.'"[70]

Again, the story amused us, but the point was not missed.

"In summary, our precious Lord does not say what the content of 'treasure in heaven' is. That we leave to Him and expect that like a father at Christmas loves to surprise his children with what's under the tree, our heavenly Father will open our treasure box at the dawning of the eternal morning. We will then be glad—glad beyond words—that we saw eternity in time and seized opportunities to send our money on ahead.

"We have covered a warehouse of information in our studies together, and I have savored every moment. As we wrap this up and tie a red ribbon on it, I'd like to review several principles from a superb book called *Going for the Gold* by Joe Wall. I imagine you could order this excellent overview of the *bema* seat of Christ from your local Christian bookstore, or online.

"In chapter 9, our brother Wall enumerates several general principles related to the criteria for rewards, some of which we have not had time to discuss. Here they are for your consideration: (1) Jesus will judge our deeds, our words, our thoughts, and our motives; (2) Only what Christ, through the Holy Spirit, produces in our lives has any value at the *bema*; (3) Jesus will reward us according to our persevering faith in God and His promises; (4) Jesus will reward us according to our faithful and wise stewardship; (5) At the bema Jesus will take into account how we responded to the Word of God; (6) At the *bema*, Jesus will be concerned with the purity of our lives; (7) At the *bema* Jesus will take into account how long we have been saved; (8) Jesus will reward us according to our secondary involvement in the ministry of others; (9) If we judge others, Jesus will apply our standards when He judges us; (10) Jesus will reward us for the results of our ministry in the lives of others; (11) Teachers will receive the stricter judgment, and (12) Not only production but contribution to production will receive reward.[71]

"When you read Wall's book you will see the biblical validation for each principle, but I felt they were worth quoting to prod your further research. Now let's see if we can once more remember the five general principles that have shaped our discussions regarding God's criteria for eternal rewards, beginning with the tour at the Gallery of Virtue."

"I think I can recall all of them," I said.

"Go for it, Ron," said Didaskolos with evident pleasure.

I began, "(1) Christ will reward us for progressing in spiritual maturity; (2) Christ will reward us for practicing our life and ministry with Spirit-led motives; (3) Christ will reward us for persevering in God-sent suffering; (4) Christ will reward us for practicing a Spirit-led ministry of evangelism and disciple-making; and (5) Christ will reward us for preaching a sound message."

"Excellent memory, brother Ron," said Didaskolos. "I hope you all will not only remember these, but allow them to govern the way you live your lives each day until you see the Lord. Then you can be assured of a hero's welcome when you meet Jesus. And then as we summarize the content of our various future rewards that we have studied, we could list the following: A royal welcome home (see 2 Pet. 1:5-11); verbal praise from God (see Matt. 25:21); special crowns of honor (see James 1:12); ruling positions in Christ's earthly and eternal kingdom (Matt. 20:20-28); full enjoyment of our inheritance-rest (see Heb. 4; 10); portrayal of God's glory through our resurrection bodies (see Dan. 12:3); and heavenly treasures (see Matt. 6:19-21). To be sure, this is not an exhaustive list, and I certainly do not claim to understand everything about this complex and fascinating aspect of Bible doctrine, but I think we can be clear on the essential criteria for rewards and the content of rewards. By the way, another book to broaden your understanding of eternal rewards is by Randy Alcorn. It is entitled, *Money, Possessions, and Eternity*. Alcorn has written many books, both fiction and non-fiction alike; he is a phenomenal writer and has done extensive research on the doctrine of rewards."

"My, how I have taken delight sharing every moment with you all during these weeks of study. And as I pondered how to end our series on the bema seat of Christ, a dramatic true story came to mind. It's about a high school junior. Her name, Kay Bothwell. Joseph Dillow tells the story:

> Kay was greatly admired by both Christians and non-Christians alike. Not only had she given her life to Christ, but she had also allowed Christ to be formed in her.
>
> "One day she was given the following assignment in her English literature class: 'State how you would spend your time if you knew this would be the last week of your life.' Her essay reads as follows:
>
> "Today I live. One week from today I die. If a situation such as this came to me I should probably weep. As soon as I realized there are many things to be done, I would try to regain my composure. The first day of my suddenly shortened life I would use to see all my loved ones and assure them that I loved them all very much. On the evening of my first day I would ask God, in the solace of my room, to give me strength to bear the rest of my precious days and give me His hand, so that I could walk with Him.
>
> "On the second day I would awaken early in order to see the rising sun, which I had often cast aside to gain a few more moments of coveted sleep. I would continue throughout the day to visit family and friends, telling each one, 'I love you. Thank you for the part

you've played in my life.'

"On the third day I'd travel alone to the woods, allowing God's goodness and creation to surround me. I would see, undoubtedly for the first time, many things I had not taken the time to notice before.

"On the fourth day I would prepare my will; all sentimental things I possess I would leave to my family and friends. I would spend the rest of the day with my mother. We have always been very close, and I would want to especially assure her of my deep gratitude for her tremendous impact on my life.

"On Friday, the fifth day, my life almost ended, I would spend the time with my pastor, speaking with him of my relationship with Christ and seeking advice for my final hours. I would spend the rest of my day visiting those who are ill, silently being thankful that I know no pain and yet I know my destiny.

"On Saturday morning I would spend my time with a special friend who is going through a difficult time with her broken family and seek to comfort her. The rest of Saturday I would spend with my treasured grandparents and elderly friends, seeking their wisdom and sharing my love. Saturday night I would spend awake in prayer, knowing that God was by my side. I would be at peace now, knowing that because of Christ I was soon going to spend an eternity in heaven.

"Upon wakening Sunday morning, I would make all my last preparations, and then taking my Bible, I would go to church to spend my last hours in worship and praise, seeking to die gracefully and with the hope that my life had influence upon others for His glorious name. The last hour would not be spent in agony but the perfect harmony of my relationship with Jesus Christ.

"One week almost to the day after she handed in this essay, Kay Bothwell was ushered into eternity when she was killed in an automobile accident just outside her home in Marion, Indiana.[72]

"Dillow shows that with intentional focus 'the final week of her life, at least, Kay Bothwell lived life with the end in mind.'"[73] Didaskolos paused, then quietly, reverently offered this prayer: "Thank you, dear Lord, for the legacy of Kay Bothwell; may those of us who come behind her know the joy of hearing your 'Well done!' May we all live a life worthy of a hero's welcome, for that is the only kind of reception by which You will be honored. And Lord, I am so grateful for each of these brothers and sisters, for the moments of fun and encouragement we have known, for the radical changes you have made in each one in view of the bema seat. To a one, keep us true to You until we breathe our last breath, or until You call us upward at the Rapture, whichever occurs first. Protect them on their way home now. And thank You again for being our Teacher these many weeks together. We do love You, Lord. In the name of Jesus, our precious Savior, we ask these things. Amen."

It was sorrow parting. Not one of us missed the opportunity to thank Didaskolos, whom we had grown to love so much, not for just his teaching but for his brotherly kindness and Christ-like love. The fragrance of Christ he exuded would linger in our hearts and inspire us to imitate him as He imitated Jesus in our midst.[74]

We strolled slowly down the red-brick sidewalk and gently embraced each other for the last time. A few talked of meeting monthly at a local coffee shop to review the things we'd learned and keep each other accountable in terms of practical application. That sounded good to me.

As I started the engine of my red Ford Escort, I took one last look at the neatly trimmed hedges bordering the sidewalk; the lush green lawn, so carefully manicured; the window boxes decorated with such variety of colorful flowers; the white house with yellow trim and the large porch with the white wooden railings. This had been a special place and I would never forget what the Master Teacher had taught me. More than ever, I wanted to see Him, and tell Him face to face how much I appreciated His love and purchasing my eternal salvation. And now, more than ever, I resolved to live each day the way I will wish I had lived each day when I stand before Him on That Day—the *bema* seat. I wanted to honor Him with an honorable life, meriting nothing less than a hero's welcome. What could be better than that? Nothing would glorify Him more.

Endnotes for Chapter 10

[1] *Hosper*, subordinating conjunction of comparison.

[2] *Paredoken*, entrusted to, to deliver over to.

[3] *Ergazomai*, to be active, to work.

[4] *De*, mild adversative serving as a structural marker regarding the crucial difference between the third man and the first two men.

[5] Cf. verse 19 where the Greek reads *polun chronon*.

[6] The Greek construction in verse 20 includes two uses of *alla*, showing a strong contrast between what the first servant was given and what he gained.

[7] *Katasteso*, from *kathistemi*, "to appoint"; same term used in the parable of the wise servant (cf. Matt. 24:47).

[8] Emphatic in Greek.

[9] In terms of the cultural backdrop here, "The Greek for this word comes from *trapeza* (table), a word seen on the front of banks in Greece today. Bankers sat at small tables and changed money (cf. 21:12)." *NIV Study Bible*, 1483.

[10] "The Greek for this word was first used in the sense of offspring, interest being the 'offspring,' of invested money." *NIV Study Bible*, 1483.

[11] *For–Gar*, to give the reason for the master's actions against the unfaithful steward.

to everyone–Dative of advantage, or reference/respect; the form is singular to signify the individual duty of faithful stewardship before the Lord.

who has–In contrast to the last man who buried his talent and therefore had none

shall more be given, and he shall have an abundance; but–Mild adversative, *de*, to reveal the literary structure of comparison and contrast, so often used by Jesus in His pedagogical style.

from the one who does not have–Namely, the third man.

even what he does have shall be taken away–Per the experience of the third man in verse 28.

[12] ‘*And cast out*–Aorist imperative, showing the finality and decisive nature of *ekbalete*.

the worthless slave–*Achreion doule*, in parallel with "wicked, lazy slave," in verse 26.

into the outer darkness; in that place there shall be–The future tense indicates a judgment yet to come.

[13] Matthew often mentions this description of the future judgment of unbelievers (cf. 8:12; 13:42, 50; 22:13). In Matthew 13:34-43, the "sons of the kingdom" stand in contrast to the "sons of the evil one" (v. 38). The latter are gathered by God's angels who will throw them into "the furnace of fire; in that place there will be weeping and gnashing of teeth" (v. 41-42). But "the righteous will shine forth as the sun in the kingdom of their Father..." (v. 43).

[14] The Greek has *tous idious doulous*.

[15] Cf. Wiersbe, *The Bible Exposition Commentary: Matthew-Galatians*, 1:92; see also Dillow, 344-53, 385. Ladd adds, "Those who have a proper foundation [referring to the foundation of faith in Christ, 1 Corinthians 3:11] but produce an unworthy work [the wood, hay and straw caliber] will not experience exclusion from the Kingdom but the loss of privilege and position in the Kingdom. We must conclude that Paul thought of graded positions in the Kingdom, which would be bestowed on the basis of Christian faithfulness." George Eldon Ladd, *A Theology of The New Testament* (Grand Rapids: Eerdmans, 1974), 521.

[16] The phrase "do you not know" occurs six times in this chapter alone, compared to only three other times in the entire NT. Paul uses the phrase to expose the moral laxity so prevalent in this carnal congregation–things they should have known and applied were being grossly neglected. The Greek construction with *ouk* expects the affirmative (cf. parallel uses of *ouk* are seen in Matt. 13:55; Luke 4:22 and 17:17). In view of this, "Paul had probably taught this doctrine in Corinth in the course of founding the church." David K. Lowery, "I Corinthians," *The Bible Knowledge Commentary: An Exposition of the Scriptures: New Testament* (Wheaton: Victor Books, 1983), 515.

[17] Perhaps the sheep-goat judgment of Matthew 25 is one example of when we shall do so, as well as during the Millennium.

[18] Keener, 463.

[19] Mare states that the expression *pragma echon* includes "different kinds of property cases." See his excellent historical background comments; Mare, "I

Corinthians," *Expositor's*, 10:221. See also Ryrie, *The Ryrie Study Bible*, 1824. Keener's discussion on the cultural backdrop here is also very helpful. Keener, 463.

[20] By way of comparison, Paul employed the civil courts of Rome to appeal to his rights as a Roman citizen for a fair trial and for proper treatment as a prisoner (cf. Acts 22:25-29; 23:37; 24:10-21; 25:4-12 and 16:37-39, respectively).

[21] The term is *adikon*, a pronominal adjective, genitive masculine plural, depicting the unjust nature of the pagan judges of the Roman court; the word signifies the general falling short of the righteous requirements of God's law (1 Pet. 3:18), and, as such, it stands in sharp contrast to *dikaios*.

[22] *Adikos* can have this semantical value, as in Luke 16:10.

[23] Charles Hodge suggests that Christians will judge even the good angels in the sense of presiding over them in the Millennial Age. Charles Hodge, *I Corinthians* (New York: A. C. Armstrong, 1891), 95-96, quoted in Mare, "I Corinthians," *Expositor's*, 10:222.

[24] The term is *hagios* and is found numerous times in Scripture; Bauer, Arndt and Gingrich categorizes the word under (1) an adjective of things such as the city of Jerusalem and the temple there, the holy age of the *eschaton*, the mountain of Transfiguration, the calling of the Christian, etc.; (2) holy persons such as God's prophets (John the Baptist), Christians; (3) angels; (4) God and Christ and (5) pure substantive uses such as sacrificial meat. Bauer, Arndt and Gingrich. 10. The term has both positional and practical nuances relative to believers (see respectively, 1 Cor. 1:2 and Rom. 12:1).

[25] Cf. Matthew 20:17-28, especially verses 20-23. See Appendix B for a more detailed treatment of this passage.

[26] The reward is for his character borne out in his actions as a good and faithful servant (v. 17).

[27] Dillow, 564. The same author asserts that in Luke 12:35-48, the articular phrase *ton apiston* (usually translated "the unbelievers") should be rendered "the unfaithful," a reference to a carnal believer who was a poor steward of what his master had left him to do and therefore forfeits the privilege of being put in charge of his master's possessions as in the case of the faithful servant of verses 43-44. Dillow, 389.

[28] Hoyt observes that "The Judgment Seat of Christ might be compared to a commencement ceremony. At graduation there is some measure of disappointment and remorse that one did not do better and work harder. However, at such an event overwhelming emotion is joy, not remorse. The graduates do not leave the auditorium weeping because they did not earn better grades. Rather, they are thankful that they have been graduated, and they are grateful for what they did achieve. To overdo the sorrow aspect of the Judgment Seat of Christ is to make heaven hell. To underdo the sorrow aspect is to make faithfulness inconsequential."

Samuel L. Hoyt, "The Judgment Seat of Christ in Theological Perspective Part 2: The Negative Aspects of the Christian's Judgment," *Bibliotheca Sacra*, 137, no. 546 (April-June 1980): 129-30. In this regard, cf. 1 John 2:28.

[29] Charles Baker lists several passages where the kinds of behavior that result in forfeiture of rewards is stated or implied (1 Cor. 5:5; 9:24-27; 11:31-33; Col. 2:18; 3:24-25). Charles F. Baker, *A Dispensational Theology* (Grand Rapids, MI: Grace Bible College Publications, 1971), 605-606.

[30] *For if*–The first of four conditional clauses, the first two being positive and the remaining two, negative. In this initial sentence, the indicative mood in the *protasis* and the *apodosis* shows a condition of reality (a simple particular instance), accepting as true what is stated.

we died–Aorist tense, *sunapethanomen*, "to die together." Rienecker, 641; showing a crisis, a definite act of the believer's co-identification with Christ in His death for sin (cf. Rom. 6:8).

with Him, we will also live–Suzesomen, from *suzaw*, to live together with, to live with someone. Rienecker, 641; refers to the believer's co-identification with Christ in His resurrection, resulting in his ability to walk in newness of life (Rom. 6:4).

with Him; If we endure–The second couplet begins with a present tense verb, *hypomenomen*, "to endure." Using the same word, Paul has just declared his willingness to "endure all things for the sake of those are chosen, so that they also may obtain the salvation which is in Christ Jesus and with it eternal glory" (v. 10). The present tense contrasts the punctiliar nature of the preceding aorist, "we have died with Him," so that this past event of the believer's union with Christ's beneficiary death enables him to be clothed with spiritual endurance for the spiritual benefit of others.

we will also reign with Him–The words "we will reign with Him" render the Greek term *sumbasileusomen* from *sumbasileuo*, "to be king together, to rule with someone." Rienecker, 641. The cause-effect relationship in the couplet is obvious: to endure here means reigning in the hereafter with Christ, part of the criteria and content of future rewards for the believer. This motif of co-rulership with Christ in the coming age is illustrated and confirmed elsewhere (Dan. 7:9, 22; Matt. 19:27-20:16; 24:47; 25:14-30; Luke 19:11-27; 1 Cor. 4:8; 6:2-3; Rev. 2:26-27; 3:12, 21; 5:9-10; 20:4-6).

If we deny Him–The word deny is *arnesometha*, again a first class conditional sentence, presenting a real condition. The term means to refuse someone, not to know or recognize him either in the face of a former relationship or better knowledge. The believer who fails to provide for his family denies the faith and is worse than an unbeliever in reference to his incredible insensitivity and lack of dependability (1 Tim. 5:8); ungodliness should be denied, rejected by believers in view of the gracious salvation received (Titus 2:12); the saints at Pergamum, amid great opposition, did not deny their faith in Christ (Rev. 2:12); Peter, on the other hand, denied his association with Christ to the slave girl (Matt. 26:70). Moses refused to be known as the son of Pharaoh's daughter (Heb. 11:24); in general, as Bauer, Arndt and Gingrich states, the term is opposite *homologein* = admit, say "yes"; in fact, in Matthew 10:32-33, the two terms are juxtaposed; often in view is "apostasy from the Christian faith." Bauer, Arndt and Gingrich, 107. It is hard to accept outright rejection here, as some would view this denial or disowning. The NIV rendering of "disown" is best since this term is "more accurate when applied to persons as its object." Ralph Earle, "2 Timothy," in *The Expositor's Bible Commentary*, ed. by Frank E. Gaebelein (Grand Rapids, MI: Zondervan, 1984), 11:401. Peter certainly experienced spiritual failure in his disowning the Lord before the crowd (see above), but remained in the faith, as does the believer who denies his faith by not taking care of his family in 1 Timothy 5:8, though his reputation is soiled deeply. Further, the pronoun "we," in verses 11-13, to be consistent, must refer, in each case, to Paul and Timothy, the recipient of the letter, and by extension to each believer. Unless one believes a falling out like Peter had evicts one from God's family (a works-righteousness versus free grace-righteousness), this disowning must be viewed as an act of carnality in contrast with "endure" in the previous couplet and in parallel with "faithless" in the following couplet. But in what sense does He deny us, as the *apodosis* states? Perhaps in withholding the reward of reigning with Him per the reward of enduring in verse 12. As Wiersbe writes, "What a pair of paradoxes! Death leads to life! Suffering leads to glory! We have nothing to fear! The important thing is that we not 'disown' our Lord; for if we disown Him here, He will disown us before the Father (Mt. 10:33). In that great 'roll call' in glory, when the 'medals' are given out, we will lose our reward if we disown His name." Wiersbe, 2:245.

He also will deny us; If we are faithless–The term faithless means to be unfaithful, untrustworthy (*apistoumen*); in the present tense it has the idea of a settled refusal to place confidence in Jesus. Confer, the use of the term in Luke 24:11, 41 regarding the disciples' doubts about Jesus' bodily resurrection, and in 1 Peter 2:7, referring to unbelievers; see also the classical example of "disloyal soldiers" in Xenophon's *Anabasis*. Bauer, Arndt and Gingrich, 84. The term is opposite *pistos*. Here the word denotes again (as with "disown Him" above) a carnal believer who proves unfaithful to Christ, but as the *apodosis* shows, Christ cannot (*dunatai*) deny (*arnesasthai*, from same word used in v. 12) Himself, i.e., He is true to His own character, this being the reason (*gar*) He remains (*menei*) faithful to His struggling child. As Liftin says, "Christ cannot disown Himself; therefore He will not deny even unprofitable members of His own body. True children of God cannot become something other than children, even when disobedient and weak. Christ's faithfulness to Christians is not contingent on their faithfulness to Him." A. Duane Liftin, "2 Timothy," in *The Bible Knowledge Commentary: An Exposition of the Scriptures: New Testament*, ed. by John F. Walvoord and

Roy B. Zuck (Wheaton: Victor Books, 1983), 754.

[31] The term loved is *agapesas*, showing that *agape* is not always used in the NT in a positive sense, though it is in almost every case, especially of God's unconditional, sacrificial love for sinners (John 3:16).

[32] See Appendix B for further details regarding the Imperishable Crown of 1 Corinthians 9:25. A further discussion of the Crown of Righteousness, 2 Timothy 4:8, is found in Appendix A: *stephanos*.

[33] See Appendix B for a brief treatment of 2 John 8.

[34] See Appendix A for a word study on the Greek term *nikon* rendered "overcomes."

[35] *Exousian*, as Vine states, refers to "the ability or strength with which one is endued then to that of the power of authority, the right to exercise power (Mt. 9:6; 12:23)." Vine, 45. The term is used also of apostolic authority (2 Cor. 10:8), the civil government (Rom. 13:1-3), the evil forces of wickedness (Eph. 6:12: demons under Satan's authority), the Lord's authority over the church (1 Cor. 11) and Jesus' authority over the nations which provides the means of success for His followers as they embrace His mandate to disciple the nations (Matt. 28:18-20)–He will "build His church and the gates of hell will not prevail against it" (Matt. 16:18).

[36] John F. Walvoord, "Revelation," in *The Bible Knowledge Commentary: An Exposition of the Scriptures: New Testament*, ed. by John F. Walvoord and Roy B. Zuck (Wheaton: Victor Books, 1983), 938.

[37] Walvoord, "Revelation," in *The Bible Knowledge Commentary*, 938.

[38] Note the present tense of the participles in parallel here: *ho nikon* and *ho teron*.

[39] Revelation 2:26-27 is explained further in Appendix B.

[40] Alan Johnson, "Revelation," in *The Expositor's Bible Commentary*, 12:459-60.

[41] Cf. verses 14-15. For all its wealth, the city suffered from a pathetic water system. Their water originated from either a hot springs or from a cooler source; in either case it arrived lukewarm via the aqueduct. Jesus drew from this reality to expose their spiritual lukewarm condition.

[42] This particular group of Christians is included in the identities of those mentioned in Revelation 20:4-6.

[43] Regarding David's role, see for example, Jeremiah 30:9; and cf. Pentecost's excellent discussion on this matter; it would only make sense to include OT saints in the future rule of Messiah in light of passages such as Daniel 7:14, 27 and Zechariah 3:7. J. Dwight Pentecost, *Things to Come: A Study in Biblical Eschatology* (Grand Rapids: Zondervan, 1978), 498ff.

[44] Daniel 7:9, 22 assert, prophetically, the dominion of the saints in Messiah's future rule. The doctrine of rewards is certainly present in the OT.

[45] Dillow, 577. Kroll states that "the incorruptible crown is given as a reward

for those who have lived a separated life unto the Lord, one constantly cleansed by confession of sin. If we constantly say 'no' to our fleshly appetites and live fully and completely for the glory of God, the incorruptible crown is ours." Woodrow Michael Kroll, *It Will Be Worth It All* (Neptune, NJ: Loizeaux Brothers, 1977), 96-97.

[46] See details in Appendix B: 1 Peter 5:1-4.

[47] Cf. Revelation 4:10 and see Appendix B. Kroll's observation is worth noting: "When our earthly life is past, what better way to continue bringing glory to God than to make another sacrifice by laying down our crowns at His feet? The very act of placing these tangible rewards at the Lord's feet is an act of transferring the glory to the One who is truly deserving of it—Jesus....By striving to obtain more crowns, we will be able to honor Him more. Our eternal destiny is to bring glory to God." Kroll, 101. It should be noted that some view the twenty-four elders as angels based upon the better reading of earlier manuscripts of the pronoun "they" versus "we" in KJV as per Revelation 5:9. In this regard, how would church saints be singing about themselves? Thus it must be angels singing about church saints and their redemption by Christ. However, if seen as representatives of the church, these literal twenty-four elders speak for the great throng of the redeemed. See Walvoord's comments in the text. Walvoord, "Revelation," 946.

[48] As Burgess aptly notes, "The reward is far above any calculations one can make. It is not commensurate. It is grace abounding. It is the divine surprise. It is beyond proportion (Mt. 25:21, 23; cf. Mt. 24:47; & Luke 12:44), a hundredfold (Mt. 19:29...), overflowing (Luke 6:38; Mt. 5:12 & Luke 6:23), undeserving (Luke 17:7-10; Mt. 20:1-16)....Nor is such abundant reward limited to the future, for it begins now (Mk. 10:30; Lk. 18:28-30)....The best illustration of what is meant by 'undeserving' is the parable of the unworthy slaves in Luke 17:7-10. Strictly speaking, slaves are never paid, for they themselves are the property of their master. Although they cannot be paid, they can be rewarded, and, when they are, it is to be entrusted with more responsibility (Mt. 25:21, 23; Luke 19:17, 19)!" Joseph A. Burgess, "Rewards, But in a Very Different Sense," in *Justification by Faith.* Lutherans and Catholics in Dialogue VII, ed. by H. George Anderson, T. Austin Murphy, and Joseph A. Burgess (Minneapolis, MN: Augsburg Publishing House, 1985), 107. To this Spicq cites St. Thomas who said, "Our works derive their merit from the fact that they proceed from the grace of the Holy Spirit." Ceslas Spicq, *Theological Lexicon of the New Testament*, trans. and ed. by James D. Ernest (Peabody: Hendrickson Publishers, 1994), 2:511. Finally, in this vein, Vos says, "The differences between the Jewish and the Pauline standpoint may be briefly formulated as follows: according to the Jewish mind the matter rests on a commercial basis; consequently God has no choice but is bound to reward; Paul never loses out of sight the prerogative of the divine sovereignty. God is not under obligation to reward such as He is under to punish sin, except in so far as He has bound Himself by implicit or explicit promise. It further follows from this

that the reward according to Paul is never meted out on the basis of strict equivalence; in this respect also God retains His full sovereignty....henceforth, it is not only a reward of grace, but specifically a reward bestowed by paternal love." Geerhardus Vos, *The Pauline Eschatology* (Grand Rapids: Eerdmans, 1972), 276.

[49] Cf. 1 Cor.3:8. The whole idea of degrees of reward is replete in Scripture; Vos lists the following references as examples: 1 Cor. 1:4-8; 3:8; 15:32,58; 2 Cor. 4:16; 5:10; 9:6-8; Gal. 6:5-10; Phil. 1:10,26; 2:16; Col. 1:5; 3:24; 1 Thess. 3:13; 5:23; 2 Thess. 1:7; I Tim. 2:18; 4:8; 5:25; 6:18,19; 2 Tim. 2:11; 4:4,8,14,16. Vos, 275.

[50] As the context shows, the era in view here is clearly the Tribulation of Revelation 6-19. Verse 3 says, "Those who have insight will shine brightly like the brightness of the expanse of heavens and those who lead the many to righteousness, like the stars forever and ever." As Wood observes, "The same basic word is used for 'brightness' as for 'shall shine' (root, *zahar*, 'to shine forth, to be brilliant')....The thought is that each of the 'wise' would shine like a star in the vastness of space....The duration of this shining will be 'forever and ever' (*leolam we'ed*, literally, 'to an age and yet'), a common Scriptural reference to eternity. Strong motivation is thus provided for faithfulness in witnessing for Christ in the world." Leon Wood, *A Commentary on Daniel* (Grand Rapids: Zondervan, 1973), 320. Citing this verse, Berkhof says, "Our good works will be the measure of our gracious reward, though they do not merit it. Notwithstanding this, however, the joy of each individual will be perfect and full." Louis Berkhof, *Systematic Theology*, 4th ed. (Grand Rapids: Eerdmans, 1977), 737.

[51] As Keener notes, "other Jewish texts also spoke of the righteous shining with glory in the future kingdom." Keener, 84. The shining could refer to "the glory of the resurrection body which will, of course, be manifested by all saints." Dillow, 203. Or it could mean that only those who practice a righteous lifestyle will shine as the stars in the future kingdom ("righteous" does not always denote forensic righteousness in Matthew; cf. 1:19; 5:45; 9:13; 10:41; 13:17; 20:4; 23:28, 29, 35).

[52] Pentecost, 226.

[53] See chapter 3 of this work for a discussion on the glory of God.

[54] Erickson suggests that "No one will be aware of the differences in range of enjoyment, and thus there will be no dimming of the perfection of heaven by regret over wasted opportunities." Millard J. Erickson, *Christian Theology* (Grand Rapids, MI: Baker Book House, 1991), 1234.

[55] *Therefore*–The *oun* serves to coordinate the previous thought in verse 34 that these believers possessed something of eternal value, therefore they should not throw away their confidence in their future inheritance as faithful believers, in spite of the persecution afflicting them.

do not throw away–The aorist subjunctive is used here with the negative *me* to denote that the action being warned against has not yet been carried out and should not be carried out.

your confidence–Parresia, "boldness, confidence," used also in 3:6; 4:16 and 10:19. Hodges states that the confidence referred to here is specifically the future glory of the eternal inheritance awaiting the faithful sons of God and the glorious nature of their co-rulership with Christ as His co-companions. Zane C. Hodges, "Hebrews," in *The Bible Knowledge Commentary: An Exposition of the Scriptures: New Testament*, ed. by John F. Walvoord and Roy B. Zuck (Wheaton: Victor Books, 1983), 2:786, 804.

which has a great reward–What they had endured for Christ's sake (e.g., v. 34) would result in a great reward (*megalen misthapodosian*). To throw it away would be tragic. As Morris says, "The NT does not reject the notion that Christians will receive rewards, though of course, that is never the prime motive of service." Leon Morris, "Hebrews," in *The Expositor's Bible Commentary*, ed. by Frank E. Gaebelein (Grand Rapids: Zondervan Publishing House, 1981), 12:111.

For you have need–Translates *chreian*, which is something absolutely necessary, not merely a want.

of endurance–Since salvation is not attained via our endurance in the Christian journey, this endurance (*hypomone*), or courageous steadfastness (the true meaning of the term) is applied as a prerequisite for future reward as in 2 Timothy 2:11-13.

[56] *For He did not subject–Hupetaxen*, aorist active indicative from *hupotasso*, "to subordinate, to subject to one's authority." Rienecker, 668.

to angels the world to come–Literally, "the coming inhabited earth (as in Luke 2:1). A reference to the millennial kingdom on earth, which will not be ruled by angels but by Christ and the redeemed." Ryrie, *The Ryrie Study Bible*, 1946. "The phrase 'the world to come' was considered by the rabbis to be the age of Messiah, the time when the Messiah would rule as king from His throne at Jerusalem (Buchannan)...The term refers to the coming age when Christ at His return shall establish His rule as the promised Davidic king (Kent)." Rienecker, 668. Finally, as Hodges writes, "While the psalm as a whole is often read as a general statement about the role of man in God's creation, it is clear in light of Hebrews 2:5 and the application that follows in verses 8b-9 that the author of Hebrews read it primarily as messianic and eschatological." Hodges, 784.

concerning which we are speaking. But one has testified somewhere–The quotation that follows is from Psalm 8:4-6; the author of Hebrews does not specify his source, but what is evident is that he views Scripture as inspired by God and thereby the final authority in what it says, here concerning its details about the future.

saying, 'What is man, that You remember him? Or the son of man, that You are concerned–Translates *episkepte*, "to look upon, to visit. The word is almost exclusively in the LXX, as in the NT, of a visitation for good (Westcott)." Rienecker, 668.

[57] A metaphor that denotes complete supremacy. Morris, 24.

[58] Ryrie, *The Ryrie Study Bible*, 1947. Keener adds, "The Old Testament and

Jewish teaching declared that God's people would reign with Him in the world to come, just as Adam and Eve had been designed to reign for him in the beginning. The writer proceeds to prove this point by appealing to a specific Old Testament text, Psalm 8:4-6, in Jewish midrashic style." Keener, 653.

[59] Romans 8:17 concurs with this same thought: "and if children, heirs also, heirs of God and fellow heirs with Christ, if indeed we suffer with Him, so that we may so be glorified with Him." As Witmer explains, "In many families children inherit their parents' estates; each child is an heir and the children together are co-heirs. Similarly, since Christians are God's children, they are His heirs (cf. Gal. 4:7), and they are co-heirs with Christ. They are recipients of all spiritual blessings (Eph. 1:3) now, and in the future they will share with the Lord Jesus in all the riches of God's kingdom (John 17:24; I Cor.3:21-23). Sharing with Jesus Christ, however, involves more than anticipating the glories of heaven. For Jesus Christ it involved suffering and abuse and crucifixion; therefore being co-heirs with Christ requires that believers share in His sufferings (cf. John 15:20; Col. 1:24; 1 Tim. 3:12; 1 Peter 4:12). In fact, believers do share in His sufferings; if indeed translates *eiper*, which means 'if, as is the fact' (cf. Rom. 8:9). Then after the suffering they will share in His glory (2 Tim. 2:12; 1 Peter 4:13; 5:10)....Paul reminded his readers that sharing in the glory of Christ in the future required sharing 'in His sufferings' in this life." Witmer, 471. In this regard, we must conclude that Paul's discussion about the prophesied freedom of the physical creation from its curse (vv. 20-22) is chiefly, if not exclusively, linked to the thought of man's restoration to his original place of authority over creation–the final significance of man as a joint-heir with Christ in His future kingdom of glory is the focus.

[60] Larson, 166.

[61] Dillow, 93-94.

[62] *Do not store up*–Literally, "do not have this habit" due to the *me* and the present imperative, *thesaurizete*. Robertson, 1:56.

for yourselves–Dative of advantage (personal interest), *humin*.

treasures–Note the play on words here, "treasure not for yourselves treasures," the same construction found in verse 20 with the cognate accusative. According to Roberston, John Wycliff translated it: "do not treasure to you treasures." Robertson, 1:56. The term "treasure" is *thesaruos*, the source of our English word "thesaurus," a treasury of words. "The Greek also carries the connotation of stacking or laying out horizontally, as one stacks coins...the idea is that of stockpiling or hoarding, and therefore pictures wealth that is not being used...to make a show of wealth or to create an environment of lazy overindulgence (cf. Luke 12:16-21)." MacArthur, *Matthew 1-7*, 409.

on earth, where moth and rust–"(*brosis*). Something that 'eats'...'gnaws' or 'corrodes.'" Robertson, 1:56.

destroy, and where thieves–Kleptai; because of thieves "...many people buried their nonperishable valuables in the ground away from the house, often in a field (see Matt. 13:44)." MacArthur, *Matthew 1-7*, 411.

break in–Diorussousin, to "dig through, to break in." Rienecker, 18. According to Robertson, "The Greeks called a burglar a 'mud-digger.'" Robertson, 1:56.

and steal. But–De, mild adversative pointing up the contrast with verse 19 regarding the wrong and right place to lay up treasures.

store up for yourselves treasures in heaven, where neither moth nor rust destroys, and where thieves do not break in or steal; for–The *gar* introduces the reason for the previous imperative: If your treasure is (*estin*) in heaven, your heart will be there (*ekei estai*) as well–you will begin seeing eternity in time, living life from God's viewpoint.

[63] Keener, 63.

[64] Ibid.

[65] Larson, 155.

[66] Ibid.

[67] MacArthur, *Matthew 1-7*, 410.

[68] Larson, 94.

[69] This story is adapted from Joe L. Wall, *Going for the Gold* (Chicago: Moody Press, 1991), 170-1.

[70] Larson, 157.

[71] Wall, 91-103.

[72] Dillow, 61-62.

[73] Ibid., 62.

[74] Cf. 2 Corinthians 11:1 for this profound principle of spiritual leadership displayed in the apostle Paul.

Appendices

Appendix A: Word Studies

In viewing the New Testament concept of future rewards for the believer, the following Greek words will be considered in accordance with their direct bearing on the doctrine: *nikon, misthos, apodidomi, and stephanos.*

Nikon

The term overcomes renders *nikon*, present substantival participle from *nikao*. Used twenty-eight times in the New Testametn, it is translated "conquer," "prevail," "get the victory" and "victory." Of the twenty-eight references, twenty-three are by John, seventeen of which appear in Revelation. Each of the seven churches of chapters 2-3 are given "overcomer" promises (to be considered below). In Revelation11:7 the antichrist overcomes God's two witnesses and kills them (temporarily) in 12:11, Tribulation saints overcome the devil "because of the blood of the Lamb and because of the word of their testimony, and they did not love their life even when faced with death." In 13:7, once again the antichrist is seen making war with the saints and overcoming them and "authority [delegated from God, implied] over every tribe and people and tongue and nation was given to him." In 17:14 the ten-nation federation headed by the antichrist "will wage war against the Lamb, and the Lamb will overcome them, because He is Lord of lords and King of kings, and those who are with Him are the called chosen and faithful." And in 21:7, the Lord says, "He who overcomes [referring to the believer] will inherit these things [the blessings of vv. 1-6] and I will be His God and He will be My son." This promise is contrasted with verse 8 where unbelievers are condemned to the lake of fire, the second death.

In identifying who the overcomers are, some say it refers to all believers, such as Revelation 21:7 would seem to indicate (otherwise why the contrast with unbelievers in the next verse who are assigned to hell?). Besides this, in the context of verses 1-6, there is the general description of "His people" referring to God's people. The passage reveals His intimate presence among His people in the new heavens and new earth (v. 3), the lifting of the curse for each of His people (v. 4) and the promise of verses 6-7: "I will give to the one who thirsts from the spring of the water of life without cost"—he who overcomes inherits these things...." But, in the passages noted above, those who overcome are conquering someone in battle, and in several instances the concept is associated with authority over those defeated. In these cases, overcoming is more than just a position, but involves victorious activity of some kind that emerges from that position. In 12:11, specifically, the saints who overcome the devil overcome not only because of the blood of the Lamb (i.e., the salvation victory Christ provides through His atoning death which defeats the devil, Col. 2:15; Heb. 2:14-15; 1 John 3:8), but also because of their own obedience. They accepted Christ's blood sacrifice as sufficient for their sins, then share His sufferings in their own stand for Christ against the devil's attacks. Their being conformed to His sufferings (Phil. 3:10) makes them overcomers in a practical sense, not just a positional sense obtained by faith in Christ.

This same active element in overcoming is seen in other uses of the term (cf. Luke 11:21f; Rom. 3:4 [a legal victory is in view here in reference to vindicating God as righteous before sinful man]; John 16:11, 33; 12:31f). As Holtz concludes, in 1 John 5:4 the use of the term "is pregnant and comprehensive: the one who is born of God overcomes the cosmos...Being born of God is made manifest in faith....With this faith believers participate in the reality of Jesus and have therefore overcome the world as power over their life. *Nikao*, in 1 John 4:4, refers to the victory of those who are from God and to the defeat of the false teachers; 2:13f addresses the group of young men with the assertion that they have overcome the evil one. The statement in verse 14 varies from that of verse 13; the context makes turning toward one's brother and turning away from the world and its dangers (v. 16) a sign of this victory."[1] As Holtz concludes, "The absolute use of *nikao* represents the eschatological trial through which participation in salvation and exaltation are achieved. At its base lies the concept of the world as the theater of the battle waged by the antigod against God, in which the historical actions of the individual can either support or oppose the antigod."[2] Bauernfeind concurs that the word group of *nikao* denotes "'Victory' or 'superiority' whether in the physical, legal or metaphorical sense, whether in moral conflict or peaceful competition...[that a *nike*] is demonstrated by an action, by the overthrow of an opposing force....*Nike* is also crowned as victor...."[3] But the same

---

[1] Traugott Holtz, "nikos victory," in *Exegetical Dictionary of the New Testament*, ed. by Horst R. Balz and Gerhard Schneider (Grand Rapids, MI: Eerdmans, 1990), 2:467.

[2] Ibid.

author concludes that "no believer, does not have the promise of the *nikon*: 'He who overcomes...,' 2:7, 11, 17, 26; 3:5, 12, 21."[4]

In surveying the general use of the term and in light of the context of the suffering churches of Asia Minor, it would seem, however, that the promises to the overcomers of Revelation 2-3 (cf. the references above cited by Bauernfeind) are not guaranteed to every believer. For instance, in Revelation 2:26 we read, "He who overcomes, *and he who he keeps My deeds until the end, to him I will give authority over the nations* [emphasis added]...." Verse 27 then compares this delegated authority to the believer in the future rule over the nations to the fact that Jesus also received authority from the Father (cf. John 5:22; 1 Cor. 15:27-8). This verse, along with 3:21, link overcoming with obedience and the resulting reward of authority in the future kingdom. It is admittedly more difficult to see how overcoming in spiritual victory is rewarded with the "tree of life" in 2:7, or deliverance from the "second death" in 2:11. Salvation (if that's what these concepts mean) is certainly not something earned by a life that consistently "overcomes" the enemy. Perhaps these are statements of comfort to suffering saints that though they endure affliction now, paradise is on the horizon—a reality that would soothe their souls and encourage perseverance. Or, as some suggest, the reference to not being hurt by the second death is an example of *litotes*.[5] Dillow also believes that "the tree of life" denotes a special intimacy with Christ shared by faithful Christians.[6] Revelation 3:11 is, however, another passage that seems to view the overcomer as a faithful Christian who has not lost his crown of

---

[3] O. Bauernfeind, "nikao," in *Theological Dictionary of the New Testament*, ed. by Gerhard Kittel and Gerhard Friedrich, trans. and ed. by Geoffrey W. Bromiley (Grand Rapids: Eerdmans, 1967), 4:942.

[4] Bauernfeind, 945.

[5] Dillow, 556.

[6] Ibid., 555.

reward due to his steadfastness, and as a result he will, according to verse 12, be made "a pillar in the temple of My God...." In this regard, "a faithful municipal servant or distinguished priest was sometimes honored by having a special pillar added to one of the temples and inscribed with his name."[7] If this is the cultural backdrop to John's description in the rest of the verse–"...I will write on him the name of My God, and the name of the city of My God...and My new name"–then, the idea of the figure is, as Johnson states, that of "identification and ownership. To those who have 'little strength' (little influence) because of being ostracized, Christ promises recognition in His kingdom worthy of the most noble hero of any society."[8] This interpretation certainly fits a host of passages on the eternal state of faithful believers as being distinctly honored as part of the content of their reward (e.g., 2 Pet. 1:5-11). Walvoord disagrees when he says the pillar in God's temple is "symbolic of the permanent place in heaven for believers...."[9]

In Revelation 3:5, we're told that the overcomer will be "dressed in white garments and his name will never be erased from the book of life and will have his name confessed before the Father and the angels. The white garments are viewed differently; some see them as figures of the imputed righteousness of God (Walvoord seems to mean this in his comments);[10] Johnson says white garments represent "the righteousness, victory, and glory of God (3:18; 6:11; 7:9, 13f., 19:14)" and states that a Christian's safe arrival into the eternal kingdom is contingent on his faithfulness (this sounds like a works-righteousness view of salvation).[11] In

---

[7] William Barclay, *Letters to the Seven Churches* (New York: Abingdon Press, 1958), 89, as quoted in Johnson, "Revelation," *Expositor's*, 12:455.

[8] Johnson, "Revelation," *Expositor's*, 12:455.

[9] Walvoord, 2:940.

[10] Ibid., 938.

[11] Johnson, "Revelation," *Expositor's*, 12:449-50.

light of verse 4, where "a few people in Sardis" had not "soiled their garments," and were thusly rewarded with intimate fellowship with Christ ("walk with Me in white, for they are worthy"), it seems consistent to see the following phrase about overcomers being thus clothed in "white garments" as parallel to the purity of the faithful few in Sardis, thereby denoting not imputed righteousness, but practical righteousness. This seems to anticipate Revelation 19:8 where the saints return with Christ in "fine linen, bright and clean; for the fine linen is the righteous acts of the saints." In this regard, verse 7 says,

> the church "made herself ready" [which] indicates she has worked for the clothes she wears. These are the garments of service, not of salvation. ... They are the "righteousness of the saints...." Not all the service of the saints will be found righteous. ... Thus, preceding this wedding [the Wedding of the Lamb], there must be an event in which the bride will be advised as to what is fit to wear and what is not.... The bride will be wrapped in the acceptable deeds or service which she has done for her bridegroom. ... Between the Rapture...and the marriage of the Church to her Bridgegroom, there is the awesome occasion of judging the life and service of the bride. This event is...the judgment seat of Christ.[12]

It should also be noted here that the term "righteous" in Revelation19:8 is plural (*dikaiomata*); as Earl Radmacher points out, the KJV has not rendered this word correctly, choosing to translate with "righteousness" (singular); it would have to be "righteousnesses," or better, as the NASB and NIV read, "righteous acts." This is not the imputed righteousness of justification, but the sanctificational righteousness of the church's obedience to Christ while on earth.[13]

---

[12] Kroll, 31.

[13] Adapted from a taped sermon given by Earl Radmacher at North Umpqua Bible Fellowship, Roseburg, Oregon, 1996.

Returning to the text of Revelation 3:5, the wool industry in Sardis intensifies the image of soiled and dirty garments, and in the pagan religions, it was forbidden to approach the gods with stained clothing. Again, this cultural backdrop points to fellowship with Christ via righteous living before Christ amid a morally filthy society. The promise in Revelation 3:5 regarding the believer not having his name erased from the book of life is a consoling statement of assurance that any believer would have, regardless of the degree of faithfulness to his Savior. As such, this would be another of John's uses of the figure of speech, *litotes*, where the positive reality is affirmed by the negation of its opposite (see also Rev. 2:11). Further, the overcomers' acknowledgement before God and the angels could denote the praise he receives for his purity (1 Cor. 4:5). Admittedly these promises are more difficult to interpret if overcomer means more than justificational salvation. But, in light of clear passages such as Revelation 2:26, which indicate that the overcomer is more than just a believer, it is this writer's opinion that the concept is best taken as signifying faithful obedience in its use in Revelation 2-3. Such faithful obedience secures various rewards in the future kingdom of Christ. That some believers, due to their carnality, would not be regarded as overcomers, would not be inconsistent with passages like 1 Corinthians 3:15 where it seems clear that not all saints will be rewarded, though all will be saved and inherit, *in the most broad sense*, the kingdom.

Misthos

In the classical period, as Bottger states, "The noun *misthos* can be traced from Homer onwards in the sense of reward for work."[14] For instance, doctors, soldiers, orators, and other vocations are cited in

[14] P. C. Bottger, "misthos," in *The New International Dictionary of New Testament Theology*, ed. by Colin Brown (Grand Rapids: Zondervan, 1975-78), 3:138.

Thucydides, Plato and Xenophon as recipients of *misthos*. In this regard, commercial and industrial venues are the more common places where the word is found. In rare cases the term may indicate the rendering of material fortune in return for "ethical endeavors."[15]

In the LXX, the same idea of "wages" is found in relation to *misthos*. Synonyms would include: reimbursement, recompense, payment and reward. For example, there is reward for military service (Ezek. 29:18); payment for Levitical services in the sanctuary (Num. 18:31); remuneration of priests (Mic. 3:11); and rent for temporary use of a beast of burden (Ex. 22:14).

Metaphorically, there is reward which God gives (e.g., Gen. 15:1; 2 Chron. 15:7; Prov. 11:21). It is imperative to note that rewards from God are not strictly a matter of contract, but a matter of His grace and blessing on the obedient. As well, this reward may consist of eternal life itself (Wis. 5:15).

As we fast-forward through time, what about the idea of rewards in Greek religion? Interestingly, the concept of *misthos*, as disclosed in the Old and New Testaments, is absent here. As Bottger maintains, "Religion did not rest on the basis of rewards."[16] What the Greeks did pursue as a consequence of their virtuous ways was, rather, glory and honor. In "Greek ethics...morality finds compensation and reward on this earth."[17] Preisker goes on to explain in definitive terms just what the Greek man's philosophy on future rewards was. He says: "The good are recompensed here and now for their uprightness and righteousness....The certainty of

---

[15] Bottger, "misthos," NIDNT, 3:138.

[16] Ibid.

[17] H. Preisker "misthos," in *Theological Dictionary of the New Testament*, ed. by Gerhard Kittel and Gerhard Friedrich, trans. and ed. by Geoffrey W. Bromiley (Grand Rapids: Eerdmans, 1967), 4:703.

the Greeks that there will be recompense on earth makes any beliefs in future rewards unnecessary...The man is not good who fulfills the moral demand merely for a good reputation or for a future reward."[18]

"Plato rarely used the term [*misthos*] in ethical contexts and even when he used the idea he thought more in terms of "living according to the immanent laws of being (Rep. 10, 612d ff.)"[19] In fact, "Plato rejects the Orphic doctrine of reward and punishment," using the term *misthos* more so in the sense of recognition and honor.[20] For Plato, righteousness carried with it its own reward. Thus moral acts are to be done for their own sake, not with the motive of some reward. The denial of future reward is even more prominent in Aristotle and Stoicism.[21]

But as the river of time coursed its way beyond the Hellenistic era, the idea of future reward began to seep into religious thought. Again, according Bottger,

> the belief in rewards and punishments in the next life begins to play a decisive role in the Hellenistic religions of Serapis-Isis and of Mithras. In Roman religion the commercial conception of payment and reward expanded to include the relationship of men to gods, illustrated by the basic phrase *to ut des*, I give (to you) so that you can give (to me); in Roman religion people carried out their stipulated obligations expecting help in return. The concept of reward is linked here, clearly, with the language of sacrifice.[22]

By the time of the Gospels, the Old Testament concept of rewards, both material and spiritual, present and future, is in full bloom. The difference in the New Testament is that more specifics are given relative to

---

[18] Preisker "misthos," TDNT, 4:703.
[19] Bottger, "misthos," NIDNTT, 3:138.
[20] Preisker "misthos," TDNT, 4:703-4.
[21] Ibid., 4:704.
[22] Bottger, "misthos," NIDNTT, 3:138.

the content and cause of future, spiritual rewards. This will be amply illustrated in Appendix B, beginning with Matthew's gospel, chapters 5, 6 and 10.

Misthos first appears in the New Testament in Matthew 5:12. "Rejoice, and be exceedingly glad; for great is your reward in heaven; for so persecuted they the prophets which were before you." As the final beatitude in Jesus' Sermon on the Mount, the Teacher pronounces God's blessing upon those reviled for His sake (see vv. 10-11). The cause for reward here is, then, a godly response to non-Christian opposition while the content of reward is heaven itself in view of verse 10: "for theirs is the kingdom of heaven" (probably an example of *litotes*; this coincides with use of *misthos* in the LXX where God's reward consists of eternal life). We note, as well, the present consequences of the great, eternal reward promised: (1) inward joy: "rejoice and be glad," and (2) honorable association with the Old Testament prophets "persecuted before you." As for the source of reward, it is God Himself, implied in the words, "great is your reward in heaven." And finally, the term "heaven" would also imply that the time of the reward is future.

Misthos next occurs in Matthew 5:46: "For if you love them which love you, what reward have you? Do not even the Publicans do the same?" Here, the cause for reward, by implication, is loving those who don't love you. The "persecutors" of verses 10-12 certainly fit this criteria. The content of reward is unidentified while the time of the reward is viewed in the future tense. In brief, God will reward those who walk in love, especially when this love is exercised toward the unlovable. God will reward godly character, because it reflects Him and thereby glorifies Him. In this vein, also see Luke 6:35, 1 John 2:28 and 1 John 4:17-18. These passages reiterate the reality that a life that loves others is a life that merits great reward from Jesus. They reveal that the Christian who treats others as Christ treats him has no need to fear a bad review at the *bema* seat (see also Rev. 3:11 which exhorts believers to persevere in godly conduct so that they will not lose potential rewards).

Matthew 6:1-2 is our next stop. Here Jesus warns of giving with wrong motives–to be seen of men–lest you "have no reward of your Father which is in heaven." On the other hand, sanctified motives for giving to God's eternal work are, by implication, worthy of reward. In fact, those who "sound their trumpets" when they place their offering in the plate will be rewarded, but not by God. Jesus says it succinctly and soberly: "they have their reward." MacArthur states that this phrase:

> was a form of technical expression used at the completion of a commercial transaction, and carried the idea of something being paid for in full and receipted. Nothing more was owed or would be paid. Those who give for the purpose of impressing others with their generosity and spirituality will receive no other reward, especially from God. The Lord owes them nothing. When we give to please men, our only reward will be that which men can give. Seeking men's blessing forfeits God's.[23]

Will those who want their name on a plaque, or a brick, or displayed in some other memorial, forfeit their heavenly reward? Perhaps not; only God knows the heart. But we must take close inventory of why we would desire public recognition. In Matthew 6:4, Jesus says that if, in contrast to showy giving, our giving is done humbly and in secret, then the Father will reward (*apodidomi*) us openly. (It's intriguing to note the interchange of *misthos* and *apodidomi* in Matthew 6; both terms are translated "reward"; *apodidomi* will be considered later.)

Finally, the actual content of reward is not identified here, and again, the time of reward appears to be future.

---

[23] MacArthur, *Matthew 1-7*, 356.

Matthew 6:5 issues more warnings, this time against ostentatious prayers: "And when thou prayest, thou shalt not be as the hypocrites are; for they love to pray standing in the synagogues and in the corners of the streets, that they may be seen of men. Verily I say unto you, they have their reward." Motives, and therefore inward character, are again the focus of Jesus' instruction. As verse 5 affirms, God will reward (*apodidomi*) those whose hearts are filled with humility when they offer public prayers. Ouch! How often have I wanted others to be impressed with how well I've learned to pray. I find myself, too often, praying "to men," in a sense, instead of to God. And that's where my reward ends. God's reward, in contrast, lasts forever.

The same polemic is hurled, in verse 16, against those who fast to impress others. They "disfigure their faces, that they may appear unto men to fast." Verse 18 then discloses the standard of heaven, that is, "That thou appear not unto men to fast, but unto thy Father which is in secret; and the Father, which seeth in secret, shall reward [*apodidomi*] thee openly." The omniscient God, who notes our very intentions, will reward us openly if we practice our fasting privately, unpretentiously.

As we continue our course through Matthew's gospel, we discover that hospitable attitudes and actions are a cause for heavenly reward, according to Matthew 10:41-42. Jesus said, "He who receives a prophet in the name of a prophet shall receive a prophet's reward; and he who receives a righteous man in the name of a righteous man shall receive a righteous man's reward. And whoever in the name of a disciple gives to one of these little ones even a cup of cold water to drink, truly I say to you, he shall not lose his reward." The context of Matthew 10 contains a call to radical discipleship and the inevitable tension, persecution and possible death that may arise in the life of the one who embraces the call. In such times, showing hospitality to Jesus' true disciples is highly commendable and worthy of reward. Even the smallest act of providing a cup of cold water does not go unnoticed by the omniscient One. Note finally, the certainty of the reward as indicated by the *ou me* construction in the Greek. This double negative reveals the emphatic nature of Jesus' promised reward.

Our trek now takes us into the epistles where Paul, in 1 Corinthians 3:8, declares, "Now he who plants and he who waters are one; but each will receive his own reward according to his own labor." What do the apostle's metaphors mean here? In context, he reviews the process God used to bring these people to Himself, specifically the evangelistic work of Paul, who planted, and Apollos who watered. Then God caused the growth. In the grand scheme of salvation, there are both divine and human elements: God's sovereign work in the heart of the unbeliever, the Christian's responsibility to preach the gospel and the unbelievers' responsibility to believe the gospel. Of himself and Apollos, Paul says, "we were servants through whom you believed, even as the Lord gave opportunity to each one" (v. 5). And as a result of their faithful stewardship of the God-given opportunity to evangelize, Paul and Apollos can expect a *misthos* from God. From verse 8 we conclude that the reward is (1) personal (each, own); (2) certain ("will receive" displays the indicative mood); (3) yet future ("will receive" denotes the future tense as does the succeeding context); and (4) judicially meted out "according to his [the Christian's] own labor." While it is true, as Bottger states, that the sole root of the Christian's reward is God's sovereign generosity,"[24] yet there is an element of equity in the final phrase of the verse: "according to his labor." In fact, this particular judicial factor behind the reward is further affirmed by the causal idea in verse 9, "*For* [emphasis mine] we are God's

---

[24] Bottger, "misthos," NIDNTT, 3:141.

fellow workers; you are God's field, God's building." Thus, the basis for rewards seems to be a harmonious blend between the justice of God and the grace of God (the grace of God is clearly seen in v. 10 of this passage). Most commentators emphasize the latter, some to an overemphasis in my opinion, but all see the undeniable fact that rewards are, in some sense, earned. As Ryrie puts it, "Salvation is a free gift, but rewards, for those who are saved, are earned."[25]

With this in view, it is easy to see Paul's progression of thought in the following verses. Having affirmed God's sure reward for the evangelistic labors of himself and Apollos, he now reveals further detail about the bema seat of Christ itself, the event at which such rewards will be dispensed. In fact, he moves from God's reward for evangelism (3:8) to God's reward for disciple-making (edification) in verses 10-17.

In verses 10-17, God tells us that as we build into another believer's life, He is assessing the quality of our work. If we are careful to build upon the foundation of another's belief in Christ as Savior (v. 10-11), by teaching sound doctrine (4:1-2, 15-17), we will "receive a reward" (*misthos*, v. 14). Of course, in addition to sound doctrine, there are other issues germane to receiving rewards at the bema seat of Christ (e.g., motives, 4:5).

Paul's use of *misthos* is later reiterated by the apostle John. In 2 John 8, he writes, "Watch yourselves, that you might not lose what we have accomplished, but that you may receive a full reward." John has emphasized both sound character (vv. 4-6) and sound doctrine (vv. 1-3, 7, 9-11) in this New Testament postcard. In the middle of these exhortations and commendations is the specific application of this warning which, in this historical setting, is one's response to peddlers of false doctrine. Such

---

[25] Ryrie, *Ryrie Study Bible*, 1730.

a person is to receive no hospitality from one who walks in the truth (vv. 10-11). It would seem, then, given the thrust of this epistle, that to lose one's future reward, one would have to stray from sound doctrine which would inevitably lead one to stray from sound character. Or, to say it positively, God promises a reward, indeed a full reward, to those who stay true to His Word and to His Way.

Let's not miss John's point: Rewards can be forfeited! In this case by doctrinal and moral slippage. How many Christians have allowed themselves to get entangled in the barbwire of false teaching while Christian friends stand tearfully by and watch their doctrinal stance mudslide into error upon error and their character into the slime of compromise? Only God knows how many of His own have slipped so, but there are seemingly plenty. Such, according to 2 John 8, will not do as well on their final report card as they could have.

As we jog our final lap, we come to Revelation 11:18 where John writes, "And the nations were enraged, and Thy wrath came, and the time came for the dead to be judged, and the time to give their reward to Thy bond-servants the prophets and to the saints and to those who fear Thy name, the small and the great, and to destroy the earth." As God's closes the book on the Tribulation and sets up His millennial reign (v. 15-17), He also takes time to reward His servants. They are described as "those who fear Thy name...." Their earthly status is of no issue; it's both the small and the great who are rewarded, showing us that future rewards are handed out impartially. After all, "there is no partiality with God" (Rom. 2:11). But who are these saints, to this point yet to be rewarded? That they are not church age saints is clear from the fact that judgment day for Christ's body occurs on the heels of the Rapture at the *bema* seat of Christ. The content of reward is not given here, but as seen time and time again, the certainty of the reward is clear and the cause of the reward is revealed, though only in a general sense: they fear God. At least we can say that God rewards godly character, a fact affirmed previously in several passages.

In recapping the twenty-nine uses of *misthos* in the New Testament, we can conclude the following as it relates to future rewards for the Christian: (1) The idea of future reward is a certainty; wise is the believer who lives in light of this reality. (2) Rewards come from God. (3) Rewards, since they come from God, are eternal by nature; this stands in contrast to man's temporary rewards. (4) Rewards are given for (a) progressing in spiritual maturity (e.g., showing love toward one's enemies; practicing hospitality to God's people, especially in times of persecution); (b) presenting our service to God with Spirit-led motives; God not only assesses what we do, but why we do it; (c) practicing a Spirit-led ministry, which includes befriending sinners to the Friend of sinners, as Paul and Apollos did at Corinth; and for (d) preaching the right message, that is, dispensing sound doctrine as good steward of the mysteries of God. Such adherence to God's truth makes our ministry for Him of great quality and enduring worth, like gold, silver and stones. Both correct behavior and correct belief are criterion for rewards. (5) Rewards will be given out at Christ's return at the Rapture. (6) Rewards are dispensed impartially, individually, and on the basis of the quality (not necessarily the quantity) of each man's work. (7) Rewards at the *bema* seat of Christ are for believers from the church age only; Tribulation saints are rewarded at the close of the Tribulation (most likely at Christ's Second Advent). (8) Rewards, if lost, due to carnal ways, do not effect one's eternal security in Christ. (9) Rewards, due to their reality, should cause the Christian great joy. (10) Rewards inject relevance into every act the Christian does for his Lord, even the seemingly insignificant activities (a cup of cold water given to someone who needs it). (11) Rewards are God's way of honoring publicly (openly) those who honor Him privately (motives) and publicly (ministry before others, both in deed and word). (12) Rewards, as to their content, are not defined in a survey of *misthos*, except to reiterate the previous principle that God wants to honor us by giving us rewards. The forthcoming study of the word *stephanos* will unveil some of the specific content of God's heavenly rewards. (13) Rewards are not wrong to seek after since (a) Jesus commands us, "Store up for yourselves treasures in heaven" (Matt. 6:19); (b) God has made it clear that He wants to reward us (see Heb. 6:10); (c) God has made clear the criteria for rewards; and (d) God has ordained a certain day to bestow rewards (1 Cor. 3:10-15; see also 2 Cor. 5:9-10).

Apodidomi

In Classical Greek, this term, attested in its general usage:

> from the time of Homer, means primarily to give up, render (Diod. Sic. 14, 84, 2), or, to give back (Xen., Hell. 2, 2, 9). In the middle voice it means accordingly, to sell. Hence it acquired the specific meaning of giving something up because of a certain obligation (thus to pay out a wage, Xen., Anab. 1, 2, 12....This gives the word the technical sense to render, requite, in both good and bad senses, Dio. Hal., 6, 73). The compound form antapodidomi, and its derivatives, express this meaning of the word still more definitely in the Hellenistic period.[26]

In the intertestamental era, the concept of "recompense came to be related exclusively to the Law. ...[In this regard, recompense] determines who has succeeded in reaching the height of fellowship with God by means of his good works."[27] Of course, this stands in sharp contrast to the Old Testament doctrine of salvation via the grace of God.

---

[26] Bottger, "apodidomi," NIDNT, 3:134.
[27] Ibid., 3:135.

> Now judgement, recompense, and salvation or condemnation are transferred completely into the future. The present state of salvation, which for the Old Testament consisted in living in the Promised Land, became lost in the hardships of the people from the time of the Babylonian captivity. This legalistic understanding of recompense leads the LXX to translate the Hebrew equivalents into the legal terms *antapodidomi*, to requite, and *antapodoma*, requital.[28]

In the New Testament, *apodidomi* is employed some forty-eight times. In Matthew, where it is found eighteen times, the term covers the following ranges of meaning: (1) fulfilling one's vows to the Lord (5:33); (2) God's reward for proper motives in giving, praying and fasting [in brief, rewards for godly character] (6:4, 6, 18); (3) recompense for every man, according to his deeds, from the Son of Man at His Second Advent (16:27); (4) payment for what is owed (18:25-25); (5) payment of wages for manual labor (20:8; (6) rendering taxes to Caesar (22:21); and (7) giving something to someone, as per the body of Christ being given to Joseph of Arimathea for burial (27:58).

In Luke 19:8, Zaccheus, showing the fruit of his recent salvation, promises to give half of his material possessions to the poor. In Acts 4:33, the apostles give witness to Christ's resurrection. Also in Acts, the word is used for selling land (5:8), or people into slavery (7:9). Romans tells us to render to all what is due them, whether it be taxes, custom, honor or fear (respect) (13:7), and adds that we should never return evil for evil, but rather leave room for God's vengeance (12:17).

Paul instructs the married couples in Corinth to fulfill their sexual responsibilities to one another. The sexual relationship in a marriage is (1) imperative (7:3-4), (2) should be normative (v. 5a), and (3) is designed to be preventative (v. 5b).

---

[28] Bottger, "apodidomi," NIDNT, 3:135.

God's welfare system for His people is, in part, children making some kind of return of financial support to their parents should the latter be in need (widowed, 1 Tim. 5:4). In 2 Timothy 4:8, God awards the Crown of Righteousness to those who "love His appearing." This, as Bullinger states, is a metonymy of cause; that is, loving Christ's return is put for the actions produced by this desire to see Christ. [29] Certainly, the actions are seen in verse 7: fighting the good fight (victorious Christian living/spiritual maturity), finishing the course God has for you, and keeping the faith (sound doctrine).

In Hebrews 12:11, God's fatherly discipline "yields the peaceful fruit of righteousness." In this same vein, the tree of life will yield twelve kinds of fruit, monthly, in the New Jerusalem (Rev. 22:2).

Revelation 22:12 is the final occurrence of *apodidomi*. Jesus says, "...My reward [*misthos*] is with Me, to render [*apodounai*] to every man according to his deeds." It should be noted that man being judged according to his deeds does not mean that salvation is based on his works. Both Matthew 16:27 and Roman 2:6, where *apodidomi* is also found, must be viewed in this same light. This is the only logical position to take, theologically, since it is abundantly clear that works and grace are incompatible when it comes to man's justification before God (cf. Rom. 3:28; 5:17; 11:6; Gal. 2:21; Eph. 2:8-10; Rev. 22:17). Salvation is a free gift (Rom. 6:23). Salvation is based upon faith, whereas, in the most general sense, judgment is based upon works to determine both the unbeliever's degree of eternal punishment and the believer's degree of eternal reward.

In summary, *apodidomi* intimates the general sense of giving something to someone, and in almost every case, giving that which is

---

[29] E. W. Bullinger, *Figures of Speech Used in the Bible* (Grand Rapids: Baker Book House, 1968), 556.

owed, or expected as a just return. It seems fair to say that a cause-effect relationship exists between what is done and what is received, whether in a negative or positive context. In connection with future rewards for the believer at the *bema* seat of Christ, *apodidomi* is used to inform us that God will graciously and judiciously bestow His favorable recompense for spiritual maturity. And within the realm of such maturity lies the inescapable issue of motives. Godly motives spring from a spiritually mature heart, being produced by the Spirit Himself. In particular, God will award those who give, pray and fast with humble motives; and He will give the Crown of Righteousness to those who look forward to His return, a longing that corresponds to and comes from godly actions. Furthermore, we can add that future rewards are an absolute certainty, as seen in the future, indicative statement of Revelation 22:12 and, such rewards are dispensed on an individual basis. He will "render to every man, according to his deeds."

Stephanos

Connected to the verb *stepho*, which means "to encircle," this term, in its core meaning, signifies "that which surrounds, as a wall or crowd."[30] Thus, in the noun form, there is the basic sense of "crown," (to crown, in the verbal form *stephanoo*). As such, an historical survey of the term from the ancient world to New Testament times reveals a host of rich symbolism. But before we track this field of meaning let's first consider the physical nature of the crown itself.

In the simplest form, the crown, the use of which is "attested in Egypt, ancient Greece, and independently in Rome," is a "bent twig or two twigs tied together."[31] Almost any material could be used to construct

---

[30] Vine, 139.

[31] W. Grundmann, "stephanos," in *Theological Dictionary of the New Testament*,

a wreath: "Acc[ording] to [Pliny in *Natural History*] the Roman victor's crown was originally a simple wreath of grass. Flowers and leaves are also used.... Demeter is crowned with a wreath made of ears of grain.... The followers of th[e] god [Dionysus] the god of life and death...crown[ed] themselves with leaves of oak. ...Acanthus as an ever-green is also employed [especially in the cult of the dead]." [32] Other expressions include laurel berries, fig leaves, the olive wreath, parsley, myrtle or ivy leaves, crowns of gold and precious stones.[33] Palm branches are also cited by Bauer, Arndt and Gingrich as forms of certain crowns.[34] But what did these crowns symbolize?

To begin with, as Grundmann states, "The crown derived from the twig which was placed on the head, often open, perhaps doubled, and granting life and fertility to its bearer is a symbol of life...and fruitfulness...."[35] As well, the crown was an integral part of cultic worship.[36] Priests crowned themselves while offering sacrifices.[37] Worshippers too, were crowned.[38] The motivation was that "through the crown the favor of the gods was won."[39] Finally, in this connection, in the form of wreaths, foliage and flowers, "crowns were even [employed] as offerings" in themselves.[40] Crowns permeated nearly every aspect of ancient society according to Grundmann: the cultus, oracles, processions and feasts, as a

---

ed. by Gerhard Kittel and Gerhard Friedrich, trans. and ed. by Geoffrey W. Bromiley (Grand Rapids: Eerdmans, 1967), 7:616.

[32] Ibid.

[33] Ibid., 7:617.

[34] Bauer, Arndt and Gingrich, 774.

[35] Grundmann, "stephanos," TDNT, 7:615.

[36] Ibid., 7:617.

[37] Ibid.

[38] Ibid.

[39] Ibid.

[40] Ibid., 7:618.

sign of salvation and protection, the mysteries, political life, the games, the army, private life, the cult and honoring of the dead.[41]

Crowns served as a sign of salvation and protection, even good luck in the New Year. For instance, "The emperor Tiberius put on a laurel crown during thunder storms because the laurel was a protection against lightning."[42] Crowns were also viewed as a vehicle of power and protection in invoking gods and demons in magic. In the Isis mysteries the neophytes bear crowns; the crown is a "sign of the light of the sun and it brings illumination and apotheosis to the neophyte."[43] Socrates "crowns Strepsiades to prepare him for initiation into his teaching."[44]

Crowns represent dignity, as seen in particular in the political life, and in the death rituals, of the ancients. Those who held public office wore crowns as a sign of propriety. In the Attic popular assembly, politicians who spoke donned crowns.[45] Even as the dead were honored with wreaths that were placed on the deceased on the day of burial: "A permanent wreath was also cared on the gravestone. The meaning of the crown for the dead is the same as that of the crown for divine images; it reminds us of the common view of antiquity that the dead are heroes."[46] In brief, the assimilation of the crown in political life shows its close relationship to cultic, religious life.

This relationship is seen in the sporting arena. "In his address to young people, Basil the Great also describes the efforts and renunciations, the discipline and practice, which contestants must accept, so that their life before the games is one long preparation for the contest. They suffer

---

[41] Grundmann, "stephanos," TDNT, 7:617-623.
[42] Ibid., 7:619.
[43] Ibid.
[44] Ibid.
[45] Ibid., 7:620.
[46] Ibid., 7:623

and do all this to attain a wreath of olive leaves or ivy and to be proclaimed victor by the herald."[47] Then, as Grundmann continues, "The victory party ended in the victor's home, which was also honored by a wreath. In this rite the victor offered his crown to the deity. A victor's crown in the games was regarded as supreme earthly fortune."[48]

Crowns were used as expressions of joy or to signify respect for another: "When a dealer in sausages tells the council that since the outbreak of war anchovies have never been so cheap as now, he is crowned as a bringer of good news."[49] Conversely, when Xenophon, while crowned for cultic sacrifice, heard that his son had died, he took off his crown. But when he then learned that his son had died as a hero, he put it on again.[50]

As a final example, crowns were also common at weddings and other festive occasions. "An amphora shows the bridal pair on a chariot; a female figure approaches the bride and gives her a crown which she carries in her hands. On the other depictions the bride herself has the crown in her hands. The guests at the feast wear crowns."[51] Beyond this, crowns were a part of festival occasions in general. They became "expression[s] of festive joy and took on a profane sense in course of time, cooling the head during the drinking of wine and expressing the joy of feasting and carousing."[52] C. J. Hemer supports Grundmann's assertion of the widespread use of crowns: "*stephanos* in fact plays its part in many ancient customs, and bore diverse connotations, of victory, festivity, worship, public office or honour, kingship or royal visitation."[53]

---

[47] Grundmann, "stephanos," TDNT, 7:620.

[48] Ibid.

[49] Ibid., 7:622.

[50] Ibid.

[51] Ibid.

[52] Ibid., 7:623.

[53] C. J. Hemer, "Crown, Sceptre, Rod," in *The New International Dictionary of*

As we transition to the Old Testament, specifically the LXX, *stephanos* and *stephanoo* render the Hebrew verb *atar*, which shares the meaning "to surround" and is a relative of the "Accadian '*etru*' (probably the 'head-band')."[54] A prime example of this usage is found in Psalm 5:12 where the righteous are given the promise from God: "...thou dost compass him as with a shield of favour." Some forty-nine instances of *stephanos* and seven occurrences of *stephanoo* have been counted in the LXX; and in like manner to the ancient world, the terms signify: (1) honor (Ps. 8:5; 21:3); (2) special worship attire (Zech. 6:13); (3) festive joy in general (Jdt. 3:7); (4) festive joy as part of the wedding ceremony (Cant. 3:11); (5) God's protective care (Ps. 103:4); (6) Israel's worth before God (Is. 62:3); (7) spiritual joy and gladness (Sir. 15:6); (8) rewards for faithful and productive labor (good administration), and for righteous character (cf. Sir. 32 (35):2 and Wis. 5:16 respectively.); (9) victory and triumph in battle (Ant., 14, 299), and (10) eschatological rewards: "For those who are merciful to the poor 'God will plait a crown in the world to come.' (bShab., 104a). The fig[urative] usage shows that in many of these examples the crown suggests radiance and glory. The crown is an eschatological reward for victory and an eschatological honour."[55] In addition to *atar*, stephanos is represented by the Hebrew *tarah*, both of a royal crown (2 Sam. 12:30 etc.), and very commonly figurative, of honour, victory or pride, especially in the poetic books"[56]

But having taken this brief survey, it is enlightening to consider Grundmann's astute observation when he says,

When one steps out of the world of Greece and Rome, of the near

---

New Testament Theology ed. by Colin Brown (Grand Rapids: Zondervan, 1971), 1:405.

[54] Grundmann, "stephanos," TDNT, 7:624.

[55] Ibid., 7:625-8.

[56] Hemer, "Crown, Sceptre, Rod," NIDNTT, 1:405.

> East and Hellenism, into that of the Old Testament, one realizes how slight in comparison is the use of "wreath," "crown" and "crowning." Only in the later strata of the Old Testament are the words more common, but then it is mainly in connection with relations outside Israel or in a figurative sense. This shows plainly that while outside Israel the crown and crowning derive from the cultus, Israel itself stands under the second commandment which forbids images and therefore their emblems as well, including the wreath of the gods and their worshippers. Thus the silence of the Old Testament confirms the cultic-magical origin of the use of crowns and is a sign of the distinctiveness of Israel.[57]

Moving on through the corridor of time, and in keeping with some of the themes noted in the LXX, Rabbinic theology speaks of at least three crowns, namely, "the Torah, the priesthood and the monarchy."[58] The crown for the priesthood is Aaron's, David owns the monarchial, but that of the Torah, we're told, is up for grabs. Anyone can win it! In reference to the crown of the Torah, there is the familiar victor's crown: "The crown of radiance is a sign of the victory of the righteous who have endured."[59]

Philo, too, refers to crowns, being especially fond of the metaphor of the sporting arena: "he compares the contestant in the stadium to the man who seeks knowledge, who lives his life without falling, and who finally, arriving at the goal, receives the deserved crowns and rewards of victory.... Philo demands: 'Oppose (to the desire of the senses) the mind which fights the serpent; fight this finest of fights and in the battle against all other dominant lusts of the sense strive to win the beautiful and glorious victor's crown...which no festal assembly of men can give thee."[60]

As we now arrive at the New Testament, several parallels will be seen

---

[57] Grundmann, "stephanos," TDNT, 7:624.
[58] Ibid., 7:628.
[59] Ibid.
[60] Grundmann, "stephanos," TDNT, 7:628.

with the above tracking of *stephanos*. To start with we see the crown as a representation of honor. Jesus was crowned with a crown of thorns in Matthew 27:29. Assuredly, this was done in mockery to the impeccable Son of God, but the gesture still implies the use of crowns in issuing public honor, especially for political leaders.

In like fashion to Philo, Paul draws upon the perishable wreath given to victors in the athletic games of his day and contrasts the imperishable award available to Christians who embrace the discipline required to maintain an evangelistic lifestyle (1 Cor. 9:24-27).

In the theme of crowns and their connection with festive joy and gladness (even spiritual joy), Paul tells his spiritual children in Philippi that they are his "joy and crown" (4:1). Likewise, the Thessalonian believers, also the fruit of the apostle's evangelistic labor, are described as Paul and his co-workers' future "crown of exultation" at the coming of Christ. This association of rewards and the coming of Christ (the Rapture in this context) assumes an understanding that the Rapture and the *bema* seat of Christ occur in close proximity, if not in direct juxtaposition.

Second Timothy 4:8 reveals a Crown of Righteousness to be given to those who "love His appearing." This correlates with figurative uses of the term "crown" in Judaism. For instance, in the Letter of Aristeas (during the time of the Maccabees), "the author replies to the king: 'Those who hate evil and...act justly' are worthy to be instituted as royal governors, 'and this is your experience, O king, to whom God has given the Crown of Righteousness.'"[61] Rabbinic, Midrash writings of the righteous being awarded in the world to come for enduring the spiritual battle may also be alluded to here by Paul. For, the verse which precedes this promise of a Crown of Righteousness speaks of fighting the good fight, keeping the

[61] Grundmann, "stephanos," TDNT, 7:627.

faith, and finishing one's course of ministry from the Lord. Further to this, if "keeping the faith" refers to staying true to sound doctrine, then there may be an additional allusion by the apostle to the "up for grabs" crown of the Torah, given to those who "accept toil for the Torah."[62] Earle's inspiring ethical insights concerning the Crown of Righteousness are worth noting. He writes, "The 'crown' which Paul knew was awaiting him was not the royal diadem (Greek, *diadema*), but the victor's wreath (*stephanos*). It would be given him by the Lord, who is the righteous 'judge', or Umpire. He stands at the end of each Christian's race, waiting to give him the victor's crown and welcome him into his eternal home. What an encouragement to all of us to keep pressing on to the end! This is the apostle's dying testimony, and it is a glorious one."[63]

James 1:12 speaks of the Crown of Life given to those who respond properly to the adversity God plans for their lives. The recipients of this crown are also given the particular quantifier, "to those who love Him." Revelation 2:10, akin to James, says to the persecuted saints in Thyatira, "Be faithful until death, and I will give you the crown of life." Again, endurance is an undeniable theme and requisite for eternal reward, as is the element of suffering hardship for righteousness. As Rogers and Rogers add, "The crown spoken of here [James 1:12], a head wreath, or circlet, was the victor's prize in the Gr. Games; it might also be given to someone the public wished to honor and worn in religious and secular feasts."[64] In terms of a biblical theology of rewards, Matthew 5:10-12 also correlates well here, though the term *misthos*, not *stephanos*, is employed there.

The apostle Peter refers to a Crown of Glory given by the Chief

---

[62] Grundmann, "stephanos," TDNT, 7:628.

[63] Ralph Earle, *Word Meanings in the New Testament* (Grand Rapids: Baker, 1989), 410.

[64] Rogers and Rogers, 554.

Shepherd to faithful under-shepherds (elders, in particular). These spiritual leaders are rewarded with such a crown for faithfully discharging their duties as overseers of Jesus' flock, and doing so with godly motives. Perhaps Peter is thinking of writings in Judaism which referred to a *stephanos* of glory as a halo around one's head. In fact, in a story about Joseph and Asenath (his Egyptian wife), Joseph is pictured with a "golden crown on his head adorned with 12 selected precious stones which radiate golden beams.... The description...of Joseph has a priestly character."[65]

The apostle John cautions the saints at Philadelphia when he commands: "hold fast what you have, in order that no one take your crown" (Rev. 3:11). By implication, spiritual slippage from their firm stand on God's Word, and choosing to deny Christ (see v. 8), would result in loss of future rewards. Specifically, honor in the New Jerusalem is promised to those who overcome moral and/or doctrinal lapses.

Finally, it is also John who, in his vision of heaven, sees twenty-four elders, their heads fit with golden crowns, casting these crowns before the throne of Christ (Rev. 4:4-10). These crowns stipulate rewards received by members of Christ's church at the *bema* seat of Christ, rewards which are cast at the feet of the One who deserves ultimately glory and honor.

As Vine aptly summarizes, *stephanos*

> denotes (a) "the victor's crown," a symbol of triumph in the games or some such contest; hence, by metonymy, a reward or prize; (b) "a token of public honor," for distinguished service, military prowess, etc., or nuptial joy, or festal gladness, especially at the *parousia* of kings. It was woven as a garland of oak, ivy, parsley, myrtle, or olive, or in imitation of these in gold. In some passages the reference to the games is clear, 1 Cor.9:25; 2 Tim.4:8 (crown of righteousness); it may be so in 1 Pet.5:4, where the fadeless character of the "crown of

---

[65] Grundmann, "stephanos," TDNT, 7:627.

> glory" is set in contrast to the garlands of the earth. In other passages, it stands as an emblem of life, joy, reward and glory, Phil.4:1; 1 Thess.2:19-20; Jas.1:12 (crown of life); Rev. 2:10 (ditto); 3:11; 4:4, 10; of triumph, 6:2; 9:7; 12:1; 14:14.[66]

In conclusion, our New Testament survey of the term *stephanos* (employed eighteen times in all[67]) reveals many parallels to a historical tracking of the term. Some of these have been noted above. But more importantly, this survey has shown basic and profound similarities with the term *misthos* and *apodidomi* relative to the general categories for rewards at the *bema* seat. The areas of personal maturity, personal ministry and personal motives are once again connected with future rewards. But now, in the overall portrait, some colorful brushstrokes have been added. We now witness the weary but pursuing soldier coming in from the battlefield to receive his victor's crown. We see his face beaming with rays of joy as he receives public honor from the One whose face he has longed to see, the One who made him an overcomer. Also coming into view is a group of new soldiers surrounding him, who themselves are his Crown Of Rejoicing before his Victorious Warrior and Righteous Judge. And inasmuch as he has provided spiritual leadership for these converts of his on the battlefront of life, he is accordingly crowned with additional honor. He has won the shepherd's crown. Then add to this glorious portrait the honor the soldier receives as he enters the New Jerusalem to serve His Lord forever, all his battles now ended.

As Jesus proclaimed, "Behold, I am coming soon! My reward is with me, and I will give to everyone according to what he has done" (Rev. 22:12).

---

[66] Vine, 139.

[67] Hemer, "Crown, Sceptre, Rod," NIDNTT, 1:405.

Appendix B: Central Passage Summaries

In this section, the goal will be to review and summarize the exegetical data in central passages regarding the doctrine of eternal rewards for the believer. The field of study will be selected Scripture in Matthew through Revelation.

Matthew 5:10–12

In the eighth beatitude of Jesus' Sermon on the Mount, the Teacher states, "Blessed are those who are persecuted because of righteousness, for theirs is the kingdom of heaven. Blessed are you when people insult you, persecute you and falsely say all kinds of evil against you because of me. Rejoice and be glad because great is your reward in heaven for in the same way they persecuted the prophets who were before you" (5:10-12).

The term "blessed," employed twice here, means "to pronounce happy." Jesus' use of the adjective echoes its frequent occurrence in the Old Testament. The Hebrew idea is that of having an enviable spiritual disposition in the eyes of others. For instance, Job was "blessed" by God for his endurance in adversity (James 5:11; see also Ps. 1 and 34:8).

But who are those so enviable here? It is those persecuted (literally, "pursued," perfect passive participle) by God's enemies (implied) for doing what is right in God's eyes. The phrase "because of righteousness" is in the genitive (adverbial of reference) showing the reason for the persecution. Such believers are "blessed" because (*hoti*, introducing the causal clause) first, "theirs is the kingdom of heaven," that is, they possess the very life of the King and will, therefore, live forever with Him as members of His eternal, heavenly kingdom. And second, they have great reward (*misthos*) in heaven.

The attributive adjective, "great," unveils the lavish nature of the King's reward upon His faithful subjects, who in this case, are honored for enduring those opposed to the King and His servants. To hate one is to hate the other, so close is their identity.

Therefore, having this assurance of future rewards should effect the very attitude with which one faces persecution, thus the two imperatives in verse 12: "Rejoice and be glad...." The term "glad" translates the Greek term *agalliao*, which means "to be overjoyed," literally to "skip and jump with happy excitement."

But such inward joy, in spite of undesirable circumstances, is not only in light of our great reward, but also in view of our link to "the prophets before you." What God-exalting company with which to be associated.

Suffering for the Savior marks us out then as members of God's kingdom, as those worthy of future reward, and identifies us with the prophets persecuted in Old Testament times.

Summary of Reward for Matthew 5:10–12

Subjects	Members of God's kingdom (context)
Content	Unspecified
Cause for (human)	Suffering for righteousness (i.e., for doing what is right in God's sight, v. 10)
Cause for (divine)	God's justice and grace (implied)
Nature	(1) Personal (implied in context); (2) Great (v. 12)
Time	Future (unspecified)
Implications	A blessed disposition, cause for exceeding joy, identification with the Savior and His servants of old (vv. 10-12)
Source	The Father in heaven (context, cf. 6:1ff.)

Matthew 6:1–18

In Matthew 6:1, Jesus discusses three Pharisaic practices and provides corrective counsel. Using the imperative (*prosechete*), He warns, "Be careful not to do your acts of righteousness before men, to be seen by them. If you do, you will have no reward (*misthos*) from your Father in heaven." "Righteousness," here, speaks of acts of piety, duties which "conform to the will of God."[68] The phrase "to be seen" is the aorist infinitive of purpose, revealing the improper motives for pious living. The term "reward" is in the emphatic position: "no reward you presently have (*echete*) in the presence of your Father in heaven."

Moving then, in deductive fashion, from the general to the particular, Jesus now offers concrete examples and application of His imperative in verse 1. Verse 2 begins with the inferential, coordinating conjunction, "so," introducing the first application: "So, when you give to the needy, do not announce it with trumpets, as [subordinating conjunction of comparison] the hypocrites do in the synagogues and on the streets, to be honored [*hopos* + *doxazo* = purpose clause] by men [*hupo* + genitive. = means of reward]. I tell you the truth, they have received their reward in full. But when you give to the needy, do not let your left hand know what your right hand is doing, so that your giving may be in secret. Then your Father, who sees what is done in secret, will reward you."

The word "full," in verse 2, means "receipting an account that is paid in full."[69] Giving to impress others exhausts one's opportunity for future reward, for there is none left to give. Such a person's account is paid in full. On the other hand, he who embraced the Jewish tradition of entering the secret chambers in the temple to deposit his gifts so the poor could

[68] Rienecker, 17.
[69] Ibid.

receive them in secret, would be rewarded by the omniscient Father who always sees (present participle) in secret. Such humble giving would be putting up "treasures in heaven" (6:19-20).

A second application regards the practice of prayer, and the parallels to the first example are striking. There is the same negative command (*me* + imperative = to prohibit current, on-going disobedience), followed by the negative examples of the hypocrites, and then Jesus' emphatic and authoritative statement, "I tell you the truth." Next, is the warning element that such ostentatious religious practice is void of reward, followed by the positive command on how to pray in secret, and then, the attending, future reward is promised. Added to the structure of this second application is a further polemic against meaningless repetition in prayer, since the omniscient Father "knows what you need before you ask Him." And finally, an example of how to pray is given in verses 9-15, though not in the sense of rote formula, but in concepts such as adoration, petition and confession.

A few particulars should be observed here. In verse 6, the pronoun "you" is placed in the emphatic position to stand in contrast to the hypocrites. The "inner room" (*tameion*) spoken of is, according to Bauer, Arndt and Gingrich, "the storeroom, the innermost secret room."[70] As in the first exhortation, motives are the focus of Jesus' instruction; one cannot seek the honor of men and hope to be honored by God, as well. God is concerned with what a man is on the inside, with the kind of inward character that produces humble motivations in our service to others and worship of God.

The final application of Jesus' imperative in verse 1 concerns the spiritual discipline of fasting. And once again, the same structure seen in

---

[70] Bauer, Arndt and Gingrich, 811.

the first two examples is noted: The negative imperative, followed by the positive imperatives and then the promise of reward. The hypocrites fast "to be seen of men," a play on words in the original: "they neglect their appearance [literally, 'they disfigure their faces'] that they may appear...."

The mild adversative, *de* (but) in verse 17, coupled with the emphatic pronoun, "you," is once again employed by Jesus to point up the different approach His followers should take to kingdom living, in this case, in the matter of fasting. The phrase, "When you fast" (present participle of circumstance, contemporaneous with the verbs "anoint" and "wash") assumes they will do so. The strong adversative, *alla* (but), in verse 18, exposes again the whole issue of motives in spiritual life. In this regard, verses 17-18a read, "But when you fast, put oil on your head and wash your face so that [*hina*, of purpose] it will not be obvious to men that you are fasting, but only to your Father, who is unseen...."

Finally, the phrase, "your Father who sees what is done in secret, will reward you," repeats verses 4 and 6 in the first two applications and also underscores the reality and requirements for future reward.

Summary of Reward for Matthew 6:1–18

Subjects	Believers (members of Christ's kingdom, implied in context)
Content	Unspecified
Cause for (human)	Spirit-led motives as the believer carries out kingdom duties (Giving, praying and fasting are the three examples given by Jesus to teach this principle, vv. 1-17)
Cause for (divine)	God's justice and grace (implied)

Nature	1) Divine remuneration (*apodidomi* and *misthos* are used interchangeably in this context, vv. 1, 2, 4, 6, 16, 18); (2) personal (implied); (3) can be lost through spiritual duties done in the power of the sinful nature (religious pride in this context)
Time	Future (indicated by future tenses, vv. 4, 6, 18, in contrast to those who receive a present "reward" from men and forfeit a future reward from God, vv. 2, 5, 16)
Source	The Father in heaven (vv. 4, 6, 18). The Lord will reward us for serving Him with right motives. The idea of motives compels us to consider the real reason we do what we do; it takes us to the why behind the what in our lives. We would all agree, would we not, that it is easy to do the right thing for the wrong reason? As Proverbs 16:2 declares, "All a man's way seem innocent to him, but motives are weighed by the Lord." In 1 Corinthians 4, God tells us that our motives will be one of the issues reviewed by Jesus on Judgment Day. Verse 5 declares, "Therefore judge nothing before the appointed time; wait till the Lord comes. He will bring to light what is hidden in darkness and will expose the motives of men's hearts. At that time each will receive his praise from God."

Matthew 16:27

In Matthew 16:24-25, Jesus articulates the clear terms of discipleship. In verse 26, He then explains the reasons for these terms: "For [explanatory conjunction, *gar*] whoever wants to save his life will lose it, but whoever loses his life for me will find it." Jesus follows with two rhetorical questions. First, "What good will it be for a man if he gains the whole world [the definition of "save his life" in v. 26], yet forfeits his life?" And then the second question, "Or what can a man give in exchange for his life?"

Verse 27 then explains why a believer will not profit eternally who chooses to save his life in worldly gain versus losing his life—and thereby finding it—by embracing Jesus' terms of discipleship. He declares, "For [explanatory *gar*] the Son of Man is going to come in his Father's glory with his angels, and then he will reward [*apodosei*, future active indicative] each person [*ekasto*, singular pronoun] according to [*kata*, preposition, accusative] his deeds [subjective genitive]." In brief, Christ's call to discipleship and warning against ignoring the call is grounded in a future day of reckoning. In *The Bible Exposition Commentary*, Wiersbe cogently summarizes Jesus' poignant comparison and contrast in Matthew 16:24-27 in the following manner (I have added the word "versus" to set off the two approaches a believer can embrace during his earthly life):

Deny yourself	*versus*	live for yourself;
Take up your cross	*versus*	ignore the cross;
Follow Christ	*versus*	follow the world;
Lose your life for His Sake	*versus*	save your life for your sake;
Forsake the world	*versus*	gain the world;
Keep your soul (life)	*versus*	lose your soul (life);*
Share His reward and glory	*versus*	lose His reward and glory.[71]

*In the parallel passage (Mark 8:31-38), Wiersbe explains that "losing your soul is the equivalent to wasting your life, missing the great opportunities God gives you to make your life count.... Discipleship is a matter of profit and loss, a question of whether we will waste our lives or invest our lives."[72] It should be noted that the Greek term, *psyche*, occurs four times in verses 25-26, and should be translated "life" not "soul."

---

[71] Wiersbe, 1:60.

[72] Ibid., 1:140.

Summary of Reward for Matthew 16:27

Subjects	Followers of Christ
Content	Unspecified (positive and negative recompense implied)
Cause for (human)	A Christian who embraces Jesus' terms of discipleship during his earthly sojourn
Cause for (divine)	God's justice and omniscience (implied)
Nature	Judicial, impartial, universal, and personal (each one, [*eskatos*, v. 27], refers to believers in this context)
Time	The Son of Man's glorious coming to earth after the Tribulation
Source	The Son of Man

Matthew 19:27-30

In Matthew 19:23-26, Jesus warns the materially rich to recognize their need for salvation. This prompts Peter to declare, "We have left everything to follow you! What then will there be for us?" The plural pronoun "we" is emphatic and contrasts the disciples with the rich young ruler who, failing to accept Jesus' challenge to love Him more than riches, "went away sad, because he had great wealth" (v. 22). Peter and the others had instead accepted the terms of discipleship. They had "left" (a perfective aorist seems best) everything, whatever meager or abundant riches they possessed, and followed Him. So, he asks the question, "What then shall there be for us?"

The coordinating conjunction "then" (adverb of time) shows the logical connection in Peter's mind between loyalty to Jesus and the potential of rewards from Jesus. The plural "us" forms an inclusion with the emphatic "we" and places the full spotlight on the Twelve. So how would Jesus answer?

In verse 28, He begins with the characteristic, "I tell you the truth" (literally, "Amen, Amen, I say to you...." This signifies the authority and certainty behind His words). Then He says, "...at the renewal of all things, when the Son of Man sits on His glorious throne, you who have followed Me will also sit on twelve thrones, judging the twelve tribes of Israel. And everyone who has left houses or brothers or sisters or father or mother or children or fields for My sake will receive a hundred times as much and will inherit eternal life. But many who are first will be last, and many who are last will be first."

The pronoun "you" in verse 28 is emphatic, directly connecting Jesus' answer to Peter's concern for himself and the others (observed in the previous inclusion). According to Guhrt in the NIDTT, the term "renewal" (*palingenesia*) is used frequently in Hellenistic Judaism. Philo employed the term to signify "the renewal of the world after the flood and also of individuals...Josephus describes the revival of Israelite national life after the exile as the *palingenesia* of the land...Jewish thought, influenced by the OT, gave the word a different meaning than that of the Stoics. The world's new existence is not simply a return of the old. Regeneration is unique, and does not occur in cycles."[73] It is, in essence, the introduction of a new state, a new order.

In the New Testament, the other lone reference to *palingenesia* is in Titus 3:5 where it denotes spiritual rebirth. In the breathtaking transaction called "salvation," God imparts His very life, eternal life, to the one who trusts in the Lord Jesus Christ alone for salvation from hell.

But here, in Matthew 19:28, the focus is on a new world, the one anticipated by the Jews since Old Testament times. In brief, the New

---

[73] J. Guhrt, "palingenesia," in *The New International Dictionary of New Testament Theology*, ed. by Colin Brown (Grand Rapids: Zondervan, 1975-78), 1:185.

Testament idea of regeneration, in general, finds its roots in Old Testament prophecy: The restoration of Israel (Ezek. 36); the New Covenant (Jer. 31; Ezek. 20:33-38); the New Jerusalem (Zech. 14); and a new heaven and earth (Isa. 65). Jesus even refers to this new world a few chapters later (Matt. 25:31-34). In fact, a comparison of the two passages reveals at least three similarities: (1) Jesus calls Himself the "Son of Man"; (2) He is pictured seated on His "glorious throne"; and (3) in both passages the concept of receiving the inheritance of eternal life is used in reference to those who belong to Him. From these comparisons, it seems safe to correlate the two references to the same event.

This being true makes it clear what there will be (at least in part) for Peter and company as a reward for forsaking material riches in exchange for the spiritual riches Jesus offers. In the new order, that is, when Christ comes in His glory to rule the earth (Matt. 25:31), those original disciples—minus, of course, Judas Iscariot—will be co-rulers with the King Himself. Again, Jesus says, "...you [emphatic] who have followed [same term as Peter used] Me will sit on twelve thrones, judging [present participle complimentary to the verb 'sit'] the twelve tribes of Israel."

The question this begs, in light of Judas' defection, is, "Who is the twelfth disciple [judge]?" Could it be Matthias (cf. Acts 1)? This we may not be able to answer, but from Jesus reply to Peter, we do know how he and the disciples will be recompensed (in part) for their loyalty to Christ. But there's more to Jesus' answer.

Verse 29 begins with the words, "And everyone [*pas*]...." The terms of reward are now expanded to every follower of Christ, not just the original disciples. Everyone who refuses to let (1) material possessions be a hindrance to Christ's wishes (houses), (2) family relationships be a hindrance to Christ's wishes (brothers and sisters, etc.), and/or (3) vocational interests be a hindrance to Christ's wishes (fields), "for My sake will receive [future indicative] a hundred times as much [emphatic] and will inherit eternal life."

The causal idea in the words "for [*eneken*] My sake," with the genitive, reveals that the motive for following Jesus is His glory, not ours. This would correct any attitude of self-aggrandizing on Peter's part. As well, this reality confirms the crucial role that motives play in our eternal rewards and forever status in the long tomorrow.

The dividends for following Christ, that which the rich young ruler did not do, but that which the disciples did do, includes having (1) innumerable spiritual brothers and sisters in the family of God, (2) physical and material needs met (cf. Matt. 6:33), and best of all, the acquisition (the literal meaning of "inherit" in v. 29) of life eternal (*aionion*, attributive adjective of *zoe*). This inheritance is another example of *litotes*, or, an emphasis on the rewards associated with the eternal kingdom which is sometimes the semantic value of "inherit." What an investment Jesus offers those who belong to Him. But, there's one more truth to underscore here.

In the world's eyes, the rich and famous deserve the front of the line; but in the kingdom of the Son of Man, the world's philosophy will be reversed: Many who are first (*protoi*), like the rich young ruler, will be last, that is, demoted. The term "last" is used here to signify rank and succession.[74] Of course, the apostles, and anyone who follows Christ, are looked upon by the world as deserving last place in line, if any place at all. But in the new order, the millennial reign of the King of Kings and His co-ruling disciples, the last will be first. Those humbled by the godless, materialistic world will be exalted by the Judge of the earth. (The parable in ch. 20 further explains the meaning of Jesus' statement in 19:30. This

---

[74] Bauer, Arndt and Gingrich, 313-14.

parable is examined below).

Peter, then, got his question answered. He may have been thinking selfishly, "What's in it for me?" or, his inquiry may have been sincere. Only the omniscient Christ knows. The point is that Jesus did not rebuke Peter for investigating the possibility of divine recompense for resolving to follow Him. Some would feel squeamish about making rewards an incentive for serving Christ, but this passage, among many others, contains no polemic for doing so, as long as our service is for His name's sake. If our motive is correct, then Jesus will happily reward us. After all, rewards are God's idea, and His to give–graciously and judiciously. This reality must have impacted Peter profoundly. After all, his loyalty to Christ took him to a cross to be crucified upside down, as history would record it.

Summary of Reward for Matthew 19:27–30

Subjects	See below under "Content of reward"
Content	1) Exalted leadership positions in the government of the millennial kingdom (judging the Twelve tribes of Israel) for the eleven original disciples (and whoever the twelfth disciple will be to replace Judas), verse 27; (2) for all Christ's true disciples, the provision of social blessings/needs in this life and the next, in the form of forever fellowship with God's universal family, verse 29. (Note: Eternal life is spoken of as a gift in the New Testament, e.g., Rom. 6:23; it is included here, not as a reward for discipleship, but as a reward for belonging to Christ as Peter did, and in contrast to the rich young ruler, who did not.) And, the inheritance of such a gift naturally includes all the things that pertain to an eternal existence with Christ, such as serving Him in various ways and positions of responsibilities.

Cause for (human)	Following the Son of Man resolutely, unconditionally, and with the correct motivation (His name's sake, v. 29).
Cause for (divine)	(1) personal (implied); (2) legitimate to pursue if done so for Jesus' glory; (3) an occasion for God's exaltation of His faithful ("the last shall be first," v. 30); (4) may be varied in kind and effect, i.e., the original disciples have a special honor of ruling the twelve tribes of Israel (v. 28).
Nature	(1) personal (implied); (2) legitimate to pursue if done so for Jesus' glory; (3) an occasion for God's exaltation of His faithful ("the last shall be first," v. 30); (4) may be varied in kind and effect, i.e., the original disciples have a special honor of ruling the twelve tribes of Israel (v. 28).
Time	(1) For the original disciples, the second advent of Christ, at least in their opportunity to judge the twelve tribes of Israel in the Millennium (an observation based on a pre-millennial return of Jesus Christ); (2) for the "everyone" of verse 29, the time of reward is not stated. Correlating other Scripture, it would seem that the rewards of fellowship with God's family begin now, only to be fully realized in eternity (Heb. 12:22-24; Rev. 21:1-5; 22:1-5).
Source	The Son of Man (v. 28)

Matthew 20:1-16

The parable in Matthew 20:1-16 begins with the explanatory conjunction "for," (*gar*) which means the parable serves to further explain 19:27-30, especially the meaning of verse 30: "Many who are first will be last; and the last, first." In this parable, Jesus says that "the kingdom of heaven is like [*omoia*, comparative adjective] a landowner [ruler of a household] who went out early in the morning to hire laborers for his vineyard" (v. 1). Each was hired for a denarius (a Roman coin worth about eighteen cents), a normal days' wages for rural workers. Additional workers were hired at 9 a.m. (v. 3), noon (v. 5), and 5 p.m. (vv. 6-7). When evening had come, the landowner ordered his foreman, "Call [imperative] the laborers and pay [imperative, from *apodidomi*, "to recompense"] them their wages [*misthon*], beginning with the last group to the first" (v. 8). Jewish law required payment at sunset (6 p.m.; see Lev. 19:3). But now, watch what happens.

Those hired at the eleventh hour (5 p.m.) each received a full denarius. Those hired earlier (from early morning to the sixth hour) consequently expected a bigger paycheck than those hired for only one hour. When they didn't, they "began to grumble" (*gogguzo*, inceptive imperfect) at the landowner, saying, "These last men [*eschatos*, v. 9] have worked one hour, and you have made them equal to us who have borne the burden and the scorching heat of the day" (vv. 11-12). The emphatic elements in the original are worth noting here. Literally, they pined, "These last men one hour have worked, and equal to us...you have made them."

But their sour grapes attitude is met with this reply from the landowner, "Friend [a 'general address to someone whose name is not known. It implies a rebuke.'[75]], I am doing you no wrong [*adikeo*, to treat unrighteously in contrast with the landowner's resolve to reward their labor with whatever is "right," i.e., fair (*dikaion*, v. 4)]; did you not agree with me for a denarius?" The use of the negative, *ouchi*, in the question expects a positive answer: "Yes, we did." Furthermore, the noun, *denarius*, is emphatic to point up the exact wages agreed to.

Then, the landowner issues two imperatives, "Take what is yours and go your way, but [*de*, mild adversative for contrast] I wish [*thelo*, used of

---

[75] Rienecker, 59.

personal desire] to give [from *didomi*, complimentary aorist infinitive following *thelo*] to these last ones [*eschato*, emphatic, 'to these last ones to give'] the same as [*hos*, subordinating conjunction of manner] to you [*soi*, dative of advantage]."

Next, a rhetorical question is fired off: "Is it not lawful for me to do what I wish with what is my own?" (Again, the grammar expects a positive answer from the disgruntled laborers.) Next, is a question with a stinger inside: "Or is your eye envious [*poneros*, literally, 'evil eye'], because [*hoti*, introduces causal clause] I am generous?" Literally, "because generous (*agathon*) I am?" Then finally, the point of the parable, which connects it with 19:27-30, is reiterated, "Thus [inferential] the last shall be first, and the first last."

Peter's original question in 19:27, "What then will there be for us?" (for following Jesus) is, therefore, thoroughly answered by the Master Teacher. In essence Jesus says, "Though you may be last on the totem pole in this world's eyes, if you serve Me willingly, and on My terms, not only will I reward you generously and fairly, but I will promote you to the top of the totem pole. You will be first! I will exalt you in My heavenly kingdom. On the other hand, those who are unwilling to serve Me and instead pursue their own interests of accumulating worldly gain, (e.g., the rich young ruler) will be demoted to last on the totem pole." Nothing is revealed here about the specific nature of divine retribution for the unsaved, merely the fact that they will be "last."

Summary of Reward for Matthew 20:1–16

Subjects	Christ's followers (from 19:27-30)

Content	Unspecified (monetary wages in the parable are not given corresponding representation regarding what the servant of God will receive on judgment day and neither is the negative recompense for those who refuse to serve God: e.g., the rich young ruler, ch. 19).
Cause for (human)	(1) Spiritual maturity, here expressed in correct motives (vv. 12-13, 15b); a sincere willingness to serve Christ is required; too much focus on rewards is wrong; (2) faithful stewardship of individual opportunities provided by Christ for service; in this connection, the quantity of one's service is not the issue, but rather the quality of it, i.e., faithfulness (vv. 1, 3, 5, 6). Ryrie's comment on the meaning of "the last shall be first, and the first last" is helpful. He states, "Not that they trade places, but that there will be an equality of rewards for equal faithfulness to differing opportunities given to each of us."[76] Some say this parable teaches that every believer is given the same reward, but other passages (e.g., Luke 19:11-27; 1 Cor. 3:10-15; 2 Cor. 5:10; Rev. 22:12) reveal differing degrees of rewards. The point of this parable is God's sovereign control and lavish generosity in the matter of rewards and the believer's need to serve God from his heart, not merely for eternal rewards.
Cause for (divine)	God's sovereignty (vv. 14-15); God's justice (fairness) (vv. 4, 13), God's goodness (v.15).
Nature	(1) Personal (v. 9); (2) honorable recompense for completion of assignment given by the Lord (v. 8).
Time	In keeping with the context of 19:27-30, the owner's return at evening to pay his workers (20:8) is symbolic of the Son of Man's return to set up His earthly kingdom (19:28).
Source	The Son of Man (see "Time" of reward).

[76] Ryrie, *Ryrie Study Bible*, 1495.

Matthew 20:17-28

On the heels of Jesus' prediction of His death and resurrection, in Matthew 20:17-19, the mother of John and James makes a reverent request of Jesus: "Command that in your Kingdom these two sons of mine may sit, one on Your right and one on Your left" (20:21). The verb "sit" (*kathizo*) is the same one found in 19:28, repeating the motif of the original disciples co-ruling with Christ in the millennial kingdom. The positions of right hand and left hand denote honor and authority. So, what would Jesus say to such a request?

"You do not know what you are asking for," He says. Then He asks, "Are you able to drink the cup that I am about to drink?" They reply, "We are able," to which He responds, "My cup you shall drink; but to sit [*kathizo*] on My right and on My left, this is not Mine to give, but it is for those for whom it has been prepared [passive voice] by My Father." The preposition "by" identifies the Father's sovereign choice as the means by which such an austere appointment is made. And true to Jesus' prophecy, they did drink His cup, a figure for suffering. James was the first to taste of it, being martyred by Herod (Acts 12:1-2).

Back to the narrative, according to verse 24, the other ten disciples were eavesdropping ("having heard this" translates an aorist participle, antecedent in time to the verb "indignant") and thus became indignant (literally, "to be moved with indignation," ingressive aorist) with the two brothers, James and John. Somehow they expressed their fiery jealously which drew the following corrective from Jesus: "You know that the rulers of the Gentiles lord it over them, and their great men exercise authority over them. It is not so among you, but whoever wishes to become great among you shall be your servant, and whoever wishes to be first among you shall be your slave; just as [*hosper*, comparative adjective] the Son of Man did not come to be served, but to serve and to give His life a ransom for many." But Jesus does not just teach servanthood; He models it. In verses 29-34, He takes time to heal two blind men on His way out of Jericho. Contrast the calloused hearts of the crowd with the compassionate heart of Christ (vv. 31-34).

In brief, Jesus exposes the indignant disciples' selfish motives for high rank in the coming kingdom. He does not condemn their aspiration for greatness, but rather the means by which it is normally achieved in this world. The Father will grant such positions of honor and authority, but only to those who realize that the way up is down, that exaltation is found in humiliation, that superiority comes through humbly serving others' needs. This is the polar opposite of the world's way (rulers of the Gentiles). The disciples should be focused on serving, not ruling.

So, once again, the concept of being "first" (*protos*) is prominent, correlating the passage with 19:27-20:16. "Many who are first" in this world will be "last" in the world to come, because they were self-serving instead of others-serving. But those considered "last" by the world will be "first" in Christ's earthly kingdom because of their willingness to embrace the standard for kingdom living now. The "first" are represented by the rich young ruler in chapter 19, whereas the "last" are depicted by the disciples. As well, we must note that the purpose of the parable is not to paint a contrast between disciples and non-disciples, but to impart the fact that external circumstances do not determine eternal reward.

In short, the request of James and John's mother is clearly answered by Jesus: "If your sons are willing to be the compassionate servants of others, then such a position of honor and authority in the future kingdom will be granted by the Father."

Summary of Reward for Matthew 20:17–18

Subjects	Those appointed by the Father as co-rulers in the Millennium (v. 23). The emphasis here, given the previous context from 19:27-20:16, may be on the appointment of Jewish believers as Christ's co-rulers; although, other passages reveal Jew and Gentile believers as His co-rulers–some from the church age and some from the Tribulation (see 1 Cor. 6:2; 2 Tim. 2:12; Rev. 20:4-6).
Content	Co-ruling with Christ in the Millennium which entails public honor and governing authority (vv. 21-23).
Cause for (human)	Godly character: leading others by serving their needs from a heart full of compassion, vv. 24-34.
Cause for (divine)	God's sovereign, just and gracious appointment to places of high rank and leadership in the millennial kingdom (v. 23).
Nature	(1) Personal (implied in vv. 21-23); (2) an occasion for honor in the coming millennial kingdom (vv. 21-23).
Time	The second advent of Christ to earth (cf. 19:27-30).
Source	God, The Father (v. 23).

Matthew 24:45-47

In Matthew 24:45, Jesus asks the question, "Who then is the faithful and wise servant, whom the master has put in charge of the servants in his household [literally, 'household slaves,' *oiketia*] to give them their food [infinitive of purpose from *dounai*] at the proper time?" This question, posed to the disciples (24:3), is a logical application of the preceding revelation regarding Jesus' Second Coming to earth (vv. 32-44).

The inferential coordinating conjunction, "then," in verse 45, shows the cause-effect relationship between the two passages. The attributive adjectives, "faithful" (*pistos*) and "wise" (*phronimos* = sensible, thoughtful) depict the kind of servant (*doulos*) worthy of reward. Charged (*katestesen*, aorist active, "to appoint to a position") with the duty of caring for the master's servants, and found faithful in his execution, he will find that "good" (*makarios*) will come his way when the master returns. For the master will "put him in charge [*katestesen*, future active] of all his possessions" (*huparchousin*, substantival participle, from *huparchon*, "to be in existence"; here, material substance is certainly in view, but the thought includes the master's slaves [subjective genitive], v. 46).

In short, based on the adjectives "faithful" and "wise," it is again clear that Jesus will reward spiritual maturity when He comes. But there is seemingly more here than a just reward for spiritual maturity. From such spiritual maturity issues faithful ministry, that is, fulfilling the practical duties and priorities assigned by the Master. The Master, upon His return, will see if His servant is "doing" what he has been assigned. Such maturity and ministry will bring increased responsibilities in the future kingdom of Messiah.

Summary of Reward for Matthew 24:45–47

Subjects	Believers in the Tribulation era (context, 24:3).
Content	(1) "Blessed" denotes an enviable spiritual disposition characterized by an inward joy independent of circumstances, v. 46; Christ's repeated use of the term "blessed" in Matthew 5:3-12 reveals such a disposition; (2) significant responsibilities as co-rulers with Christ during the millennial kingdom.
Cause for (human)	Being a faithful and wise servant of Christ, that is, being and doing what Christ wants, characterized by an attitude of expectancy concerning His imminent return; in general, spiritual maturity and faithful ministry are what's being rewarded (vv. 45-47).

Cause for (divine)	Just and gracious recompense for faithful stewardship of assigned responsibilities from the Master.
Nature	(1) Personal (v. 45); (2) public honor from God (v. 47).
Time	Second Advent of Christ (v. 46).
Source	The Son of Man (vv. 35-44).

Matthew 25:14-30

Continuing His similes on the kingdom of heaven, Jesus, in Matthew 25:14-30, tells the parable of the talents. Verse 14 begins with the explanatory conjunction "for" (*gar*) to reveal why one should obey the imperative in verse 13: "Be on the alert then, for you do not know the day nor the hour." This syntactical observation makes it clear, then, that this parable serves to generate spiritual readiness for Christ's Second Advent (the point of the previous parable, the Ten Virgins).

Jesus says that the kingdom of heaven is "just like [*hosper*, subordinating conjunction of comparison] a man about to go on a journey, who calls his own slaves, and entrusted his possessions to them," (v. 14). To one he gave (*paredoken*, entrusted to, to deliver over to) five talents, to another two, and to another, one talent, "each according to his own ability" (v. 15). It should be pointed out that a talent was a measure of weight. The size varied anywhere from 58-80 pounds. Customarily, it was used to weigh precious metals. What's more, one talent was worth about 6,000 denarii, one denarius being one day's wage. This was a lot of money. And, in this story, the possessions entrusted were silver, as the term for "money" in verse 18 indicates. So what kind of stewards would these three men be?

The first man immediately traded (*ergazomai*, to be active, to work) with his five talents and gained five more. Likewise, the one receiving two talents doubled his money (vv. 16-17). But, in contrast (*de*, mild adversative) to these industrious stewards, the third fellow buried his master's money (v. 18). Bad decision.

After a long time (*polun chronon*), the master returned to settle accounts with his servants. The phrase "settle accounts" translates *sunairo logon* in the Greek, found only here and in Matthew 18:23-24. It is a commercial term meaning "to compare accounts, to make a reckoning." It denotes the principle of accountability.

The first man proved his faithful stewardship by revealing ten talents in contrast (*alla*, strong adversative) to the five entrusted to him (v. 20). And for this, he was exonerated with praise from his master: "Well done, good and faithful servant; you were faithful with a few things, I will put you [emphatic in Greek] in charge [*katasteso*, same term used in Matt. 24:47 in the parable of the wise servant] of many things, enter into the joy of your master."

The term "servant" (*doule*) is in the vocative case here, drawing special attention to the man. Then the two attributive adjectives, "good" (*agathe*) and "faithful" (*piste*) follow to describe the kind of servant he was. The reward is both verbal and practical as he is not only praised but promised greater responsibility in his master's kingdom. Of course, the ultimate reward is the privilege of coming into the joyous presence of his master.

As regards the second man, it is the same song, second verse. For though the two men received different opportunities and abilities, they received the same reward. So what's the point? Faithfulness. The master was simply looking for fidelity to the individual stewardships given.

But the beautiful chords of faithfulness played by the first two men are followed by the dissonant sounds of the third man's song. This man proves his poor stewardship of his master's gifts by his fear-driven act of hiding his talent in the ground. His assessment of his master as "hard" and unfair (v. 24) had prompted such foolish action, and the result was severe.

First, his master rebukes him, calling him a "wicked, lazy slave" (*doule, ponere kai oknere*, in contrast to "good and faithful servant," above) and advises him as to what he should have done (vv. 26-27). Next, his talent is stripped from him and given to the first man, who now has eleven talents (v. 28). Then comes the explanation for such retribution: "For (*gar*) to everyone [dative of respect/reference, singular in number to indicate the individual responsibility of faithful stewardship before the Lord] who has [in contrast to the last man, who buried his talent and, therefore, had none] shall more be given, and he shall have an abundance; but [*de*, mild adversative] from the one who does not have [i.e., the third man], even what he does have shall be taken away" (v. 29; the principle here is illustrated precisely in v. 28). But the axe is still falling on this man's unfaithful stewardship.

Verse 30 concludes with, "And cast out [imperative] the worthless slave [*achreion doule*, in correlation with 'wicked, lazy, slave' in v. 26] into the outer darkness; in that place there shall be weeping and gnashing of teeth."

In brief, this parable paints a sharp contrast between believers who use their God-given abilities and opportunities in life for Him—and are, therefore, eternally rewarded—and unbelievers who do not know the Lord and are, therefore, assigned to eternal punishment. Some teach that the third servant is an unfaithful believer who loses eternal rewards through his poor stewardship of what the Master gave him.

A Hero's Welcome

Summary of Reward for Matthew 25:14–30

Subjects	Believers in the Tribulation era (context of Matt. 24-25).
Content	(1) Verbal praise; (2) exalted positions of service (co-rulers with Christ) in the Millennial age (vv. 21, 23).
Cause for (human)	Spiritual maturity (good and faithful servant) which produces faithful activity as stewards of the few individual responsibilities assigned and corresponding abilities given (vv. 15, 21, 23).
Cause for (divine)	(1) God's just recompense for faithful stewardship (the principle of accountability); (2) God's grace to even grant rewards, especially to give greater privileges and responsibilities to His faithful servants (good work rewarded with more work); (3) God's sovereign distribution of individual abilities (v. 15) and opportunities (contrast between various number of talents given) (v. 15).
Nature	(1) Personal (v. 15, 29); (2) public honor from God.
Time	Future (Second Advent of Christ, context).
Source	Son of Man (context).

Romans 14:10-12

Within the body of Christ, there are differing levels of spiritual maturity and cultural backgrounds. This reality makes it imperative that in amoral issues such as food, drink, observance of days, etc., each believer restrains himself from foisting his own convictions on those different than him. This kind of mutual respect demonstrates the love required to preserve the unity enjoyed by all members of God's family. And further, this devotion to unity proves the validity of one's dedication to God as called for in Romans 12:1-2. In brief, Romans 12:1-2 exhorts the believer to present himself to God, and 12:3-16:27 tells him how this dedication should express itself. Romans 14 and 15, in particular, tell him how to keep unity with those in the body who are different than him in amoral matters. This being true, how does Romans 14:10-12 specifically fit into this context?

Verse 10 asks the probing question, "...why do you judge your brother? Or you again, why do you regard your brother with contempt? For we shall all stand before the judgment seat of God." This indicative statement is followed up in verse 11 by two quotes from Isaiah's prophecy (49:18 and 45:23). Both quotes are preceded by the common preface in the Pauline corpus: "for it is written...." These words translate the Greek word *gegraptai*, which, in the perfect tense, discloses the permanent and authoritative nature of God's Word. And what does He say here? "As I live [emphatic], says the Lord, 'Every knee shall bow to Me, and every tongue shall give praise to God.'" But how is the apostle using these prophetic words in his argument?

Isaiah's worldwide evangelistic appeal, "turn to God and be saved" (Isa. 45:22), is grounded in the fact that every knee will bow and every tongue will confess God's righteousness and strength (45:23). Paul simply applies God's universal appeal to unbelievers to the universal body of Christ to show that every believer will also humble himself and acknowledge God's worth. This is clear by the inferential conjunction, "so then" (*ara oun*), which begins verse 12. Drawing from the realities of verses 10-11, Paul states, "So then, each one [*ekastos*] of us shall give account [*logon*] of himself [literally, 'concerning himself'] to God."

The singular pronoun, "himself," is emphatic and reveals the personal nature of this tribunal called "the judgment seat of God," referred to in verse 10 (*bema* seat of God, subjective genitive). In 2 Corinthians 5:10, this same event is called "the judgment seat of Christ." This comparison, by the way, lends clear evidence for the deity of Christ.

But the word, "himself," is also significant for another reason, namely, it is the most comprehensive term in all references to the judgment seat of Christ. Everything about our Christian lives and ministry are a stewardship before God and subject to personal accountability. However, it should be noted that, contextually, Paul's specific focus is the matter of interpersonal relationships in the body of Christ, especially as they touch on issues of Christian liberty.

So back to our original question, "How does Romans 14:10-12 fit into the context of Paul's argument in Romans 14 and 15?" Succinctly, God is telling us here that another Christian's personal convictions in amoral issues are out of our jurisdiction. We can't sit on our tribunal, peer down our proud noses at him in a spirit of contempt and pronounce final verdict on his actions and motives. And why not? We go back to verse 10 for our answer: "For [explanatory *gar*] we must all stand before the judgment seat of God." God alone reserves the right to pass final judgment on His servants. And this He will do, in the ultimate sense, at the *bema* seat. And every believer will be there for a personal evaluation of his life and ministry. In this vein, it is interesting to note that the verb "stand before" is in the middle voice, signifying the intense personal involvement of our appointment with God on that day.

One final observation regards some basic New Testament background concerning the concept of the bema seat. According to Ralph Earle, "...you can see the very term today carved on the wall where Gallio once sat on the judgment seat at Corinth (Acts 18:12-16); Pilate sat on the bema seat (Matt. 27:19; John 19:13), as did Festus (Acts 25:6-7, 17). All these were Roman governors, so it refers to an official tribunal where the governor could pass judgment on offenders or exonerate the innocent."[77]

---

[77] Ralph Earle, *Word Meanings in the New Testament* (Grand Rapids: Baker, 1989), 209.

Summary of Reward for Romans 14:10–12

Subjects	All Christians (see Rom. 1:7).
Content	Unspecified.
Cause for (human)	A stewardship of life and ministry that meets the Lord's standard of holiness and love. More specifically, in this context the reward is for spiritual maturity manifested in interpersonal relationships with other believers (here exemplified in a loving, non-judgmental spirit in matters of Christian liberty).
Cause for (divine)	God's justice, grace and sovereign jurisdiction over each of His servants to evaluate and honor them.
Nature	(1) Personal; (2) honor from God (based in the meaning and historical background of the phrase "*bema* seat").
Time	Future (unspecified).
Implications	Every believer must leave the final evaluation of another believer's personal convictions to God.
Source	God (v. 10).

1 Corinthians 3:10-15

There was chaos in Corinth. Disunity had erupted in the church due to exalting certain Christian leaders. Some said, "I am of Paul"; another, "I am of Apollos"; another, "I will follow Cephas'; still another, "I follow Christ" (1:12). What's more, these carnal Christians placed too much emphasis on human wisdom (1:18-2:5) and needed, therefore, a lesson on the primacy of God's wisdom revealed through the agency of the Holy Spirit–wisdom taught by the Spirit and received by those who are spiritual (2:6-16; see especially vv. 15-16). And here's precisely where the root of the Corinthians' problem lies. In one word, they were not spiritual, they were "carnal."

If one spent a week with the Corinthian Christians, he might leave with a question in his mind, "Are those people really Christians?" Yet, as the Apostle Paul begins his first letter to these people, he says, "to the church of God in Corinth, to those sanctified in Christ Jesus..." (1:2).

But though positionally "in Christ," practically, they were worldly. In fact, as Paul begins chapter 3 he says, "Brothers, I could not address you as spiritual but as worldly—mere infants in Christ..." (v. 1). Believers? Indeed. Mature believers? No!

The fact that Paul calls them "worldly" (*sarkinos*) means that their living was ruled by the promptings of the flesh, the sin nature (the outlook oriented to the self[78]). And one of the many evidences of their carnality was the disunity among them—disunity characterized by jealousy and strife. According 1:10-12 and 3:4 some were bragging of their allegiance to Paul, others to Apollos, others to Cephas, and still others to Christ. Paul is thus stirred to fire off the stinging, rhetorical question, "Are you not mere men?" But he doesn't stop there. Following his exhortations to spiritual maturity (3:1-4), he explains who these leaders of the church really are (3:5-9). It's a perspective they desperately need.

"What, after all is Apollos? And what is Paul? Only servants, through whom you came to believe, as the Lord has assigned to each his task. I planted the seed, Apollos watered it, but God made it grow" (vv. 5-6). What observations can we make here?

In brief, evangelism is a partnership between God and His people. The Godward side is to "assign to each his task" and to cause the work done to "grow." The human side is to plant and water, figurative expressions for preaching the gospel (see 2:1-5). Thus, Paul says of himself and Apollos, we are only "servants through whom [*dia*, preposition of

---

[78] A. C. Thiselton, "sarx," in *The New International Dictionary of New Testament Theology*, ed. by Colin Brown (Grand Rapids: Zondervan, 1975-78), 1:680.

means] you believed [ingressive aorist = denotes the act of becoming a believer]." Evangelism is a partnership between God and His people.

Then a second principle emerges from verse 7: The fruits of evangelism exalt God, not His servants. The inferential conjunction "so" which begins verse 7 shows that since God makes the work of His evangelists grow (v. 6), "neither he who plants nor he who waters is anything, but only God, who makes things grow" (present participle, "the one causing things to grow"). The carnal Corinthians were exalting God's servants, not God. Paul sought to correct this immature perspective.

A third principle surfaces in verse 8: God rewards His servants for their faithful labor. Paul continues, "The man who plants and the man who waters have one purpose [literally, "are one," the neuter indicating that their aim and result are identical; they work in harmony, not in competition[79]], and each will be rewarded [*misthos* = wages, salary; a commercial term here used metaphorically to denote the recompense given to God's workers] according to his own labor."

God rewards faithful endeavors to win people to His Son; and these rewards are dispensed individually. The term "each" is the Greek *ekastos*, precisely illustrated in the context by the two individuals, Paul and Apollos, who each did their respective task of planting and watering. Also noteworthy, in this regard, are the emphatic words "his own reward." "Own" translates *idiom* (attributive adjective) and highlights the personal nature of God's rewards.

Verse 8 also reveals the future timing of God's disbursement of rewards: "each will be rewarded...." And finally, the basis for rewards is God's justice: "each will be rewarded according to his own labor." Surely, these rewards issue from God's gracious heart. He does not have to reward

---

[79] Rienecker, 394.

anyone. But they are also grounded in the holy standards expected of His servants. The Christian life is a stewardship of various responsibilities, including the evangelistic emphasis in this context. And he who discharges his duties faithfully will be justly recompensed.

Having established the reality of rewards in verse 8, Paul explains the reason for rewards in verse 9: "For [*gar*] we are God's fellow workers; you are God's field, God's building." Since we work with God in this partnership, and with His servants as fellow workers (cf. v. 8, "he who plants and he who waters are one"), God will not let our labor go unnoticed, much less unrewarded. As the writer to the Hebrews declares, "God is not unjust; He will not forget your work and the love you have shown as you have helped His people and continue to help them" (6:10).

It's important to note the continued agricultural metaphor in verse 9: "You are God's field," an allusion to "I planted...Apollos watered...God made it grow," in verse 6. But the metaphor changes in the last part of verse 9: "you are...God's building." Most likely this is an allusion to the many temples and buildings in Corinth. This change in metaphors is significant to Paul's argument as he now introduces, in verses 10-15, the *bema* seat of Christ, a future event the worldly saints at Corinth should be profoundly interested in. For, at this event, Christ will pass out the rewards spoken of above. There will be rewards for those who are spiritual (faithful in their labors for Christ), but loss of rewards for those who are unfaithful. In particular, Paul discusses the divine resources for spiritual labor, the nature of spiritual labor, and the rewards for spiritual labor.

In verse 10, the apostle reveals the divine resources for spiritual labor. He says, "By the grace God has given me, I laid a foundation as an expert builder, and someone else is building on it. But each one should be careful how he builds." The building metaphor, introduced in verse 9c, is now extended. And Paul is keenly aware of the means by which he, as a wise master builder (*architekton*, skilled craftsman), laid a foundation in Corinth. It was by God's grace, here not a reference to God's undeserved mercy which provides eternal salvation for believing sinners (Eph. 2:8-9), but to God's enabling power imparted to those who believe. This power enables them to do His assigned tasks (v. 5; see also 1 Cor. 15:10 for another example of this same nuance of the term grace: *charis*). But what foundation did he lay?

The figurative expression references his joint efforts with Apollos in winning the Corinthians to Christ (v. 5). Of course, laying this foundation meant preaching Christ crucified (2:1-5), since, according to verse 12, "...no one can lay any foundation other than the one already laid, which is Jesus Christ." In brief, Paul preached the glad news about Christ to the Corinthians, and they believed the message. And this he did, not only by God's grace, but by God's wisdom as well.

Paul describes himself as a "wise master builder" in verse 10, an indirect rebuke, perhaps, to the carnal Corinthians' emphasis on human wisdom and their subsequent failure to exalt the wisdom of God (cf. 1:18-2:5). By God's enabling grace and God's wisdom, Paul labored in Corinth.

But now someone else was building (literally, "continually building," present active) upon the foundation Paul had laid (that is, "laid once and for all," culminative or perfective aorist). And due to the sacred and true nature of this foundation laid—Jesus Christ Himself in the hearts of the Corinthians—and due to the coming judgment of rewards (vv. 12-15), "each one [who is building] must be careful [*blepete*] how he builds" (v. 10c). The words "each one" (*ekastos*) remind the reader of the aforementioned reality that God's rewards are individually dispensed. Each believer is accountable to God for how he has labored (see "each one" in v. 8.). But what is the criteria for our labor? What kind of labor yields God's eternal reward? And which kind does not? Paul answers such questions in verses 12-15: "If any man builds on this foundation using gold, silver, costly stones, wood, hay or straw, his work will be shown for what is, because the Day will bring it to light. It will be revealed with fire, and the fire will test the quality of each man's work. If what he has built survives, he will receive his reward. If it is burned up, he will suffer loss; he himself will be saved, but only as one escaping through the flames." Several observations must be made here.

First, the context here focuses on making disciples of new believers. Paul is addressing those who are actively and consistently building on "this foundation," that is, the foundation of belief in Jesus Christ as one's redeemer (cf. 1:30 and 3:5: "servants through who you believed"). And in view of the emphasis on teaching God's truth in the following context (4:1-2, 15-17), it seems safe to say that Paul's definitive focus here is on those teaching God's Word to the Corinthians. Each teacher's message is being evaluated to see if it represents gold, silver and costly stones, metaphors for that which is valuable and enduring in God's eyes, namely, sound doctrine about Jesus Christ. Or, "wood, hay and straw", metaphors for that which is worthless and of no lasting value, namely, false doctrine (teaching which does not correspond to the true gospel and wisdom of Christ).

By further comparison, gold, silver, and costly stones would represent the qualitative labor that the Holy Spirit alone can produce, as Paul's ministry in Corinth illustrates (see 2:1-5). The apostle's discussion about receiving the Spirit at conversion, the subsequent understanding of what God has "freely given us" (v. 12), and then teaching God's wisdom as you are "taught by the Spirit" (v. 13), should be correlated here.

By stark contrast, wood, hay and straw would signify non-qualitative labor, that which is done in the flesh (the carnality the Corinthians were accused of in 3:1-4, and in chapters 12-14 in the use of spiritual gifts).

Culturally, "costly stones" (*timios*), such as marble and granite, were used to erect strong, quality buildings, and "straw" (*kalame*) as building material for thatched roofs of low quality.

Verse 13 then continues the thought of verse 12: "his work will be shown for what it is, because [*hoti*, introducing causal clause] the Day will bring it to light." These words reveal that this judgment will occur on a well-known day (the noun "day" is articular). But what day is in view? 1 Corinthians 4:5 gives the answer: "Therefore, judge nothing before the appointed time; wait till the Lord comes. He will bring to light what is hidden in darkness and will expose the motives of men's hearts. At that time each will receive his praise from God."

It is obvious that both passages have the same event in mind. Given this fact, the "day" spoken of in 1 Corinthians 3:13 is clarified in 1 Corinthians 4:5 as Christ's coming at the Rapture. And on that day each man's work (*ton ergon*) will be brought to light, that is manifested (*phaneroo*) in its true character, (*phaneroo* is employed in both verses, showing yet another link in the two references to the same event). And, according to the end of verse 13, the reason (*hoti*, to introduce a causal clause) it will be so clearly manifest is that "with fire [emphatic] it will be revealed, and the fire will test the quality of each man's work."

"Fire" is a metaphor here of the thorough examination by the omniscient Christ, who, according to 1 Corinthians 4:5, will even take into account the very motives in the believer's heart. The term "quality" translates a term (*hopoion*) that was used of testing metal for genuine character. Once "put through the fire," the metal was found to be approved or disapproved.

So also, Christ will examine the messages we preach, the Bible studies and counsel we give, and see if it rightly divides His truth (2 Tim. 2:15). If it does, we will individually be approved for reward: "If any man's work which he has built upon it remains [*menei*, 'shall abide'], he shall receive a reward" (literally, "a reward [emphatic] he shall receive"). Such sound teaching honors the Lord who gave it by His Spirit (2:6-16) and is, therefore, of great worth and enduring quality, like gold, silver and precious stones.

But not every believer will be found completely faithful to those things "taught by the Spirit" and will see their work go up in smoke: "If any man's work is burned up, he shall suffer loss; but he himself shall be saved, yet so as through fire" (v. 15).

The verb "burned up" has the idea of total consumption by fire (*katakaestai*; the prefix *kata* intensifies the meaning). But note that the non-rewarded work is not to be confused with the security of salvation. True, the errant teacher of the Word will suffer loss of reward (the passive voice in the verb "suffer loss" shows that Christ, the Judge, will exact this just penalty), but he himself (emphatic) shall be saved (*sothesetai*, future passive, "he shall be rescued..."). His teaching will be worthless and non-durable like wood, hay and straw, but his salvation is as stable and secure as the Christ who gave it. This fact is further confirmed by the final words of verse 15, "yet so as through fire." The Greek phrase is *hos dia puros*. As Rienecker states, "The prep[osition] is to be taken in a local sense; that is 'as one who dashes through the flames safe, but w[ith] the smell of fire upon him' (Barrett)."[80]

A final observation here regards the first class condition of both declarative sentences in verses 14-15. This means that the assumptions (if) in both cases are assumed as true.

As we arrive at verses 16-17, Paul continues his warning to those whose teaching is not reflective of the careful master builder (v. 10). First,

---

[80] Rienecker, 394-395.

he asks the rhetorical question, "Do you not know that you [plural, referring to the church at Corinth] are a temple of God, and that the Spirit of God dwells in you?" The answer expected is "Yes, this is a fact." The Corinthians had received the Spirit (2:12) and needed to know that as part of God's people, they were the special dwelling place of the Spirit. This aspect of their position in Christ is a continuous reality as signified by the "to be" verb, "you are."

The noun "temple" sustains the building metaphor and denotes the idea of an inward shrine or sanctuary. Used forty-six times in the New Testament, it sometimes refers to the temple in Jerusalem and the holy of holies. God's people are now God's holy of holies. The Spirit's indwelling presence makes us sacred. This reveals Paul's high view of the church and sets the stage for the polemical words of verse 17: "If any man destroys the temple of God, God will destroy him, for [explanatory *gar*] the temple of God is holy, and that is what you are."

In context, this siren-like warning must be made to those whose work (teaching) was akin to wood, hay and straw. Observe the parallel phrase that begins verse 17 and verses 14 and 15: "If any man...." The term "destroys" (*phtheirie*) in verse 17 is used in 1 Corinthians 15:33 of bad company destroying (corrupting, NASB) good morals. In his second letter to these believers, the apostle asks them to make room for him in their hearts, for he had wronged no one, corrupted no one, nor taken advantage of anyone (7:2). Elsewhere, the term speaks of the old self-being corrupted with deceit (Eph. 4:22), the harlot of Revelation 18 corrupting the earth with her immorality, and in Jude 18 speaks of the eternal destruction of the ungodly.

So, what is Paul's point here? True to the context, the apostle is affirming that anyone who causes the collapse of a local church is subject to the severe discipline of God. It's worth noting that the verb "destroy," found twice in this sentence–once of the effects of the errant teacher and once of God's discipline on such a teacher–is actually juxtaposed in the Greek sentence.

But what is the content of this destructive teaching by the errant teacher? In context, most assuredly it includes the divisive ideas referred to earlier, that is, those which promoted making celebrities out of Christian leaders. In a brief survey, the letter as a whole addresses such issues as disunity (1:10-13), worldly wisdom so highly prized by the Corinthians (1:18-30), misunderstandings about the Spirit's ministry (2:1-16) and God's servants (3:1-4:21; ch. 9), immorality (ch. 5; 6:12-20), litigation in pagan courts (6:1-11), marriage and divorce (ch. 7), Christian liberty matters (chs. 8 and 10), the role of women in worship and abuses of the Lord's supper (ch. 11), the abuse and misuse of spiritual gifts (chs. 12-14), and incorrect teachings regarding the doctrine of the resurrection (ch. 15).

To sum up, a myriad of misguided beliefs and eye-popping practices characterized this church. Errant teachers were having a field day. Paul, therefore, informed the church of the *bema* seat of Christ (1) to lend encouragement to those who, as careful master builders, were building up the church by speaking those things "taught by the Spirit" and (2) to give firm admonition to those whose teaching was as worthless as wood, hay and straw and, therefore, destructive to the church.

In the final verses of the chapter (18-23), these destructive teachers in Corinth are exhorted to embrace God's wisdom and become wise master builders (18-20; cf. 2:6-3:10). And, they are exhorted to embrace the right perspective on God's servants: Paul, Apollos, and Cephas (21-23). And, it is this need for proper perspective that propels the apostle into his discussion in chapter 4. But before we examine that discussion, let's summarize chapter 3.

Summary of Reward for 1 Corinthians 3:10–15

Subjects	All Christians (3:1).
Content	Unspecified.
Cause for (human)	(1) Spirit-directed labors in evangelism and discipleship (2:4; 3:5-7); (2) teaching sound doctrine (vv. 10-11); (3) quality spiritual service—that which is of enduring value like gold, silver and stone (vv. 12-13).
Cause for (divine)	God's justice (vv. 8, 12-17).
Nature	(1) Personal (vv. 8, 10-17); (2) an occasion for honor from God (implied in context); (3) can be forfeited through incorrect teaching which corrupts the body of Christ (vv. 15-17).
Time	A fixed (future) day on God's prophetical calendar (vv. 8, 13).
Source	The Lord (4:5).

1 Corinthians 4:1-5

The chapter division must be ignored here as Paul continues to educate the Corinthians on a correct perspective of his ministry in their lives, a discussion that began at 3:5. In 4:1, he issues the imperative, "Let a man regard us in this manner, as servants of Christ, and stewards of the mysteries of God." The term "servants" (*huperetes*), used twenty times in the New Testament, signifies "one in service of another." Thus, it implies the subordination of one person to another, in this case, of Paul and Apollos to Christ. They were "servants of Christ" (subjective genitive). Originally, the term was used of an under-rower in a *trireme*, a ship with three banks of oars.

But not only should the Corinthians view Paul and Apollos as servants, but also as stewards (*oikonomois*). Found ten times in the New Testament, this term pictures one entrusted with a large estate, an administrator or manager. It denotes one to whom certain responsibilities have been given, with corresponding accountability. Examples of stewards include a trusted slave in charge of a whole household, official attendants of a magistrate, pastors in charge of God's people (Titus 1:7), and every Christian as a steward of the spiritual gift he has received (1 Pet. 4:10).

But here in 1 Corinthians 4:1, the stewardship pertains to "the mysteries of God." In general, this refers to God's revelation, and in particular to things formerly unrevealed in Old Testament times (e.g. Matt. 13:11; Rom. 11:25; 1 Cor. 15:51-52; Eph. 3:3, 5:32, 6:19; Col. 1:27, 2:2, 4:3; 2 Thess. 2:7; 1 Tim. 3:16; Rev. 1:20, 17:5,7). In this context, the concept refers, in general sense, to the inspired Word of God as spoken and written by God's servants, such as Paul. In fact, Paul had just revealed his communication of God's wisdom via the revelatory ministry of the Spirit (2:6-16; see also 7:39, 40). The mysteries of God would, no doubt, include as well, the Old Testament Scripture.

Having imparted a divine perspective concerning his God-given role among the Corinthians, Paul now asserts the one criteria for servants and stewards, namely, faithfulness (v. 3). The term "faithful" translates *pistos* in the Greek and intimates one who is reliable, trustworthy. The owner of an estate could not leave his possessions and personnel in the hands of an undependable slave (steward). The slave must be reliable. Likewise, those who speak God's word must teach it accurately. They must embrace heavenly wisdom, not earthly wisdom (3:18). This theme began in 3:10 where Paul said, "According to the grace of God which was given to me, as a wise master builder, I laid a foundation, and another is building upon it. But let each man be careful how he builds upon it."

A careful and faithful stewardship of God's revelation brings reward from God (3:12-14), but being reckless and untrustworthy with God's Word (using words taught by human wisdom, 2:13) forfeits potential rewards and, instead, brings God's severe chastisement (3:15-17). So then, what are the practical implications of this reality that we are stewards of God's mysteries, either faithful or unfaithful, rewarded or unrewarded? The answer is found in verses 3-5.

Since God is the one to whom every teacher of His Word shall give an account of his stewardship, it follows that final judgment must rest with Him, not others—or even ourselves. Thus, Paul rebuffs the Corinthians scrutiny about his person and ministry (v. 3) and then adds, "I don't even examine myself. I am conscious of nothing against myself [Paul viewed himself as a faithful steward of God's truth], yet I am not by this acquitted; but the one who examines me is the Lord. Therefore, do no go on passing judgment before the time, but wait until the Lord comes who will both bring to light the things hidden in the darkness and disclose the motives of men's hearts; and then each man's praise will come to him from God" (vv. 4-5).

What stands out here is the sovereignty of God over His servants. His Lordship supersedes all human wisdom and opinion. Another believer's examination of me and my ministry and/or my own self-examination of the same, holding some value as they may, are inferior and incomplete when compared to the ultimate verdict of God. God, in His omniscience, knows me through and through, even my very motives—why I do and say what I do and say. This reality forms the basis for Paul's stern corrective to the judgmental, arrogant Corinthians. With this general observation of these verses, let's now take a closer look.

First, we note that the Lord's examination of our earthly lives and ministries is continual. The end of verse 4 reads, "...the one who examines [literally, continually examines] me is the Lord." Class is always in session, and the Master Teacher is evaluating my work, my stewardship from Him.

Second, as already alluded to, it is not my place to draw final conclusions about another's life or ministry. This is the implication from the fact that the Lord examines us continually. In this regard, note that verse 5 begins with the inferential conjunction "therefore" (*hoste*): "Therefore, do not go on passing judgment before the time..." (The Greek construction here of the negative *me* + imperative shows that Paul is placing restriction on current inappropriate activity). The final verdict on every Christian's life and ministry is up to God alone. I have no input on my Christian brother's or sister's final report card–even though sometimes I think I have the insight necessary, and even the right to such input.

Third, the time of this "final exam" will be "when the Lord comes" (v. 5). This fact fits several other New Testament passages where the judgment seat of Christ is aligned with His coming.

Fourth, the criteria for reward will include the very motives for ministry. Verse 5 tells us that the Lord will both "bring to light [*photisei*, 'to illumine'; same term found in 3:13: 'the day will show it'] the things hidden in the darkness and disclose the motives of men's hearts." "Motives" translates *boulas*, used twelve times in the New Testament. Often, it speaks of God's purposes and intentions (Acts 2:23), but there of man's intentions. And the locus of these intentions is said to be in the "heart" (*kardia*). Even the reasons why Christians did what they did and said what they did will be clearly revealed, brought out in the open. In this regard, the term rendered "disclose" translates *phaneroo*, seen also in 3:13 concerning the open manifestation of each man's work at the bema seat of Christ.

In short, another's evaluation of me is largely limited to the outward; my evaluation can include the outward and the inward, but even then I am handicapped by a heart that has the potential of being deceitful and desperately wicked (Jer. 17:9). Only God knows the whole truth about who and what I am outwardly and inwardly. As God said to Samuel when the man of God was selecting Saul's successor to lead Israel, "Man looks on the outward appearance, but God looks on the heart" (1 Sam. 16:7). And who was God's pick? None else but David, for God knew the young shepherd was a man after His own heart.

As one last comment on this issue of motives, the context calls us back to the description of God's leaders as servants and stewards, and the faithfulness required of them (vv. 1-2). Certainly, a faithful servant realizes he is under the Lord's authority, whom he serves, and is not out to preach himself, but his Master. Paul exemplifies this very thing in his testimony in 2:1-5 (see also 2 Cor. 4:5).

Arriving at the end of the verse we read, "...and then each man's praise will come to him from God." The adverb "then" (*tote*, adverb of time) indicates that God will supervise a certain order of events at this judgment for His servants. Following His omniscient scrutiny of each Christian's life and ministry, he will then dispense the appropriate praise. We note, as we have elsewhere, that this judgment is personal: "each man's praise...." One day I will stand alone before the Lord Jesus at this tribunal.

There is also the seeming reality that each Christian will receive a measure of praise from God, although some, according to 1 Corinthians 3:15, will suffer loss of reward (though not their salvation). Admittedly, however, 3:15 indicates that receiving no reward will be the experience of those who are not careful master builders of God's Word into the lives of other believers. It seems, from the context, that this warning refers only to the area of teaching sound doctrine. Most commentators, however, interpret verse 15 in the more general sense of overall Christian living, not restricting it to the issue of sound teaching.

This takes us to our final observation here. To begin with, we learn the amazing truth that God wants to honor His servants. He wants to praise them, a thought that conjures up the words of Jesus' parable in Matthew 25:21: "Well done, good and faithful servant…." It's worth noting that the term "faithful" (*pistos*), used by Jesus, is the same one used here in 1 Corinthians 4:2. Literally, the end of 1 Corinthians 4:5 says, "…and for each man [dative of advantage] praise will come [future indicative, showing the absolute reality of this event] from God" ("from" is the preposition *apo*, signifying God as the source of a man's praise at the judgment seat of Christ).

Summary of Reward for 1 Corinthians 4:1–5

Subjects	Christians (context, 3:1, 4:1).
Content	Praise from God (v. 5).
Cause for (human)	(1) Spiritual character—in this case, Spirit-led motives in ministry (2:6-16, 4:5); and (2) faithful stewardship of God's truth (4:1-2).
Cause for (divine)	God's just judgment and omniscience (vv.4–5).
Nature	Personal honor from God (v. 5, "each man").
Time	The future coming of the Lord at His coming (v. 5).
Implications	Passing final judgment on another believer's ministry and motives is God's place, not mine (vv. 3-5).
Source	Lord (Jesus Christ), God (the Father) (v.5).

1 Corinthians 9:24-27

By way of context, 1 Corinthians 9 finds Paul in defense (v. 3) of his rights as an apostle before the carnal critics at Corinth. How unfortunate the need for such an apologetic, for God-ordained church leaders should be honored, not criticized. In fact, those who serve God vocationally should even be supported financially. As Paul illustrates, the soldier, the farmer, the dairyman and the ox are rewarded materially for their labor. And what's more, the Levites and Priests of the Old Testament were supported by the contributions of the Israelites, so also the Lord directed those who proclaim the gospel to get their living from the gospel (v. 14).

This chapter is, then, an application in Paul's life of the truth he preached 8:13: "...if food causes my brother to stumble, I will never eat meat again, that I might not cause my brother to stumble." But how did the apostle apply this charitable restriction? He resolved to never take advantage of his personal rights as an apostle appointed by the Lord Jesus. In sum, the chapter looks at Paul's rights as an apostle (vv. 1-14), Paul's personal restrictions and resolve as an apostle (vv. 15-23) and Paul's reward for preaching the gospel (vv. 24-27). The focus here will be on Paul's reward.

Verse 24 poses the rhetorical question, "Do you not know that those who run in a race all run, but only one receives the prize?" Paul draws upon the Corinthians' knowledge of the Isthmian games held every two years in Corinth, of which the foot race was the all-important event. These games were not mere amusement for the Greeks, but a matter of passionate, patriotic pride (like unto the Super Bowl of modern USA). In the employment of this illustration, the apostle makes several comparisons between the Greek games and the Christian evangelist.

First, only one person could win the foot race and take home the coveted prize (*brabeion*), namely, a pine wreath (v. 25). Of course, along with this wreath came fame and popularity. This being true meant that each competitor should run in such a way that he could win (v. 24b).

But secondly, this goal would demand something of the competitor, that is, large doses of self-discipline. As Paul says, "And everyone who competes in the games exercises self-control in all things...." The term translated "self-control" (*agonizomenos*) is found only here and in 1

Corinthians 7:9. From it we derive the English word, "agonize." The middle voice denotes the intense personal involvement of the Greek athlete to avoid anything ("self-control in all things," an accusative of genitive reference) which represents harm to his physical body and thus hinders his goal to win the prize. Equally noteworthy is the gnomic present here which signifies the idea of something that is always true. In this case the agonizing discipline of the body for the sake of the prize was the norm, not the exception.

A final element of comparison in these verse regards the possibility of being disqualified from competition and thereby forfeiting any reward. Changing the metaphor in verse 27, Paul speaks of his own body as an opponent. He says: "But I buffet my body and make it my slave, lest possibly after I have preached to others, I myself should be disqualified." This is an allusion to the Greek athlete who broke the training rules and forfeited his opportunity to enter the race and win the prize. With this athletic analogy in view, let's now examine the spiritual principles extracted by Paul.

To begin with, the context is about evangelizing the unsaved. Verse 23 says, "And I do all things for the sake of the gospel, that I may become a fellow partaker of it." The "all things" comprehends Paul's resolve in verses 19-22 to find common ground with unsaved Jews (v. 20) and Gentiles (v. 21) in order to win a hearing for the gospel and thereby win souls to salvation. Verse 22 may represent a third group in the apostle's mind, namely, weak Christians: "To the weak, I became weak, that I might win the weak...." In light of the context of Paul's whole argument it is best to see this as a reference to the weak Christian of 8:9-13.

As already cited, Paul was willing to regulate his own personal liberty in non-moral matters in order to keep another believer with different convictions from stumbling. Thus, he would not eat meat offered to idols in the presence of those believers who thought it wrong to do so, even though "...food does not bring us near to God; we are not worse if we do not eat, and no better if we do" (8:8).

So in what sense did Paul seek to "win" these believers? In the sense of sanctification, not justification. He hoped that his sensitivity and instruction would lead them to a better understanding of such non-moral issues and to greater spiritual maturity. In all, *Paul did everything he could, short of moral compromise, to befriend sinners to the Friend of sinners and to bring up the saints to be like the Savior.* All these things he did "for the sake of the gospel." For even the practice of charity toward weak believers would have impact on unbelievers looking on. As Jesus said, "By this will all men know that you are my disciples, if you have love for one another" (John 13:34-35). The focus, then, of the context is primarily on an evangelistic lifestyle. With this perspective, the following principles are drawn.

First, an evangelistic lifestyle must be embraced with earnest. Several points in Paul's comparison speak to this reality: (1) the sentence, "Run in such a way that you may win" (v. 24b) not only features the imperative, "run," but as well the purpose element: "that you may win" (*hina* clause). The verb "win" means "to grasp and hold onto something," and with the prepositional attachment (*katalabnte*) the meaning is intensified; (2) the picture in verse 25 of the Greek athlete agonizing (exercising self-control in all things) adds to this imagery of earnestness; (3) in verse 26, Paul makes the statement, "Therefore I run [present tense indicates on-going commitment] in such a way, as not without aim." The words "without aim" translate *adelos*, signifying Paul's fixed and certain goal to be evangelistic in his lifestyle. The new metaphor which follows illustrates the point: "I box in such a way, as not beating the air; but I buffet my body and make it my slave...."

To "box" is to fight with the fist. The image calls to mind the rigorous training required of a boxer and echoes the agonizing self-discipline of verse 25. And Paul does not merely shadow box, that is, he's not just "beating the air" (present participle), "but [*alla*, strong adversative] I buffet my body," he says, "and [*kai*, coordinating conjunction] make it my slave...." To "buffet" is literally to "strike under the eye and make black and blue" (perhaps Paul has in view all the physical abuse he has taken for being a herald of the gospel; see 2 Cor. 11:23-33.). Then, in connection with this buffeting, he makes his body his slave. The idea is that of an athlete eliminating every potential hindrance to his goal. His body serves him to this desired end. The point is that "the spirit should dominate the body, not vice versa."[81]

This entire right-brain analogy, drawn from the sports arena of the Greek world, vividly portrays the left-brain propositions of verses 19 and 23: "For though I am free from all men, I have made myself a slave to all, that I might win the more" (19). "And I do all things for the sake of the gospel, that I may become a fellow partaker of it" (23). Paul would let nothing stand in the way of his goal to win people to his Savior. This resolve was woven into the fabric of his lifestyle. Thus the first principle learned here, as stated above, is: An evangelistic lifestyle must be embraced with earnest.

The second and final principle found here concerns the rewards of such a lifestyle. We could state it like this: An evangelistic lifestyle carries with it the expectation of future reward. But where is this principle found in the passage?

Once again, in verse 25, Paul says, "And everyone who competes in the games exercises self-control in all things. They then do it ['do it' supplied by the translators as inferred in the context] to receive a

---

[81] Earle, 232.

perishable wreath, but we an imperishable." "They" refers to the Greek athletes in Paul's analogy, those who run the race mentioned in verse 24 ("race" translates *stadio*, a track 200 yards long and 30 yards wide, a long parallelogram). These runners enjoined the strictest of training programs to put themselves in a position to win the big race—all for a pine wreath that would soon wither and perish. "But we an imperishable [wreath]," says Paul in contrast. Paul anticipated a reward of eternal value, one that will never perish, a reward for embracing an evangelistic lifestyle.

Thus, it was for this very reason that the apostle made his body his slave, not allowing the physical sufferings attached to true discipleship—not to mention laziness, overeating, lack of exercise, etc.—to hinder his earnest resolve to evangelize. For should he yield to the comfort zones of the body, allowing the body to dominate the spirit, he would forfeit his opportunity to obtain future reward for the self-discipline required to maintain an evangelistic lifestyle. This is the point of verse 27: "but I buffet my body and make it my slave, lest possibly after I have preached to others, I myself should be disqualified." The term "disqualified" is the operative word in this regard. What does it mean?

The Greek term is *adokomos*, meaning that which is rejected as unusable. Metals and coins not able to stand the test of refining fire were rejected. But we don't have to venture into the world of mining to define this term. All we need to do is ignore the chapter division and notice the explanatory conjunction "for" which begins 10:1. In 10:1-14, the apostle appeals to the missed opportunity of the Israelites under Moses, to possess and enjoy the Promised Land. This reality illustrates the word "disqualified" in 9:27. And why did they miss such a wonderful reward as those redeemed from literal bondage from Egypt and spiritual bondage from sin? Because (1) they craved evil things, v. 6; (2) they acted immorally, vv. 7-8; (3) they tempted the Lord, v. 9; and (4) they grumbled before God, v. 10.

Consequently, they did not please God, and were laid low in the wilderness (v. 5). They did not lose the salvation received in Egypt (Ex. 12), but they did lose the reward of Canaan. Their lack of moral self-control in actions, words and thoughts denied them of God's full reward. So also, Paul is concerned that he not forfeit his full future reward via lack of self-control, particularly as it pertains to an evangelistic lifestyle. To do "all things for the sake of the gospel" will take steady concentration and self-discipline.

Summary of Reward for 1 Corinthians 9:24–27

Subjects	Christians (context).
Content	An imperishable crown (v. 26).
Cause for (human)	An evangelistic lifestyle (v. 23), signifying a faithful stewardship of God-given responsibility (vv. 16-17, 23-27). (It may be more accurate and comprehensive to include, as a cause for reward, a commitment to building up believers in their faith in view of Paul's mention of his ministry to the "weak" in v. 22).
Cause for (divine)	Unspecified.
Nature	(1) Eternal; (2) a symbol of spiritual victory over laziness and moral compromise, and, an occasion for personal joy and honor from God (v. 25); (3) able to be lost due to a lack of moral self-control (unfaithfulness to the goal of evangelizing the unsaved, v. 27; see this principle illustrated in 10:1-11 regarding the Israelites in the wilderness).
Time	Unspecified.
Source	The Lord (context).

James 1:12

As James pens his epistle to certain persecuted Christians in the first century, he senses the need to instruct them about adversity. This instruction includes (1) the proper response to trials: be joyful (v. 2), be pliable (vv. 3-4), and be prayerful (v. 5); (2) the nature of trials: multifaceted ("many trials," i.e., they come in all shapes, colors and sizes); (3) the reality of trials: "Count it all joy, my brethren, when you encounter various trials" (v. 2) and (4) the reward for a proper response to life's trials (v. 12). Thus, verse 12 is our focus here. James writes, "Blessed is the man who perseveres under trial...."

The emphatic position of the adjective *makarios* (blessed) is the same term Christ used in the beatitudes (see Matt. 5:3-12). It means someone who is inwardly happy, in spite of circumstances, and thereby possesses a spiritual disposition that is enviable in the eyes of others. In the predicate position, the term makes an assertion about the noun it modifies, namely, "man." Thus, "Blessed is the man...." This man is happy on the inside though things on the outside are not so happy.

The noun "man" is *aner*, usually a reference to the male gender, but here employed in a generic sense.[82] The context demands this interpretation since those addressed are called "brethren," a term used elsewhere to refer to a whole group of believers (e.g., Rom. 12:1). As well, 1:7 uses the same term in the generic sense. See also Romans 4:8 for yet another example of this particular use of *aner*. But who qualifies to be so blessed?

"Blessed is the man [Christian person] who perseveres under trial..." The word "perseveres" is *hupomenei* and means to endure patiently adverse circumstances. It is employed seventeen times in the New Testament and

[82] Bauer, Arndt and Gingrich, 66.

is the same term found in 1:4 ("...let endurance have its perfect result") and in 5:11 (twice) where the endurance of Job is exonerated. Thus, "perseveres" is a good translation.

The word "trial" is *peirasmon* which means "to put to the test." Here it is used in a positive sense in contrast to verse 13 where it is used to denote a solicitation to evil. In context, the trials referred to are the "many trials" of verse 2. Chapter 5 then depicts the content of these trials as persecution from wealthy unbelievers (cf. 5:1-11). Of course, in light of the example of Job in verse 11, the multifaceted nature of trials could include (though not necessarily with James' audience) the death of a loved one, the loss of material possessions and the loss of physical health—all of which in Job's case were trials allowed by God and disseminated by Satan.

The next word in the sentence is the preposition "for." It renders the Greek conjunction *hoti* which here has a causal force. We are now told why the Christian in view (man) is "blessed." He is blessed because "after being approved [aorist participle temporal, antecedent in time to the following verb], he shall receive the crown of life." The word "approved" (*dokimos*) means to be approved after testing. In the LXX, the term is used of coins and metals which underwent the removal of impurities (alloys, etc.). For example, in Zechariah 11:13 we read, "Cast them [30 pieces of silver] into a furnace and I will see if it is good [approved] metal." As such, the word "approved" is parallel to the previous word *peirasmon* as part of the contextual motif of God testing His people, via the furnace of various trials, for spiritual character. And those who pass the test receive the Crown of Life.

The promise is "he shall receive the crown of life" (the future tense verb is in the indicative mood). By contrast, the double-minded, doubt-driven saints of 1:6 will receive nothing from their Lord, their unbelief showing an improper response to God-sent trials. They are not approved after the testing and do not qualify for any reward, or for the wisdom mentioned in verse 5. This wisdom is necessary for knowing how to suffer successfully on earth and thereby be rewarded eternally.

To sum up, the contrast between the loss of rewards for the doubting believer and the assurance of future reward (the Crown of Life) for the faith-filled, persevering believer is sobering. (cf. Heb. 11:6 in this general regard.) But what is this Crown of Life?

The phrase, "the crown of life," functions as the direct object of the sentence. It should be noted that this is a particular crown, signified by the articular construction of the noun "crown" (*stephanos*). "Crown," from its historical background and biblical usage, indicates a figurative expression of spiritual victory (over the temptation to wilt under the blistering heat of life's trials), the resultant honor from God and the joy experienced by the rewarded saint. Job's wife urged her afflicted husband to curse God and die, but Job endured. His response to adversity reaps God's reward. But how do we take the genitive here, "the crown of life"?

It could be taken in the attributive sense: "living crown," in contrast to the fading crowns of the Greek culture. But James' readers were Jewish. Would they understand this comparison? Perhaps we should take it as reference to the gift of eternal life secured by faith in the Lord Jesus Christ as one's Savior (cf. Rom. 6:32). But, such a view would introduce a severe contradiction in the context. That is, James has already identified his readers as Christians. He calls them "brethren," in verse 2, and reaffirms this spiritual identity fourteen more times in the letter. As well, James would be telling his Christian recipients that they must suffer well to receive eternal life. Such a thought would contradict the nature of salvation in the rest of the New Testament as a gift of God's grace (Eph. 2:8-10). Maybe the meaning of the word "life" can shed some light on the matter.

The term "life" (*zoe*) emphasized the quality of life that God gives to His own. It is the life that He Himself possesses. It is nothing but the best, qualitatively. And of course, it never ends, quantitatively, since God, who gave it, is Himself eternal. Could James be saying then, that those believers who react properly to God-sent trials will receive a special quality of spiritual life? One could argue this way since the double-minded of verse 6 receive nothing from the Lord, the implication being that their quality of spiritual life on earth is less than those who trust God in trials. But the entire theme of crowns in the New Testament, especially in the epistles where the eschatological element is present, would place the reception of this crown at the *bema* seat of Christ. A current reward of abundant Christian living is certainly the reward of those who follow the Shepherd (John 10:10), but the emphasis here is eschatological. In *The Expositor's Bible Commentary*, Donald Burdick rightly observes the following about the Crown of Life: "It is evident that this 'life' that God has promised is more than the eternal life given to every believer at the time of his salvation (John 5:24). Since it is a reward for an accomplishment subsequent to initial faith, it must refer to a still higher quality of life."[83] In this sense, the phrase "crown of life" is appositional, in nature, that is, the crown itself is life.

In brief, "the crown which is itself life" refers to ultimate enjoyment—abundant eternal life—in God's eternal kingdom. This correlates well with (1) Matthew 5:12 where Jesus promises His persecuted followers "great reward" and (2) the other reference to "the crown of life" in Revelation 2:10. There also, suffering believers are in view and the promise of being faithful to death guarantees them the same crown (more

---

[83] Donald Burdick, "James," in *The Expositor's Bible Commentary*, ed. by Frank E. Gaebelein (Grand Rapids, MI: Zondervan, 1981), 12:171.

on that passage later).

The last part of James 1:12 exposes both the reality of reward and the motive that produces the reward. James says, "Blessed is the man who perseveres under trial, for once he has been approved, he shall receive the crown of life, which [relative pronoun pointing back to the crown mentioned] the Lord has promised to those who love Him" (the term "promised" may best be viewed as a constative aorist).

But standing next to the reality of future reward is the motive that earns it, namely, a personal love for Christ. The phrase "those who love Him" translates a present participle showing the characteristic disposition of those rewarded. As a way of life, they love Jesus, and this is nowhere better demonstrated than when they face adversity (the same motive for Christian living is seen in 2 Tim. 4:8 regarding the Crown of Righteousness). Anyone can say they love Jesus when there are blue skies and sunshine, but when the storms come, those who love Him enough to still bless Him—and not curse Him—stand out. They are subsequently rewarded with the Crown of Life. The highest quality of life in eternity possible. In God's infinite goodness, He employs adversity to our eternal advantage.

Summary of Reward for James 1:12

Subject	Christians (context, v. 2).
Content	An enviable spiritual disposition (blessed) that results in the bestowment of the Crown of Life.
Cause for (human)	A godly response to suffering allowed by God, a response that proves one' personal love for God (motives and a mature response to adversity form the grounds for this reward).
Cause for (divine)	God's justice and grace (implied).

A Hero's Welcome

Nature	(1) Personal; (2) symbolic of victory, honor and joy; (3) that which is promised by the Lord Himself; (4) eternal.
Time	Future (unspecified).
Source	The Lord.

1 Peter 1:6-9

Like James, Peter writes to a group of persecuted believers. These saints were "scattered throughout Pontus, Galatia, Cappodocia, Asia, and Bithynia" (1 Pet. 1:1). And it should not surprise us that the doctrine of salvation is the first matter he writes about. For what will bring more comfort to the afflicted than the reminder of heaven?

In verses 1b-2, the apostle reveals the sovereign orchestration of the Godhead in making salvation possible: The selection of the Father, the sanctifying work of the Spirit and the blood sacrifice of the Son. Verses 3-5 follow with a call to praise for this great salvation. This salvation is (1) grounded in God's mercy, (2) imparts spiritual life (and with it a living hope), (3) comes via the resurrection of Christ, and (4) provides an inheritance which, due to God's protective power, is eternally secure. Wow! What encouragement for shell-shocked saints. In fact, verse 6 declares, "In this [the salvation just described] you greatly rejoice, even though now for a little while, if necessary, you have been distressed by various trials...." Focusing on their future hope will steady them in present adversity. But there's something else waiting in the future as part of their glorification experience, something else that will also provide present encouragement.

In verse 7, Peter shows one of God's purposes for sending these various trials, namely, "that the proof of your faith, being more precious than gold, which is perishable, even though tested by fire, may be found to result in praise and glory and honor at the revelation of Jesus Christ...." Why does God allow adversity in His children's lives? For one, He permits it so that one day He can exalt them in His presence. Let's take a closer look at the verse.

Verse 6 begins with a purpose clause, framed by the term *hina*, plus the subjunctive: "that the proof [of your faith]...." The term "proof" translates the Greek *dokimon*, the same word James uses in his discourse on trials and rewards (1:12). To review, it means to be "approved after examination," picturing the gold refiner's fire as he tests precious metals for genuineness. Here, the hot furnace of "various trials" (same Greek phrase found in James 1:2) provides a laboratory where the believer proves that he trusts in God during his trials. It's worth noting, at this juncture, that the original phrase "that the proof of your faith" ("your faith," subjective genitive) finds the noun "faith" (*pistis*) in the place of emphasis. This emphasis is then echoed by Peter's description of faith as being "more precious than gold which is perishable, even though tested by fire...." Such precious faith, when vindicated by rejoicing amid distressing trials, brings certain veneration from God. This takes us to the final phrase of verse 7.

The purpose clause which began the verse is now completed: "that the proof of your faith...may be found to result in praise and glory and honor at the revelation of Jesus Christ...." The verbal phrase "may be found" is a rendering of *eurethe*. The passive voice shows that this discovery of proven faith is not ultimately the believer's doing, but God's, who, in His omniscience, knows all about His children's sufferings and their faith-driven response to suffering. The preposition "to" translates the Greek preposition *eis*. In the accusative case, the construction expresses the purpose and result of the testing, namely, the exaltation of the suffering saint. And three terms designate this exaltation.

The triplet phrase, "praise and glory and honor," is linked to the believer who handles trials in a way that pleases God, that is, with joy-producing faith (note the attributive adjective construction, "greatly rejoice," in v. 6). In this regard, it is worth noting that the same word translated "praise" here (*epainon*) is also used by Paul in 1 Corinthians 4:5: "...then [at Christ's return at the Rapture] each man will receive praise from God." The *bema* seat of Christ is in Peter's mind. His instruction is of profound encouragement, then, to these afflicted believers. There will be a future day when not only will their salvation be completed (v. 5), but God will honor them for steadfast faith amid adversity.

The verse concludes by showing the time of this veneration to be "the revelation of Jesus Christ." This correlation of Christ's return at the Rapture with believer's rewards is found in many other passages in the New Testament, as 1 Corinthians 4:5 reveals.

Finally, it is vital to observe verses 8-9 where the motives for maintaining one's spiritual balance in times of turmoil is disclosed. Peter affirms his readers by saying, "and though you have not seen Him, you love Him, and though you do not see Him now, but believe in Him, you greatly rejoice with joy inexpressible and full of glory, obtaining as the outcome of your faith the salvation of your souls." Here is yet one more parallel to James 1:12, namely, the motivation of a personal love for Christ which carries the Christian through his trial.

Summary of Reward for 1 Peter 1:6–9

Subject	Christians (1:1-12).
Content	Praise, glory and honor from God (v. 7).

Cause for (human)	(1) Spiritual maturity shown in a proper response to various trials (in this case, persecution for their Christian faith; see 2:18-25; 3:13-18; 4:12-19; 5:8-11); (2) Spirit-led motives, namely, a personal love for Christ (v. 8).
Nature	(1) Personal; (2) an occasion for exaltation from Christ (v. 7).
Time	The revelation of Jesus Christ (The Rapture, v. 7).
Source	Jesus Christ (v. 7).

1 Peter 5:1-4

The last chapter of Peter's first epistle imparts a firm charge to the elders in his readership. Verse 2 begins with an imperative: "Shepherd the flock of God among you, exercising oversight...." This is the what of the apostle's charge. Next comes the how, in two parts.

First, the matter of motives again surfaces. Peter says we should shepherd Gods' flock "not under compulsion, but voluntarily, according to the will of God [literally, 'according to God']; and not for sordid gain [for money], but with eagerness...." Note the two lines of contrast: compulsion (the negative element) versus a volunteer spirit (the positive element) followed by "not for sordid gain" (negative) versus "eagerness" (positive). In regards to how the under-shepherd is to fulfill his ministry to the Chief Shepherd (v. 4), the matter of motives is crucial. But so is the issue of attitudes. Peter continues in verse 3: "nor yet as lording it over those allotted to your charge, but proving to be examples to the flock." Once again, using contrast as his teaching tool, the apostle juxtaposes a negative attitude–lording it over the sheep as an abuse of one's authority–with a positive attitude, that of being humble examples to the flock. The attitudes of pride and humility stand side by side here. Most likely, Peter's instruction at this point is an allusion to the words of Christ in Mark

A Hero's Welcome

10:42-52.

Verse 4 begins with the coordinating conjunction *kai*, signifying the continuation of Peter's thought in verses 1-3. He has revealed the elder's requirements as under-shepherds. Now, he unveils the reward for embracing such requirements. He writes, "and when the Chief Shepherd appears, you will receive the unfading crown of glory." Let's analyze this encouraging promise to God's under-shepherds.

First, note that the time of this reward will be "when the Chief Shepherd appears...." This connection of Christ's return with the dispensing of rewards has become a common theme in this New Testament survey on the doctrine of rewards. In fact, this same correlation was seen in 1 Peter 1:6-9. Concerning this, we observe that the aorist participle "when He appears" is contemporaneous with the verb "you shall receive" that follows. But who shall dispense this reward?

The Chief Shepherd will hand over the Crown of Glory to his faithful under-shepherds. But who is this Chief Shepherd? It is Jesus Christ, as 1 Peter 2:20-25 makes clear. There He is called "the Shepherd and Guardian of your souls" (v. 25). The term translated "Chief Shepherd" occurs only here in the New Testament. It is a combination of *archi*, which denotes "high office and dignity," and *poimenos*, which means "shepherd." Jesus is the Master Shepherd, par excellence. In John 10:11 He is called the Good Shepherd (compare with Ps. 22), in Hebrews 13:20, the Great Shepherd (compare with Ps. 23) and here the Chief Shepherd (compare with Ps. 24). What a glorious Shepherd He is. How marvelous it is that the Christian can say, "The Lord is my Shepherd" (Ps. 23:1).

But what is this unfading Crown of Glory that the Chief Shepherd promises His faithful under-shepherds? First, the term "unfading" translates *amarantinos* (*hapax legomena*) which is positioned emphatically in the sentence. This term gave name to the flower, *amaranth*, because it never withers if moistened with water. Thus, in the Greek world, it became the symbol of immortality.[84]

In this regard, nouns with the *inos* ending emphasize the quality of material in view. Of course, the unfading nature of this crown is in antithesis to the floral crowns awarded to the victorious Greek athletes, crowns which quickly perished. This crown, however, will never lose its attractiveness and beauty. But what is the significance of the genitive case here: "crown of glory"?

Is it best to translate the construction attributively, "glorious crown," or, is a genitive of apposition preferable: "the crown that consists of glory?" Concerning the possible attributive use, it is intriguing to note that the modifying terms "unfading" and "glory" are placed attributively between the article (the) and the noun (crown) to signify the characteristics of the crown.

As regards an appositional nuance, Jesus, the Chief Shepherd, according to Hebrews 2:9, is crowned with glory and honor by virtue of His substitutionary death. His humiliation brought about exaltation from the Father. Could it be that the Chief Shepherd shares, then, His own unfading Crown of Glory with those under-shepherds who discharge their duties with the proper motives and attitudes? Thus, their crown consists of heavenly glory.

In any case, the attributive, or the appositional concepts, do not seem far from one another in meaning. Perhaps we cannot be dogmatic on the choice, but the point is clear: Christ wants to honor His faithful under-shepherds when He returns. He wants to crown them with the eternal Crown of Glory, which in keeping with the meaning of *stephanos* (crown) indicates a reward for their victory over improper motives and

---

[84] F. W. Beare, *The First Epistle of Peter* (Oxford: Basil Blackwell, 1958), quoted in Rienecker, 744.

attitudes (compulsion, sordid gain, lording it over others) as they fulfill their duties as shepherds. It also indicates (per *stephanos*) the aspect of the authority to rule and fullness of joy.

Summary of Reward for 1 Peter 5:1–4

Subject	Elders in the body of Christ (v. 1).
Content	Crown of Glory (v. 4).
Cause for (human)	Faithful stewardship of duties given to elders, including the motives and attitudes behind these duties (vv. 2-3).
Cause for (divine)	God's justice and grace (implied in v. 4).
Nature	(1) Personal (implied in context); (2) eternal (unfading, v. 4); (3) an occasion for public honor for victory over fleshly motivations in serving God's flock (vv. 2-3).
Time	The Rapture ("when the Chief Shepherd appears," v. 4).
Source	The Chief Shepherd (v. 4).

2 Peter 1:5-11

As we continue our trek through Petrine territory, we come to his second epistle, chapter 1. The apostle starts by revealing the divine resources available to his readers for godly living (vv. 3-4). This is followed by a kind of ladder of spiritual growth wherein divine resources are appropriated in human responsibility. Christian growth is a partnership between God and his child.

This so-called spiritual ladder begins with faith (*pistis*, v. 5). The term suggests devotion to Christian teaching.[85] The top rung of the ladder is

---

[85] Rienecker, 769.

the virtue of love (*agape*, v. 7). Verse 8, beginning with the conjunction *gar*, explains that he who continually climbs this spiritual ladder, thereby possessing increasing spirituality ("increasing" translates *pleonazo*, present participle), is neither useless (*argos* = inactive, idle) nor unfruitful (*akarpos*; NIV renders it "unproductive") in the true knowledge of our Lord Jesus Christ.

The term "knowledge" denotes intimate friendship with Christ (*epiginosko*). Later, the apostle will utilize the same term as he commands his readers to "grow in the grace and knowledge of our Lord Jesus Christ..." (3:18). The point is that obedience to Christ, evident in on-going spiritual progress (vv. 5-7), results in Christ disclosing Himself to His child, a clear allusion to Jesus' teaching in John 14:21. Intimacy with God always comes by way of obedience to God (see also James 4:8, in this regard).

Verse 9 then paints a contrast to further explain his point. He says, "For (*gar*) he who lacks these qualities [the ascending virtues listed in vv. 5-7], is blind or shortsighted, having forgotten his purification from his former sins." The term "blind" translates *tuphlos*. The root is *tuph* meaning "to burn or smoke." Though sometimes used of physical blindness, here the metaphor of spiritual blindness is in view, that is, the dulling of the intellect (see John 12:40 and 2 Cor. 4:4 in this vein). This fact is strengthened by the following participle, *myopazon* (*hapax legomena*), rendered "short-sighted." But what causes such spiritual blindness in Christians?

The following participle explains that the spiritually blind believer has "forgotten [literally, "having received forgetfulness"] his purification [literally, cleansing, *katharismos*] from his former sins." The participle is causal in force signifying that spiritual blindness in the Christian is caused by a failure to remember what a wonderful thing Christ has done for him in purifying him from his sins.

Verse 10, beginning with the inferential "therefore" (*dio*), draws a conclusion from the two contrasting spiritual dispositions just stated in verses 8-9, namely, increasing Christ-likeness, or degenerating carnality. Note that Peter calls them "brethren" lest we think the description of spiritual nearsightedness (v. 9) is a reference to the unregenerate. Clearly, as the rest of the New Testament shows, there are two kinds of Christians, the spiritual and the carnal (e.g., 1 Cor. 2-3).

Therefore, with carnal Christianity a possibility in his readership, Peter issues the imperative in verse 10, "be all the more diligent to make certain about His calling and choosing you...." The words "all the more" are a rendering of *mallon*, a comparative adverb in Greek. Compared to where they were presently on the spiritual ladder, they needed to climb ever higher. One is either going up or down this ladder. When it comes to spiritual growth, neutrality is a myth.

The term "diligent" is a strong word in the original. From *spoudazo*, it means to exert much effort, to toil and labor with urgency. Peter uses the same term in verse 5 when he portrays the ladder of spiritual growth: "Now for this very reason [i.e., because of the divine resources available to you for growth], applying all diligence, in your faith...." The contrast between such diligence and the spiritual dullness of verse 9 is striking.

In the next phrase, "to make certain," the words "to make" render the aorist infinitive, *poieisthai*, which functions epexegetically relative to the imperative *spoudazo*. It explains what to be diligent about. The term rendered "certain" was used in the papyri of a legally guaranteed security.[86] It is the term *bebaios* in Greek, meaning "to certify something."

As Bob Deffinbaugh states,

---

[86] Rienecker, 770.

> Peter is not urging us to "make certain about" our election and calling. Our election and calling are from God, and they are not reversible (see Romans 8:29-30; 11:29)....On the other hand, we are not to be passive in our salvation and sanctification. We must believe in the Lord Jesus Christ and receive the salvation God has provided through Him (see John 6:28-29; Acts 2:38; 16:31; Romans 10:8-15). Likewise, while faith is a gift from God (2 Peter 1:1), we must add to our faith through the provisions God has given to us (2 Peter 1:3-7). I believe the exhortation in verse 10 is but an intensified repetition of that given in verses 5-7....We are to continually strive to grow in our faith and in the godly qualities Peter spells out in verses 5-7. As we do so, we *confirm, or establish* [emphasis mine], that which God began and which He is committed to establish in and through us. To make our calling and election sure is to make it stable. It is to set our lives on a course that cannot, and will not, be changed or moved away from the faith. It is to become so solid and stable that we will not be moved, especially by those who come to us with another gospel.[87]

Peter's command in verse 10, "make your calling and election sure," is not intended to call into question whether his readers were believers—verse 1 affirms the reality that they are. As well, it is not intended to provide solidifying proof of one's justification, but rather steadfast progress in the matter of establishing, on an increasing basis, the practice of the virtues of verses 5-7. This would sanctify the believer from spiritual blindness and spiritual amnesia (v. 9) and spiritual stumbling (v. 10). Peter's own three-fold denial of Jesus prior to Jesus' crucifixion may be in the apostle's mind here. He wanted to spare his Christian readers from the bitter taste of falling from one's own steadfastness, the very theme of

---

[87] Robert L. Deffinbaugh, "Standing On the Promises–A Study in 2 Peter: 4. A Secured Faith That Keeps the Saints from Stumbling," Bible.org, July 3, 2004, accessed May 23, 2016, https://bible.org/seriespage/4-secured-faith-keeps-saints-stumbling-2-peter-18-11.

the close of his letter (2 Pet. 3:17-18). As verse 10 further reveals, such steadfast, sure-footed growth in Christ-likeness is the purpose of God's "calling [*klesis*] and choosing [*ekloge*] you." The term "you" is emphatic which drives Peter's point right to the heart of the reader.

The end of verse 10 says, "...for as long as you practice ["continually practice," present participle] these things [virtues in vv. 5-7], you will never stumble...." The words "you will never stumble" contain the double negative *ou me* in Greek, indicating the utter impossibility of something. Here, that something is to live a carnal Christian life. There is no way, says Peter, that a Christian can embrace the virtues of verses 5-7 and the carnal disposition depicted in verse 9 at the same time. The idea, then, of the word "stumble" (*ptaio*) is the same as in James 2:10 and 3:2, namely, "to morally err." This is not a reference to losing one's salvation, an idea completely foreign to Scripture, but to a carnal Christian life. It should be noted that God's goal for our election, seen here in verse 10, is echoed in Ephesians 1:4: "Just as He chose us in Him [Christ] before the foundation of the world that we should be holy and blameless before Him...."

His warning completed, the apostle now explains further ramifications of choosing to climb the ladder spiritual growth. Verse 11 states, "For [*gar*] in this way the entrance into the eternal kingdom of our Lord and Savior Jesus Christ will be abundantly supplied to you." So then, not only will the believer avoid a moral fall (stumble) if he chooses to grow in Christ, but his entrance to heaven will be abundantly supplied. But what does that mean?

The words "will be supplied" translate a strengthened form of *choregeo* which means to outfit the chorus with additional and complete supplies, to lead a stage chorus or dance and to defray the expenses of a chorus. With the proposition in compound (*epichoregesate*) the verb has accumulative force signifying "to add further supplies, to provide more than was expected."

Peter's vivid metaphor describes, then, the Lord rolling out the red carpet, so to speak, for the child of His that embraced spiritual growth with all diligence. Placed too, in the emphatic position, these words "will be supplied" should grab his readers' attention and motivate them to climb that spiritual ladder.

Finally, this future verb, "will be supplied," is in the passive voice, implying that the Lord is the One who will supply the grand entrance to His eternal kingdom. The believer will simply sit back and enjoy the ride. This will be his reward for taking seriously His Savior's call to establish a godly life.

With all this in view, it is intriguing to note that winners of the Greek Olympic Games were given a lavish reception when they returned home. This whole concept conjures up the profuse praise bestowed on the faithful servant of Matthew 25 where Christ says, "Well done, good and faithful servant, enter into the joy of your Lord."

Also, could it be that this grand welcome, in connection with the mention of Christ's "eternal kingdom," implies an exalted position in that kingdom for the believer who progresses spiritually as he should? Again, Peter's whole discussion here could be an allusion to Christ's parables in Matthew 24 and 25 where faithful service to Christ now brings honorable positions in His future kingdom.

To sum up, if a believer furnishes his faith with the necessary additions of moral excellence, knowledge, self-control, perseverance, godliness, brotherly kindness and love, then God will furnish his heavenly arrival with abundant honor and recognition in His eternal kingdom. The opposite is true for the spiritually blind, stumbling Christian. He will make it into the kingdom, but will forfeit potential rewards (see 1 Cor. 3:15). The issue here is not whether a believer should have doubts about going to heaven—Peter's readers were believers (see 2 Pet. 1:1). The issue is, rather, what kind of entrance he will have and what kind of opportunities he will have to serve God in the eternal kingdom.

Summary of Reward for 1 Peter 1:5–11

Subjects	Christians (v. 1).
Content	(1) A lavish welcome into heaven; (2) exalted position in the eternal kingdom (v. 11).
Cause for (human)	Diligence in one's pursuit of spiritual maturity (vv. 5-11).
Cause for (divine)	God's justice and grace (implied).
Nature	(1) Personal (v. 11, implied); (2) part of one's reward can be lost via carnal Christian living (implied in vv. 8-11); (3) an occasion for honor from Christ (v. 11).
Time	Entry into Christ's kingdom (v. 11).
Source	Christ (implied, v. 11).

2 John 8

In this short epistle, the apostle John addresses a local church ("chosen lady"; some view this description as a reference to a Christian sister to whom John is writing). He declares his God-like love (vv. 1-2), extends Christian greetings (v. 3), commends those who walk in truth (v. 4), issues an exhortation to "love one another" (vv. 5-6), warns against heretical teachers (vv. 7-11), declares his desire to see them (v. 12, note plural pronouns) and passes on a final greeting (v. 13).

In the polemical section (vv. 5-8), the aged apostle gives some sage advice: "Watch yourselves [literally, 'keep on watching yourselves,' present imperative] that [*hina* of purpose] you might not lose [from *apollumi*, 'to suffer loss' (loss of reward in this context)] the things [neuter plural] we [better manuscripts read 'you' plural] have accomplished, but [strong adversative, *alla*] that you may receive a full reward [*misthos* is emphatic: 'a full reward, you may receive']."

In context, this stern warning regards the cruciality of guarding oneself from falling prey to heretical doctrine, to the teachings of the deceiver and the antichrist (v. 7). The group John addresses has learned "the truth." The articular construction here reflects a familiar theme in the letter. The same construction is seen in 1:1-2 where the body of truth embraced by Christians is in view. This motif is repeated in vv. 9-10 concerning the teachings of Christ. Thus, the prepositional phrase here, "in truth," refers to Christian doctrine.

But these saints have not only believed the truths of Christianity, but have behaved accordingly: "I was very glad to find some of [*ek*, 'some from among you'] your children walking in truth" (v. 4). Their accomplishments (v. 8, from *ergazomai*, "to work") of correct belief and behavior were an occasion for great joy and commendation in the present. And in the future they could be an occasion for full reward (v. 8). Therefore, they are warned in verses 10-11 not to endorse false teachers and their doctrine, lest they lose out on full compensation from the Lord. Note the contrast between "lose" and "receive" in verse 8. It should be noted that such doctrinal defection would not cut off salvation, but full reward.

The term "reward" (*misthon*) is a metaphor borrowed from the commercial world since it signifies the payment of labor, workman's wage. This term frequently appears in passages on the judgment seat of Christ.

Summary of Reward for 2 John 8

Subject	Christians (v. 1).
Content	Unspecified.

Cause for (human)	Adherence to sound doctrine in belief and behavior (belief and behavior being essentially inseparable in a cause-effect relationship: what one believes will determine his behavior.).
Cause for (divine)	(1) God's justice and grace (implied); (2) God's truth (vv. 7-11).
Nature	(1) Personal (implied); (2) part of one's reward can be lost via defection from sound doctrine (v. 8).
Time	Unspecified.
Source	Unspecified.

Revelation 2:10

The seaport city of Smyrna was about 35 miles north of Ephesus (present day Ismir), the center of the imperial cult of Rome. When John penned his letters to the seven churches of Asia (Rev. 1:4), the Smyrnan saints were among them. To these believers John wrote, "Do not fear what you are about to suffer. Behold, the devil is about to cast some of you into prison, that you may be tested, and you will have tribulation ten days. Be faithful until death and I will give you the crown of life" (2:10).

Staring persecution in the face, these saints were in need of supreme encouragement, thus the imperative, "Stop being afraid..." (*meden phobou*). Fear is the normal human response to such adversity, but the promise of future reward supplies the courage to stand. The words "about to suffer" indicate that their trauma is lurking around the corner ("about to" translates *melleis* future tense). And where is this persecution coming from?

The source of this persecution is the devil himself (*ho diabolos*) who was about to cast (*ballein*, present active infinivite) some of (*ex humon*) the believers into prison for the purpose of testing them (*hina* + subjunctive [*pierasthete*] = purpose clause). In this same connection, verse 9 indicates that these believers were the objects of "blasphemy by those who say they are Jews and are not, but are a synagogue of Satan." Obviously, these blasphemers were instruments in the devil's hand to roughly oppose the saints at Smyrna.

In this regard, it should be understood that the prisons of the ancient world were a place where the accused awaited sentencing which resulted either in execution or banishment. No wonder John felt the need to calm their fears. The words "you will have tribulation" show the Lord's omniscient awareness of what the future holds for His children. They also echo Paul's words to Timothy that "all who live godly in Christ Jesus will suffer persecution" (2 Tim. 3:12).

There is no evident reason to take the reference to "ten days" other than literal, or if taken figuratively, to an undetermined but relatively brief period of time. History does show, however, that a host of Christians were martyred over the next several centuries. (Some view this figuratively as the ten periods of persecution in Church history, beginning with Nero and ending with Diocletian.) And should this intense period of persecution lead to martyrdom, Christ's command and promise to these saints is, "Be faithful until death, and I will give you the crown of life."

The imperatival phrase, "Be faithful," (*ginou pistis*) could be literally rendered "prove yourself loyal and true." Such loyalty included a readiness to die for Christ's sake. Furthermore, the word "faithful" conjures up Jesus' applause to the faithful servants in the parables of Matthew 24 and 25. In fact, the term *pistis* is the one found in both places (see Matt. 24:45 and 25:21). Once again, the virtue of faithfulness (a fruit of the Spirit according to Gal. 5:22) is seen as a prerequisite for future rewards. And what is the reward here?

In like fashion to James 1:12, the promised reward here is "the crown of life." How intriguing that in both contexts, the theme is that of suffering saints. As even the stench of death fills the air, the fragrant aroma of God's favor and reward enables the discouraged saint to face the future with a smile. The words "I will give you" (dative of advantage) signify not only the future reality of the rewards that await His people, but as well the personal warmth of Jesus and His sensitive heart toward His own, especially in their hour of agony—He Himself has been there (Heb. 2:18; 4:14-16).

As for the Crown of Life itself, it is seemingly the special reward, then, for those who remain faithful in the fiery furnace of trials. It is interesting to note that the particular description Jesus gives of Himself to the church at Smyrna is, "The first and the last, who was dead, and has come to..." (v. 8). The very source of life, the self-existent eternal One, indeed the resurrected Christ, promises this unique reward called "the crown of life." The word "life" is the same Greek term in both verse 8 and 10. What's more, as already concluded in James 1:12, this crown cannot be purely a reference to the eternal life promised to the believer at conversion (John 3:15-16), but must be in addition to such a promise. Verse 11 helps us interpret the concept.

Verse 11 issues the wonderful assurance, "He who overcomes shall not be hurt by the second death." Revelation 20:14 makes it clear that the second death is the lake of fire, the destiny of those whose names are not written in the Lamb's book of life (see Rev. 20:11-15). Thus, the promise of verse 11 is the promise of sure deliverance from hell itself, an example of a rhetorical device called *litotes,* where one thing is diminished with the effect that the plainness of the statement is magnified all the more. The idea is that the believer who is victorious even when faced with the threat of martyrdom will, of course, be saved from eternal doom. Again, the Crown of Life is a specific reward for those who are already believers and have remained faithful to the living Christ. They are overcomers, even in suffering.

Summary of Reward for Revelation 2:10

Subject	Christians (context, 1:7).
Content	Crown of Life (v. 10).
Cause for (human)	Faithful to God (even until death) in persecution (v. 10).
Cause for (divine)	God's justice and grace (v. 10).
Nature	(1) Personal (implied); (2) occasion for honor to celebrate spiritual victory amid suffering (vv. 9-10).
Time	Future (unspecified).
Source	Christ (v. 8).

Revelation 2:26-27

Thyatira was the fifth of seven Asian churches addressed by John. This city was known for its many trade guilds, but also for its wool and dyeing industry (see Acts 16:14). It was located about 35 miles southeast of Pergamum. The saints at Thyatira receive words of commendation from Christ for their overall spiritual progress (v. 19), but words of confrontation for areas of compromise. Specifically, they had tolerance for a woman named Jezebel. Perhaps this wasn't her real name, but her ways made her a modern day parallel to the notorious Jezebel of 1 Kings 16 and 2 Kings 9. In any case, this woman's teaching was leading some of Christ's bondservants in Thyatira into immorality and idolatry (v. 20). Christ had given her time to repent, but she refused His call (v. 21). Therefore, the axe of judgment was about to fall, not only upon her but upon "all who commit adultery with her..." (v. 22). Even her children would die via pestilence (v. 23a).

All such judgment would come because Christ wanted all the churches to know this: "that I am He who searches the minds and hearts; and I will give to each one according to his deeds" (v. 23b). This fierce judgment grounded in both the omniscience and justice of Christ vividly illustrates His introductory self-disclosure to the church as "The Son of God, who has eyes like a flame of fire, and His feet are like burnished bronze..." (v. 18).

But, according to verse 24, there were some in Thyatira "who do not hold this teaching [i.e., the teaching of Jezebel, v. 20], who have not known the deep things of Satan, as they call them...." And to this sanctified group, Jesus says, "I place no other burden on you. Nevertheless what you have, hold fast until I come. And he who overcomes, and he who keeps My deeds until the end, to him I will give authority from My Father; and I will give him the morning star" (vv. 24b-28).

In discerning the angles on the doctrine of rewards here, it seems best to first analyze verse 25: "Nevertheless what you have, hold fast until I come." What did they have that they were to hold on to? In context, what they had would certainly include the commendation of verse 19: "I know your deeds, and your love and faith and service and perseverance, and that your deeds of late are greater than at first." This particular profile seems to emphasize the progressively spiritually mature behavior of the church, aside from those involved in the immorality and idolatry of the woman, Jezebel.

Added to this, in light of the second commendation in verse 24, would be the spiritually mature beliefs of the faithful in Thyatira: "But I say to the rest who are in Thyatira [i.e., the 'non-compromisers'], who do not hold this teaching...the deep things of Satan...I place no other burden on you." The term "teaching" is the noun form (*didachen*) of the verb *didaskei* in verse 20. Christ commends those in the assembly who neither compromised their belief nor their behavior in spite of the alluring enticements of Jezebel's teaching and the errant behavior it produced.

Here it is important to note that belief and behavior are inexorably wedded to one another, for what one believes will be manifest in his behavior; the former determines the latter. They are commanded, then, to hold fast what they have, namely, their correct doctrine and their corresponding correct duty. But what is the reward for such perseverance?

Verse 26 begins with the coordinating conjunction "and" to show the connection between the requirement for reward in verse 25 and the reward itself in verses 26-28. The next three words, "he who overcomes" are repeated at the end of John's message to each of the seven churches in chapters 2-3. The conjunction "and" coordinates the phrases: "...he who overcomes *and* he who keeps My deeds until the end...." This reveals that to qualify for the reward spoken of here, one must consistently keep (*teron*, present participle) Christ's deeds "until the end." This last phrase translates *achri telous* and is linked to the phrase "until I come" (*achri ekso*) in verse 25. As in 2 Timothy 4:8, perseverance to the end of one's journey is rewarded by Christ, whether that "end" be the termination of one's life via the corridor of physical death, as with Paul, or via Jesus' coming at the Rapture. The saints at Smyrna were given a similar charge, "Be faithful until death, and I will give you the crown of life" (Rev. 2:10). God honors faithfulness.

The term "deeds" (*erga*) represents a common motif in this passage. Twice, in verse 19, it refers to godly actions; in verse 22, the ungodly actions in verses 20-21 are in view; and in verse 23 the believer's deeds are the basis for Christ's future recompense ("I will give," *doso*); and in verse 26 we read "My deeds," that is, Christ's deeds.

But how should we understand this genitive construction, "My deeds"? It could be taken in an objective sense, i.e., "the deeds, or works, that pertain to serving Christ." On the contrary, if the nuance is subjective, the idea would have to center on Christ's own activity. But in what sense could a believer keep that?

One could argue that Christ's deeds, the ones which He Himself did in His incarnation, are in view here and that His followers are to emulate those. And such emulation guarantees rewards from Him. Also, the genitive construction "her deeds" (in reference to Jezebel) in verse 22, is an obvious subjective genitive, i.e., the deeds that she does. It could be that John intends to contrast "her deeds" with "My deeds," using the subjective genitive in both cases for emphasis and style.

In the end, the outcome is not much different, but the first choice seems best, especially in view of the commendation of verse 19 that the faithful in Thyatira had a reputation themselves for increasingly doing godly deeds. These godly deeds stand in contrast to the immorality and idolatry of the compromisers of verses 20-21. In this respect, they were doing what Christ expected of them. They embraced the activity (*erga*) that pertains to Christ, not the wicked activity associated with Jezebel. Such behavior, stemming from Christ-centered beliefs, is worthy of reward. By contrast, those involved in the ungodly deeds of Jezebel would be severely chastised and, by implication, forfeit the rewards mentioned here.

In short, those overcomers whose lives, in contrast to the compromisers of verses 20-22, were consistently about the business (deeds) of their Savior could expect the Savior's generous recompense. For as verse 23 declares, "...I will give to each one of you according to your deeds." With the requirement for the reward in view, let's now consider the reward itself.

First, there is the promise, "...to him [dative of advantage] I will give authority over the nations." This is a reference to Psalm 2:8 where the Father promises Christ the right and authority to rule in the yet future millennial kingdom. John simply applies the reward of co-rulership to Christ's faithful followers. As He has received authority from His Father (v. 27c), He now delegates authority to saints who overcome. The term "authority" renders the Greek term *exousia*, which denotes the "right to exercise power."[88]

As to the extent of this authority, it will be "over the nations" (*epi ton ethon*). As for the time of this rule, it must refer to the Millennium in view of John's use of Psalm 2 and the anticipated millennial context there. As further support, Revelation 12:5 and 19:15 use the same description of the rule seen here in verse 27, that of severe retribution against sin. Verse 27 reads, "And he shall rule [*poimanei*, 'to shepherd'; a mild term in general, but perhaps here the picture of the shepherd wielding his staff to ward off marauding beasts, an exercise in exacting authority] them with a rod of iron, as the vessels of the potter are broken to pieces...." The harsh imagery here is in keeping with other descriptions of Christ's future rule (cf. Ps. 2; Rev. 11:15-18; 19:11-21). In particular, 19:15 describes Christ's Second Coming to earth which is followed, in chapter 20, by details of His earthly, millennial rule. There, in verses 1-6, this rule is depicted as being free from Satan's presence, lasting 1,000 years, and is shared by His resurrected saints as co-rulers. But what of this "thousand years?"

The term "thousand years" is found six times in Revelation 20:1-7. It must be taken in a literal sense, otherwise, the rest of the events and personages in the passage could not be taken literally. A consistent hermeneutic leads one to see Christ's coming followed by a literal thousand year reign, a reign assisted by His saints as a part of the content of their reward for faithful service on earth.

A final note is the obvious link between this promise of delegated, millennial authority in Revelation 2:26-27 and the rewards Jesus promises in Matthew 24 and 25. There also, faithful service to Christ is

[88] Vine, 45; this use of *exousia* by John is the first of twenty-one uses in Revelation.

recompensed with future positions and privileges in His future kingdom. Following the reward of kingdom authority, authority delegated by Christ who has received the same from His Father, there is the additional promise, "and [*kai*, coordinating conjunction] I will give him the morning star." What does this mean?

The word "star" is *aster* in Greek. The term refers to literal stars in Matthew 2:2-10 and 1 Corinthians 15:41, and to the "angels of the seven churches" in Revelation 2-3 (see Rev. 1:20). These "angels" could be actual guardian angels over the churches or a figurative expression for human leaders in each church. In Luke 9:52 and James 2:25 the word "angel" is used of human beings.

Aster is also used of false teachers in Jude 13 "as if the stars, intended for light and guidance, became the means of deceit by irregular movements."[89] And finally, the term is used metaphorically of Christ in Revelation 22:16 where Jesus calls Himself "the bright Morning Star." This may be the way Peter uses the figure as well. In his second epistle he writes, "And we have the word of the prophets made more certain, and you will do well to pay attention to it, as a light shining in a dark place, until the day dawns and the morning star rises in your hearts" (2 Pet. 1:19).

Commenting on Peter's words, Rienecker asserts that the "imagery lay ready at hand, for the famous prophecy in Numbers 24:17 'there shall come a star out of Jacob,' was understood in Judaism as pointing to the Messiah (Kelly) and the coming of the Messiah is also compared to the dawn in Malachi 4:2 (Mayor).... In Greek and Roman times the term was applied not only to the morning star (Venus), but also to royal and divine persons."[90] This historical perspective would provide evidence for Jesus

[89] Vine, 598.

Himself being the morning star. But let's think further.

The adjective "morning" (*troinon*) qualifies *astar* in an attributive sense. The articular construction, "the morning star," maybe another reason to view this expression as a reference to Christ Himself, especially in light of its repetition later by the same author in the same book. The question arises as to why Christ would refer to Himself in the third person in this way. But this seems to be the preferable interpretation. The expression could, however, be figurative of the immortality promised to the believer.

In sum, Vine sees the figure as referring to Christ: "For Israel He will appear as 'the sun of righteousness'; as the 'morning' Star which precedes, He will appear for the rapture of the church."[91] But Rienecker is not so dogmatic. He writes, "No completely satisfactory answer for this symbol has been offered."[92]

Summary of Reward for Revelation 2:26–27

Subject	Christians (v. 18).
Content	1) Authority to be co-rulers with Christ in the future (millennium) (vv. 26-27); (2) the morning star (v. 28).
Cause for (human)	Remaining faithful in correct doctrine and progressing in spiritual maturity (vv. 24-26a).
Cause for (divine)	God's justice and grace (implied in vv. 24-26a but also in view of the contrast with the retribution promised to the carnal element in the church, vv. 20-23).

[90] Rienecker, 773.
[91] Vine, 416-417.
[92] Rienecker, 818.

Nature	(1) Personal (implied); (2) an occasion for public honor; (3) can be forfeited by compromising in sound doctrine and godly behavior (vv. 20-24).
Time	Future, Christ's coming (Rapture) (v. 25).
Source:	Christ (v. 26-28).

Revelation 3:11-12

The sixth church to whom John writes in Revelation 2-3 is the "church in Philadelphia" (3:7). "Philadelphia" means "brotherly love." This city was a lesser city than others addressed and was located approximately 38 miles southeast of Sardis. Its chief deity was Dionysus, the god of wine.[93]

To these saints Christ has nothing to say but words of commendation. But in light of the potential compromise that any believer or church is capable of, and in view of Christ's imminent return, Jesus says in verse 11, "I am coming quickly, hold fast *what you have* [emphasis added], in order that no one take your crown." What can be said about this exhortation?

First, note the cause-effect relationship between Christ's promised coming and His command to remain steadfast. In brief, the return of Christ should never be reduced to some static doctrine we embrace in discussions on eschatology, rather it ought to shape the very way we live. Second, the verb "hold fast" is a present imperative (*kratei*, "to grasp") which, in an expanded translation could read, "keep holding a tight grip on what you now have." But what did they have to hold on to?

According to verse 8, Christ tells them, "...you have a little power, and have kept My word, and have not denied My Name." What's more, in

[93] Cf. Ryrie, *Ryrie Study Bible*, 1899n3:7.

the face of persecution perpetrated by Satan (v. 9), He says, in verse 10, "...you have kept the word of My perseverance...." Essentially, they hold in their possession a reputation of spiritual steadfastness. Even amidst persecution, they had not denied the Lord's name. They had remained obedient to His Word. They must hold a firm grip on this spiritual disposition "in order that [*hina,* clause of purpose] no one take your crown."

The term "crown" (*stephanos*) is the term seen repeatedly in contexts regarding the believer's future rewards. As already established, in these contexts it signifies spiritual victory, inward gladness and kingly honor from Christ. These Christians who honor Christ on earth will be honored by Him in heaven, and such honor will indicate their spiritual triumph over the world, the flesh and the devil. Here the potential of losing such reward is again observed (see 2 John 8).

Should these believers stray from adherence to Christ's word and deny Him before the world, their crown would be taken, a figurative expression for loss of reward. But what specific reward is promised here?

In verse 12, Jesus declares, "He who overcomes, I will make him a pillar in the temple of My God, and he will not go out from it anymore; and I will write upon him the name of My God, and the name of the city of My God, the New Jerusalem, which comes down out of heaven from My God, and My new name."

The familiar phrase "he who overcomes" (*nikon*, present participle) describes the victorious believer, as observed previously. Christ's promise to make the faithful believer a "pillar [*stulon*] in the temple of My God" is a figurative expression of the permanent relationship the overcomer will enjoy with Christ in the eternal temple of God, identified here as the "New Jerusalem." It should be noted, in this connection, that historically this city experienced the threat of frequent earthquakes, earthquakes which only the huge stone temple columns survived. The believer is eternally secure in his personal relationship with Jesus Christ. His position in Christ's eternal kingdom is unshakable.

But there's more here to this figure of a temple pillar. It also denotes the honor Christ desires to bestow in His kingdom on His faithful ones. In view here is, no doubt, the custom of the day in which a magistrate was publicly venerated by the placement of a pillar in his name in one of the temples in Philadelphia. In fact, the rest of verse 12 unveils both the security and the honor granted to Christ's followers. The element of security is seen in the promise, "and he will not go out from it anymore," and the aspect of honor in the words, "and I will write on him the name of My God, and the name of the city of My God, the new Jerusalem...and My new name." And all of this is Christ's very own doing as is revealed in the future active verb, "I will make him" (*poieso*), in verse 12.

A final note concerns the promise in verse 10 that believers (which these Philadelphian saints represent) will be kept from "the hour." The articular construction denotes a certain, specific hour on God's prophetic calendar—a period of time which is about to come upon the whole world, "to test those who dwell on the earth." Due to the global nature of this "testing" (*peirasmou*), the Tribulation era described in Revelation 6-19 must be in view. The promise here that the church will be kept "out of" (*ek*) this specific time of testing supports a pre-tribulation Rapture.

Summary of Reward for Revelation 3:11–12

Subject	Christians (v. 7).
Content	Personal and public honor in the New Jerusalem (v. 12).

Cause for (human)	Spiritual maturity (faithfulness to God's word and unashamedly identifying with Christ, even amid persecution, vv. 8-10).
Cause for (divine)	God's justice and grace (implied in the cause-effect elements regarding certain behavior and subsequent rewards in addition to the warning about losing one's crown, vv. 11-12).
Nature	(1) Personal (implied); (2) occasion for honor; (3) can be forfeited via disobedience to Christ and denial of Christ (vv. 8, 11).
Time	Christ's coming (implied in v. 11).
Source	Christ (v. 12).

Revelation 4:10

The scene here is John's Spirit-enabled vision of heaven itself (vv. 1-2). After seeing the majestic manifestation of Christ Himself (v. 3), he sees twenty-four elders who are seated on twenty-four thrones, clothed in white garments and who have golden crowns upon their heads. So who are these twenty-four elders? Evidence shows that they are the bride of Christ, the church.

The term elder (*presbuteros*) is never used of angels. It refers to elder women in 1 Timothy 5:2 (elder in the respect to physical age and maturity) and, in every other place, to men. Both physical and spiritual maturity are in view (respectively, cf. Luke 15:25 and 1 Tim. 3:1; in Num. 22:7 the emphasis is on societal rank as regards the elders of Moab and Midian).

The description, "clothed in white garments," is used in the surrounding context to denote the inner purity of Christ's faithful bride (cf. 3:4, 18; 6:9-11; 7:13-14).

The mention of crowns (*stephanous*) correlates 2:10 and 3:11 where crowns of reward are linked with the church, not angels. Revelation 4:10

then shows the redeemed falling down before God, our Creator, to worship (*proskuneo*) Him and to cast (*ballousin*) their crowns (*stephanous*) before Him. While it is true that *stephanos* is used as a symbol of temporary triumph in connection with the antichrist (6:2), and as a symbol of honor with regard to Israel (12:1) and Christ (14:4), the crowns mentioned in Revelation 4:4, 10 are best seen as crowns of reward associated with the church, especially due to (1) the identity of the twenty-four elders as the church and (2) the contextual proximity of these crowns to the seven churches addressed in chapters 2-3 and references to crowns there (again cf. 2:10 and 3:11).

A final issue here concerns the particular timeframe of the events described in Revelation 4. In this regard, note that chapters 4-5 concern the church worshipping God, the Father, and Jesus, the Lamb slain for sinners. This worship occurs in heaven, a fact that fits well with Revelation 3:10 where Christ promised to keep the church out of the period of worldwide testing, the period that begins in Chapter 6. The church is not mentioned again until this global Tribulation is over. In Revelation19:7-9, the church returns with Christ to earth having been already rewarded. As Revelation 19:8 declares, "And it was given to her to clothe herself in fine linen, bright and clean; for the fine linen is the righteous acts of the saints."

Such a chain of events lends evidence to a pre-tribulational Rapture of the church. Also, the idea that the Rapture is followed closely by the *bema* seat of Christ could be implied, here, in view of the sequence of events. The apparent juxtaposition of these two events is seen in many passages (e.g., 2 Tim. 4:8).

Finally, crowns of reward are cast before God (Rev. 4:10) to signify believers' absolute surrender of their authority to rule to the all-sovereign, Creator. As well, this act expresses recognition of the enablement He gave them to earn such crowns (see Phil. 2:12-13). Casting crowns before Him reveals that *Ultimate Honor is His alone* (v. 11). This act, however, does not mean that the amount of reward received by each believer does not determine his disposition in the millennial kingdom and throughout eternity future (e.g., Luke 19:11-19; James 1:12). In this regard, every moment matters forever. The garments we weave today we will wear forever. Every day, our forever and ever can get better and better.

Summary of Reward for Revelation 4:10

Subjects	All church saints (v. 10).
Content	Crowns (symbols of authority to rule with Christ; honor; spiritual triumph during earthly life; and joy, v. 10).
Cause for (human)	Unspecified.
Cause for (divine)	Unspecified.
Nature	Personal, and perhaps universal (both may be implied since every saint [each of the 24 elders] possesses a crown to cast before God, though 1 Cor. 3:15 may show that a believer, due to consistent carnal living, will receive no reward at all).
Time	After the church age is complete (immediate and general context of the book).
Source	God, the Father (implied, vv. 10-11).

Appendix C: Crowns

Crowns	Passages	Recipient
Incorruptible crown	1 Cor. 9:25	The Christian who maintains a healthy fear that eternal rewards can be lost and therefore embraces the self-mastery required to live a Gospel-centered life.
Crown of rejoicing	1 Thess. 2:19	The Christian who embraces a lifestyle of befriending sinners to the Friend of sinners and bringing up saints to be like the Savior.
Crown of righteousness	2 Tim. 4:8	The Christian who finishes well...who perseveres in his love for Jesus to the end of his earthly life.
Crown of life	James 1:12; Rev. 2:10	The Christian who remains in love with Jesus amidst the various earthly trials sent by Jesus.
Crown of glory	1 Pet. 5:4	The elder over God's flock who faithfully discharges his duties with an exemplary life and sanctified motives.

Bibliography

Bibles and Scripture Versions

Aland, Kurt, et al., eds. *The Greek New Testament*. 3rd ed. New York: United Bible Societies, 1975.

Barker, Kenneth L., ed. *Zondervan NIV Study Bible: New International Version*. Grand Rapids, MI: Zondervan Publishing House, 1985.

Elliger, K. and W. Rudolph, eds. *Biblia Hebraica Stuttgartensia*. Stuttgart: Gesamtherstellun Biblia-Druck, 1977.

Ryrie, Charles C. *The Ryrie Study Bible: New American Standard*. Exp. ed. Chicago: Moody Press, 1995.

Language Resources

Alford, Henry. *The Greek Testament*. Revised by Everett F. Harrison. 4 vols. Chicago: Moody, 1968.

Balz, Horst R., and Gerhard Schneider, eds. *Exegetical Dictionary of the New Testament*. 3 Vols. Grand Rapids, MI: Eerdmans, 1990.

Bauer, Walter. *A Greek-English Lexicon of the New Testament and Other Early Christian Literature*. Translated and adapted by William F. Arndt and F. Wilbur Gingrich. Chicago: University of Chicago Press, 1957.

Brown, Colin, ed. *The New International Dictionary of New Testament Theology*. 3 vols. Grand Rapids, MI: Zondervan, 1975-78.

Brown, Francis, S. R. Driver, and Charles A. Briggs. *Hebrew and English Lexicon of the Old Testament*. London: Oxford University Press, 1966.

Bullinger, E. W. *Figures of Speech Used in the Bible*. Grand Rapids, MI: Baker Book House, 1968.

Chapman, Benjamin. *New Testament-Greek Notebook*. 2nd ed. Grand Rapids, MI: Baker, 1978.

Dana, H. E., and Julius R. Mantey. *A Manual Grammar of the Greek New Testament*. New York: Macmillan, 1955.

Earle, Ralph. *Word Meanings in the New Testament*. Grand Rapids, MI: Baker, 1989.

Friberg, Barbara, and Timothy Friberg, eds. *Analytical Greek New Testament*. Grand Rapids, MI: Baker, 1981.

Goetchius, Eugene Van Ness. *The Language of the New Testament*. New York: Charles Scribner's Sons, 1965.

Kittel, Gerhard, and Gerhard Friedrich, eds. *Theological Dictionary of the New Testament*. Translated and abridged by Geoffrey W. Bromiley. Grand Rapids, MI: Eerdmans, 1985.

———. *Theological Dictionary of the New Testament*. Translated and edited by Geoffrey W. Bromiley. 10 Vols. Grand Rapids, MI: Eerdmans, 1967-1976.

Moule, C. F. D. *An Idiom Book of New Testament Greek*. Cambridge: University Press, 1959.

Owens, John Joseph. *Analytical Key to The Old Testament*. 4 vols. Grand Rapids, MI: Baker, 1989-92.

Rienecker, Fritz. *A Linguistic Key to the Greek New Testament*. Edited by Cleon Rogers, Jr. Grand Rapids, MI: Zondervan, 1980.

Robertson, Archibald Thomas. *Word Pictures of the New Testament*. 6 vols. Nashville, TN: Broadman, 1933.

Rogers, Cleon L. Jr., and Cleon L. Rogers III. *The New Linguistic and Exegetical Key to the Greek New Testament*. Grand Rapids, MI: Zondervan, 1998.

Smith, J. B. *Greek-English Concordance to the New Testament*. Scottdale, PA: Herald Press, 1955.

Spicq, Ceslas. *Theological Lexicon of the New Testament*. Vol. 2. Translated and edited by James D. Ernest. Peabody, MA: Hendrickson Publishers, 1994.

Trench, Richard Chenevix. *Synonyms of the New Testament*. Grand Rapids, MI: Eerdmans, 1953.

Vine, W. E. *Vine's Complete Expository Dictionary of Old and New Testament Words*. Edited by Merrill Frederick Unger and William White. Nashville, TN: Thomas Nelson, 1985.

Zodhiates, Spiros. *The Hebrew-Greek Study Bible: King James Version*. Chattanooga, TN: AMG Publishers, 1992.

Commentaries

Barclay, William. *The Daily Study Bible*. Rev. ed. Toronto: G. R. Welch, 1975-76.

————. *Letters to the Seven Churches*. New York: Abingdon Press, 1958.

Bigg, Charles. *A Critical and Exegetical Commentary on the Epistles of St. Peter and St. Jude*. International Critical Commentary 42. Edinburgh: T. & T. Clark, 1901.

Bruce, F. F. *1 & 2 Thessalonians*. Word Biblical Commentary 45. Waco, TX: Word Books, 1982.

Bruce, F. F., ed. *The New International Commentary on the New Testament*. 18 vols. Grand Rapids, MI: Eerdmans, 1959–.

Cranfield, C. E. B. *A Critical and Exegetical Commentary on the Epistle to the Romans*. The International Critical Commentary. 2 vols. Edinburgh: T & T. Clark, 1975-79.

DeHaan, Richard W. *Studies in Second Peter.* Wheaten, IL: Victor Books, 1977.

Gaebelein, Frank E., ed. *The Expositor's Bible Commentary.* 12 vols. Grand Rapids, MI: Zondervan Publishing House, 1981-84.

Green, Michael. *The Second Epistle General of Peter and the General Epistle of Jude: An Introduction and Commentary.* Tyndale New Testament Commentary 18. Grand Rapids, MI: Eerdmans, 1984.

Hailey, Homer. *Revelation, an Introduction and Commentary.* Grand Rapids, MI: Baker Book House, 1979.

Heibert, D. Edmond. *First Peter.* Chicago: Moody Press, 1984.

————. *The Thessalonian Epistles: A Call to Readiness.* Chicago: Moody Press, 1971.

Hendriksen, William. *Exposition of I and II Thessalonians [and] the Pastoral Epistles (I and II Timothy, Titus).* New Testament Commentary. Grand Rapids, MI: Baker, 1983.

————. *Matthew.* New Testament Commentary. Grand Rapids, MI: Baker, 1973.

Inrig, Gary. *The Parables: Understanding What Jesus Meant.* Grand Rapids, MI: Discovery House, 1991.

Keener, Craig S. *The IVP Bible Background Commentary: New Testament.* Downers Grove, IL: IVP, 1983.

MacArthur, John, Jr. *Matthew 1-7.* The MacArthur New Testament Commentary. Chicago: Moody Press, 1985.

Marshall, I. Howard. *The Gospel of Luke: A Commentary on the Greek Text.* The New International Greek Testament Commentary. Grand Rapids, MI: Eerdmans, 1979.

Mason, A. J., Alfred Plummer, and William M. Sinclair. *The Epistles of Peter,*

John, and Jude: With Commentaries. Layman's Handy Commentary, ed. by C. J. Ellicott. Grand Rapids, MI: Zondervan Pub. House, 1957.

Mayor, Joseph B. *The Epistle of St. James*. Grand Rapids, MI: Zondervan, 1954.

Mitton, C. Leslie. *The Epistle of James*. Grand Rapids, MI: Eerdmans, 1966.

Moo, Douglas J. *The Letter of James: An Introduction and Commentary*. Tyndale New Testament Commentaries. Grand Rapids, MI: Eerdmans, 1985.

Nieboer, Joe. *Practical Exposition of II Peter: Verse by Verse*. Erie, PA: Our Daily Walk Publishers, 1952.

O'Brien, Peter T. *Colossians, Philemon*. Word Biblical Commentary 44. Waco, TX: Word Books, 1982.

Plummer, Alfred. *A Critical and Exegetical Commentary on the Second Epistle to the Corinthians*. Edinburgh: T&T Clark, 1975.

Robertson, Archibald Thomas. *Word Pictures in the New Testament: The General Epistles and The Revelation of John*. Vol. 6. Nashville, TN: Broadman Press, 1933.

Ropes, James H. *A Critical and Exegetical Commentary on the Epistle of St. James*. The International Critical Commentary. Edinburgh: T. T. & Clark, 1954.

Walvoord, John F., and Roy B. Zuck, eds. *The Bible Knowledge Commentary: An Exposition of the Scriptures*. 2 vols. Wheaton, IL: Victor Books, 1983-85.

Wiersbe, Warren W. *The Bible Exposition Commentary*. 2 vols. Wheaton, IL: Victor Books, 1989.

Wood, Leon. *A Commentary on Daniel*. Grand Rapids, MI: Zondervan, 1973.

Theology Works

Anderson, H. George T., Austin Murphy, and Joseph A. Burgess, eds. *Justification by Faith*. Lutherans and Catholics in Dialogue VII. Minneapolis, MN: Augsburg Publishing House, 1985.

Baker, Charles F. A *Dispensational Theology*. Grand Rapids, MI: Grace Bible College Publications, 1971.

Berkhof, Louis. *Systematic Theology*. 4th ed. Grand Rapids, MI: Eerdmans, 1977.

Erickson, Millard J. *Christian Theology*. Grand Rapids, MI: Baker Book House, 1991.

Guthrie, Donald. *New Testament Theology*. Downers Grove, IL: IVP, 1981.

Ladd, George Eldon. A *Theology of the New Testament*. Grand Rapids, MI: Eerdmans, 1974.

———. *Prophecy for Today: A Discussion of Major Themes of Prophecy*. Grand Rapids, MI: Zondervan, 1961.

Pentecost, J. Dwight. *Things to Come: A Study in Biblical Eschatology*. Grand Rapids, MI: Zondervan, 1978.

Ryrie, Charles C. *Basic Theology*. Wheaton, IL: Victor Books, 1986.

Schreiner, Thomas R., and Ardel B. Caneday. *The Race Set Before Us: A Biblical Theology of Perseverance & Assurance*. Downers Grove, IL: InterVarsity Press, 2001.

Strauss, Lehman. *God's Plan for the Future*. Grand Rapids, MI: Zondervan, 1965.

Strong, Augustus Hopkins. A *Systematic Theology*. Philadelphia: Judson Press, 1907.

Thiessen, Henry C. *Introductory Lectures in Systematic Theology*. Grand Rapids,

MI: Eerdmans, 1949.

Vos, Geerhardus. *The Pauline Eschatology*. Grand Rapids, MI: Eerdmans, 1972.

Other Books

Alcorn, Randy C. *Money, Possessions, and Eternity*. Wheaton, IL: Tyndale House Publishers, 2003.

Barker, William. *Who's Who in Church History*. Old Tappan, NJ: F. H. Revell, 1969.

Deffinbaugh, Robert L. "Standing On The Promises–A Study in 2 Peter: 4. A Secured Faith That Keeps The Saints from Stumbling." Bible.org. July 3, 2004. Accessed May 23, 2016. https://bible.org/seriespage/secured-faith-keeps-saints-stumbling-2-peter-18-11.

Dillow, Joseph C. *The Reign of the Servant Kings*. Hayesville, NC: Schoettle Publishing, 1992.

Hodges, Zane C. *Grace in Eclipse*. Dallas: Rendencion Viva, 1987.

Kroll, Woodrow Michael. *It Will Be Worth It All*. Neptune, NJ: Loizeaux Brothers, 1977.

Larson, Craig Brian, ed. *Illustrations for Preaching & Teaching from Leadership Journal*. Grand Rapids, MI: Baker, 1993.

Lewis, Ralph L., and Gregg Lewis. *Learning to Preach Like Jesus*. Westchester, IL: Crossway Books, 1989.

Our Daily Times with God: Favorite Selections from Our Daily Bread. Grand Rapids, MI: Discovery House Publishers, 1988.

Robinson, Haddon W. *The Christian Salt and Light Company*. Grand Rapids, MI: Discovery House Publishers, 1988.

———. *The Solid Rock Construction Company: How to Build Your Life on the Right Foundation*. Grand Rapids, MI: Discovery House Publishers, 1989.

Schaeffer, Francis A. *A Christian View of the Church*. Vol. 4, *The Complete Works of Francis A. Schaeffer: A Christian Worldview*, 2nd ed. Wheaton, IL: Crossway Books, 1994.

Swindoll, Charles R. *The Grace Awakening*. Waco, TX: Word, 1982.

Tan, Paul Lee. *Encyclopedia of 7700 Illustrations: Signs of the Times*. Rockville, MD: Assurance Publishers, 1979.

Wall, Joe L. *Going For The Gold*. Chicago: Moody Press, 1991.

Periodicals

Barnes, Ron. "Why Your Motives Count Forever." *Kindred Spirit* 19, no.4 (Winter 1995): 10-11.

Noonan, Tim. "The Greatest Treasure Ever Found: Gold." *Life*, March 1992.

Hoyt, Samuel L. "The Judgment Seat of Christ in Theological Perspective Part 2: The Negative Aspects of the Christian's Judgment," *Bibliotheca Sacra*, 137, no. 546 (April-June 1980): 125-131.

Fedarko, Kevin, and Mark Thompson. "All for One." *Time*, June 1995.

Made in the USA
San Bernardino, CA
12 October 2017